Contents

Tips to Help You Do Your Best

Before the Exam:

1. Don't wait until a week before the test to start preparing for it. Well before the date, begin a systematic program of study, using the material in this book. When you feel that you are ready, take the model test. Use the results and the analysis of answers to pinpoint areas that require further study.

2. Get adequate rest the night before. "Cramming" until midnight will get you nowhere.

3. Leave home in plenty of time. There is nothing more nerve wracking than dashing into the room just as the exam is about to start.

4. Know what materials you will need, for example, your admission ticket, a supply of sharpened #2 pencils, and a good eraser, and have them ready.

During the Exam:

1. Keep calm. If you have prepared faithfully and systematically and have followed up each weakness as it was revealed, you are well prepared.

2. Read the directions carefully, so that you know what each question calls for.

3. Work as steadily and quickly as you can. Do first the questions to which you know the answers. If you have time, go back to the ones you have skipped.

4. Since wrong answers carry a penalty, don't guess wildly. If, however, you can eliminate one or two choices as clearly wrong, it may be wise to make an educated guess.

5. Don't become panic-stricken if you encounter a series of difficult questions. There will be some that even superior students cannot answer. No one is expected to score 100%.

GOOD LUCK!

SAT and Achievement Test Dates

Test Dates		Registration Deadlines	
National	New York State	Regular	Late
1985			
†October 12		September 20	September 20
November 2	November 2	September 27	October 9
December 7	December 7	November 1	November 13
1986			
January 25	*January 25	December 20	January 2
**March 15		February 7	February 19
May 3	May 3	March 28	April 9
June 7	June 7	May 2	May 14

† SAT given in California, Florida, Georgia, Illinois, North Carolina, South Carolina, and Texas.
* Only Achievement Tests given
**SAT only

NOTE: Students taking the SAT in November, December, May, and June may obtain copies of the test questions, correct answers, and their answer sheets. Ask your guidance counselor for an order form.

BARRON'S

BASIC TIPS

on the Scholastic Aptitude Test

SAT

Third Edition

Samuel C. Brownstein
Formerly Chairperson, Science Department
George W. Wingate High School, Brooklyn, New York

Mitchel Weiner
Formerly Member, Department of English
James Madison High School, Brooklyn, New York

Barron's Educational Series Inc.
Woodbury, N.Y. • London • Toronto • Sydney

Preface

Are you ready for the College Boards? Will your score reflect your true scholastic ability? Are you familiar with the type of questions encountered on the college entrance examinations? This booklet may be the eye-opener you need. The selected word list should be a check on the extent of your vocabulary as well as a means of building a more powerful vocabulary. This third edition also provides review and practice exercises for the analogy, sentence completion, and reading comprehension questions, as well as for the Test of Standard Written English.

In addition, this third edition contains a chapter with review and a practice exercise, as well as answers and analysis of the answers, for the various types of mathematics questions that are typical of the SAT. Do these questions before taking the sample aptitude test. Thus you will get a truer picture of your ability to score high on the actual exams.

How would you score on the College Boards if you took the test now? The sample test in this book will answer that question so that you will be in a position to evaluate yourself realistically and to determine how much more review you need. This test simulates the one you will be taking with its antonyms, sentence completions, analogies, reading comprehension, and standard English PLUS the various types of mathematics questions, including quantitative comparisons.

Study the word list. Do the practice exercises. Take the sample aptitude test. Score your results. Analyze your errors. Refer to the explanation of answers, especially for questions you were not sure of or answered incorrectly. If you feel you need more review and drill, if your mathematics is weak, if you should immediately begin working with the most widely used SAT review book — Barron's How to Prepare for College Entrance Examinations. This book has nearly 700 pages of drill material in word study, reading comprehension, technical English, and review of high school mathematics from algebra to geometry. Finally, it has a diagnostic test and six complete simulated scholastic aptitude tests with correct answers explained.

Timetable for the SAT*   Total time: 3 hours

Time	Section	Questions
9:00 to 9:30	**Section I** **Verbal Aptitude Test**	15 Antonym Questions 10 Analogy Questions 10 Sentence Completion Questions 10 Reading Comprehension Questions
9:30 to 10:00	**Section II** **Mathematics Aptitude Test**	25 to 40 Questions
10:00 to 10:05	BREAK	
10:05 to 10:35	**Section III** **Test of Standard Written English**	35 Usage Questions 15 Sentence Correction Questions
10:35 to 11:05	**Section IV** **Verbal Aptitude Test**	10 Antonym Questions 10 Analogy Questions 5 Sentence Completion Questions 15 Reading Comprehension Questions
11:05 to 11:10	BREAK	
11:10 to 11:40	**Section V** **Mathematics Aptitude Test**	25 to 40 Questions (There is a total of 60 math questions in Sections II and V.)
11:40 to 12:10	**Section VI** **Verbal Aptitude Test** or	40 Questions
	Mathematics Aptitude Test or	25 to 40 Questions
	Test of Standard Written English	50 Questions

*Actual times will vary in accordance with the time the proctor completes the preliminary work and begins the actual test. Format and timing are subject to change.

Truth in Testing

Why Truth-in-Testing?

For some time consumer organizations have been advocating laws to remove the secrecy that prevails in the standardized testing industry. These groups claim that the tests play too important a role in education and that the rights of test takers are not protected. They feel that applicants are entitled to know more about the test questions in advance and should be permitted to verify the grading of their papers. As a result truth-in-testing has been receiving much attention along with freedom-of-information, truth-in-lending, and truth-in-packaging.

The Pros and Cons

Consumer activists claim these laws would provide closer monitoring of cultural biases and economic class biases on test questions. However, testing sponsors claim that all questions are pretested and questions that prove to have any of these characteristics are discarded from actual tests. The College Board objected to general public scrutiny of its services since it is already accountable to its member educational institutions and the thousands of colleges that use its program.

To answer the charge that there is too much secrecy in admissions testing, the College Board contended that applicants are provided with information about the tests, their purpose, what they intend to measure, and their reliability. Are students in the dark about test questions? Sample questions are supplied to students with the application for the test. Publications like this book not only give the students a very good idea what to expect but also supply sufficient drill and practice to enable them to walk into the examination room with confidence.

What Is the New York Admissions Test Law of 1979?

According to this law, after January 1, 1980, agencies administering college and university entrance examinations must file a copy of each test along with correct answers with the State Department of Education within 30 days after the results are distributed. Nevertheless, the achievement tests do not follow this procedure. As of June 30, 1980, one form of each achievement test must be disclosed every three years. This procedure also applies, with a minor variation, to certain low-volume college entrance examinations (for the handicapped and for students who, for religious reasons, will not take the test on Saturdays). There will now be an equal number of Saturday and Sunday test dates; at least one of the Sunday administrations will be designated for 30-day disclosure. Students may receive a copy of their graded test with the correct answers after the payment of a special fee.

Nationwide Truth-in-Testing

In a March, 1981 meeting the College Entrance Examination Board voted to make truth-in-testing nationwide for the Scholastic Aptitude Test (SAT). As a result, it was decided to give the SAT on five Saturdays and two Sundays during the 1981–82 school year with the provision that applicants may request to see their scored answers as well as the questions with the correct answers. In addition, the Board decided to add other test dates without this provision, since test questions once disclosed cannot be used again, and it would be impossible to produce sufficient questions during this period.

How Does Test Disclosure Affect You?

Now that you have the option of inspecting your scored answer sheet, you can analyze your errors. Discovering your areas of weakness offers you the opportunity to establish a realistic and time-saving program for study. Thus you can concentrate on those specific areas in this book.

There are some disadvantages. You will most probably have to pay more for the test. Also, you can expect to have fewer dates for taking the test. You may also be penalized if you are unable to pay for expensive tutoring courses. Since the tests will be open to the public, coaching schools will coach with actual tests. Opponents of standardized tests claim that when the ability to pay for extra test preparation becomes a factor, the validity of the entire testing program is open to question.

How Will Test Disclosure Affect College Admission?

Most authorities feel it will have no effect. Colleges use test scores to compare applicants from private and public schools, from rural areas, and urban regions. As far as choosing students for admission is concerned they use test scores along with secondary grades, teacher recommendations, personal interviews, and extracurricular activities to decide whom to admit. Admission officers are trained to identify poor test takers who have academic promise.

1 The College Entrance Examinations

The basic purpose of this chapter is to help you to understand the general scope and nature of the various college entrance examinations. It will answer some fundamental questions about these tests and prepare the groundwork for the study material that follows.

What Are College Entrance Examinations?

These are standardized tests required for admission to most colleges. About 850 colleges and 300 scholarship sponsors require applicants to take the Scholastic Aptitude Tests (SAT) and often, in addition, the Achievement Tests of the College Entrance Examination Board.

What Is the Scholastic Aptitude Test (SAT)?

This is a three-hour test of objective questions designed to measure the ability to do college work. Part of the test deals with verbal skills such as the ability to read with understanding, use words correctly, and reason with them. Another part of the test measures the ability to use and reason with numbers or mathematical concepts. The verbal parts of the Scholastic Aptitude Test measure the extent of your vocabulary, your ability to interpret and relate ideas, and your ability to reason logically and to draw conclusions correctly. The SAT now also includes a 30-minute test to identify a student's ability to write clearly and correctly. A separate score is given on this part, and colleges are expected to use this score for placement purposes. The questions in this section test for competence in the use of standard written English and deal with the basic rules of grammar and usage and acceptable sentence structure. The mathematics section tests ability to handle general number concepts rather than specific achievement in mathematics. There is no premium here for the applicant who has carefully memorized formulas. The emphasis is on ability to apply fundamental mathematical knowledge to new situations.

What Is the PSAT/NMSQT?

This test is similar to the SAT except that it is a two-hour test basically designed for high school juniors. It serves to give high school juniors experience with the type of questions they will encounter on the SAT in their senior year. Scores on this test are used by college guidance counselors to give advice about college planning. This test is also the first step in the competition for the scholarship program administered by the National Merit Scholarship Corporation. High scorers on this test may become semifinalists and become eligible for Merit Scholarships, special scholarships, or achievement scholarships. It is generally given in October. A fee of $5.00 is collected by the school administering the test. The school may waive this fee in the case of needy students and may add an additional fee to cover costs of administering the test.

What Are Achievement Tests?

The Achievement Tests are one-hour tests designed to measure your level of achievement in a particular subject. Tests are offered in English composition, literature, American history and social studies, European history and world cultures, mathematics level I, mathematics level II, French, Hebrew, German, Latin, Russian, Spanish, biology, chemistry, and physics.

These tests serve many functions. Some colleges use such tests to confirm or verify the secondary school record of the applicant. Since the marking systems of schools differ, such standardized tests are sometimes used by colleges to choose applicants. More often these tests are used for placement purposes. For example, in a foreign language, the performance on the Achievement Test may be a deciding factor in determining whether the freshman will be registered in the elementary, intermediate, or advanced course of that language. In some cases, a college may even excuse a student from taking a foreign language in college on the basis of the accomplishments of the secondary school course as demonstrated by the score on the appropriate Achievement Test.

How Do I Apply for College Entrance Examinations?

If a registration form is not available at your school, request one by mail. You can obtain a form from the College Entrance Examination Board, Box 592, Princeton, New Jersey 08540 or Box 1025, Berkeley, California 94701.

What Are the Fees for College Entrance Examinations?

The fee for the SAT is $11.00 nationally ($12 in New York State). The fee for one, two, or three Achievement Tests taken on a single date is $18. If you feel you cannot afford these fees, consult your school guidance counselor. The fees are waived for members of low-income families.

When Are College Entrance Examinations Given?

The College Board Scholastic Aptitude Tests are given in January, March, May, June, November, and December. Achievement Tests are given on the same days, except that Achievement Tests in European history and world cultures, Hebrew, Latin, and Russian are given only in December. The regularly scheduled dates fall on Saturdays, but applicants who, for religious reasons, do not wish to appear on these dates may apply for testing on the Sunday following the regularly scheduled day. (In New York there are now equal numbers of Saturday and Sunday test dates.)

How Does the SAT Differ from Other Tests?

This is an objective test. Your scrap work is not subject to inspection so it should be kept to a minimum. Since wrong answers carry a penalty, haphazard guessing should be avoided. The penalty for guessing is a percentage of the wrong answers subtracted from the number of correct answers. Thus a candidate who answers 20 out of 30 questions correctly and 10 questions incorrectly, and does not omit any, has a Raw Score of 20 minus penalty (10 ÷ 4) or 17½. Speed is important on this test. You will be given a specific time limit for each part of the test. Since your score depends upon how many questions you do correctly, you should not waste your time on questions that seem too difficult for you.

How Are College Board Scores Reported?

Unlike examinations which you may take in school, there is no passing mark on College Entrance Examinations. Scores are reported on a scale of 200 to 800 in which your performance is compared with other high school seniors of other years. In addition, you will receive a score from 20 to 80 on the separate Test of Standard Written English.

How Do I Interpret My College Board Scores?

To compare your scores with those other students who also took the test, refer to the charts which follow. For example, if you have a score of 500 on your verbal SAT you will observe that 15% of the senior boys of previous years and 16% of the senior girls of previous years did better than you. Column B indicates that 31% of the previous senior boys who later entered college did better than you. Column D indicates that of the girls who later went to college 42% of them did better than you. Since the meaning of a score remains the same from year to year, the percentages given for seniors of previous years applies to you.

Interpretation of SAT — Verbal Scores

SAT — Verbal Score	Column A	Column B	Column C	Column D
800	0	0	0	0
750	<1	<1	<1	<1

Interpretation of SAT — Verbal Scores *(Continued)*

SAT — Verbal Score	Column A	Column B	Column C	Column D
700	<1	1	1	2
650	1	5	2	8
600	3	11	6	17
550	9	19	5	28
500	15	31	16	42
450	24	56	24	57
400	35	63	36	73
350	50	78	51	82
300	68	86	69	91
250	88	99	88	96
200	97	99+	98	99+

Column A — Percentage of senior boys of previous years who scored higher than you

Column B — Percentage of senior boys of previous years who scored higher than you entering college later

Column C — Percentage of senior girls of previous years who scored higher than you

Column D — Percentage of senior girls of previous years who scored higher than you entering college later

    A senior boy examining the chart of SAT mathematical scores would follow the same procedure. If his score is 550 he would conclude that 20% of the senior boys of previous years did better than he did, and of the boys who eventually entered college, 39% scored higher than he did. A senior girl with the same 550 score in the SAT mathematics would conclude that 9% of the previous senior girls did better than she did and 24% of the senior girls who later entered college scored higher than she did.

    If your score falls between two of the 50-point intervals, you may use the data for the score that is nearest to your own. In all cases use the data for your sex.

Interpretation of SAT — Mathematical Scores

SAT — Mathematical Score	Column A	Column B	Column C	Column D
800	0	0	0	0
750	1	1	1	1
700	1	4	1	1
650	5	13	2	6
600	11	24	4	13
550	20	39	9	24
500	31	56	16	39
450	43	69	25	55
400	59	82	38	72
350	75	91	57	85
300	91	98	80	97
250	99	99+	97	99+
200	99+	99+	99+	99+

Column A — Percentage of senior boys of previous years who scored higher than you

Column B — Percentage of senior boys of previous years who scored higher than you entering college later

Column C — Percentage of senior girls of previous years who scored higher than you

Column D — Percentage of senior girls of previous years who scored higher than you entering college later

Interpretation of SAT — Standard Written English Scores

Grading on this new part of the Scholastic Aptitude Test is from 20 to 80. Comparison with other scores is not possible because these scores are not meant to be competitive. Schools are expected, however, to use this part of the examination as a basis for determining placement in freshman English courses, rather than as a standard for admission.

How Important Are College Board Scores?

Colleges hesitate to officially announce cut-off points, but the year-to-year inspection of average college board scores of entering freshmen would lead one to believe that admissions officers regard a certain score minimal for successful work in their particular college. A poor score on an entrance examination, even if accompanied by a fairly good high school record, makes academic promise a serious question. A good college entrance examination score with an accompanying mediocre high school record is not uncommon. Although an unusually high score is a sign of good potential, admissions officers may attempt to explore the reason for this discrepancy. Temporary ill health as a reason for some low marks in school will probably be forgiven.

The results of college entrance examinations are important because they are a scientific way of comparing all candidates in regard to their abilities to do college work. A high school record alone cannot be a yardstick of academic promise. Marking standards differ among high schools. Class standing in a small high school is not as significant as it is in a large city school. The standing in a specialized school is of little significance except for those at the very top. Entrance examinations afford equal opportunity to each college-bound student.

What Is a Good College Board Score?

The publicity given to average scores on the Scholastic Aptitude Tests (SAT) of accepted applicants by certain colleges tends to frighten and alarm high school students planning to go to college. To allay these fears, let us analyze the meaning of these scores and interpret their significance.

Bear in mind that the average scores on a national basis are somewhere between 400 and 500 for the SAT, which is reported on a scale of 200-800. Secondly, *median*, or *average*, scores should not be regarded as *required* scores.

A college that reported a median score of 610 on the verbal part of the SAT for its freshman class indicates that 25% of its freshmen scored between 550 and 599, 14% between 500 and 549, and 6% between 400 and 450. For the mathematics part of the SAT the same school reported a median score of 700, but 29% of the admitted students received scores between 500 and 599.

Another school, reporting an average of 669 in the verbal part of the SAT for the 500 accepted applicants, indicated that 33 of them scored 550-599 and 10 scored below 550. It is interesting to note that this school failed to accept 15 applicants with SAT verbal scores of 700-749 and one unsuccessful applicant had a score above 750.

Thus we see that College Board scores are important, but additional criteria are used. It is well to repeat that SAT scores are used to *supplement* such factors as high school grades, class rank, and personal qualities obtainable from the application form and the personal interview. In addition, admissions officers are reporting that they are giving special consideration to applicants with low SAT scores from deprived areas or to applicants for whom English is not the native language. Of course, these college-bound students must present some evidence of academic promise.

How Good Are Your College Board Scores?

Use your PSAT scores or your SAT scores of the College Boards taken in your junior year to determine whether your choice of college is realistic. Compare the median scores reported for the college with your own scores. Eliminate as a choice any college whose scores are far above yours. Be realistic and choose a college that will most probably accept your SAT scores. Remember that a *median* score is given only as a guideline. Actually all the median score indicates is that as many applicants accepted were above that score as were below it.

How Can This Book Help You Score High on the College Boards?

Obviously no book used for a few months in the sophomore or junior year of high school is the complete answer to superior SAT scores. As one admissions officer has put it, the books in the home of the kindergarten child are more important than the books in the hands of the high school junior. The home environment and the emphasis on in-school and outside-school educational and cultural agencies throughout a child's formative years are the most important reasons for high scores on these examinations, which measure general background as well as specific subject abilities.

This book will help the superior, the average, and the below-average student to achieve better scores. Throughout, emphasis is placed on efficient test techniques. Vocabulary building is followed by exercises using words in the format of examination questions. A complete practice SAT is presented and correct answers are supplied. In addition, all answers are completely explained.

The student who uses the subsequent chapters diligently will add words to his or her vocabulary and will be able to use them correctly, will be able to read more efficiently, and will improve his or her ability to think mathematically.

For Further Study

You will find extensive review chapters and additional practice examinations in *Barron's How to Prepare for College Entrance Examinations*. This book also contains model Achievement Tests for some of the more commonly taken examinations. For additional practice and review for Achievement Tests, you may find these books useful; all are published by Barron's Educational Series, Inc., Woodbury, New York 11797.

How to Prepare for the College Board Achievement Tests:
     Biology, Bleifeld
     Chemistry, Mascetta

English, Shostak
European History/World Cultures, James
French, Cabat, Godin & Warner
German, Newmark, Scherer & Walz
Latin, Gerwig
Mathematics Level I, Rizzuto
Physics, Gewirtz
Social Studies/American History, Midgley
Spanish, Cabat, Godin & López

2 Sample Questions

The purpose of this chapter is to familiarize you with the kinds of questions that appear on Scholastic Aptitude Tests. Knowing what to expect when you take the examination is an important step in preparing for the test and succeeding on it. Begin by attempting to answer all questions and then checking your answers.

The Verbal Section

You will observe that the verbal section measures your ability to understand relationships among words and ideas in addition to comprehension of reading material. These skills are measured in several ways. In the *antonym* type of question you are given a word and are asked to select the word nearly opposite in meaning. Students who have read extensively in and out of the high school classrooms will be familiar with the vocabulary. All students will profit from the vocabulary building exercises in Chapter 3. In the *sentence completion* type of question you are asked to complete a sentence from which one or several words have been removed. Here your ability to recognize logical organization, clarity, and good style is tested. While the sentences may be in music, art, literature, philosophy, or social studies, choosing a correct answer will depend basically upon your ability to use the English language. Next, the *reading comprehension* type of question is presented. This constitutes about one-half of the verbal part of the test. The questions test your understanding of the material presented, your ability to apply the opinions presented by the author, as well as your ability to evaluate the style and method of presentation of facts by the author. Finally, in the *analogy* type of question you are tested in your understanding of relationships among words. Here you may find a cause-effect relationship or a concrete-to-abstract relationship. The practice exercises in Chapter 4 will help you become proficient in handling these three types of questions. For additional practice,

11

use *Barron's Verbal Aptitude Workbook for College Entrance Examinations*.

The Mathematics Section

In the mathematics part your ability to understand and to reason with mathematical symbols is tested, in addition to your ability to solve problems and to interpret data. The subject matter of the test consists of algebra and simple geometric concepts. No advanced mathematics is required. Since these questions are designed to test your power to think rather than to do mathematical computations or to recall complicated formulas it is well to bear in mind that any proposed solution on your part that is time-consuming is open to question. Close inspection, insight, and reasoning may often yield the correct answer without much, if any, computational work. Thousands of students have found that with diligent practice they walk into the examination with confidence. Do the exercises in Chapter 6 and, for additional practice, use *Barron's Mathematics Workbook for College Entrance Examinations*.

The Test of Standard Written English

This new part of the SAT uses two types of questions to establish your familiarity with clearly written prose. To develop skill necessary for answering these questions you should do the exercises in Chapter 5 and take the practice SAT. If you still need improvement, refer to *Barron's How to Prepare for College Entrance Examinations*.

Guessing

Some college entrance and scholarship examinations invoke no penalty for guessing. For example on the New York State Scholarship test no deductions are made for incorrect answers. In such examinations it is unwise to leave any answers blank. However, in the examinations of the College Entrance Examination Board the directions to the candidates make it clear that a percentage of the wrong answers is subtracted from the number of right answers. Let us cite the case of a student who omits 10 questions and correctly answers 20 out of 30 questions. His Raw Score would be 20. If this pupil had attempted to answer all 30 questions, his Raw Score would have been 20 minus Penalty (10 ÷ 4) or 17½.

Advice on guessing must differentiate between wild, haphazard guessing and intelligent reasoning. The pupil who feels that it would be a pity to leave answers blank and therefore chooses the answer which "looks good" will probably lower his score. The pupil who is not certain of the question and can eliminate one or more choices as being unreasonable, contradictory, or entirely incorrect has a fairly good chance of choosing the correct answer. Some students regard an answer to a question as a guess when actually it is a shrewd analysis. As you do the exercises and tests in this book, keep a record of your guesses. Determine how many of these are correct. If you label yourself "a good guesser" actually you may be employing reasoned guessing with great proficiency. In taking college entrance and scholarship examinations, listen carefully to the proctor's instructions about guessing. Read the directions in bulletins of information and on the examination booklet for announcements of methods of scoring.

Some Mechanical Details

Most standardized tests today are so designed that the answers may be marked by machine. If you are given a special pencil before you take the examination, you may confidently expect your paper will be so marked. You may be instructed to blacken a circular area to indicate your choice of the correct answer. The circles will appear thus:

1. Ⓐ Ⓑ Ⓒ Ⓓ Ⓔ   4. Ⓐ Ⓑ Ⓒ Ⓓ Ⓔ
2. Ⓐ Ⓑ Ⓒ Ⓓ Ⓔ   5. Ⓐ Ⓑ Ⓒ Ⓓ Ⓔ
3. Ⓐ Ⓑ Ⓒ Ⓓ Ⓔ   6. Ⓐ Ⓑ Ⓒ Ⓓ Ⓔ

SAMPLE:
1.   Reno is _____ .   1. Ⓐ Ⓑ Ⓒ ● Ⓔ
     (A) a country   (B) a mountain
     (C) an island   (D) a city   (E) a state

Since you mark your paper either with the special pencil sometimes provided or with a No. 2 pencil which you may be instructed to bring with you, you must observe the following precautions:

1.   Darken the entire area of the circle selected.
2.   Avoid all stray pencil marks on your answer paper.
3.   If you change your mind, erase the pencil markings very carefully.

Speed

Speed is an important factor in these examinations. Many of them are constructed so that it is almost impossible for even brilliant students to finish them in the time allotted. If you cannot see a short method of solving an example on the mathematics tests, for instance, it is advisable to leave the question and go on to the next problem. In a multiple-choice test, a score of 40 correct and 20 wrong is a much better score than 20 correct and none wrong. Do not spend too much time on any single question.

SAMPLE SAT QUESTIONS*

The sample questions that follow illustrate most of the kinds of questions you will find in the verbal, mathematical, and Standard Written English sections of the SAT and the range of difficulty within each group of questions. It is possible that types of questions not illustrated here may appear in any one edition of the test, and that types of questions illustrated here may not appear.

Verbal Questions

Your academic success in college undoubtedly will be closely bound up with your verbal abilities — among them your grasp of the meaning of printed materials, the breadth and depth of your vocabulary, and your understanding of relationships among ideas. The SAT assesses these abilities through a number of different kinds of objective test questions. Some of these types are discussed and illustrated in the following pages.

Antonyms

Questions of this sort test the extent and quality of your vocabulary. In each question you are given a word and are asked to select, from the five choices that follow it, the word that is most nearly *opposite* in meaning. The vocabulary used in this section includes words that most high school students should have met in their general reading, although some words may not be of the kind you use in everyday speech.

The directions given in the test for this type of question follow

Each question below consists of a word in capital letters, followed by five lettered words or phrases. Choose the word or phrase that is most nearly opposite in meaning to the word in capital letters. Since some of the questions require you to distinguish fine shades of meaning, consider all the choices before deciding which is best.

Example:

GOOD: (A) sour   (B) bad   (C) red
(D) hot   (E) ugly
                                    Ⓐ ● Ⓒ Ⓓ Ⓔ

1. AMBULATORY: (A) bedridden   (B) hostile
   (C) contagious   (D) frail   (E) glum

2. BUTTRESS: (A) straighten   (B) forward
   (C) undermine   (D) show off
   (E) observe secretly

3. SACCHARINE: (A) caustic   (B) allergic
   (C) magnetic   (D) reticent   (E) polluted

Sentence completions

This type of question requires you to complete a sentence from which one or two words have been omitted. That is, you must identify, from a list of five choices, the word or words that would make the most sense if inserted in the sentence. Such questions provide a measure of one aspect of reading comprehension: the ability to recognize logical and stylistic consistency among the elements in a sentence. If you understand the implications of a sentence, you should be able to select the answer that best fulfills the meaning of the sentence — that is, the element that makes the sentence lucid, logical, and stylistically consistent.

The sentences cover a wide variety of topics of the sort you are likely to have encountered in your general reading. Your understanding of any one sentence will inevitably depend to some degree on your knowledge of the subject matter involved: science, literature, music, philosophy, social studies, or other fields. But your success in answering each question will depend primarily on your ability to understand and use the English language.

The directions given for sentence completion questions are as follows:

Each sentence below has one or two blanks, each blank indicating that something has been omitted. Beneath the sentence are five lettered words or sets of words. Choose the word or set of words that <u>best</u> fits the meaning of the sentence as a whole.

Example:

Although its publicity has been . . . . . . , the film itself is intelligent, well-acted, handsomely produced, and altogether . . . .
(A) tasteless..respectable   (B) extensive..moderate
(C) sophisticated..amateur   (D) risqué..crude
(E) perfect..spectacular

4. The reactor is a tool of enormous ----: its energy is turned to the service of many disciplines, from metallurgy to archaeology.

(A) versatility   (B) disparity   (C) vagueness
(D) fragility   (E) fluctuation

5. The ---- of music these days provides the exposure that enables any person to discover that he or she has an ---- for some sort of music.

(A) polyphony. .esteem
(B) enrichment. .articulation
(C) classicism. .aptitude
(D) vibrance. .antipathy
(E) accessibility. .appreciation

6. There is little chance of ---- in a static society in which all people think and live alike.

(A) consensus   (B) boredom   (C) regularity
(D) tranquility   (E) innovation

Analogies

Questions of this kind test your understanding of relationships among words and ideas. You are asked to recognize pairs that are similar or parallel in nature. For example, some of the questions ask you to recognize a specific type of relationship, such as cause and effect; others may ask you to establish a relationship between concrete terms that is analogous to a relationship between abstract terms. Consider each relationship critically and then select the answer choice that comes closest to satisfying all the demands.

The directions given for analogy questions are approximately as follows:

Each question below consists of a related pair of words or phrases, followed by five lettered pairs of words or phrases. Select the lettered pair that best expresses a relationship similar to that expressed in the original pair.

Example:

> YAWN : BOREDOM ::   (A) dream : sleep   (B) anger : madness
> (C) smile : amusement   (D) face : expression
> (E) impatience : rebellion   Ⓐ Ⓑ ⬤ Ⓓ Ⓔ

7. MOTH : CLOTHING ::   (A) woodpecker : hole
    (B) bear : trap   (C) lamb : wool
     (D) puncture : tire   (E) termite : house

8. FILTER : LIQUID ::   (A) melt : ice
    (B) grind : solid   (C) sift : powder
     (D) inflate : air   (E) chisel : rock

9. ANNULMENT : MARRIAGE ::
    (A) nullification : contract
    (B) negation : opinion
    (C) refutation : authority
    (D) invalidation : discovery
    (E) denial : permission

Reading comprehension

Approximately half the testing time for the verbal sections of the SAT is devoted to reading comprehension because college students must be able to read with understanding, insight, and discrimination. The reading passages are taken from a variety of fields, and reading comprehension is tested at several levels. Some of the questions merely test your understanding of the plain sense of what has been stated directly. To answer other questions, you must be able to interpret and analyze what you have read. Still other questions test your ability to recognize reasonable applications of the principles or opinions expressed by the author. And some of the questions require you to judge what you have read — to observe

good and bad points in the presentation, to recognize how far the
author has supported his statements by evidence, and to recognize
and evaluate the means used by the author to get his points across.

The directions for reading comprehension questions are
as follows:

Each passage below is followed by questions based on its
content. Answer all questions following a passage on the
basis of what is <u>stated</u> or <u>implied</u> in that passage.

Can poverty in the United States be abolished within
the limits of the welfare state?

The answer is clear enough. The government's
own figures demonstrate that the current antipoverty
programs are basically inadequate. I do not, however,
want to dismiss completely the government's antipoverty programs. Current serious discussion of
poverty in this country is a gain which one owes in
part to that program. But there is no point in pretending that a little more welfarism will do away with
a national shame.

Today's poor are different from the pre-Second
World War poor. The "old" poor lived at a time when
economic opportunity was the national trend, when the
net income from the growth of American manufacturing
increased by 4,500 per cent. It was the "old" poor,
mostly Eastern European immigrants unified by language and culture, who created the big-city political
machines and participated in the organization of unions
and the political struggle for the New Deal. They had
objective, realistic reason for hope.

An analysis of the first phase and second phase of
the New Deal of the Roosevelt administration is quite
relevant at this point. The first phase of the New Deal,
supported by American business and dominated by the
National Recovery Act, gave recognition to an old
corporate dream—economy planned by business. The

second phase of the New Deal (the source of today's welfare theory and antipoverty wisdom) moved away from the concept of planning and toward a "free market." The assumption was that in its intervention the government should not plan but should stimulate the economy and that the private sector and initiative would continue to be the mainspring of progress.

After the Second World War, the government started emphasizing training programs because some workers were not participating in the general economic advance. However, these training programs have missed the fundamental problem. The novelty of impoverishment today is that it takes place in a time of automation. The government offers education and training and at the same time admits that the jobs for its graduates are obsolete. Such hypocrisy reinforces the cynicism and resistance to organization which characterizes poor communities.

It is therefore crucial that the federal government generate jobs and create an environment of economic hope. The essence of the "third phase" of the New Deal would be social investment, a conscious and political allocation of resources to meet public needs. This New Deal would be dependent upon a coalition, which would include, but not be confined to, the poor, that would see to it that planning and social investment were extended in a democratic way.

10. It can be inferred that the first phase of the New Deal

(A) discouraged investment in industry

(B) was the source of today's welfare theory

(C) stimulated the growth of big-city political machines

(D) provided programs to prepare workers for jobs in automated industry

(E) gave business an opportunity to extend control over the economy

11. The primary purpose of the passage is to

(A) expose those who support government antipoverty programs
(B) distinguish between the pre- and post-Second
World War poor
(C) argue for social investment by the federal
government to alleviate poverty
(D) reveal the practices of society that perpetuate
poverty
(E) distinguish among the first, second, and
third New Deal approaches to reducing
unemployment

12. According to the passage, today's poor differ from
the "old" poor in which of the following ways?

I. The "old" poor enjoyed a higher average
income.
II. The "old" poor had a realistic hope for
economic opportunity.
III. The "old" poor were better educated.

(A) II only   (B) III only   (C) I and III only
(D) II and III only   (E) I, II, and III

13. The author's attitude toward the government's
current poverty program can best be described as

(A) unqualified appreciation
(B) fundamental dissatisfaction
(C) apathetic acceptance
(D) self-righteous pomposity
(E) violent indignation

The assumption that chlorofluorocarbons would be
innocuous in the environment because they were chemi-
cally inert might have gone unchallenged for some time,
but at a conference someone mentioned their curious
persistence in the atmosphere to F. Sherwood Rowland,
a chemist, who began to wonder what ultimately became

of the synthetic compounds. In 1973, Rowland got a
research grant to study the question, and he and his
associate, Mario J. Molina, set out to prove that
chlorofluorocarbons must be floating unchanged to the
stratosphere, where the strong ultraviolet rays in sunlight would cause them to release chlorine atoms. These
atoms would act as catalysts to destroy ozone, with each
chlorine atom capable of setting off a chain reaction involving thousands of ozone molecules. These ozone
molecules are part of the atmospheric ozone layer that
protects the earth from solar ultraviolet rays. It is
thought that if this layer is depleted, the results could
be increased incidences of skin cancer, damage to plant
life, and even global climatic changes.

Even though the depletion of the ozone layer
would be lessened if production of the compounds
ceased immediately, Rowland and Molina concluded
that a twenty to forty per cent reduction of the layer
was a strong possibility. The most disturbing conclusion was that the full effect of chlorofluorocarbons
already in the atmosphere would not be felt for at least
a decade, since the gases floated up and down until
they gradually ascended to the ozone layer. "There
was no moment of triumph," Rowland recalled. "I
just came home one night and told my wife, 'The work
is going very well, but it looks like the end of the
world.'"

14. The passage primarily concerns the

     (A) effects of ozone on plant and animal life
     (B) interaction of ultraviolet rays with ozone
     (C) potentially dangerous uses for chlorofluoro-
         carbons
     (D) discovery of the effect of chlorofluorocarbons
         on the ozone layer
     (E) variety of gases in the atmosphere surround-
         ing the earth

15.   It can be inferred that before the publication of
      the study of Rowland and Molina, it was widely
      assumed that chlorofluorocarbons in the environ-
      ment

      (A) were harmless
      (B) absorbed ultraviolet rays
      (C) reacted with ozone
      (D) were rapidly increasing
      (E) could not be reproduced in a laboratory

16.   According to the hypothesis of Rowland and
      Molina, the chlorofluorocarbons would release
      chlorine atoms when

      (A) the ozone broke up the chlorofluorocarbon
           molecules
      (B) they were subjected to the lowered air pres-
           sure of the stratosphere
      (C) they were exposed to strong ultraviolet rays
           in the stratosphere
      (D) they floated down from the stratosphere
           closer to the earth's surface
      (E) the amount of ozone in the stratosphere was
           more than twenty per cent

Mathematical Questions

The mathematical questions in the SAT are designed to measure abilities closely related to college-level work in the liberal arts, engineering, and other fields requiring mathematics by providing a general answer to three questions: (1) How well do you understand elementary mathematics? (2) How well can you apply what you already know to new situations? (3) How well can you use what you know in insightful or nonroutine ways of thinking? Your ability in these areas will make an important contribution to your success not only in mathematics, but also in a wide variety of fields such as chemistry, physics, engineering, statistics, economics, and accounting.

In some questions you will be asked to apply graphic, spatial, numerical, and symbolic techniques to types of problems that are familiar; these may be similar to exercises in your textbooks. In other questions, you will work with types of problems that are not familiar, problems that require insightful reasoning, or combinations of these. In any case, you do not have to use mathematical subject matter beyond elementary algebra and geometry. Advanced mathematics is not required in the solution or interpretation of any of the questions.

Special mention should be made of certain questions that emphasize insightful reasoning. Any mathematical question requires insight in the sense that one must find the proper technique for its solution. In certain questions in the SAT, however, an even greater emphasis is placed on this kind of nonroutine approach. In question 22, for example, the correct solution can readily be obtained, once an appropriate insightful approach has been discovered, but could be obtained only at the cost of much time and labor if a routine approach were used.

On the other hand, questions 18 and 26 may reasonably be solved by either method, although an insightful approach would still be quicker than a routine one. When you take the SAT, however, do not spend too much time searching for nonroutine solutions. If you cannot find such a solution, try a routine approach or go on to the next question.

Two kinds of multiple-choice questions may appear in the mathematical portion of the SAT and are described in this booklet:

1. Standard multiple-choice
2. Quantitative comparison

Of these, type two requires special directions.

In the quantitative comparison questions you are given two quantities that are sometimes accompanied by information that concerns either or both quantities. Answering the question properly depends upon your ability to decide which, if either, is the greater quantity. In general, quantitative comparison questions require less time to answer, involve less reading, and require somewhat less computation than the usual multiple-choice questions. This type of question reflects the contemporary emphasis in school mathematics on inequalities; you must use the concepts of "greater than," "less than," and "equal to" to decide which choice is correct. Observe that the note about figures for quantitative comparison questions differs from that for other questions in the test. Several clarifying examples are included in the directions.

Directions, reference formulas, and sample questions are provided on the following pages for each type of question described. Directions for the quantitative comparison questions require special study, and it is to your advantage to become familiar with them before the test. *All such directions are a part of the timed test.*

Standard multiple-choice questions

Sample questions 1-10 illustrate the range of difficulty and content in the standard multiple-choice question, and they provide a representative sample of the variety of questions you may expect to encounter. Standard multiple-choice questions will appear with the following instructions:

DIRECTIONS: In this section solve each problem using any available space on the page for scratchwork. Then indicate the *one* correct answer in the appropriate space on the answer sheet.

The following information is for your reference in solving some of the problems.

Circle of radius r:

Area $= \pi r^2$

Circumference $= 2\pi r$

The number of degress of arc in a circle is 360.

The measure in degrees of a straight angle is 180.

Triangle:

The sum of the measures in degrees of the angles of a triangle is 180.

If $\angle CDA$ is a right angle, then

(1) area of $\triangle ABC = \dfrac{AB \times CD}{2}$

(2) $AC^2 = AD^2 + DC^2$

Definitions of symbols:

$=$ is equal to	$\leqq$ is less than or equal to
$\neq$ is unequal to	$\geqq$ is greater than or equal to
$<$ is less than	$\parallel$ is parallel to
$>$ is greater than	$\perp$ is perpendicular to

NOTE: Figures which accompany problems in this test are intended to provide information useful in solving the problems. They are drawn as accurately as possible EXCEPT when it is stated in a specific problem that its figure is not drawn to scale. All figures lie in the plane unless otherwise indicated. All numbers used are real numbers.

1. If $x^3 + y = x^3 + 5$, then $y =$

(A) -5 (B) $-\sqrt[3]{5}$ (C) $\sqrt[3]{5}$ (D) 5 (E) 5^3

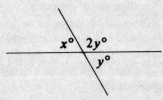

2. In the figure above, two lines intersect as shown. What is the value of x ?

(A) 30   (B) 60   (C) 90   (D) 120   (E) 180

3. The number 99,999,999 is NOT divisible by

   (A) 9
   (B) 11
   (C) 99
   (D) 111
   (E) 9,999

Sun.	Mon.	Tue.	Wed.	Thu.	Fri.	Sat.
						30
29	28	27	26	25	24	23
22	21	20	19	18	17	16

4. If the days of a month are numbered consecutively backward as shown on the partial calendar above, on what day of the week will the day numbered 1 occur?

   (A) Sunday
   (B) Monday
   (C) Tuesday
   (D) Friday
   (E) Saturday

5. Of the following numbers, which is the LEAST?

   (A) 0.102
   (B) 0.11
   (C) 0.1201
   (D) 0.101
   (E) 0.1001

6. If $x^2 - y^2 = 27$, then $3(x + y)(x - y) =$

    (A) 9   (B) 24   (C) 27   (D) 36   (E) 81

7. Points A, B, X, and Y lie on the same line but
    not necessarily in that order. Given the lengths
    $AB = 12$, $BX = 2$, and $XY = 8$, what is
    length AY?

    (A) 2
    (B) 6
    (C) 18
    (D) 22
    (E) It cannot be determined from the information
         given.

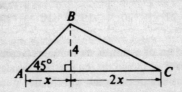

8. In $\triangle ABC$ above, what is the length of side AC?

    (A) 24   (B) 18   (C) 12   (D) 8
    (E) It cannot be determined from the information
        given.

9. A jar contains 10 pencils, some sharpened and some
    unsharpened. Each of the following could be the
    ratio of sharpened to unsharpened pencils EXCEPT

    (A) $1 : 1$
    (B) $3 : 2$
    (C) $4 : 1$
    (D) $5 : 1$
    (E) $9 : 1$

10. Initially, there are exactly 18 bananas on a tree. If one monkey eats $\frac{1}{3}$ of the bananas and another monkey eats $\frac{1}{3}$ of the bananas that are left, how many bananas are still on the tree?

(A) 4
(B) 6
(C) 8
(D) 10
(E) 16

Quantitative comparison questions

Questions 11–15 are examples of quantitative comparison questions. There are only four (4) choices to choose an answer from in this type of question. Quantitative comparison questions will appear with the following instructions:

Questions 11–15 each consist of two quantities, one in Column A and one in Column B. You are to compare the two quantities and on the answer sheet blacken space

A if the quantity in Column A is greater;
B if the quantity in Column B is greater;
C if the two quantities are equal
D if the relationship cannot be determined from the information given.

Notes: 1. In certain questions, information concerning one or both of the quantities to be compared is centered above the two columns.
2. In a given question, a symbol that appears in both columns represents the same thing in Column A as it does in Column B.
3. Letters such as x, n, and k stand for real numbers.

EXAMPLES		Answers
Column A	Column B	
E1. 2×6	$2 + 6$	● Ⓑ Ⓒ Ⓓ
E2 $180 - x$	$x°$ $y°$ y	Ⓐ Ⓑ ● Ⓓ
E3. $p - q$	$q - p$	Ⓐ Ⓑ Ⓒ ●

	Column A	Column B

11.   0 0×2

---

12. $a + 25$ $a - 5$

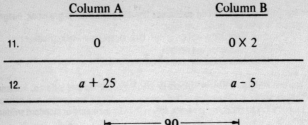

Note: Figure not drawn to scale.

On segment AD, length AB is not equal to length CD.

13.   Length AC Length BD

When a certain pitcher contains 3 cups of water, the pitcher contains half its capacity.

14.   The capacity, in cups,   6 cups
       of the pitcher

---

15.   The cost of a stereo that   The cost of a television
       is marked "15% off"   set that is marked "20% off"

The Test of Standard Written English

The Test of Standard Written English is graded separately from the standard verbal and mathematical portions and is to be used by the colleges primarily as a means for determining student abilities in English composition for placement purposes. Grading is in a range from 20 to 80; the section contains a total of 50 questions. The following are two types of questions which appear on this section.

The questions in this section measure skills that are important to writing well. In particular, they test your ability to recognize and use language that is clear, effective, and correct according to the requirements of standard written English, the kind of English found in most college textbooks.

Directions: The following sentences contain problems in grammar, usage, diction (choice of words), and idiom.

> Some sentences are correct.
> No sentence contains more than one error.

You will find that the error, if there is one, is underlined and lettered. Assume that elements of the sentence that are not underlined are correct and cannot be changed. In choosing answers, follow the requirements of standard written English.

If there is an error, select the one underlined part that must be changed to make the sentence correct and blacken the corresponding space on your answer sheet.

If there is no error, blacken answer space Ⓔ .

EXAMPLE: **SAMPLE ANSWER**

The region has a climate <u>so severe that</u> plants   Ⓐ Ⓑ ● Ⓓ Ⓔ
                          A

growing there rarely <u>had been</u> more than twelve
       B   C

inches high. <u>No error</u>
        D   E

---

1. Idealists are <u>not always</u> as <u>ignorant of</u> realities as <u>his</u>
                       A   B   C

    critics would <u>like to</u> believe. <u>No error</u>
                      D   E

2. <u>Once an</u> Italian colony, Eritrea <u>was captured</u> by
        A   B

    the British in 1941 and was <u>united with</u> Ethiopia
                                      C

    in <u>the early</u> 1950's. <u>No error</u>
          D   E

Directions: In each of the following sentences, some part or all of the sentence is underlined. Below each sentence you will find five ways of phrasing the underlined part. Select the answer that produces the most effective sentence, one that is clear and exact, without awkwardness or ambiguity, and blacken the corresponding space on your answer sheet. In choosing answers, follow the requirements of standard written English. Choose the answer that best expresses the meaning of the original sentence.

Answer (A) is always the same as the underlined part. Choose answer (A) if
you think the original sentence needs no revision.

EXAMPLE: **SAMPLE ANSWER**

Laura Ingalls Wilder published her first book   Ⓐ ● Ⓒ Ⓓ Ⓔ
and she was sixty-five years old then.
  (A) and she was sixty-five years old then
  (B) when she was sixty-five years old
  (C) at age sixty-five years old
  (D) upon reaching sixty-five years
  (E) at the time when she was sixty-five

---

3. Because dodo birds could not <u>fly, so they were
   killed</u> by the hogs and monkeys brought to the
   islands by the explorers.

   (A) fly, so they were killed
   (B) fly, they were killed
   (C) fly and they were killed
   (D) fly, and this allowed them to be killed
   (E) fly, killing them

4. Performing before an audience for the first time,
   <u>fear suddenly overcame the child and she could
   not remember her lines.</u>

   (A) fear suddenly overcame the child and she
       could not remember her lines
   (B) the lines could not be remembered by the
       child because she was overcome by fear
   (C) the child was suddenly overcome by fear and
       could not remember her lines
   (D) the child was suddenly overcome by fear,
       she could not remember her lines
   (E) suddenly the child was overcome by fear, and
       consequently not remembering her lines

Answers to Sample Questions

Verbal

1.	A	7.	E	12.	A
2.	C	8.	C	13.	B
3.	A	9.	A	14.	D
4.	A	10.	E	15.	A
5.	E	11.	C	16.	C
6.	E				

Mathematical

1.	D	8.	C
2.	B	9.	D
3.	D	10.	C
4.	A	11.	C
5.	E	12.	A
6.	E	13.	B
7.	E	14.	C
		15.	D

Standard Written English

1. C
2. E
3. B
4. C

3   Building Your Vocabulary

Procedure

The original Basic Word List of more than 2,000 words in thirty sections has been retained in this edition. For even more study material, refer to Barron's full-length publication *How to Prepare for College Entrance Examinations*, where ten more vocabulary sections have been added in response to the many requests of students and teachers.

All the words are defined and illustrated in the thirty word lists which follow. We recommend that you follow the procedure described below in order to use the word lists and the exercises most profitably:

1. Allot a definite time each day for the study of a list.
2. Devote one hour to each list.
3. Pay particular attention to those words in each section which have unusual definitions that are not commonly known. Many tests make use of these secondary definitions.
4. List unusual words on index cards which you can shuffle and review from time to time.
5. Take the test which follows each list at least one day after studying the words. In this way, you will check your ability to remember what you have studied.
6. If you can answer correctly 15 of the 20 questions in the test, you may proceed to the next list; if you cannot answer this number, restudy the list.
7. Keep a record of your guesses and your success as a guesser in the chart which follows.

This chart has been developed by the authors because of the uncertainty that exists in many students' minds about the nature of the penalties imposed for wrong answers on many tests. The advice given in the preceding chapter is too general for the student who is worried about the outcome of the examination. All too often, good students are afraid to guess "intelligently." They are skeptical of the statement that it is advisable to guess when one or more of the choices can be eliminated.

By keeping systematic records of the guessing done while taking many tests in this book, a student can find out how intelligently and profitably he or she can guess.

Self-evaluation

1. In each test, answer those questions which you know. (You will probably make some mistakes in these; however, these errors do not enter into the guessing chart.)

2. Examine the unanswered questions. If you are *totally* ignorant of the word or concept tested, leave it blank. If you find any clue or have a "hunch" about an answer, if you can eliminate one or more of the choices, guess.

3. Enter the number of guesses made in each test and the number right and wrong in the spaces provided in the chart.

4. Apply the formula. Score equals the number right minus one-quarter of the number wrong. Thus, a student who guesses the answer to 20 questions and gets 6 right and 14 wrong

$$R - \frac{1}{4}W \quad \text{or } 6 - \frac{14}{4} \quad \text{or } 6 - 3\frac{1}{2} \quad \text{or } 2\frac{1}{2}$$

has gained two and a half points. A student who gets 3 right and 17 wrong

$$R - \frac{1}{4}W \quad \text{or } 3 - \frac{17}{4} \quad \text{or } 3 - 4\frac{1}{4} \quad \text{or } -1\frac{1}{4}$$

has lost one and a quarter points.

5. If you keep records of your results in the thirty Word Study tests, you will be able to determine whether you should "guess" on the actual test. If you con-

sistently gain, you should guess. If you lost credit, you should be very careful not to answer questions which puzzle you.

	Page on which test appears	Number of questions in test	Number of guesses	Number of guesses right	Number of guesses wrong	Result + or −
WORD STUDY TEST 1	44	20				
WORD STUDY TEST 2	50	20				
WORD STUDY TEST 3	57	20				
WORD STUDY TEST 4	63	20				
WORD STUDY TEST 5	69	20				
WORD STUDY TEST 6	75	20				
WORD STUDY TEST 7	81	20				
WORD STUDY TEST 8	87	20				
WORD STUDY TEST 9	92	20				
WORD STUDY TEST 10	99	20				
WORD STUDY TEST 11	105	20				
WORD STUDY TEST 12	110	20				
WORD STUDY TEST 13	116	20				
WORD STUDY TEST 14	122	20				
WORD STUDY TEST 15	127	20				
WORD STUDY TEST 16	133	20				
WORD STUDY TEST 17	139	20				
WORD STUDY TEST 18	145	20				
WORD STUDY TEST 19	150	20				
WORD STUDY TEST 20	156	20				
WORD STUDY TEST 21	162	20				
WORD STUDY TEST 22	168	20				
WORD STUDY TEST 23	175	20				
WORD STUDY TEST 24	180	20				

	Page on which test appears	Number of questions in test	Number of guesses	Number of guesses right	Number of guesses wrong	Result + or −
WORD STUDY TEST 25	186	20				
WORD STUDY TEST 26	192	20				
WORD STUDY TEST 27	198	20				
WORD STUDY TEST 28	203	20				
WORD STUDY TEST 29	209	20				
WORD STUDY TEST 30	214	20				

The approximately 2,000 words in this list have been compiled from various sources. They have been taken from the standard literature read by high school students throughout the country and from the many tests taken by high school and college students. Ever since the list first appeared in 1954, countless students have reported that mastering this list has been of immense value in the taking of all kinds of college entrance and scholarship tests. It has been used with profit by people preparing for civil service examinations, placement tests, and promotion examinations in many industrial fields.

For each word, the following is provided:

1. The word is printed in heavy type (words are arranged in strict alphabetical order for ease in locating).
2. Its part of speech is given.
3. Where needed, the pronunciation of a difficult syllable or sound is indicated. For this, a simplified key is used:

KEY

ā — ale	ə — event, allow	ou — out
ă — add	ī — ice	th — thin
ä — arm	ĭ — ill	ū — use
à — ask	ō — old	ŭ — up
ē — ever	ŏ — odd	zh — pleasure
e — end	ô — orb	
ê — err, her	oo — food	

4. A brief definition of the word is given.

5. A sentence illustrates the use of the word.

6. Whenever useful, related words are provided.

7. Following each list of words will be a group of common prefixes, suffixes, and stems. Studying these can be of help to many students in reinforcing the impression the word has made. It will help the student interpret other words he encounters. However, it must be remembered that many words have lost their original meanings and have taken on more specific and limited meanings. These prefixes, suffixes, and roots should be used as a guide when in doubt about the meaning of a strange word. There is no substitute for learning the exact meaning of each word as it is used today.

8. Answer Key for all Word Study Tests is on pages 336-339.

Basic Word List

Word List 1   abase - allegory

abase V. lower; humiliate. His refusal to *abase* himself in the eyes of his followers irritated the king, who wanted to humiliate the proud leader.

abash V. embarrass. He was not at all *abashed* by her open admiration.

abdicate V. renounce; give up. When Edward VIII *abdicated* the British throne, he surprised the entire world.

abettor N. encourager. He was accused of being an aider and *abettor* of the criminal. abet, V.

abeyance (-*bā´*-) N. suspended action. The deal was held in *abeyance* until his arrival.

abhor V. detest; hate. He *abhorred* all forms of bigotry. abhorrence, N.

abjure V. renounce upon oath. He *abjured* his allegiance to the king. abjuration N.

ablution N. washing. His daily *ablutions* were accompanied by loud noises which he humorously labeled "Opera in the Bath."

abominate V. loathe; hate. Moses scolded the idol worshippers in the tribe because he *abominated* the custom.

aboriginal ADJ., N. being the first of its kind in a region; primitive; native. His studies of the primitive art forms of the *aboriginal* Indians were widely reported in the scientific journals. aborigines, N.

abortive ADJ. unsuccessful; fruitless. We had to abandon our *abortive* attempts.

abrade V. wear away by friction; erode. The skin of his leg was *abraded* by the sharp rocks. abrasion, N.

abrogate V. abolish. He intended to *abrogate* the decree issued by his predecessor.

abscond V. depart secretly and hide. The teller *absconded* with the bonds and was not found.

absolve V. pardon (an offense). The father confessor *absolved* him of his sins. absolution, N.

abstemious (-*stē´*-) ADJ. temperate; sparing in drink, etc. The drunkards mocked him because of his *abstemious* habits.

abstinence N. restraint from eating or drinking. The doctor recommended total *abstinence* from salted foods. abstain, V.

ā—ale; ă—add; ä—arm; à—ask; ē—eve; ĕ—end; ê—err, her; ə—allow; even; ī—ice; ĭ—ill; ō—oll; ŏ—odd; ô—orb; ōō—food; ŏŏ—foot, put; o—oŭt; th—thin; ū—use; ŭ—up; zh—pleasure

abstruse ADJ. obscure; profound; difficult to understand. He read *abstruse* works in philosophy.

accelerate V. move faster. In our science class, we learn how falling bodies *accelerate.*

accessory N. additional object; useful but not essential thing. The *accessories* she bought cost more than the dress. also ADJ.

acclivity (*-klĭv´-*) N. sharp upslope of a hill. The car could not go up the *acclivity* in high gear.

accolade (*ak´-ə-lād*) N. award of merit. In Hollywood, an "Oscar" is the highest *accolade.*

accomplice N. partner in crime. Because he had provided the criminal with the lethal weapon, he was arrested as an *accomplice* in the murder.

accord N. agreement. He was in complete *accord* with the verdict.

accost V. approach and speak first to a person. When the two young men *accosted* me, I was frightened because I thought they were going to attack me.

accoutre (*-kōōt´-*) V. equip. The fisherman was *accoutred* with the best that the sporting goods store could supply. accoutrements, N.

accretion (*-krē´-*) N. growth; increase. The *accretion* of wealth marked the family's rise in power.

accrue V. come about by addition. You must pay the interest which has *accrued* on your debt as well as the principal sum. accrual, N.

acetic (*-sēt´-*) ADJ. vinegary. The salad had an exceedingly *acetic* flavor.

acidulous (*-sĭd´-*) ADJ. slightly sour; sharp, caustic. James was unpopular because of his sarcastic and *acidulous* remarks.

acknowledge V. recognize; admit. When pressed for an answer, he *acknowledged* the existence of another motive for the crime.

acme (*ăk´-mē*) N. top; pinnacle. His success in this role marked his *acme* as an actor.

acoustics (*-kōō´-*) N. science of sound; quality that makes a room easy or hard to hear in. Carnegie Hall is liked by music lovers because of its fine *acoustics.*

acquiescent (*-w-ĕs´-*) ADJ. accepting passively. His *acquiescent* manner did not indicate the extent of his reluctance to join the group. acquiesce, V.

acquittal N. deliverance from a charge. His *acquittal* by the jury surprised those who had thought him guilty. acquit, V.

ā—ale; ă—add; ä—arm; à—ask; ē—eve; ĕ—end; ê—err, her; ə—allow; even; ī—ice; ĭ—ill; ō—oll; ŏ—odd; ô—orb; ōō—food; ŏŏ—foot, put; o—out; th—thin; ū—use; ŭ—up; zh—pleasure

acrid ADJ. sharp; bitterly pungent. The *acrid* odor of burnt gunpowder filled the room after the pistol had been fired.

acrimonious ADJ. stinging; caustic. His tendency to utter *acrimonious* remarks alienated his audience. acrimony, N.

actuarial ADJ. calculating; pertaining to insurance statistics. According to recent *actuarial* tables, life expectancy is greater today than it was a century ago.

actuate V. motivate. I fail to understand what *actuated* you to reply to this letter so nastily.

acumen (-*kū´*-) N. mental keenness. His business *acumen* helped him to succeed where others had failed.

adage (*ăd´*-) N. wise saying; proverb. There is much truth in the old *adage* about fools and their money.

adamant (*ăd´*-) ADJ. hard; inflexible. He was *adamant* in his determination to punish the wrongdoer. adamantine, ADJ.

adapt V. alter; modify. Some species of animals have become extinct because they could not *adapt* to a changing environment.

addiction N. compulsive, habitual need. His *addiction* to drugs caused his friends much grief.

addle ADJ. rotten; muddled; crazy. This *addle*-headed plan is so preposterous that it does not deserve any consideration. also V.

adduce V. present as evidence. When you *adduce* evidence of this nature, you must be sure of your sources.

adept (-*dĕpt´*) ADJ. expert at. He was *adept* at the fine art of irritating people. also N.

adhere V. stick fast to. I will *adhere* to this opinion until proof that I am wrong is presented. adhesion, N.

adipose (*ăd´*-) ADJ. fatty. Excess *adipose* tissue should be avoided by middle-aged people.

adjuration (*ăj-a-rā´*-) N. solemn urging. His *adjuration* to tell the truth did not change the witnesses' testimony. adjure, V.

admonish V. warn; reprove. He *admonished* his listeners to change their wicked ways. admonition, N.

adroit ADJ. skillful. His *adroit* handling of the delicate situation pleased his employers.

adulation N. flattery; admiration. He thrived on the *adulation* of his henchmen.

adulterate V. make impure by mixing with baser substances. It is a crime to *adulterate* foods without informing the buyer.

adumbration (-*brā´*-) N. foreshadowing; outlining. The *adumbration* of the future in science fiction is often extremely fantastic.

ā—ale; ă—add; ä—arm; à—ask; ē—eve; ĕ—end; ê—err, her; ə—allow; even; ī—ice; ĭ—ill; ō—oll; ŏ—odd; ô—orb; o͞o—food; o͝o—foot, put; o—out; th—thin; ū—use; ŭ—up; zh—pleasure

adventitious (*-tĭsh´-*) ADJ. accidental; casual. He found this *adventitious* meeting with his friend extremely fortunate.

adverse (*-vêrs´*) ADJ. unfavorable; hostile. *Adverse* circumstances compelled him to close his business.

adversity N. poverty; misfortune. We must learn to meet *adversity* gracefully.

advocate V. urge; plead for. The abolitionists *advocated* freedom for the slaves. also N.

aesthetic (*ĕs-thĕt´-*) ADJ. artistic; dealing with or capable of appreciation of the beautiful. Because of his *aesthetic* nature, he was emotionally disturbed by ugly things. aesthete, N.

affected ADJ. artificial; pretended. His *affected* mannerisms irritated many of us who had known him before his promotion. affectation, N.

affiliation N. joining; associating with. His *affiliation* with the political party was of short duration for he soon disagreed with his colleagues.

affinity N. kinship. He felt an *affinity* with all who suffered; their pains were his pains.

affirmation N. solemn pledge by one who refuses to take an oath. The Constitution of this country provides for oath or *affirmation* by officeholders.

affluence (*ăf´-*) N. abundance; wealth. Foreigners are amazed by the *affluence* and luxury of the American way of life.

affray N. public brawl. He was badly mauled by the fighters in the *affray*.

agape (*ə-gāp´*) ADJ. openmouthed. He stared, *agape*, at the many strange animals in the zoo.

agglomeration N. collection; heap. It took weeks to assort the *agglomeration* of miscellaneous items he had collected on his trip.

aggrandize (*-grăn-*) V. increase or intensify. The history of the past quarter century illustrates how a President may *aggrandize* his power to act aggressively in international affairs without considering the wishes of Congress.

aggregate ADJ. sum; total. The *aggregate* wealth of this country is staggering to the imagination. also V.

aghast ADJ. horrified. He was *aghast* at the nerve of the speaker who had insulted his host.

agility N. nimbleness. The *agility* of the acrobat amazed and thrilled the audience.

agitate V. stir up; disturb. His fiery remarks *agitated* the already angry mob.

ā—ale; ă—add; ä—arm; à—ask; ē—eve; ĕ—end; ê—err, her; ə—allow; even; ī—ice; ĭ—ill; ō—oll; ŏ—odd; ô—orb; ōō—food; ŏŏ—foot, put; o—out; th—thin; ū—use; ŭ—up; zh—pleasure

agnostic N. one who is skeptical of the existence or knowability of a god or any ultimate reality. The *agnostic* demanded proof before he would accept the statement of the minister. also ADJ.

alacrity N. cheerful promptness. He demonstrated his eagerness to serve by his *alacrity* in executing the orders of his master.

albeit (ôl-bē´-ĭt) CONJ. although. *Albeit* fair, she was not sought after.

alchemy N. medieval chemistry. The changing of baser metals into gold was the goal of the students of *alchemy*. alchemist, N.

alias (ā´-lē-əs) N. an assumed name. John Smith's *alias* was Bob Jones. also ADV.

alienate V. make hostile; separate. His attempts to *alienate* the two friends failed because they had complete faith.

alimentary ADJ. supplying nourishment. The *alimentary* canal in our bodies is so named because digestion of foods occurs there.

alimony N. payment by a husband to his divorced wife. Mrs. Jones was awarded $200 monthly *alimony* by the court when she was divorced from her husband.

allay V. calm; pacify. The crew tried to *allay* the fears of the passengers by announcing that the fire had been controlled.

allege V. state without proof. It is *alleged* that he had worked for the enemy. allegation, N.

allegory N. story in which characters are used as symbols; fable. *Pilgrim's Progress* is an *allegory* of the temptations and victories of man's soul. allegorical, ADJ.

ETYMOLOGY 1

AB, ABS (from, away from) prefix
    abduct lead away, kidnap
    abjure renounce (swear away from)
    abscond depart secretly and hide

ABLE, IBLE (capable of) adjective suffix
    portable able to be carried
    legible able to be read
    interminable unable to be ended

AC, IC (like, pertaining to) adjective suffix
    cardiac pertaining to the heart
    aquatic pertaining to water
    dramatic pertaining to drama

AC, ACR (sharp)
    acrimonious bitter

ā—ale; ă—add; ä—arm; à—ask; ē—eve; ĕ—end; ê—err, her; ə—allow; even; ī—ice; ĭ—ill; ō—oll; ŏ—odd; ô—orb; o͞o—food; o͝o—foot, put; o—out; th—thin; ū—use; ŭ—up; zh—pleasure

acerbity bitterness of temper

acidulate make somewhat acidic or sour

AD (to, forward) prefix

adjure request earnestly

admit allow entrance

Note: By assimilation, the AD prefix is changed to

AC in accord

AF in affliction

AG in aggregation

AN in annexation

AP in apparition

AR in arraignment

AS in assumption

AT in attendance

AEV (age, era)

primeval of the first age

coeval of the same age or era

medieval (*mediaeval*) of the middle ages

AG, ACT (to do)

act deed

agent doer

retroactive having a backward or reversed action

AGOG (leader)

demagogue false leader of people

pedagogue teacher (leader of children)

synagogue house of worship (leading together of people)

AGRI, AGRARI (field)

agrarian one who works in the fields; farmer

agriculture cultivation of fields

ALI (another)

alias assumed (another) name

alienate estrange (divert from another)

inalienable unable to be diverted from another

TEST—Word List 1—Synonyms

Each of the questions below consists of a word printed in italics, followed by five words or phrases numbered 1 to 5. Choose the numbered word or phrase which is most nearly similar in meaning to the word in italics and write the number of your choice on your answer paper.

ā—ale; ă—add; ä—arm; à—ask; ē—eve; ĕ—end; ê—err, her; ə—allow; even; ī—ice; ĭ—ill; ō—oll; ŏ—odd; ô—orb; ōō—food; ŏŏ—foot, put; o—out; th—thin; ū—use; ŭ—up; zh—pleasure

1. *aborigines* 1 first designs 2 absolutions 3 finales 4 concepts 5 primitive inhabitants
2. *abeyance* 1 obedience 2 discussion 3 excitement 4 suspended action 5 editorial
3. *abjure* 1 discuss 2 renounce 3 run off secretly 4 perjure 5 project
4. *ablution* 1 censure 2 forgiveness 3 mutiny 4 survival 5 washing
5. *abortive* 1 unsuccessful 2 consuming 3 financing 4 familiar 5 fruitful
6. *abasement* 1 incurrence 2 taxation 3 ground floor 4 humility 5 humiliation
7. *abettor* 1 conception 2 one who wagers 3 encourager 4 evidence 5 protection
8. *abstruse* 1 profound 2 irrespective 3 suspended 4 protesting 5 not thorough
9. *acclivity* 1 index 2 report 3 upslope of a hill 4 character 5 negotiator
10. *accoutre* 1 compromise 2 equip 3 revise 4 encounter 5 visit
11. *accrue* 1 come about by addition 2 reach summit 3 create a crisis 4 process 5 educate
12. *accretion* 1 mayonnaise 2 ban 3 increase 4 protection 5 ceremony
13. *acme* 1 pinnacle 2 skin disease 3 basement 4 congestion 5 pinnacle
14. *acidulous* 1 recommended 2 witty 3 realistic 4 slightly sour 5 very generous
15. *abstinence* 1 restrained eating or drinking 2 vulgar display 3 deportment 4 reluctance 5 population
16. *acrid* 1 sour 2 bitterly pungent 3 sweetish 4 slightly acid 5 very hard
17. *adipose* 1 sandy 2 round 3 fatty 4 alkali 5 soft
18. *adventitious* 1 incidental 2 happy 3 courageous 4 accidental 5 foretelling
19. *affluence* 1 wealth 2 fear 3 persuasion 4 consideration 5 neglect
20. *allegory* 1 fable 2 poem 3 essay 4 anecdote 5 novel

Word List 2   alleviate - aptitude

alleviate (-*lē̄'-vē̄*-) v. relieve. This should *alleviate* the pain; if it does not, we shall have to use stronger drugs.

allocate v. assign. Even though the Red Cross had *allocated* a large sum

---

ā—ale; ă—add; ä—arm; à—ask; ē—eve; ĕ—end; ê—err, her; ə—allow; even; ī—ice; ĭ—ill; ō—oll; ŏ—odd; ô—orb; ōō—food; ŏŏ—foot, put; o—oŭt; th—thin; ū—use; ŭ—up; zh—pleasure

for the relief of the sufferers of the disaster, many people
perished.

alloy N. a mixture as of metals. *Alloys* of gold are used more frequently
than the pure metal.

allude V. refer indirectly. Try not to *allude* to this matter in his presence
because it annoys him to hear of it.

allusion N. indirect reference. The *allusions* to mythological characters
in Milton's poems bewilder the reader who has not studied
Latin.

alluvial ADJ. pertaining to soil deposits left by rivers, etc. The farmers
found the *alluvial* deposits at the mouth of the river very fertile.

aloof ADJ. apart; reserved. He remained *aloof* while all the rest con-
versed.

altercation N. wordy quarrel. Throughout the entire *altercation,* not one
sensible word was uttered.

altruism (ăl'-troō-) N. unselfish aid to others; generosity. The philanthropist was noted for his *altruism.* altruistic, ADJ.

amalgamate (-măl'-) V. combine; unite in one body. The unions will attempt to *amalgamate* their groups into one national body.

amass (-măs') V. collect. The miser's aim is to *amass* and hoard as much
gold as possible.

ambiguous (-bĭg'-) ADJ. doubtful in meaning. His *ambiguous* directions
misled us; we did not know which road to take. ambiguity,
N.

amble N. moving at an easy pace. When she first mounted the horse, she
was afraid to urge the animal to go faster than a gentle *amble.*
also V.

ambrosia (-brō'-zhə) N. food of the gods. *Ambrosia* was supposed to give
immortality to any human who ate it.

ambulatory (ăm'-) ADJ. able to walk. He was described as an *ambulatory*
patient because he was not confined to his bed.

ameliorate (-mēl'-) V. improve. Many social workers have attempted to
ameliorate the conditions of people living in the slums.

amenable (-mē'-) ADJ. readily managed; willing to be led. He was *amenable* to any suggestions which came from those he looked up
to; he resented advice from his inferiors.

amenities (-mĕn'-) N. agreeable manners; courtesies. He observed the
social *amenities.*

amiable (ā̄-mē-) ADJ. agreeable; lovable. His *amiable* disposition pleased
all who had dealings with him.

ā—ale; ă—add; ä—arm; à—ask; ē—eve; ĕ—end; ê—err, her; ə—allow;
even; ī—ice; ĭ—ill; ō—oll; ŏ—odd; ô—orb; ōō—food; oŏ—foot, put;
o—out; th—thin; ū—use; ŭ—up; zh—pleasure

amicable (*ăm'-*) ADJ. friendly. The dispute was settled in an *amicable* manner with no harsh words.

amnesia N. loss of memory. Because she was suffering from *amnesia,* the police could not get the young girl to identify herself.

amnesty N. pardon. When his first child was born, the king granted *amnesty* to all in prison.

amorphous ADJ. shapeless. He was frightened by the *amorphous* mass which had floated in from the sea.

amphibian ADJ. able to live both on land and in water. Frogs are classified as *amphibian.* also N.

amphitheater N. oval building with tiers of seats. The spectators in the *amphitheater* cheered the gladiators.

ample ADJ. abundant. He had *ample* opportunity to dispose of his loot before the police caught up with him.

amplify V. enlarge. His attempts to *amplify* his remarks were drowned out by the jeers of the audience.

amputate V. cut off part of body; prune. When the doctors decided to *amputate* his leg to prevent the spread of gangrene, he cried that he preferred death to incapacity.

amuck ADV. in a state of rage. The police had to be called in to restrain him after he ran *amuck* in the department store.

amulet (*ăm'-*) N. charm; talisman. Around his neck he wore the *amulet* which the witch doctor had given him.

analogous (*-năl'-ə-gəs*) ADJ. comparable. He called our attention to the things that had been done in an *analogous* situation and recommended that we do the same.

analogy N. similarity; parallelism. Your *analogy* is not a good one because the two situations are not similar.

anarchy (*ăn'-*) N. absence of governing body; state of disorder. The assassination of the leaders led to a period of *anarchy.*

anathema (*-năth'-*) N. solemn curse. He heaped *anathema* upon his foe.

ancillary (*ăn'-sə-*) ADJ. serving as an aid or accessory; auxiliary. In an *ancillary* capacity he was helpful; however, he could not be entrusted with leadership. also N.

andirons N. metal supports in a fireplace for cooking utensils or logs. She spent many hours in the department stores looking for a pair of ornamental *andirons* for her fireplace.

anemia (*-nē'-*) N. condition in which blood lacks red corpuscles. The doctor ascribes his tiredness to *anemia.* anemic, ADJ.

anesthetic (*-thĕt'-*) N. substance that removes sensation with or without

ā—ale; ă—add; ä—arm; à—ask; ē—eve; ĕ—end; ê—err, her; ə—allow; even; ī—ice; ĭ—ill; ō—oll; ŏ—odd; ô—orb; ōo—food; ŏŏ—foot, put; o—out; th—thin; ū—use; ŭ—up; zh—pleasure

loss of consciousness. His monotonous voice acted like an *anesthetic;* his audience was soon asleep. anesthesia, N.

animadversion (-vêr´-) N. critical remark. He resented the *animadversions* of his critics, particularly because he realized they were true.

animated ADJ. lively. Her *animated* expression indicated a keenness of intellect.

animosity N. active enmity. He incurred the *animosity* of the ruling class because he advocated limitations of their power.

annals N. records; history. In the *annals* of this period, we find no mention of democratic movements.

annihilate (-nī´-ə-) V. destroy. The enemy in its revenge tried to *annihilate* the entire population.

annuity N. yearly allowance. The *annuity* he set up with the insurance company supplements his social security benefits so that he can live very comfortably without working.

annul (-nŭl´) V. make void. The parents of the eloped couple tried to *annul* the marriage.

anomalous (-nŏm´-) ADJ. abnormal; irregular. He was placed in the *anomalous* position of seeming to approve procedures which he despised.

anomaly N. irregularity. A bird that cannot fly is an *anomaly.*

anonymous (-nŏn´-) ADJ. having no name. He tried to ascertain the identity of the writer of the *anonymous* letter.

antagonism (-tăg´-) N. active resistance. We shall have to overcome the *antagonism* of the natives before our plans for settling this area can succeed.

antecede V. precede. The invention of the radiotelegraph *anteceded* the development of television by a quarter of a century.

antediluvian (-lōō´-) ADJ. antiquated; ancient. The *antediluvian* customs had apparently not changed for thousands of years. also N.

anthropoid (ăn´-) ADJ. manlike. The gorilla is the strongest of the *anthropoid* animals. also N.

anthropologist (-pŏl´-) N. a student of the history and science of mankind. *Anthropologists* have discovered several relics of prehistoric man in this area.

anticlimax (-klī´-) N. letdown in thought or emotion. After the fine performance in the first act, the rest of the play was an *anticlimax.* anticlimactic, ADJ.

antipathy (-tĭp´-) N. aversion; dislike. His extreme *antipathy* to dispute caused him to avoid argumentative discussions with his friends.

ā—ale; ă—add; ä—arm; à—ask; ē—eve; ĕ—end; ê—err, her; ə—allow; even; ī—ice; ĭ—ill; ō—oll; ŏ—odd; ô—orb; ōō—food; ŏŏ—foot, put; o—out; th—thin; ū—use; ŭ—up; zh—pleasure

antiseptic N. substance that prevents infection. It is advisable to apply an *antiseptic* to any wound, no matter how slight or insignificant. also ADJ.

antithesis (*-tĭth'-ə-*) N. contrast; direct opposite of or to. This tyranny was the *antithesis* of all that he had hoped for, and he fought it with all his strength.

apathetic ADJ. indifferent. He felt *apathetic* about the conditions he had observed and did not care to fight against them. apathy, N.

aperture (*ăp'-*) N. opening; hole. He discovered a small *aperture* in the wall, through which the insects had entered the room.

apex N. tip; summit; climax. He was at the *apex* of his career.

aphorism (*ăf'-ə-rĭzm*) N. pithy maxim. An *aphorism* differs from an adage in that it is more philosophical or scientific. aphoristic, ADJ.

aplomb N. poise. His nonchalance and *aplomb* in times of trouble always encouraged his followers.

apocryphal (*-pŏk'-*) ADJ. not genuine; sham. His *apocryphal* tears misled no one.

apogee (*ăp'-ə-jē*) N. highest point. When the moon in its orbit is furthest away from the earth, it is at its *apogee*.

apostate (*-pŏs'-*) N. one who abandons his religious faith or political beliefs. Because he switched from one party to another, his former friends shunned him as an *apostate*.

apothecary (*-pŏth'-*) N. druggist. In the *apothecaries'* weight, twelve ounces equal one pound.

apothegm (*ăp'-ə-thĕm*) N. pithy, compact saying. Proverbs are *apothegms* that have become familiar sayings.

apotheosis (*-thē-ō'-səs*) N. deification; glorification. The *apotheosis* of a Roman emperor was designed to insure his eternal greatness.

apparition N. ghost; phantom. Hamlet was uncertain about the identity of the *apparition* that had appeared and spoken to him.

appease V. pacify; soothe. We have discovered that, when we try to *appease* our enemies, we encourage them to make additional demands.

appellation N. name; title. He was amazed when the witches hailed him with his correct *appellation*.

append V. attach. I shall *append* this chart to my report.

apposite (*ăp'-*) ADJ. appropriate; fitting. He was always able to find the *apposite* phrase, the correct expression for every occasion.

appraise V. estimate value of. It is difficult to *appraise* the value of old paintings; it is easier to call them priceless. appraisal, N.

ā—ale; ă—add; ä—arm; à—ask; ē—eve; ĕ—end; ê—err, her; ə—allow; even; ī—ice; ĭ—ill; ō—oll; ŏ—odd; ô—orb; ōō—food; ŏŏ—foot, put; o—out; th—thin; ū—use; ŭ—up; zh—pleasure

apprehend (-*hĕnd´*) v. arrest (a criminal); dread; perceive. The police will *apprehend* the culprit and convict him before long.

apprehensive ADJ. fearful; discerning. His *apprehensive* glances at the people who were walking in the street revealed his nervousness.

apprise (-*prīz´*) v. inform. When he was *apprised* of the dangerous weather conditions, he decided to postpone his trip.

appurtenances N. subordinate possessions. He bought the estate and all its *appurtenances*.

aptitude N. fitness; talent. The counselor gave him an *aptitude* test before advising him about the career he should follow.

ETYMOLOGY 2

AMBI (both) prefix
      ambidextrous skillful with both hands
      ambiguous of double meaning
      ambivalent possessing conflicting (both) emotions

AN (without) prefix
      anarchy lack of government
      anemia lack of blood
      anesthetize deprive of feeling

ANIM (mind, soul)
      animadvert cast criticism upon (turn one's mind)
      unanimous of one mind
      magnanimity greatness of mind or spirit

ANN, ENN (year)
      annuity yearly remittance
      biennial every two years
      perennial flowering yearly; a yearly flowering plant

ANTE (before) prefix
      antecedent preceding event or word
      antediluvian ancient (before the flood)
      ante-nuptial before the wedding

ANTHROP (man)
      anthropology study of man
      misanthrope recluse (hater of mankind)
      philanthropy love of mankind; charity

TEST—Word List 2—Antonyms

Each of the questions below consists of a word printed in italics, followed by five words or phrases numbered 1 to 5.

ā—ale; ă—add; ä—arm; ȧ—ask; ē—eve; ĕ—end; ê—err, her; ə—allow; even; ī—ice; ĭ—ill; ō—oll; ŏ—odd; ô—orb; ōō—food; ŏŏ—foot, put; o—oŭt; th—thin; ū—use; ŭ—up; zh—pleasure

Choose the numbered word or phrase which is most nearly opposite in meaning to the word in italics and write the number of your choice on your answer paper.

21. *alleviate* 1 endure 2 worsen 3 enlighten 4 maneuver 5 humiliate
22. *amalgamate* 1 equip 2 separate 3 generate 4 materialize 5 repress
23. *amass* 1 concentrate 2 rotate 3 concern 4 separate 5 recollect
24. *antediluvian* 1 transported 2 subtle 3 isolated 4 celebrated 5 modern
25. *antipathy* 1 profundity 2 objection 3 willingness 4 abstention 5 fondness
26. *appease* 1 agitate 2 qualify 3 display 4 predestine 5 interrupt
27. *apposite* 1 inappropriate 2 diagonal 3 exponential 4 unobtrusive 5 discouraging
28. *apprehend* 1 obviate 2 set free 3 shiver 4 understand 5 contrast
29. *aloof* 1 triangular 2 gregarious 3 comparable 4 honorable 5 savory
30. *amicable* 1 penetrating 2 compensating 3 unfriendly 4 zig-zag 5 unescapable
31. *amorphous* 1 nauseous 2 obscene 3 providential 4 definite 5 happy
32. *amplify* 1 distract 2 infer 3 publicize 4 decrease 5 pioneer
33. *antithesis* 1 velocity 2 maxim 3 similarity 4 acceleration 5 reaction
34. *anomaly* 1 desperation 2 requisition 3 registry 4 regularity 5 radiation
35. *aptitude* 1 sarcasm 2 inversion 3 adulation 4 lack of talent 5 gluttony
36. *anathematize* 1 locate 2 deceive 3 regulate 4 radiate 5 bless
37. *altruism* 1 good nature 2 height 3 descent 4 modernity 5 miserliness
38. *ambiguous* 1 salvageable 2 corresponding 3 responsible 4 clear 5 auxiliary
39. *anemic* 1 pallid 2 cruel 3 red-blooded 4 ventilating 5 hazardous
40. *anonymous* 1 desperate 2 signed 3 defined 4 expert 5 written

---

Word List 3   aquiline - bantering

aquiline (*ăk-wə-līn*) ADJ. curved, hooked. He can be recognized by his *aquiline* nose, curved like the beak of the eagle.

arable ADJ. fit for plowing. The land was no longer *arable;* erosion had removed the valuable topsoil.

arbiter (*är'-*) N. a person with power to decide a dispute; judge. As an

ā—ale; ă—add; ä—arm; ȧ—ask; ē—eve; ĕ—end; ê—err, her; ə—allow; even; ī—ice; ĭ—ill; ō—oll; ŏ—odd; ô—orb; o͞o—food; o͝o—foot, put; o—out; th—thin; ū—use; ŭ—up; zh—pleasure

arbiter in labor disputes, he has won the confidence of the workers and the employers.

arbitrary ADJ. fixed or decided; despotic. Any *arbitrary* action on your part will be resented by the members of the board whom you do not consult.

arcade N. a covered passageway, usually lined with shops. The *arcade* was popular with shoppers because it gave them protection from the summer sun and the winter rain.

archaeology (*-kē-ŏl´-*) N. study of artifacts and relics of early mankind. The professor of *archaeology* headed an expedition to the Gobi Desert in search of ancient ruins.

archaic (*-kā´-ĭk*) ADJ. antiquated. "Methinks," "thee," and "thou" are *archaic* words which are no longer part of our normal vocabulary.

archipelago (*är-kə-pĕl´-*) N. group of closely located islands. When he looked at the map and saw the *archipelagoes* in the South Seas, he longed to visit them.

ardor N. heat; passion; zeal. His *ardor* was contagious; soon everyone was eagerly working.

arduous ADJ. hard; strenuous. His *arduous* efforts had sapped his energy.

argot (*är´-gət*) N. slang. In the *argot* of the underworld, he "was taken for a ride."

aromatic ADJ. fragrant. Medieval sailing vessels brought *aromatic* herbs from China to Europe.

arraign (*-rān´*) V. charge in court; indict. After his indictment by the Grand Jury, the accused man was *arraigned* in the County Criminal Court.

arrant (*ăr´-*) ADJ. thorough; complete; unmitigated. *"Arrant* knave," an epithet found in books dealing with the age of chivalry, is a term of condemnation.

arrogance N. haughtiness. The *arrogance* of the nobility was resented by the middle class.

artifacts N. products of primitive culture. Archaeologists debated the significance of the *artifacts* discovered in the ruins of Asia Minor and came to no conclusion.

artifice N. deception; trickery. The Trojan War proved to the Greeks that cunning and *artifice* were often more effective than military might.

artisan N. a manually skilled worker. Artists and *artisans* alike are necessary to the development of a culture.

ā—ale; ă—add; ä—arm; à—ask; ē—eve; ĕ—end; ê—err, her; ə—allow; even; ī—ice; ĭ—ill; ō—oll; ŏ—odd; ô—orb; ōō—food; ŏŏ—foot, put; o—oüt; th—thin; ū—use; ŭ—up; zh—pleasure

ascertain (-*tān´*) V. find out for certain. Please *ascertain* his present address.

ascetic (*ă-sĕt´-*) ADJ. practicing self-denial; austere. The cavalier could not understand the *ascetic* life led by the monks. also N.

asceticism N. doctrine of self-denial. We find *asceticism* carried on in many parts of the world.

ascribe (-*skrīb´*) V. refer; attribute; assign. I can *ascribe* no motive for his acts.

ashen ADJ. ash-colored. His face was *ashen* with fear.

asinine ADJ. stupid. Your *asinine* remarks prove that you have not given this problem any serious consideration.

askance (-*skăns´*) ADV. with a sideways or indirect look. Looking *askance* at her questioner, she displayed her scorn.

askew (-*skū´*) ADV. crookedly; slanted; at an angle. When he placed his hat *askew* upon his head, his observers laughed.

asperity N. sharpness (of temper). These remarks, spoken with *asperity,* stung the boys to whom they had been directed.

aspersion N. slanderous remark. Do not cast *aspersions* on his character.

aspirant N. seeker after position or status. Although I am an *aspirant* for public office, I am not willing to accept the dictates of the party bosses. also ADJ.

aspiration N. noble ambition. Man's *aspirations* should be as lofty as the stars.

assail V. assault. He was *assailed* with questions after his lecture.

assay (-*sā´*) V. analyze; evaluate. When they *assayed* the ore, they found that they had discovered a very rich vein. also N.

asseverate (-*sĕv´-*) V. make a positive statement or solemn declaration. I will *asseverate* my conviction that he is guilty.

assiduous (-*sĭj´-ə-wəs*) ADJ. diligent. He worked *assiduously* at this task for weeks before he felt satisfied with his results. assiduity, N.

assuage (-*swāj´*) V. ease; lessen (pain). Your messages of cheer should *assuage* his suffering. assuagement, N.

asteroid N. small planet. *Asteroids* have become commonplace to the readers of interstellar travel stories in science fiction magazines.

astral ADJ. relating to the stars. He was amazed at the number of *astral* bodies the new telescope revealed.

astringent ADJ. binding; causing contraction. The *astringent* quality of the unsweetened lemon juice made swallowing difficult. also N.

ā—āle; ă—add; ä—arm; à—ask; ē—eve; ĕ—end; ê—err, her; ə—allow; even; ī—ice; ĭ —ill; ō—oll; ŏ—odd; ô—orb; ōō—food; ŏŏ—foot, put; o—out; th—thin; ū—use; ŭ—up; zh—pleasure

astronomical ADJ. enormously large or extensive. The government seems willing to spend *astronomical* sums on weapons development.

astute ADJ. wise; shrewd. That was a very *astute* observation. I shall heed it.

atheistic ADJ. denying the existence of God. His *atheistic* remarks shocked the religious worshippers.

athwart PREP. across; in opposition. His tendency toward violence was *athwart* the philosophy of the peace movement. also ADV.

atrocity N. brutal deed. In time of war, many *atrocities* are committed by invading armies.

atrophy (a'-) N. wasting away. Polio victims need physiotherapy to prevent the *atrophy* of affected limbs. also V.

attenuate V. make thin; weaken. By withdrawing their forces, the generals hoped to *attenuate* the enemy lines.

attest V. testify, bear witness. Having served as a member of the Grand Jury, I can *attest* that our system of indicting individuals is in need of improvement.

attribute (a'-) N. essential quality. His outstanding *attribute* was his kindness.

attrition N. gradual wearing down. They decided to wage a war of *attrition* rather than to rely on an all-out attack.

atypical (ā-tĭp'-) ADJ. not normal. You have taken an *atypical* case. It does not prove anything.

audacity N. boldness. His *audacity* in this critical moment encouraged us.

audit N. examination of accounts. When the bank examiners arrived to hold their annual *audit,* they discovered the embezzlements of the chief cashier. also V.

augment V. increase. How can we hope to *augment* our forces when our allies are deserting us?

augury (ô'-gyə-) N. omen; prophecy. He interpreted the departure of the birds as an *augury* of evil. augur, V.

auspicious ADJ. favoring success. With favorable weather conditions, it was an *auspicious* moment to set sail.

austere ADJ. strict, stern. His *austere* demeanor prevented us from engaging in our usual frivolous activities.

austerity N. sternness; severity. The *austerity* and dignity of the court were maintained by the new justices.

authenticate V. prove genuine. An expert was needed to *authenticate* the original Van Gogh painting from its imitation.

ā—ale; ă—add; ä—arm; à—ask; ē—eve; ĕ—end; ê—err, her; ə—allow; even; ī—ice; ĭ—ill; ō—oll; ŏ—odd; ô—orb; ōō—food; ŏŏ—foot, put; o—out; th—thin; ū—use; ŭ—up; zh—pleasure

autocrat N. monarch with supreme power. The nobles tried to limit the powers of the *autocrat* without success. autocracy, N.

automaton (-tŏm´-) N. mechanism which imitates actions of humans. Long before science fiction readers became aware of robots, writers were presenting stories of *automatons* who could outperform men.

autonomous ADJ. self-governing. This island is a colony; however, in most matters, it is *autonomous* and receives no orders from the mother country. autonomy, N.

autopsy (ô´-tŏp-sē) N. examination of a dead body; post-mortem. The medical examiner ordered an *autopsy* to determine the cause of death. also V.

auxiliary ADJ. helper, additional or subsidiary. To prepare for the emergency, they built an *auxiliary* power station. also N.

avarice N. greediness for wealth. King Midas's *avarice* has been famous for centuries. avaricious, ADJ.

aver (ə-vêr´) V. state confidently. I wish to *aver* that I am certain of success.

averse ADJ. reluctant. He was *averse* to revealing the sources of his information.

avid ADJ. greedy; eager for. He was *avid* for learning and read everything he could get. avidity, N.

avouch V. affirm; proclaim. I am willing to employ your friend if you will *avouch* his integrity.

avow V. declare openly. I must *avow* that I am innocent.

avuncular (-vŭn-) ADJ. like an uncle. *Avuncular* pride did not prevent him from noticing his nephew's shortcomings.

awe N. solemn wonder. The tourists gazed with *awe* at the tremendous expanse of the Grand Canyon.

awry (-rī´) ADV. distorted; crooked. He held his head *awry*, giving the impression that he had caught cold in his neck during the night. also ADJ.

axiom N. self-evident truth requiring no proof. Before a student can begin to think along the lines of Euclidean geometry, he must accept certain principles or *axioms*.

azure ADJ. sky blue. *Azure* skies are indicative of good weather.

babble V. chatter idly. The little girl *babbled* about her doll. also N.

bacchanalian (băk-ə-nāl´-) ADJ. drunken. Emperor Nero attended the *bacchanalian* orgy.

badger V. pester; annoy. She was forced to change her telephone number because she was *badgered* by obscene phone calls.

ā—ale; ă—add; ä—arm; à—ask; ē—eve; ĕ—end; ê—err, her; ə—allow; even; ī—ice; ĭ—ill; ō—oll; ŏ—odd; ô—orb; ōō—food; ŏŏ—foot, put; o—out; th—thin; ū—use; ŭ—up; zh—pleasure

baffle V. frustrate; perplex. The new code *baffled* the enemy agents.

baleful ADJ. deadly; destructive. The drought was a *baleful* omen.

balk (*bôk*) V. foil. When the warden learned that several inmates were planning to escape, he took steps to *balk* their attempt.

balmy ADJ. mild; fragrant. A *balmy* breeze refreshed us after the sultry blast.

banal (*bə-năl´-*) ADJ. hackneyed; commonplace; trite. His frequent use of clichés made his essay seem *banal*. banality, N.

bandanna N. large, bright-colored handkerchief. She could be identified by the gaudy *bandanna* she wore as a head covering.

baneful ADJ. ruinous; poisonous. His *baneful* influence was feared by all.

bantering ADJ. good-natured ridiculing. They resented his *bantering* remarks because they thought he was being sarcastic.

ETYMOLOGY 3

AQUA, AQUE (water)

    aqueduct a passageway for conducting water; a conduit

    aquatic living in water

    aqua fortis nitric acid (strong water)

ARCH (chief, first) prefix

    archetype original model

    archbishop chief bishop

    archaeology study of antiquities (study of first things)

ARCH (government, ruler, first)

    monarch sole ruler

    anarchy lack of government

    oligarchy government by the few

ASTER, ASTR (star)

    astronomy study of the stars

    asterisk starlike type character (*)

    disaster catastrophe (contrary star)

AUD, AUDIT (to hear)

    audible able to be heard

    auditorium place where people may be heard

    audience hearers

AUTO (self)

    autocracy rule by self (one person)

    automobile vehicle that moves by itself

    autobiography story of a person's life written by himself

---

ā—ale; ă—add; ä—arm; à—ask; ē—eve; ĕ—end; ê—err, her; ə—allow; even; ī—ice; ĭ—ill; ō—oll; ŏ—odd; ô—orb; o͞o—food; o͝o—foot, put; o—out; th—thin; ū—use; ŭ—up; zh—pleasure

TEST—Word List 3—Synonyms and Antonyms

Each of the following questions consists of a word printed in italics, followed by five words or phrases numbered 1 to 5. Choose the numbered word or phrase which is most nearly the same as or the opposite of the word in italics and write the number of your choice on your answer paper.

41. *aquiline*   1 watery 2 hooked 3 refined 4 antique 5 rodentlike
42. *archaic*   1 youthful 2 cautious 3 antiquated 4 placated 5 buttressed
43. *ardor*   1 zeal 2 paint 3 proof 4 group 5 excitement
44. *artifice*   1 spite 2 exception 3 anger 4 candor 5 loyalty
45. *artisan*   1 educator 2 decider 3 sculptor 4 discourser 5 unskilled laborer
46. *ascertain*   1 amplify 2 master 3 discover 4 retain 5 explode
47. *asteroid*   1 Milky Way 2 radiance 3 large planet 4 rising moon 5 setting moon
48. *asperity*   1 anguish 2 absence 3 innuendo 4 good temper 5 snake
49. *assuage*   1 stuff 2 describe 3 wince 4 worsen 5 introduce
50. *astute*   1 sheer 2 noisy 3 astral 4 unusual 5 foolish
51. *atrocity*   1 endurance 2 fortitude 3 session 4 heinous act 5 hatred
52. *atypical*   1 superfluous 2 booming 3 normal 4 clashing 5 lovely
53. *audacity*   1 boldness 2 asperity 3 strength 4 stature 5 anchorage
54. *avarice*   1 anxiety 2 generosity 3 statement 4 invoice 5 power
55. *balmy*   1 venturesome 2 dedicated 3 mild 4 fanatic 5 memorable
56. *awry*   1 recommended 2 commiserating 3 startled 4 straight 5 psychological
57. *banal*   1 philosophical 2 original 3 dramatic 4 heedless 5 discussed
58. *baleful*   1 doubtful 2 virtual 3 deadly 4 conventional 5 virtuous
59. *auxiliary*   1 righteous 2 prospective 3 assistant 4 archaic 5 mandatory
60. *baneful*   1 intellectual 2 thankful 3 decisive 4 nonpoisonous 5 remorseful

---

Word List 4   barb - cadaverous

barb N. sharp projection from fishhook, etc. The *barb* from the fishhook caught in his finger as he grabbed the fish. barbed, ADJ.

ā—ale; ă—add; ä—arm; à—ask, ē—eve; ĕ—end; ê—err, her; ə—allow; even; ī—ice; ĭ—ill; ō—oll; ŏ—odd; ô—orb; ōō—food; ŏŏ—foot, put; o—oüt; th—thin; ū—use; ŭ—up; zh—pleasure

baroque (-rōk) ADJ. highly ornate. They found the *baroque* architecture amusing.

barrage (-äzh) N. barrier laid down by artillery fire. The company was forced to retreat through the *barrage* of heavy cannons.

barrister (băr-ə-) N. counselor-at-law. Galsworthy started as a *barrister*, but, when he found the practice of law boring, turned to writing.

barterer N. trader. The *barterer* exchanged trinkets for the natives' furs.

bate (bāt) V. let down; restrain. Until it was time to open the presents, the children had to *bate* their curiosity. bated, ADJ.

batten V. grow fat; thrive upon others. We cannot accept a system where a favored few can *batten* in extreme comfort while others toil.

bauble (bô-) N. trinket; trifle. The child was delighted with the *bauble* she had won in the grab bag.

beatific (bē-ə-tǐf) ADJ. giving bliss; blissful. The *beatific* smile on the child's face made us very happy.

bedizen (bǐ-dīz-) V. dress with vulgar finery. The witch doctors were *bedizened* in all their gaudiest costumes.

bedraggle V. wet thoroughly. We were so *bedraggled* by the severe storm that we had to change into dry clothing. bedraggled, ADJ.

beguile (-gīl) V. delude; cheat; amuse. He *beguiled* himself during the long hours by playing solitaire.

behoove V. suited to; incumbent upon. In this time of crisis, it *behooves* all of us to remain calm and await the instructions of our superiors.

belabor V. beat soundly; assail verbally. He was *belaboring* his opponent.

belated ADJ. delayed. He apologized for his *belated* note of condolence to the widow of his friend and explained that he had just learned of her husband's untimely death.

beleaguer V. besiege. As soon as the city was *beleaguered,* life became more subdued as the citizens began their long wait for outside assistance. beleaguered, ADJ.

bellicose ADJ. warlike. His *bellicose* disposition alienated his friends.

benediction N. blessing. The appearance of the sun after the many rainy days was like a *benediction.*

benefactor N. gift giver; patron. Scrooge later became Tiny Tim's *benefactor.*

beneficiary N. person entitled to benefits or proceeds of an insurance policy or will. You may change your *beneficiary* as often as you wish.

ā—ale; ă—add; ä—arm; à—ask; ē—eve; ĕ—end; ê—err, her; ə—allow; even; ī—ice; ĭ—ill; ō—oll; ŏ—odd; ô—orb; ōō—food; ŏŏ—foot, put; o—out; th—thin; ū—use; ŭ—up; zh—pleasure

benevolent (-*nĕv*-) ADJ. generous; charitable. His *benevolent* nature prevented him from refusing any beggar who accosted him.

benighted ADJ. overcome by darkness. In the *benighted* Middle Ages, intellectual curiosity was discouraged by the authorities.

benign (-*nīn*) ADJ. kindly; favorable; not malignant. The old man was well liked because of his *benign* attitude toward friend and stranger alike.

berate V. scold strongly. He feared she would *berate* him for his forgetfulness.

bereft ADJ. deprived of; lacking. The foolish gambler soon found himself *bereft* of funds.

berserk (*bêr-sêrk*) ADV. frenzied. Angered, he went *berserk* and began to wreck the room.

besmirch V. soil, defile. The scandalous remarks in the newspaper *besmirch* the reputations of every member of the society.

bestow V. confer. He wished to *bestow* great honors upon the hero.

bête noire (*bĕt-nwär´*) N. aversion; person or thing strongly disliked or avoided. Going to the opera was his personal *bête noire* because high-pitched sounds irritated him.

betroth (-*trōth*) V. become engaged to marry. The announcement that they had become *betrothed* surprised their friends who had not suspected any romance. betrothal, N.

bicameral (*bī-*) ADJ. two-chambered, as a legislative body. The United States Congress is a *bicameral* body.

biennial (*bī-*) ADJ. every two years. The plant bore *biennial* flowers. also N.

bigotry N. stubborn intolerance. Brought up in a democratic atmosphere, the student was shocked by the *bigotry* and narrowness expressed by several of his classmates.

bilious ADJ. suffering from indigestion; irritable. His *bilious* temperament was apparent to all who heard him rant about his difficulties.

bivouac (*bĭv´-ə-wăk*) N. temporary encampment. While in *bivouac*, we spent the night in our sleeping bags under the stars. also V.

bizarre (*bə-zär*) ADJ. fantastic; violently contrasting. The plot of the novel was too *bizarre* to be believed.

bland ADJ. soothing; mild. She used a *bland* ointment for her sunburn.

blandishment N. flattery. Despite the salesperson's *blandishments*, the customer did not buy the outfit.

blasphemous (*blăs-fə-*) ADJ. profane; impious. The people in the room were shocked by his *blasphemous* language.

ā—ale; ă—add; ä—arm; à—ask, ē—eve; ĕ—end; ê—err, her; ə—allow; even; ī—ice; ĭ—ill; ō—oll; ŏ—odd; ô—orb; ōō—food; ŏŏ—foot, put; o—oüt; th—thin; ū—use; ŭ—up; zh—pleasure

blatant (*blāt -*) ADJ. loudly offensive. I regard your remarks as *blatant* and ill-mannered. blatancy, N.

blazon (*blāz -*) V. decorate with an heraldic coat of arms. *Blazoned* on his shield were the two lambs and the lion, the traditional coat of arms of his family. also N.

bleak ADJ. cold; cheerless. The Aleutian Islands are *bleak* military outposts.

blighted ADJ. suffering from a disease; destroyed. The extent of the *blighted* areas could be seen only when viewed from the air.

blithe ADJ. gay; joyous. Shelley called the skylark a *"blithe* spirit" because of its happy song.

bloated ADJ. swollen or puffed as with water or air. The *bloated* corpse was taken from the river.

bludgeon (*blŭj -*) N. club; heavy-headed weapon. His walking stick served him as a *bludgeon* on many occasions. also V.

bode V. foreshadow; portend. The gloomy skies and the sulphurous odors from the mineral springs seemed to *bode* evil to those who settled in the area.

bogus ADJ. counterfeit; not authentic. The police quickly found the distributors of the *bogus* twenty-dollar bills.

boisterous ADJ. violent; rough; noisy. The unruly crowd became even more *boisterous* when he tried to quiet them.

bolster V. support; prop up. I do not intend to *bolster* your hopes with false reports of outside assistance; the truth is that we must face the enemy alone. also N.

bombastic ADJ. pompous; using inflated language. The orator spoke in a *bombastic* manner. bombast, N.

bootless ADJ. useless. I "trouble deaf heaven with my *bootless* cries."

bouillon (*bōo̅l -yän*) N. clear beef soup. The cup of *bouillon* served by the stewards was welcomed by those who had been chilled by the cold ocean breezes.

bountiful ADJ. generous; showing bounty. She distributed gifts in a *bountiful* and gracious manner.

bourgeois (*bo̅orzh-wä*) N. middle class. The French Revolution was inspired by the *bourgeois*. also ADJ.

braggadocio (*-dō -shē-ō*) N. boasting. He was disliked because his manner was always full of *braggadocio*.

bravado (*-väd -ō*) N. swagger; assumed air of defiance. The *bravado* of the young criminal disappeared when he was confronted by the victims of his brutal attack.

ā—ale; ă—add; ä—arm; à—ask; ē—eve; ĕ—end; ê—err, her; ə—allow; even; ī—ice; ĭ—ill; ō—oll; ŏ—odd; ô—orb; o̅o̅—food; o̅o̅—foot, put; o—out; th—thin; ū—use; ŭ—up; zh—pleasure

brazen (*brāz*-) ADJ. insolent. Her *brazen* contempt for authority angered the officials.

brazier (*brā-zhər*) N. open pan in which live coals are burned. On chilly nights, the room was warmed by coals burning in *braziers* set in the corners of the room.

breach N. breaking of contract or duty; fissure; gap. They found a *breach* in the enemy's fortifications and penetrated their lines. also V.

brevity N. conciseness. *Brevity* is essential when you send a telegram or cablegram; you are charged for every word.

bristling ADJ. rising like bristles; showing irritation. The dog stood there, *bristling* with anger.

broach V. open up. He did not even try to *broach* the subject of poetry.

brocade N. rich, figured fabric. The sofa was covered with expensive *brocade*.

brochure (*brō-shoŏr*) N. pamphlet. This *brochure* on farming was issued by the Department of Agriculture.

brooch (*brōch*) N. ornamental clasp. She treasured the *brooch* because it was an heirloom.

brusque (*brŭsk*) ADJ. blunt; abrupt. She was offended by his *brusque* reply.

bucolic (*bū-kŏl*-) ADJ. rustic; pastoral. The meadow was the scene of *bucolic* gaiety.

buffoonery N. clowning. Jimmy Durante's *buffoonery* was hilarious.

bullion (*boŏl-yən*) N. gold and silver in the form of bars. Much *bullion* is stored in the vaults at Fort Knox.

bulwark (*boŏl*'-) N. earthwork or other strong defense; person who defends. The navy is our principal *bulwark* against invasion.

bumptious ADJ. self-assertive. His classmates called him a show-off because of his *bumptious* airs.

bungle V. spoil by clumsy behavior. I was afraid you would *bungle* this assignment but I had no one else to send.

burgeon (*bêr-jən*) V. grow forth; send out buds. In the spring, the plants that burgeon are a promise of the beauty that is to come.

burlesque V. give an imitation that ridicules. In his caricature, he *burlesqued* the mannerisms of his adversary. also N.

burnish V. make shiny by rubbing; polish. The *burnished* metal reflected the lamplight.

buttress N. support or prop. The huge cathedral walls were supported by flying *buttresses*. also V.

buxom (*bŭk-səm*) ADJ. plump; vigorous; jolly. The soldiers remembered

ā—ale; ă—add; ä—arm; à—ask, ē—eve; ĕ—end; ê—err, her; ə—allow; even; ī—ice; ĭ—ill; ō—oll; ŏ—odd; ô—orb; oō—food; oŏ—foot, put; o—out; th—thin; ū—use; ŭ—up; zh—pleasure

the *buxom* nurse who had always been so pleasant to them.

cabal (-*băl*) N. small group of persons secretly united to promote their own interests. The *cabal* was defeated when their scheme was discovered.

cache (*kăsh*) N. hiding place. The detectives followed the suspect until he led them to the *cache* where he had stored his loot. also V.

cacophony (*kă-kŏf-*) N. discord. Some people seem to enjoy the *cacophony* of an orchestra that is tuning up.

cadaver (*kə-dăv-*) N. corpse. In some states, it is illegal to dissect *cadavers*.

cadaverous ADJ. like a corpse; pale. By his *cadaverous* appearance, we could see how the disease had ravaged him.

ETYMOLOGY 4

BELLI (war)
  bellicose inclined to fighting
  belligerent engaged in war
  rebellious warring against authority

BEN, BON (well, good) prefix
  benefactor one who does good
  benevolence charity (wishing good)
  bonus something extra above regular pay

BI (two) prefix
  bicameral legislature consisting of two houses
  biennial every two years
  bicycle two-wheeled vehicle

BIBLI (book)
  bibliography list of books
  bibliophile lover of books
  Bible the sacred scriptures ("The Book")

BIO (life)
  biology study of living things
  biography writing about a person's life
  biochemist a student of the chemistry of living things

BREV, BREVE (short)
  brevity briefness
  abbreviate shorten
  breve mark placed over a vowel to indicate that it is short (*ă* as in *hăt*)

ā—ale; ă—add; ä—arm; à—ask, ē—eve; ĕ—end; ê—err, her; ə—allow; even; ī—ice; ĭ —ill; ō—oll; ŏ—odd; ô—orb; ōō—food; oŏ—foot, put; o—out; th—thin; ū—use; ŭ—up; zh—pleasure

CAD, CAS (to fall)

    decadent deteriorating
    cadence intonation, terminal musical phrase
    cascade waterfall

TEST—Word List 4—Synonyms

Each of the questions below consists of a word printed in italics, followed by five words or phrases numbered 1 to 5. Choose the numbered word or phrase which is most nearly similar in meaning to the word in italics and write the number of your choice on your answer paper.

61. *baroque* 1 polished 2 constant 3 transformed 4 highly ornate 5 aglow
62. *benign* 1 tenfold 2 peaceful 3 blessed 4 wavering 5 favorable
63. *boisterous* 1 conflicting 2 noisy 3 testimonial 4 grateful 5 adolescent
64. *brazen* 1 shameless 2 quick 3 modest 4 pleasant 5 melodramatic
65. *barrister* 1 specialist 2 teacher 3 attorney 4 conductor 5 professor
66. *biennial* 1 yearly 2 every two years 3 favorable 4 impressive 5 celebrated
67. *bombastic* 1 sensitive 2 pompous 3 rapid 4 sufficient 5 expensive
68. *bucolic* 1 diseased 2 repulsive 3 rustic 4 twinkling 5 cold
69. *bauble* 1 mainstay 2 gas 3 soap 4 trifling piece of jewelry 5 expense
70. *bigotry* 1 arrogance 2 approval 3 mourning 4 promptness 5 intolerance
71. *bouillon* 1 insight 2 chowder 3 gold 4 clear soup 5 stew
72. *buxom* 1 voluminous 2 indecisive 3 convincing 4 plump 5 bookish
73. *beatific* 1 glorious 2 blissful 3 theatrical 4 crooked 5 handsome
74. *bland* 1 mild 2 meager 3 soft 4 uncooked 5 helpless
75. *braggadocio* 1 Cyrano 2 boasting 3 skirmish 4 encounter 5 position
76. *cache* 1 lock 2 hiding place 3 tide 4 automobile 5 grappling hook
77. *bellicose* 1 warlike 2 navel 3 amusing 4 piecemeal 5 errant
78. *blithe* 1 spiritual 2 profuse 3 gay 4 hybrid 5 comfortable
79. *brochure* 1 opening 2 pamphlet 3 censor 4 bureau 5 pin
80. *cacophony* 1 discord 2 dance 3 applause 4 type of telephone 5 rooster

ā—ale; ă—add; ä—arm; à—ask; ē—eve; ĕ—end; ê—err, her; ə—allow; even; ī—ice; ĭ—ill; ō—oll; ŏ—odd; ô—orb; ōō—food; ŏŏ—foot, put; o—out; th—thin; ū—use; ŭ—up; zh—pleasure

---

Word List 5 cajole - churlish

cajole (-*jōl*) v. coax; wheedle. I will not be *cajoled* into granting you your wish.

caliber N. ability; capacity. A man of such *caliber* should not be assigned such menial tasks.

callous ADJ. hardened; unfeeling. He had worked in the hospital for so many years that he was *callous* to the suffering in the wards. callus, N.

calorific (kăl-ə-rĭf-) ADJ. heat-producing. Coal is much more *calorific* than green wood.

calumniate (-*lŭm*-) v. slander. Shakespeare wrote that love and friendship were subject to envious and *calumniating* time.

calumny (kăl-) N. malicious misrepresentation; slander. He could endure his financial failure, but he could not bear the *calumny* that his foes heaped upon him.

cameo N. shell or jewel carved in relief. Tourists are advised not to purchase *cameos* from the street peddlers of Rome who sell poor specimens of the carver's art.

canard (-*närd*) N. unfounded rumor; exaggerated report. It is almost impossible to protect oneself from such a base *canard*.

candor N. frankness. The *candor* and simplicity of his speech impressed all. candid, ADJ.

canker N. any ulcerous sore; any evil. Poverty is a *canker* in the body politic; it must be cured.

canny ADJ. shrewd; thrifty. The *canny* Scotsman was more than a match for the swindlers.

cant N. jargon of thieves; pious phraseology. Many listeners were fooled by the *cant* and hypocrisy of his speech.

cantankerous ADJ. ill humored; irritable. Constantly complaining about his treatment and refusing to cooperate with the hospital staff, he was a *cantankerous* patient.

cantata (-*tät*-) N. story set to music, to be sung by a chorus. The choral society sang the new *cantata* composed by its leader.

canter N. slow gallop. Because the racehorse had outdistanced its competition so easily, the reporter wrote that the race was won in a *canter*. also V.

canto N. division of a long poem. In *The Man without a Country*, Philip Nolan is upset when he reads one of Sir Walter Scott's *cantos*.

ā—ale; ă—add; ä—arm; à—ask, ē—eve; ĕ—end; ê—err, her; ə—allow; even; ī—ice; ĭ—ill; ō—oll; ŏ—odd; ô—orb; ōō—food; ŏŏ—foot; put; o—out; th—thin; ū—use; ŭ—up; zh—pleasure

canvass V. determine votes, etc. After *canvassing* the sentiments of his constituents, the congressman was confident that he represented the majority opinion of his district. also N.

capacious ADJ. spacious. In the *capacious* areas of the railroad terminal, thousands of travelers lingered while waiting for their train.

caparison N, V. showy harness or ornamentation for a horse; put showy ornamentation on a horse. The audience admired the *caparison* of the horses as they made their entrance into the circus ring.

capitulate V. surrender. The enemy was warned to *capitulate* or face annihilation.

caprice (-*prēs*) N. whim. Do not act on *caprice*. Study your problem.

capricious (-*prĭsh*-) ADJ. fickle; incalculable. The storm was *capricious* and changed course constantly.

caption N. title; chapter heading; text under illustration. I find the *captions* which accompany these cartoons very clever and humorous. also V.

captious ADJ. faultfinding. His criticisms were always *captious* and frivolous, never offering constructive suggestions.

carat N. unit of weight for precious stones; measure of fineness of gold. He gave her a three-*carat* diamond mounted in an eighteen -*carat* gold band.

caricature N. distortion; burlesque. The *caricatures* he drew always emphasized a personal weakness of the people he burlesqued. also V.

carmine (*kär'-mən*) N. rich red. *Carmine* in her lipstick made her lips appear black in the photographs.

carnage N. destruction of life. The *carnage* that can be caused by atomic warfare adds to the responsibilities of our statesmen.

carnal ADJ. fleshly. The public was more interested in *carnal* pleasures than in spiritual matters.

carnivorous ADJ. meat-eating. The lion is a *carnivorous* animal. carnivore, N.

carousal (-*rou-zəl*) N. drunken revel. The party degenerated into an ugly *carousal*.

carping ADJ. finding fault. A *carping* critic disturbs sensitive people.

carrion N. rotting flesh of a dead body. Buzzards are nature's scavengers; they eat the *carrion* left behind by other predators.

carte blanche (*kärt-blänsh*) N. unlimited authority or freedom. Use your own discretion in this matter; I give you *carte blanche*.

cascade N. small waterfall. We could not appreciate the beauty of the

ā—ale; ă—add; ä—arm; à—ask, ē—eve; ĕ—end; ê—err, her; ə—allow; even; ī—ice; ĭ—ill; ō—oll; ŏ—odd; ô—orb; o͞o—food; o͝o—foot, put; o—out; th—thin; ū—use; ŭ—up; zh—pleasure

many *cascades* as we were forced to make detours around each of them. also V.

castigate V. punish. He decided to *castigate* the culprit personally.

casualty N. serious or fatal accident. The number of *casualties* on this holiday weekend was high.

cataclysm N. deluge; upheaval. A *cataclysm* such as the French Revolution affects all countries. cataclysmic, ADJ.

catapult N. slingshot; a hurling machine. Airplanes are sometimes launched from battleships by *catapults*. also V.

catastrophe N. calamity. The Johnstown flood was a *catastrophe*.

catechism N. book for religious instruction; instruction by question and answer. He taught by engaging his pupils in a *catechism* until they gave him the correct answer.

cathartic N. purgative. Some drugs act as laxatives when taken in small doses but act as *cathartics* when taken in much larger doses.

catholic ADJ. broadly sympathetic; liberal. He was extremely *catholic* in his reading tastes.

caustic ADJ. burning; sarcastically biting. The critic's *caustic* remarks angered the hapless actors who were the subjects of his sarcasm.

cauterize (*kôt*-) V. burn with hot iron or caustic. In order to prevent infection, the doctor *cauterized* the wound.

cavalcade N. procession; parade. As described by Chaucer, the *cavalcade* of Canterbury pilgrims was a motley group.

cavil (*kăv*-) V. make frivolous objections. I respect your sensible criticisms, but I dislike the way you *cavil* about unimportant details. also N.

cede (*sēd*) V. transfer; yield title to. I intend to *cede* this property to the city.

celestial ADJ. heavenly. He wrote about the music of "*celestial* spheres."

celibate (*sĕl-ə-bət*) ADJ. unmarried; abstaining from sexual intercourse. He vowed to remain *celibate*. celibacy, N.

censor N. overseer of morals; person who reads to eliminate inappropriate remarks. Soldiers dislike having their mail read by a *censor* but understand the need for this precaution. also V.

censure (*sĕn-chər*) V. blame; criticize. He was *censured* for his ill-advised act. also N.

centaur (*sĕn-tôr*) N. mythical figure, half man and half horse. I was particularly impressed by the statue of the *centaur* in the Roman Hall of the museum.

centigrade ADJ. measure of temperature used widely in Europe. On the

ā—ale; ă—add; ä—arm; à—ask, ē—eve; ĕ—end; ê—err, her; ə—allow; even; ī—ice; ĭ—ill; ō—oll; ŏ—odd; ô—orb; o͞o—food; o͝o—foot, pu̱t; o—ou̱t; th—thin; ū—use; ŭ—up; zh—pleasure

centigrade thermometer, the freezing point of water is zero degrees.

centrifugal (-*trĭf-*) ADJ. radiating; departing from the center. Many automatic drying machines remove excess moisture from clothing by *centrifugal* force.

centurion N. Roman army officer. Because he was in command of a company of one hundred soldiers, he was called a *centurion.*

cerebral (*sə-rē´-*) ADJ. pertaining to the brain or intellect. The content of philosophical works is *cerebral* in nature and requires much thought.

cerebration (*sĕr-*) N. thought. Mathematics problems sometimes require much *cerebration.*

cessation N. stopping. The workers threatened a *cessation* of all activities if their demands were not met. cease, V.

cession N. yielding to another; ceding. The *cession* of Alaska to the United States is discussed in this chapter.

chafe (*chāf*) V. warm by rubbing; make sore by rubbing. The collar *chafed* his neck. also N.

chaffing ADJ. bantering; joking. Sometimes his flippant and *chaffing* remarks annoy us.

chagrin (*shə-grĭn*) N. vexation; disappointment. His refusal to go with us filled us with *chagrin.*

chalice N. goblet; consecrated cup. In a small room adjoining the cathedral, many ornately decorated *chalices* made by the most famous European goldsmiths were on display.

chameleon (*kə-mēl-yən*) N. lizard that changes color in different situations. Like the *chameleon,* he assumed the political thinking of every group he met.

champ V. chew noisily. His dining companions were amused by the way he *champed* his food.

champion V. support militantly. Martin Luther King, Jr., won the Nobel Peace Prize because he *championed* the oppressed in their struggle for equality.

chaotic (*kā-ŏt-*) ADJ. in utter disorder. He tried to bring order into the *chaotic* state of affairs. chaos, N.

charisma (*kə-rĭz-*) N. divine gift; great popular charm or appeal of a political leader. Political commentators have deplored the importance of a candidate's *charisma* in these days of television campaigning.

charlatan (*shär-*) N. quack; pretender to knowledge. Because he was unable to substantiate his claim that he had found a cure for

ā—ale; ă—add; ä—arm; á—ask, ē—eve; ĕ—end; ê—err, her; ə—allow; even; ī—ice; ĭ—ill; ō—oll; ŏ—odd; ô—orb; ōō—food; ŏŏ—foot; put; o—out; th—thin; ū—use; ŭ—up; zh—pleasure

the dread disease, he was called a *charlatan* by his colleagues.

chary (*chăr-ē*) ADJ. cautiously watchful. She was *chary* of her favors.

chasm (*kăzm*) N. abyss. They could not see the bottom of the *chasm*.

chassis (*shăs-ē*) N. framework and working parts of an automobile. Examining the car after the accident, the owner discovered that the body had been ruined but that the *chassis* was unharmed.

chaste (*chāst*) ADJ. pure. Her *chaste* and decorous garb was appropriately selected for the solemnity of the occasion. chastity, N.

chastise V. punish. I must *chastise* you for this offense.

chattel N. personal property. When he bought his furniture on the installment plan, he signed a *chattel* mortgage.

chauvinist (*shō -*) N. blindly devoted patriot. A *chauvinist* cannot recognize any faults in his country, no matter how flagrant they may be.

checkered ADJ. marked by changes in fortune. During his *checkered* career he had lived in palatial mansions and in dreary boardinghouses.

chicanery (*shĭk-ān -*) N. trickery. Your deceitful tactics in this case are indications of *chicanery*.

chide V. scold. Grandma began to *chide* Steven for his lying.

chimerical (*kĭ-mĕr -*) ADJ. fantastic; highly imaginative. Poe's *chimerical* stories are sometimes too morbid for reading in bed. chimera, N.

chiropodist (*kə-rŏp -*) N. one who treats disorders of the feet. The *chiropodist* treated the ingrown nail on the boy's foot.

choleric (*kŏl'-*) ADJ. hot-tempered. His flushed, angry face indicated a *choleric* nature.

chronic ADJ. long established as a disease. The doctors were able finally to attribute his *chronic* headaches and nausea to traces of formaldehyde gas in his apartment.

churlish ADJ. boorish; rude. Dismayed by his *churlish* manners at the party, the girls vowed never to invite him again.

ETYMOLOGY 5

CAP, CAPT, CEP, CIP (to take)

        participate take part

        precept a wise saying (originally, a command)

        capture seize

CAP (head)

        decapitate behead

ā—ale; ă—add; ä—arm; à—ask, ē—eve; ĕ—end; ê—err, her; ə—allow; even; ī—ice; ĭ—ill; ō—oll; ŏ—odd; ô—orb; o͞o—food; o͝o—foot, put; o—out; th—thin; ū—use; ŭ—up; zh—pleasure

captain chief
capital major city or site; first-rate

CATA (down) prefix

catastrophe disaster (turning down)
cataract waterfall
catapult hurl (throw down)

CED (to yield, to go)

recede go back, withdraw
antecedent that which goes before
concede yield, agree with

CENT (one hundred)

century one hundred years
centennial hundredth anniversary

CHRONOS (time)

chronology timetable of events
anachronism a thing out of time sequence, as Shakespeare's reference to clocks in *Julius Caesar*
chronicle register events in order

TEST—Word List 5—*Antonyms*

Each of the questions below consists of a word printed in italics, followed by five words or phrases numbered 1 to 5. Choose the numbered word or phrase which is most nearly opposite in meaning to the word in italics and write the number of your choice on your answer paper.

81. *candid* 1 vague 2 secretive 3 experienced 4 anxious 5 sallow
82. *carnivorous* 1 gloomy 2 tangential 3 productive 4 weak 5 vegetarian
83. *celibate* 1 investing 2 married 3 retired 4 commodious 5 dubious
84. *chimerical* 1 developing 2 wonderful 3 disappearing 4 economical 5 realistic
85. *capacious* 1 warlike 2 cordial 3 curious 4 not spacious 5 not capable
86. *carousal* 1 awakening 2 sobriety 3 acceleration 4 direction 5 production
87. *censure* 1 process 2 enclose 3 interest 4 praise 5 penetrate
88. *choleric* 1 irascible 2 episodic 3 coolheaded 4 global 5 seasonal
89. *capricious* 1 satisfied 2 insured 3 photographic 4 scattered 5 steadfast

---

ā—ale; ă—add; ä—arm; à—ask, ē—eve; ĕ—end; ê—err, her; ə—allow; even; ī—ice; ĭ—ill; ō—oll; ŏ—odd; ô—orb; ōō—food; ŏŏ—foot, put; o—oüt; th—thin; ū—use; ŭ—up; zh—pleasure

90. *catholic* 1 religious 2 pacific 3 narrow 4 weighty 5 funny
91. *cessation* 1 premium 2 gravity 3 beginning 4 composition 5 stoppage
92. *churlish* 1 marine 2 economical 3 polite 4 compact 5 young
93. *captious* 1 tolerant 2 capable 3 frivolous 4 winning 5 recollected
94. *carte blanche* 1 capitalistic 2 investment 3 importance 4 restriction 5 current
95. *chaste* 1 clean 2 clear 3 curt 4 wanton 5 outspoken
96. *chaffing* 1 achieving 2 serious 3 capitalistic 4 sneering 5 expensive
97. *carnal* 1 impressive 2 minute 3 spiritual 4 actual 5 private
98. *centrifugal* 1 centripetal 2 ephemeral 3 lasting 4 barometric 5 algebraic
99. *chide* 1 unite 2 fear 3 record 4 skid 5 praise
100. *carping* 1 acquiescent 2 mean 3 limited 4 farming 5 racing

---

Word List 6   ciliated - concise

ciliated ADJ. having minute hairs. The paramecium is a *ciliated,* one-celled animal.

circlet N. small ring; band. This tiny *circlet* is very costly because it is set with precious stones.

circuitous (-*kū*-) ADJ. roundabout. Because of the traffic congestion on the main highways, he took a *circuitous* route. circuit, N.

circumscribe V. limit; confine. Although I do not wish to *circumscribe* your activities, I must insist that you complete this assignment before you start anything else.

circumspect ADJ. prudent; cautious. Investigating before acting, he tried always to be *circumspect.*

circumvent V. outwit; baffle. In order to *circumvent* the enemy, we will make two preliminary attacks in other sections before starting our major campaign.

citadel N. fortress. The *citadel* overlooked the city like a protecting angel.

cite V. quote; commend. He could *cite* passages in the Bible from memory. citation, N.

clairvoyant (*klăr-vôĭ*-) ADJ., N. having foresight; fortuneteller. Cassandra's *clairvoyant* warning was not heeded by the Trojans. clairvoyance, N.

clamber V. climb by crawling. He *clambered* over the wall.

ā—ale; ă—add; ä—arm; à—ask; ē—eve; ĕ—end; ê—err, her; ə—allow; even; ī—ice; ĭ —ill; ō—oll; ŏ—odd; ô—orb; ōō—food; ŏŏ—foot, put; o—oŭt; th—thin; ū—use; ŭ—up; zh—pleasure

clandestine (-dĕs-tən) ADJ. secret. After avoiding their chaperon, the lovers had a *clandestine* meeting.

clarion ADJ. shrill trumpetlike sound. We woke to the *clarion* call of the bugle.

claustrophobia (klô-) N. fear of being locked in. His fellow classmates laughed at his *claustrophobia* and often threatened to lock him in his room.

clavicle N. collarbone. Even though he wore shoulder pads, the football player broke his *clavicle* during a practice scrimmage.

cleave V. split asunder. The lightning *cleaves* the tree in two. cleavage, N.

cleft N. split. There was a *cleft* in the huge boulder. also ADJ.

clemency N. disposition to be lenient; mildness, as of the weather. The lawyer was pleased when the case was sent to Judge Smith's chambers because Smith was noted for his *clemency* toward first offenders.

cliché (klĭ-shā) N. phrase dulled in meaning by repetition. High school compositions are often marred by such *clichés* as "strong as an ox."

climactic ADJ. relating to the highest point. When he reached the *climactic* portions of the book, he could not stop reading. climax, N.

clique (klēk) N. small exclusive group. He charged that a *clique* had assumed control of school affairs.

cloister N. monastery or convent. The nuns lived in the *cloister*.

coadjutor (kō-ə-jōōt-) N. assistant; colleague. He was assigned as *coadjutor* of the bishop.

coalesce V. combine; fuse. The brooks *coalesce* into one large river.

cockade N. decoration worn on hat. Members of that brigade can be recognized by the green and white *cockade* in their helmets.

coerce (kō-êrs) V. force; repress. Do not *coerce* me into doing this; I hate force.

coeval ADJ. living at the same time as; contemporary. *Coeval* with the dinosaur, the pterodactyl flourished during the Mesozoic era.

cog N. tooth projecting from a wheel. On steep slopes, *cog* railways are frequently used to prevent slipping.

cogent (kō-jənt) ADJ. convincing. He presented *cogent* arguments to the jury.

cogitate V. think over. *Cogitate* on this problem; the solution will come.

cognate ADJ. allied by blood; of the same or kindred nature. In the phrase

ā—ale; ă—add; ä—arm; å—ask, ē—eve, ĕ—end; ê—err, her; ə—allow; even; ī—ice; ĭ—ill; ō—oll; ŏ—odd; ô—orb; ōō—food; oŏ—foot, put; o—out; th—thin; ū—use; ŭ—up; zh—pleasure

"die a thousand deaths," the word "death" is a *cognate* object.

cognizance (kŏg´-) N. knowledge. During the election campaign, the two candidates were kept in full *cognizance* of the international situation.

cognomen (kŏg-nō´-) N. family name. He asked the court to change his *cognomen* to a more American-sounding name.

cohere V. stick together. Solids have a greater tendency to *cohere* than liquids.

cohesion N. force which keeps parts together. In order to preserve our *cohesion,* we must not let minor differences interfere with our major purposes.

cohorts N. armed band. Caesar and his Roman *cohorts* conquered almost all of the known world.

coincident ADJ. occurring at the same time. Some people find the *coincident* events in Hardy's novels annoying.

collaborate V. work together. Two writers *collaborated* in preparing this book.

collate V. examine in order to verify authenticity; arrange in order. They *collated* the newly found manuscripts to determine their age.

collateral N. security given for loan. The sum you wish to borrow is so large that it must be secured by *collateral.*

collation N. a light meal. Tea sandwiches and cookies were offered at the *collation.*

collier N. worker in coal mine; ship carrying coal. The extended cold spell has prevented the *colliers* from delivering the coal to the docks as scheduled.

colloquy (kŏl´-ə-kwē) N. informal discussion. I enjoy our *colloquies,* but I sometimes wish that they could be made more formal and more searching.

collusion N. conspiring in a fraudulent scheme. The swindlers were found guilty of *collusion.*

colossal ADJ. huge. Radio City Music Hall has a *colossal* stage.

combustible ADJ. easily burned. After the recent outbreak of fires in private homes, the fire commissioner ordered that all *combustible* materials be kept in safe containers. also N.

comely (kŭm´-) ADJ. attractive; agreeable. I would rather have a *comely* wife than a rich one.

comestible (-mĕs´-) N. something fit to be eaten. The roast turkey and other *comestibles,* the wines, and the excellent service made this Thanksgiving dinner particularly memorable.

ā—ale; ă—add; ä—arm; à—ask, ē—eve; ĕ—end; ê—err, her; ə—allow; even; ī—ice; ĭ—ill; ō—oll; ŏ—odd; ô—orb; ōō—food; ŏŏ—foot, put; o—out; th—thin; ū—use; ŭ—up; zh—pleasure

comity N. courtesy; civility. A spirit of *comity* should exist among nations.

commandeer V. to draft for military purposes; to take for public use. The policeman *commandeered* the first car that approached and ordered the driver to go to the nearest hospital.

commensurate ADJ. equal in extent. Your reward will be *commensurate* with your effort.

commiserate V. feel or express pity or sympathy for. Her friends *commiserated* with the widow.

commodious ADJ. spacious and comfortable. After sleeping in small roadside cabins, they found their hotel suite *commodious*.

compact N. agreement; contract. The signers of the Mayflower *Compact* were establishing a form of government.

compatible ADJ. harmonious; in harmony with. They were *compatible* neighbors, never quarreling over unimportant matters.

compilation N. listing of statistical information in tabular or book form. The *compilation* of available scholarships serves a very valuable purpose.

complacent (-*plās*-) ADJ. self-satisfied. There was a *complacent* look on his face as he examined his paintings. complacency, N.

complaisant ADJ. trying to please; obliging. The courtier obeyed the king's orders in a *complaisant* manner.

complement N. that which completes. A predicate *complement* completes the meaning of the subject. also V.

compliant ADJ. yielding. He was *compliant* and ready to conform to the pattern set by his friends.

comport V. bear one's self; behave. He *comported* himself with great dignity.

compunction N. remorse. The judge was especially severe in his sentencing because he felt that the criminal had shown no *compunction* for his heinous crime.

compute V. reckon; calculate. He failed to *compute* the interest.

concatenate V. link as in a chain. It is difficult to understand how these events could *concatenate* as they did without outside assistance.

conceit N. whimsical idea; extravagant metaphor. He was an entertaining companion, always expressing himself in amusing *conceits* and witty turns of phrase.

concentric ADJ. having a common center. The target was made of *concentric* circles.

conception N. beginning; forming of an idea. At the first *conception* of the work, he was consulted. conceive, V.

ā—ale; ă—add; ä—arm; à—ask; ē—eve; ĕ—end; ê—err, her; ə—allow; even; ī—ice; ĭ—ill; ō—oll; ŏ—odd; ô—orb; ōō—food; ŏŏ—foot, put; o—oŭt; th—thin; ū—use; ŭ—up; zh—pleasure

conciliate V. pacify; win over. She tried to *conciliate* me with a gift.
      conciliatory, ADJ.

concise ADJ. brief and compact. The essay was *concise* and explicit.

ETYMOLOGY 6

CID, CIS (to cut, to kill)
>   **incision** a cut (surgical)
>   **homicide** killing of a man
>   **fratricide** killing of a brother

CIRCUM (around) prefix
>   *circumnavigate* sail around the world
>   **circumspect** cautious (looking around)
>   **circumscribe** place a circle around

CIT, CITAT (to call, to start)
>   *incite* stir up, start up
>   **excite** stir up
>   **recitation** a recalling (or repeating) aloud

CIVI (citizen)
>   *civilization* society of citizens, culture
>   **civilian** member of a community
>   **civil** courteous

CLAM, CLAMAT (to cry out)
>   *clamorous* loud
>   **declamation** speech
>   **acclamation** shouted approval

CLAUD, CLAUS, CLOS, CLUD (to close)
>   *claustrophobia* fear of close places
>   **enclose** close in
>   **conclude** finish

CLE, CULE (small) noun suffix
>   **molecule** small mass
>   **corpuscle** blood cell
>   **follicle** small sac

COGNOSC, COGNIT (to learn)
>   **agnostic** lacking knowledge, skeptical
>   **incognito** traveling under an assumed identity (without
>   knowledge)
>   **cognition** knowledge

COM (with, together) prefix
>   **combine** merge with

ā—ale; ă—add; ä—arm; à—ask, ē—eve; ĕ—end; ê—err, her; ə—allow;
evən; ī—ice; ĭ—ill; ō—oll; ŏ—odd; ô—orb; ōō—food; ŏŏ—foot, pŭt;
o—oŭt; th—thin; ū—use; ŭ—up; zh—pleasure

commerce trade with
communicate correspond with
Note: By assimilation,
coeditor associate editor
collateral connected
conference meeting
corroborate confirm

COMP (to fill)

complete filled out
complement that which completes something
comply fulfill

TEST—Word List 6—Synonyms and Antonyms

Each of the following questions consists of a word printed in italics, followed by five words or phrases numbered 1 to 5. Choose the numbered word or phrase which is most nearly the same as or the opposite of the word in italics and write the number of your choice on your answer paper.

101. *clandestine* 1 abortive 2 secret 3 tangible 4 doomed 5 approved
102. *cognomen* 1 family name 2 dwarf 3 suspicion 4 kind of railway 5 pseudopod
103. *combustible* 1 flammable 2 industrious 3 waterproof 4 specific 5 plastic
104. *compliant* 1 numerous 2 veracious 3 soft 4 adamant 5 livid
105. *ciliated* 1 foolish 2 swift 3 early 4 constructed 5 hairy
106. *cleft* 1 split 2 waterfall 3 assembly 4 parfait 5 surplus
107. *cohesion* 1 independence 2 pedestrian 3 shift 4 pharmacy 5 climbing
108. *comestible* 1 vigorous 2 fit to be eaten 3 liquid 4 beautiful 5 circumvented
109. *circuitous* 1 direct 2 complete 3 obvious 4 aware 5 tortured
110. *cliché* 1 increase 2 vehicle 3 morale 4 original 5 pique
111. *coincidental* 1 simultaneous 2 changing 3 fortuitous 4 startling 5 trivial
112. *collation* 1 furor 2 emphasis 3 distillery 4 spree 5 lunch
113. *claustrophobia* 1 lack of confidence 2 fear of spiders 3 love of books 4 fear of grammar 5 fear of closed places
114. *cite* 1 galvanize 2 visualize 3 locate 4 quote 5 signal

ā—ale; ă—add; ä—arm; à—ask, ē—eve; ĕ—end; ê—err, her; ə—allow; even; ī—ice; ĭ—ill; ō—oll; ŏ—odd; ô—orb; o͞o—food; o͝o—foot, put; o—out; th—thin; ū—use; ŭ—up; zh—pleasure

115. *coerce* 1 recover 2 total 3 force 4 license 5 ignore
116. *cognizance* 1 policy 2 ignorance 3 advance 4 omission 5 examination
117. *colloquy* 1 dialect 2 diversion 3 announcement 4 discussion 5 expansion
118. *conciliate* 1 defend 2 activate 3 integrate 4 quarrel 5 react
119. *commiserate* 1 communicate 2 expand 3 repay 4 diminish 5 sympathize
120. *commodious* 1 numerous 2 accommodating 3 leisurely 4 limited 5 expensive

---

Word List 7 conclave - crux

conclave N. private meeting. He was present at all their *conclaves* as a sort of unofficial observer.

concoct V. prepare by combining; make up in concert. How did you ever *concoct* such a strange dish? concoction, N.

concomitant N. that which accompanies. Culture is not always a *concomitant* of wealth. also ADJ.

concurrent ADJ. happening at the same time. In America, the colonists were resisting the demands of the mother country; at the *concurrent* moment in France, the middle class was sowing the seeds of rebellion.

condescend V. bestow courtesies with a superior air. The king *condescended* to grant an audience to the friends of the condemned man. condescension, N.

condign (-*dīn*) ADJ. adequate; deservedly severe. The public approved the *condign* punishment.

condiments N. seasonings; spices. Spanish food is full of *condiments*.

condole V. express sympathetic sorrow. His friends gathered to *condole* with him over his loss. condolence, N.

condone V. overlook; forgive. We cannot *condone* your recent criminal cooperation with the gamblers.

confiscate V. seize; commandeer. The army *confiscated* all available supplies of uranium.

conformity N. harmony; agreement. In *conformity* with our rules and regulations, I am calling a meeting of our organization.

congeal (-*jēl*) V. freeze; coagulate. His blood *congealed* in his veins as he saw the dread monster rush toward him.

ā—ale; ă—add; ä—arm; à—ask, ē—eve; ĕ—end; ê—err, her; ə—allow; even; ī—ice; ĭ—ill; ō—oll; ŏ—odd; ô—orb; ōō—food; oŏ—foot, put; o—out; th—thin; ū—use; ŭ—up; zh—pleasure

congenital ADJ. existing at birth. His *congenital* deformity disturbed his parents.

conglomeration N. mass of material sticking together. In such a *conglomeration* of miscellaneous statistics, it was impossible to find a single area of analysis.

congruence N. correspondence of parts; harmonious relationship. The student demonstrated the *congruence* of the two triangles by using the hypotenuse-arm theorem.

conifer N. pine tree; cone-bearing tree. According to geologists, the *conifers* were the first plants to bear flowers.

conjugal ADJ. pertaining to marriage. Their dreams of *conjugal* bliss were shattered as soon as their temperaments clashed.

connivance N. pretense of ignorance of something wrong; assistance; permission to offend. With the *connivance* of his friends, he plotted to embarrass the teacher. connive, V.

connoisseur (*kŏn-ə-sŭr*) N. person competent to act as a judge of art, etc.; a lover of an art. He had developed into a *connoisseur* of fine china.

connotation N. suggested or implied meaning of an expression. Foreigners frequently are unaware of the *connotations* of the words they use.

connubial (*-nū-*) ADJ. pertaining to marriage or the matrimonial state. In his telegram, he wished the newlyweds a lifetime of *connubial* bliss.

consanguinity N. kinship. The lawsuit developed into a test of the *consanguinity* of the claimant to the estate.

consecrate V. dedicate; sanctify. We shall *consecrate* our lives to this noble purpose.

consensus N. general agreement. The *consensus* indicates that we are opposed to entering into this pact.

consequential ADJ. pompous; self-important. Convinced of his own importance, the actor strutted about the dressing room with a *consequential* air.

consort V. associate with. We frequently judge people by the company with whom they *consort*. also N.

constraint N. compulsion; repression of feelings. There was a feeling of *constraint* in the room because no one dared to criticize the speaker. constrain, V.

construe V. explain; interpret. If I *construe* your remarks correctly, you disagree with the theory already advanced.

consummate (*-sŭm-*) ADJ. complete. I have never seen anyone who

ā—ale; ă—add; ä—arm; à—ask, ē—eve; ĕ—end; ê—err, her; ə—allow; even; ī—ice; ĭ—ill; ō—oll; ŏ—odd; ô—orb; ōō—food; oŏ—foot, put; o—oŭt; th—thin; ū—use; ŭ—up; zh—pleasure

makes as many stupid errors as you do; you must be a *consummate* idiot. also V.

contaminate V. pollute. The sewage system of the city so *contaminated* the water that swimming was forbidden.

contemn V. regard with contempt; disregard. I will not tolerate those who *contemn* the sincere efforts of this group.

contentious ADJ. quarrelsome. We heard loud and *contentious* noises in the next room.

context N. writings preceding and following the passage quoted. Because these lines are taken out of *context,* they do not convey the message the author intended.

contiguous ADJ. adjacent to; touching upon. The two countries are *contiguous* for a few miles; then they are separated by the gulf.

continence N. self-restraint; sexual chastity. He vowed to lead a life of *continence.* continent, ADJ.

contingent ADJ. conditional. The continuation of this contract is *contingent* on the quality of your first output. contingency, N.

contortions N. twistings; distortions. As the effects of the opiate wore away, the *contortions* of the patient became more violent and demonstrated how much pain he was enduring.

contraband N, ADJ. illegal trade; smuggling. The Coast Guard tries to prevent traffic in *contraband* goods.

contravene V. contradict; infringe on. I will not attempt to *contravene* your argument for it does not affect the situation.

contrite ADJ. penitent. Her *contrite* tears did not influence the judge when he imposed sentence. contrition, N.

controvert V. oppose with arguments; contradict. To *controvert* your theory will require much time but it is essential that we disprove it.

contumacious ADJ. disobedient; resisting authority. The *contumacious* mob shouted defiantly at the police. contumacy, N.

contumely (kŭn-tū-mə-lē) N. scornful insolence; insult. The "proud man's *contumely*" is distasteful to Hamlet.

contusion N. bruise. He was treated for *contusions* and abrasions.

convene V. assemble. Because much needed legislation had to be enacted, the governor ordered the legislature to *convene* in special session by January 15.

conversant (-vərs-) ADJ. familiar with. The lawyer is *conversant* with all the evidence.

conveyance N. vehicle; transfer. During the transit strike, commuters used various kinds of *conveyances.*

ā—ale; ă—add; ä—arm; à—ask; ē—eve; ĕ—end; ê—err, her; ə—allow; even; ī—ice; ĭ—ill; ō—oll; ŏ—odd; ô—orb; ōō—food; ŏŏ—foot, put; o—oŭt; th—thin; ū—use; ŭ—up; zh—pleasure

convivial ADJ. festive; gay; characterized by joviality. The *convivial* celebrators of the victory sang their college songs.

convoke V. call together. Congress was *convoked* at the outbreak of the emergency. convocation, N.

copious ADJ. plentiful. He had *copious* reasons for rejecting the proposal.

coquette (*kō-kĕt*) N. flirt. Because she refused to give him any answer to his proposal of marriage, he called her a *coquette.* also V.

cornice N. projecting molding on building (usually above columns). Because the *cornice* stones had been loosened by the storms, the police closed the building until repairs could be made.

corporeal (*-pôr-ē-əl*) ADJ. bodily; material. He was not a churchgoer; he was interested only in *corporeal* matters.

corpulent ADJ. very fat. The *corpulent* man resolved to reduce. corpulence, N.

corroborate V. confirm. Unless we find a witness to *corroborate* your evidence, it will not stand up in court.

corrosive ADJ. eating away by chemicals or disease. Stainless steel is able to withstand the effects of *corrosive* chemicals.

corsair (*kôr-*) N. pirate; pirate ship. The *corsairs,* preying on shipping in the Mediterranean, were often inspired by racial and religious hatreds as well as by the desire for money and booty.

cortege (*kôr-tĕzh*) N. procession. The funeral *cortege* proceeded slowly down the avenue.

cosmic ADJ. pertaining to the universe; vast. *Cosmic* rays derive their name from the fact that they bombard the earth's atmosphere from outer space. cosmos, N.

coterie (*kōt-*) N. group that meets socially; select circle. After his book had been published, he was invited to join the literary *coterie* that lunched daily at the hotel.

countermand V. cancel; revoke. The general *countermanded* the orders issued in his absence.

counterpart N. a thing that completes another; things very much alike. Night and day are *counterparts.*

covenant N. agreement. We must comply with the terms of the *covenant.*

covert (*kō-*) ADJ. secret; hidden; implied. He could understand the *covert* threat in the letter.

covetous ADJ. avaricious; eagerly desirous of. The child was *covetous* by nature and wanted to take the toys belonging to his classmates. covet, V.

cower V. shrink quivering, as from fear. The frightened child *cowered* in the corner of the room.

ā—ale; ă—add; ä—arm; à—ask; ē—eve; ĕ—end; ê—err, her; ə—allow; even; ī—ice; ĭ—ill; ō—oll; ŏ—odd; ô—orb; ōō—food; ŏŏ—foot, put; o—out; th—thin; ū—use; ŭ—up; zh—pleasure

coy ADJ. shy; modest; coquettish. She was *coy* in her answers to his offer.

crabbed (*krăb -əd*) ADJ. sour; peevish. The *crabbed* old man was avoided by the children because he scolded them when they made noise.

crass ADJ. very unrefined; grossly insensible. The philosophers deplored the *crass* commercialism.

craven (*krā-*) ADJ. cowardly. His *craven* behavior in this critical period was criticized.

credence (*krēd-*) N. belief. Do not place any *credence* in his promises.

credulity (*krĭ-dū-*) N. belief on slight evidence. The witch doctor took advantage of the *credulity* of the superstitious natives. credulous, ADJ.

creed N. system of religious or ethical belief. In any loyal American's *creed,* love of democracy must be emphasized.

crestfallen ADJ. dejected; dispirited. We were surprised at his reaction to the failure of his project; instead of being *crestfallen,* he was busily engaged in planning new activities.

crevice N. crack; fissure. The mountain climbers found footholds in the tiny *crevices* in the mountainside.

criterion N. standard used in judging. What *criterion* did you use when you selected this essay as the prizewinner? criteria, PL.

crone N. hag. The toothless *crone* frightened us when she smiled.

crux N. crucial point. This is the *crux* of the entire problem.

ETYMOLOGY 7

CONTRA (against) prefix
> **contradict** disagree
> **controversy** dispute (turning against)
> **contrary** opposed

CORD (heart)
> **accord** agreement (from the heart)
> **cordial** friendly
> **discord** lack of harmony

CORPOR (body)
> **incorporate** organize into a body
> **corporeal** pertaining to the body or physical mass
> **corpse** dead body

CRED (to believe)
> **incredulous** not believing, skeptical

ā—ale; ă—add; ä—arm; à—ask, ē—eve; ĕ—end; ê—err, her; ə—allow; even; ī—ice; ĭ—ill; ō—oll; ŏ—odd; ô—orb; ōō—food; ŏŏ—foot, put; o—out; th—thin; ū—use; ŭ—up; zh—pleasure

credulity gullibility
credence belief

TEST—Word List 7—Synonyms

Each of the questions below consists of a word printed in italics, followed by five words or phrases numbered 1 to 5. Choose the numbered word or phrase which is most nearly similar in meaning to the word in italics and write the number of your answer on your answer paper.

121. *condone* 1 stop 2 evaluate 3 pierce 4 infuriate 5 overlook
122. *consanguinity* 1 kinship 2 friendship 3 bloodletting 4 relief 5 understanding
123. *continence* 1 humanity 2 research 3 embryology 4 bodies of land 5 self-restraint
124. *confiscate* 1 discuss 2 discover 3 seize 4 exist 5 convey
125. *consensus* 1 general agreement 2 project 3 insignificance 4 sheaf 5 crevice
126. *conformity* 1 agreement 2 ambition 3 confinement 4 pride 5 restraint
127. *construe* 1 explain 2 promote 3 reserve 4 erect 5 block
128. *congenital* 1 slight 2 obscure 3 thorough 4 existing at birth 5 classified
129. *contaminate* 1 arrest 2 prepare 3 pollute 4 beam 5 inform
130. *connoisseur* 1 gourmand 2 lover of art 3 humidor 4 delinquent 5 interpreter
131. *contentious* 1 squealing 2 surprising 3 quarrelsome 4 smug 5 creative
132. *contraband* 1 purpose 2 rogue 3 rascality 4 difficulty 5 smuggling
133. *copious* 1 plentiful 2 cheating 3 dishonorable 4 adventurous 5 inspired
134. *contrite* 1 smart 2 penitent 3 restful 4 recognized 5 perspiring
135. *corpulent* 1 regenerate 2 obese 3 different 4 hungry 5 bloody
136. *controvert* 1 turn over 2 contradict 3 mind 4 explain 5 swing
137. *craven* 1 desirous 2 direct 3 cowardly 4 civilized 5 controlled
138. *contumely* 1 sensation 2 noise 3 silence 4 insult 5 classic
139. *crux* 1 acne 2 spark 3 events 4 crucial point 5 belief

ā—ale; ă—add; ä—arm; à—ask, ē—eve; ĕ—end; ê—err, her; ə—allow; even; ī—ice; ĭ—ill; ō—oll; ŏ—odd; ô—orb; ōō—food; ŏŏ—foot; put; o—oŭt; th—thin; ū—use; ŭ—up; zh—pleasure

140. *conversant* 1 ignorant 2 speaking 3 incorporated 4 familiar 5 pedantic

---

Word List 8   cryptic - despoil

cryptic ADJ. mysterious; hidden; secret. His *cryptic* remarks could not be interpreted.

cuisine (*kwĭ-zēn*) N. style of cooking. French *cuisine* is noted for its use of sauces and wines.

culinary (*kŭl-*) ADJ. relating to cooking. Many chefs attribute their *culinary* skill to the wise use of spices.

cull V. pick out; reject. Every month the farmer *culls* the nonlaying hens from his flock and sells them to the local butcher. also N.

culmination N. attainment of highest point. His inauguration as President of the United States marked the *culmination* of his political career.

culpable ADJ. deserving blame. Corrupt politicians who condone the activities of the gamblers are equally *culpable*.

cupidity N. greed. The defeated people could not satisfy the *cupidity* of the conquerors, who demanded excessive tribute.

curry V. dress; treat leather; seek favor. The courtier *curried* favors of the king.

cursory ADJ. casual; hastily done. A *cursory* examination of the ruins indicates the possibility of arson; a more extensive study should be undertaken.

curtail V. shorten; reduce. During the coal shortage, we must *curtail* our use of this vital commodity.

cynic N. one who is skeptical or distrustful of human motives. A *cynic* at all times, he was suspicious of all altruistic actions of others. cynical, ADJ.

dais (*dā-əs*) N. raised platform for guests of honor. When he approached the *dais,* he was greeted by cheers from the people who had come to honor him.

dally V. trifle with; procrastinate. Laertes told Ophelia that Hamlet could only *dally* with her affections.

dank ADJ. damp. The walls of the dungeon were *dank* and slimy.

dastard N. coward. This sneak attack is the work of a *dastard*. dastardly, ADJ.

daunt V. intimidate. Your threats cannot *daunt* me.

ā—ale; ă—add; ä—arm; à—ask; ē—eve; ĕ—end; ê—err, her; ə—allow;
even; ī—ice; ĭ—ill; ō—oll; ŏ—odd; ô—orb; ōō—food; ŏŏ—foot, put;
o—oūt; th—thin; ū—use; ŭ—up; zh—pleasure

dauntless ADJ. bold. Despite the dangerous nature of the undertaking, the *dauntless* soldier volunteered for the assignment.

dawdle V. loiter; waste time. Inasmuch as we must meet a deadline, do not *dawdle* over this work.

dearth (*dêrth*) N. scarcity. The *dearth* of skilled labor compelled the employers to open trade schools.

debase V. reduce to lower state. Do not *debase* yourself by becoming maudlin.

debauch (*-bôch*) V. corrupt; make intemperate. A vicious newspaper can *debauch* public ideals. debauchery, N.

debilitate V. weaken; enfeeble. Overindulgence *debilitates* character as well as physical stamina.

debonair ADJ. friendly; aiming to please. The *debonair* youth was liked by all who met him, because of his cheerful and obliging manner.

debutante (*děb -yoŏ-*) N. young woman making formal entrance into society. As a *debutante,* she was often mentioned in the society columns of the newspapers.

decadence (*děk -*) N. decay. The moral *decadence* of the people was reflected in the lewd literature of the period.

decant (*-kǎnt*) V. pour off gently. Be sure to *decant* this wine before serving it.

deciduous ADJ. falling off as of leaves. The oak is a *deciduous* tree.

declivity N. downward slope. The children loved to ski down the *declivity.*

decorous ADJ. proper. Her *decorous* behavior was praised by her teachers. decorum, N.

decoy (*dē -kôĭ*) N. lure or bait. The wild ducks were not fooled by the *decoy.* also V.

decrepit ADJ. worn out by age. The *decrepit* car blocked traffic on the highway.

decry V. disparage. Do not attempt to increase your stature by *decrying* the efforts of your opponents.

deducible ADJ. derived by reasoning. If we accept your premise, your conclusions are easily *deducible.*

defalcate (*-fǎl -*) V. misuse money held in trust. Legislation was passed to punish brokers who *defalcated* their clients' funds.

defamation N. harming a person's reputation. Such *defamation* of character may result in a slander suit.

default N. failure to do. As a result of her husband's failure to appear in court, she was granted a divorce by *default.* also V.

ā—ale; ă—add; ä—arm; à—ask, ē—eve; ĕ—end; ê—err, her; ə—allow; even; ī—ice; ĭ—ill; ō—oll; ŏ—odd; ô—orb; ōō—food; ŏŏ—foot, put; o—oŭt; th—thin; ū—use; ŭ—up; zh—pleasure

defeatist ADJ. attitude of one who is ready to accept defeat as a natural outcome. If you maintain your *defeatist* attitude, you will never succeed. also N.

defection N. desertion. The children, who had made him an idol, were hurt most by his *defection* from our cause.

deference (dĕf-) N. courteous regard for another's wish. In *deference* to his desires, the employers granted him a holiday.

defile V. pollute; profane. The hoodlums *defiled* the church with their scurrilous writing.

definitive ADJ. final; complete. Carl Sandburg's *Abraham Lincoln* may be regarded as the *definitive* work on the life of the Great Emancipator.

deflect V. turn aside. His life was saved when his cigarette case *deflected* the bullet.

defunct ADJ. dead; no longer in use or existence. The lawyers sought to examine the books of the *defunct* corporation.

deign (dān) V. condescend. He felt that he would debase himself if he *deigned* to answer his critics.

delete V. erase; strike out. If you *delete* this paragraph, the composition will have more appeal.

deleterious (-tĭr-) ADJ. harmful. Workers in nuclear research must avoid the *deleterious* effects of radioactive substances.

delineation N. portrayal. He is a powerful storyteller, but he is weakest in his *delineation* of character.

delirium N. mental disorder marked by confusion. The drunkard in his *delirium* saw strange animals.

delude V. deceive. Do not *delude* yourself into believing that he will relent.

delusion N. false belief; hallucination. This scheme is a snare and a *delusion*.

delusive ADJ. deceptive; raising vain hopes. Do not raise your hopes on the basis of his *delusive* promises.

demagogue N. person who appeals to people's prejudice; false leader of people. He was accused of being a *demagogue* because he made promises which aroused futile hopes in his listeners.

demean V. degrade; humiliate. He felt that he would *demean* himself if he replied to the scurrilous letter.

demeanor N. behavior; bearing. His sober *demeanor* quieted the noisy revelers.

demise (-mīz) N. death. Upon the *demise* of the dictator, a bitter dispute about succession to power developed.

ā—ale; ă—add; ä—arm; à—ask, ē—eve; ĕ—end; ê—err, her; ə—allow; even; ī—ice; ĭ—ill; ō—oll; ŏ—odd; ô—orb; ōō—food; ŏŏ—foot, put; o—out; th—thin; ū—use; ŭ—up; zh—pleasure

demolition N. destruction. One of the major aims of the air force was the complete *demolition* of all means of transportation by bombing of rail lines and terminals.

demoniac (-*mō*-) ADJ. fiendish. The Spanish Inquisition devised many *demoniac* means of torture. demon, N.

demur V. delay; object. To *demur* at this time will only worsen the already serious situation; now is the time for action.

demure ADJ. grave; serious; coy. She was *demure* and reserved.

denizen (*dĕn*-) N. inhabitant of. Ghosts are *denizens* of the land of the dead who return to earth.

depict V. portray. In this book, the author *depicts* the slave owners as kind and benevolent masters.

depilate (*dĕp*-) V. remove hair. Many women *depilate* their legs.

deplete V. reduce; exhaust. We must wait until we *deplete* our present inventory before we order replacements.

deploy V. move troops so that the battle line is extended at the expense of depth. The general ordered the battalion to *deploy* in order to meet the offensive of the enemy.

deposition (*dĕp*-) N. testimony under oath. He made his *deposition* in the judge's chamber.

depravity N. corruption; wickedness. The *depravity* of his behavior shocked all.

deprecate (*dĕp*-) V. disapprove regretfully. I must *deprecate* your attitude and hope that you will change your mind.

deprecatory ADJ. disapproving. Your *deprecatory* criticism has offended the author.

depreciate V. lessen in value. If you neglect this property, it will *depreciate.*

depredation N. plundering. After the *depredations* of the invaders, the people were penniless.

deranged ADJ. insane. He was mentally *deranged.*

derelict ADJ. abandoned. The *derelict* craft was a menace to navigation. also N.

deride V. scoff at. The people *derided* his grandiose schemes.

derision N. ridicule. They greeted his proposal with *derision* and refused to consider it seriously.

dermatologist N. one who studies the skin and its diseases. I advise you to consult a *dermatologist* about your acne.

derogatory ADJ. expressing a low opinion. I resent your *derogatory* remarks.

descant (*dĕs*-) V. discuss fully. He was willing to *descant* upon any topic

ā—ale; ă—add; ä—arm; à—ask; ē—eve; ĕ—end; ê—err, her; ə—allow; even; ī—ice; ĭ—ill; ō—oll; ŏ—odd; ô—orb; ōō—food; ŏŏ—foot, put; o—out; th—thin; ū—use; ŭ—up; zh—pleasure

of conversation, even when he knew very little about the subject under discussion. also N.

descry (-skrī) V. catch sight of. In the distance, we could barely *descry* the enemy vessels.

desecrate V. profane; violate the sanctity of. The soldiers *desecrated* the temple.

desiccate V. dry up. A tour of this smokehouse will give you an idea of how the pioneers used to *desiccate* food in order to preserve it.

despicable (-spĭk-) ADJ. contemptible. Your *despicable* remarks call for no reply.

despise V. scorn. I *despise* your attempts at a reconciliation at this time.

despoil V. plunder. If you do not yield, I am afraid the enemy will *despoil* the buildings.

ETYMOLOGY 8

CUR (to care)
> **curator** person in charge
> **sinecure** position without responsibility
> **secure** safe

CURR, CURS (to run)
> **excursion** journey
> **cursory** brief
> **precursor** forerunner

CY (state of being) noun suffix
> **democracy** a democratic state
> **obstinacy** state of being stubborn
> **accuracy** state of being accurate

DA, DAT (to give)
> **data** facts, statistics
> **mandate** command
> **date** given time

DE (down, away) prefix
> **debase** lower in value
> **decadence** deterioration
> **decant** pour off

DEB, DEBIT (to owe)
> **debt** something owed
> **indebtedness** debt
> **debenture** bond

ā—ale; ă—add; ä—arm; à—ask, ē—eve; ĕ—end; ê—err, her; ə—allow; even; ī—ice; ĭ—ill; ō—oll; ŏ—odd; ô—orb; ōō—food; ŏŏ—foot; put; o—oŭt; th—thin; ū—use; ŭ—up; zh—pleasure

DEMOS (people)
>   **democracy**   rule of the people
>   **demagogue**   (false) leader of the people
>   **epidemic**   widespread disease (among the people)

DERM (skin)
>   **epidermis**   skin
>   **pachyderm**   thick-skinned quadruped
>   **dermatology**   study of the skin and its disorders

TEST—Word List 8—Antonyms

Each of the questions below consists of a word printed in italics, followed by five words or phrases numbered 1 to 5. Choose the numbered word or phrase which is most nearly opposite in meaning to the word in italics and write the number of your choice on your answer paper.

141. *cryptic*   1 tomblike   2 secret   3 famous   4 candid   5 coded
142. *dank*   1 dry   2 guiltless   3 warm   4 babbling   5 reserved
143. *cupidity*   1 anxiety   2 tragedy   3 generosity   4 entertainment   5 love
144. *dastard*   1 illegitimacy   2 hero   3 presence   4 warmth   5 idol
145. *curtail*   1 mutter   2 lengthen   3 express   4 burden   5 shore
146. *dauntless*   1 stolid   2 weak   3 irrelevant   4 peculiar   5 particular
147. *cynical*   1 trusting   2 effortless   3 conclusive   4 gallant   5 vertical
148. *debilitate*   1 bedevil   2 repress   3 strengthen   4 animate   5 deaden
149. *debonair*   1 awkward   2 windy   3 balmy   4 sporty   5 stormy
150. *declivity*   1 trap   2 quadrangle   3 quarter   4 activity   5 upward slope
151. *derogatory*   1 roguish   2 immediate   3 opinioned   4 praising   5 conferred
152. *decrepit*   1 momentary   2 emotional   3 suppressed   4 youthful   5 unexpected
153. *depravity*   1 goodness   2 sadness   3 heaviness   4 tidiness   5 seriousness
154. *defection*   1 determination   2 joining   3 invitation   4 affection   5 cancellation
155. *deranged*   1 sane   2 announced   3 neighborly   4 alphabetical   5 arranged
156. *defalcate*   1 abscond   2 elope   3 observe   4 panic   5 use money held in trust properly
157. *desecrate*   1 desist   2 integrate   3 confuse   4 intensify   5 consecrate

ā—ale; ă—add; ä—arm; à—ask, ē—eve; ĕ—end; ê—err, her; ə—allow; even; ī—ice; ĭ—ill; ō—oll; ŏ—odd; ô—orb; ōō—food; ŏŏ—foot, put; o—oüt; th—thin; ū—use; ŭ—up; zh—pleasure

158. *defile* 1 manicure 2 ride 3 purify 4 assemble 5 order
159. *despicable* 1 steering 2 worthy of esteem 3 inevitable 4 featureless 5 incapable
160. *deleterious* 1 delaying 2 experimental 3 harmless 4 graduating 5 glorious

---

Word List 9   despotism - diverse

despotism N. tyranny. The people rebelled against the *despotism* of the king.

destitute ADJ. extremely poor. The illness left the family *destitute*.

desuetude (dĕs-wĭ-) N. disused condition. The machinery in the idle factory was in a state of *desuetude*.

desultory (dĕs-) ADJ. aimless; jumping around. The animals' *desultory* behavior indicated that they had no awareness of their predicament.

detergent N. cleansing agent. Many new *detergents* have replaced soap.

detonation N. explosion. The *detonation* could be heard miles away.

detraction N. slandering; aspersion. He is offended by your frequent *detractions* of his ability as a leader.

detriment N. harm; damage. Your acceptance of his support will ultimately prove to be a *detriment* rather than an aid to your cause.

deviate (dē-) V. turn away from. Do not *deviate* from the truth.

devious ADJ. going astray; erratic. Your *devious* behavior in this matter puzzles me since you are usually direct and straightforward.

devoid ADJ. lacking. He was *devoid* of any personal desire for gain in his endeavor to secure improvement in the community.

devolve V. deputize; pass to others. It *devolved* upon us, the survivors, to arrange peace terms with the enemy.

devout ADJ. pious. The *devout* man prayed daily.

dexterous ADJ. skillful. The magician was so *dexterous* that we could not follow him as he performed his tricks.

diabolical ADJ. devilish. This scheme is so *diabolical* that I must reject it.

diadem (dī-ə-) N. crown. The king's *diadem* was on display at the museum.

dialectic N. art of debate. I am not skilled in *dialectic* and, therefore, cannot answer your arguments as forcefully as I wish.

ā—ale; ă—add; ä—arm; à—ask; ē—eve; ĕ—end; ê—err, her; ə—allow; even; ī—ice; ĭ—ill; ō—oll; ŏ—odd; ô—orb; ōō—food; ŏŏ—foot, put; o—out; th—thin; ū—use; ŭ—up; zh—pleasure

diaphanous (dī-ăf-) ADJ. sheer; transparent. They admired her *diaphanous* and colorful dress.

dichotomy (dī-kŏt-) N. branching into two parts. The *dichotomy* of our legislative system provides us with many safeguards.

dictum N. authoritative and weighty statement. He repeated the statement as though it were the *dictum* of the most expert worker in the group.

diffidence N. shyness. You must overcome your *diffidence* if you intend to become a salesperson.

diffusion N. wordiness; spreading in all directions like a gas. Your composition suffers from a *diffusion* of ideas; try to be more compact. diffuse, ADJ. and V.

digressive ADJ. wandering away from the subject. His book was marred by his many *digressive* remarks.

dilapidation N. ruin because of neglect. We felt that the *dilapidation* of the building could be corrected by several coats of paint.

dilate V. expand. In the dark, the pupils of your eyes *dilate*.

dilatory (dĭl-) ADJ. delaying. Your *dilatory* tactics may compel me to cancel the contract.

dilemma N. problem; choice of two unsatisfactory alternatives. In this *dilemma,* he knew no one to whom he could turn for advice.

dilettante (-tänt) N. aimless follower of the arts; amateur; dabbler. He was not serious in his painting; he was rather a *dilettante*.

diminution N. lessening; reduction in size. The blockaders hoped to achieve victory as soon as the *diminution* of the enemy's supplies became serious.

dint N. means; effort. By *dint* of much hard work, the volunteers were able to place the raging forest fire under control.

dipsomaniac N. one who has a strong craving for intoxicating liquor. The picture *The Lost Weekend* was an excellent portrayal of the struggles of the *dipsomaniac*.

dire ADJ. disastrous. People ignored his *dire* predictions of an approaching depression.

dirge N. lament with music. The funeral *dirge* stirred us to tears.

disapprobation N. disapproval; condemnation. The conservative father viewed his daughter's radical boyfriend with *disapprobation*.

disarray N. a disorderly or untidy state. After the New Year's party, the once orderly house was in total *disarray*.

disavowal N. denial; disclaiming. His *disavowal* of his part in the conspiracy was not believed by the jury.

ā—ale; ă—add; ä—arm; à—ask; ē—eve; ĕ—end; ê—err, her; ə—allow; even; ī—ice; ĭ—ill; ō—oll; ŏ—odd; ô—orb; ōō—food; ŏŏ—foot, put; o—out; th—thin; ū—use; ŭ—up; zh—pleasure

discernible ADJ. distinguishable; perceivable. The ships in the harbor were not *discernible* in the fog.

discerning ADJ. mentally quick and observant; having insight. Because he was considered the most *discerning* member of the firm, he was assigned the most difficult cases.

disclaim V. disown; renounce claim to. If I grant you this privilege, will you *disclaim* all other rights?

discomfit V. put to rout; defeat; disconcert. This ruse will *discomfit* the enemy. discomfiture, N.

disconcert V. confuse; upset; embarrass. The lawyer was *disconcerted* by the evidence produced by his adversary.

disconsolate ADJ. sad. The death of his wife left him *disconsolate*.

discordant ADJ. inharmonious; conflicting. He tried to unite the *discordant* factions.

discrete ADJ. separate; unconnected. The universe is composed of *discrete* bodies.

discretion N. prudence; ability to adjust actions to circumstances. Use your *discretion* in this matter.

discursive ADJ. digressing; rambling. They were annoyed and bored by his *discursive* remarks.

disdain V. treat with scorn or contempt. You make enemies of all you *disdain*. also N.

disgruntle V. make discontented. The passengers were *disgruntled* by the numerous delays.

disheartened ADJ. lacking courage and hope. His failure to pass the bar exam *disheartened* him.

disheveled (dĭsh-ĕv-) ADJ. untidy. Your *disheveled* appearance will hurt your chances in this interview.

disingenuous ADJ. not naive; sophisticated. Although he was young, his remarks indicated that he was *disingenuous*.

disinterested ADJ. unprejudiced. The only *disinterested* person in the room was the judge.

disjointed ADJ. disconnected. His remarks were so *disjointed* that we could not follow his reasoning.

dismember V. cut into small parts. When the Austrian Empire was *dismembered,* several new countries were established.

disparage V. belittle. Do not *disparage* anyone's contribution; these little gifts add up to large sums.

disparate ADJ. basically different; unrelated. It is difficult, if not impossible, to organize these *disparate* elements into a coherent whole.

ā—ale; ă—add; ä—arm; å—ask; ē—eve; ĕ—end; ê—err, her; ə—allow; even; ī—ice; ĭ—ill; ō—oll; ŏ—odd; ô—orb; ōō—food; ŏŏ—foot, put; o—out; th—thin; ū—use; ŭ—up; zh—pleasure

disparity N. difference; condition of inequality. The *disparity* in their ages made no difference at all.

dispersion N. scattering. The *dispersion* of this group throughout the world may be explained by their expulsion from their homeland.

dispirited ADJ. lacking in spirit. The coach used all the tricks at his command to buoy up the enthusiasm of his team, which had become *dispirited* at the loss of the star player.

disport V. amuse. The popularity of Florida as a winter resort is constantly increasing; each year, thousands more *disport* themselves at Miami and Palm Beach.

disputatious (*-ta* -) ADJ. argumentative; fond of argument. People avoided discussing contemporary problems with him because of his *disputatious* manner.

disquisition N. a formal systematic inquiry; an explanation of the results of a formal inquiry. In his *disquisition*, he outlined the steps he had taken in reaching his conclusions.

dissection (*dĭs-ĕk*-) N. analysis; cutting apart in order to examine. The *dissection* of frogs in the laboratory is particularly unpleasant to some students.

dissemble V. disguise; pretend. Even though you are trying to *dissemble* your motive in joining this group, we can see through your pretense.

disseminate V. scatter (like seeds). The invention of the radio has helped propagandists to *disseminate* their favorite doctrines very easily.

dissertation N. formal essay. In order to earn a graduate degree from many of our universities, a candidate is frequently required to prepare a *dissertation* on some scholarly subject.

dissimulate V. pretend; conceal by feigning. She tried to *dissimulate* her grief by her gay attitude.

dissipate V. squander. The young man quickly *dissipated* his inheritance.

dissolute ADJ. loose in morals. The *dissolute* life led by these people is indeed shocking.

dissonance N. discord. Some contemporary musicians deliberately use *dissonance* to achieve certain effects.

dissuade (*dĭs-wād*) V. advise against. He could not *dissuade* his friend from joining the conspirators.

dissuasion N. advice against. All his powers of *dissuasion* were useless.

distend V. expand; swell out. I can tell when he is under stress by the way the veins *distend* on his forehead.

ā—ale; ă—add; ä—arm; à—ask, ē—eve; ĕ—end; ê—err, her; ə—allow;
even; ī—ice; ĭ —ill; ō—oll; ŏ—odd; ô—orb; ōō—food; ŏŏ—foot, put;
o—out; th—thin; ū—use; ŭ—up; zh—pleasure

distortion N. twisting out of shape. It is difficult to believe the newspaper accounts of this event because of the *distortions* and exaggerations written by the reporters.

distrait (-*strā*) ADJ. absentminded. Because of his concentration on the problem, the professor often appeared *distrait* and unconcerned about routine.

distraught ADJ. upset; distracted by anxiety. The *distraught* parents searched the ravine for their lost child.

diurnal (*dī-êrn*-) ADJ. daily. A farmer cannot neglect his *diurnal* tasks at any time; cows, for example, must be milked regularly.

diva (*dē*-) N. operatic singer; prima donna. Although world famous as a *diva,* she did not indulge in fits of temperament.

diverge (*də-vêrj*-) V. vary; go in different directions from the same point. The spokes of the wheel *diverge* from the hub.

divers (*dī*-) ADJ. several; differing. We could hear *divers* opinions of his ability.

diverse ADJ. differing in some characteristics; various. There are *diverse* ways of approaching this problem.

ETYMOLOGY 9

DI, DIURN (day)
      diary daybook
      diurnal pertaining to daytime
      journey day's travel
DIA (across) prefix
      diagonal across a figure
      diameter across a circle
      diagram outline drawing (writing across)
DIC, DICT (to say)
      abdicate renounce
      diction speech
      verdict statement of jury
DIS, DIF (not) prefix
      discord lack of harmony
      differ disagree (carry apart)
      distrust lack of trust

TEST—Word List 9—Synonyms and Antonyms

Each of the questions below consists of a word printed in italics, followed by five words or phrases numbered 1 to 5.

ā—ale; ă—add; ä—arm; à—ask; ē—eve; ĕ—end; ê—err, her; ə—allow; even; ī—ice; ĭ —ill; ō—oll; ŏ—odd; ô—orb; ōō—food; ŏŏ—foot, put; o—oŭt; th—thin; ū—use; ŭ—up; zh—pleasure

Choose the numbered word or phrase which is most nearly the same as or the opposite of the word in italics and write the number of your choice on your answer paper.

161. *disingenuous* 1 uncomfortable 2 eventual 3 naïve 4 complex 5 enthusiastic
162. *destitute* 1 reckless 2 dazzling 3 wanton 4 characteristic 5 explanatory
163. *dilate* 1 procrastinate 2 expand 3 conclude 4 participate 5 divert
164. *devout* 1 quiet 2 dual 3 impious 4 loyal 5 faithless
165. *diminution* 1 expectation 2 context 3 validity 4 appreciation 5 difficulty
166. *devoid* 1 latent 2 eschewed 3 full of 4 suspecting 5 evident
167. *disconsolate* 1 examining 2 thankful 3 theatrical 4 joyous 5 prominent
168. *diabolical* 1 mischievous 2 lavish 3 seraphic 4 azure 5 red
169. *disheveled* 1 recognized 2 unkempt 3 short 4 written 5 witty
170. *diffidence* 1 sharpness 2 boldness 3 malcontent 4 dialogue 5 catalog
171. *dissonance* 1 admonition 2 splendor 3 discord 4 reflection 5 consonance
172. *distrait* 1 clever 2 industrial 3 absentminded 4 narrow crooked
173. *disinterested* 1 prejudiced 2 horrendous 3 affected 4 arbitrary 5 bored
174. *dissipate* 1 economize 2 clean 3 accept 4 anticipate 5 withdraw
175. *disjointed* 1 satisfied 2 carved 3 understood 4 connected 5 evicted
176. *distend* 1 bloat 2 adjust 3 exist 4 materialize 5 finish
177. *dispirited* 1 current 2 dented 3 drooping 4 removed 5 dallying
178. *diurnal* 1 containing 2 daily 3 weekly 4 monthly 5 annual
179. *disparity* 1 resonance 2 elocution 3 relief 4 difference 5 symbolism
180. *dilatory* 1 narrowing 2 procrastinating 3 enlarging 4 portentous 5 sour

---

Word List 10   diversity - enigma

diversity N. variety; dissimilitude. The *diversity* of colleges in this country indicates that many levels of ability are being cared for.

divest (*dĭ-věst*) v. strip; deprive. He was *divested* of his power to act.

ā—ale; ă—add; ä—arm; à—ask, ē—eve; ĕ—end; ê—err, her; ə—allow; even; ī—ice; ĭ—ill; ō—oll; ŏ—odd; ô—orb; ōō—food; ŏŏ—foot, put; o—out; th—thin; ū—use; ŭ—up; zh—pleasure

divination N. foreseeing the future with aid of magic. I base my opinions not on any special gift of *divination* but on the laws of probability.

divulge V. reveal. I will not tell you this news because I am sure you will *divulge* it prematurely.

docile ADJ. obedient; easily managed. As *docile* as he seems today, that old lion was once a ferocious, snarling beast.

docket N. program as for trial; book where such entries are made. The case of Smith vs. Jones was entered in the *docket* for July 15. also V.

doff V. take off. He *doffed* his hat to the lady.

doggerel N. poor verse. Although we find occasional snatches of genuine poetry in his work, most of his writing is mere *doggerel*.

dogmatic ADJ. positive; arbitrary. Do not be so *dogmatic* about that statement; it can be easily refuted.

dolorous (*dōl*-) ADJ. sorrowful. He found the *dolorous* lamentations of the bereaved family emotionally disturbing and he left as quickly as he could.

dolt N. stupid person. I thought I was talking to a mature audience; instead, I find myself addressing a pack of *dolts* and idiots.

domicile N. home. Although his legal *domicile* was in New York City, his work kept him away from his residence for many years. also V.

dormant ADJ. sleeping; lethargic; torpid. Sometimes *dormant* talents in our friends surprise those of us who never realized how gifted our acquaintances really are. dormancy, N.

dorsal ADJ. relating to the back of an animal. A shark may be identified by its *dorsal* fin, which projects above the surface of the ocean.

dotage (*dōt*-) N. senility. In his *dotage,* the old man bored us with long tales of events in his childhood.

doughty (*dout*-) ADJ. courageous. Many folk tales have sprung up about this *doughty* pioneer who opened up the New World for his followers.

dour (*dour*) ADJ. sullen; stubborn. The man was *dour* and taciturn.

dowdy ADJ. slovenly; untidy. She tried to change her *dowdy* image by buying a new fashionable wardrobe.

dregs N. sediment; worthless residue. The *dregs* of society may be observed in this slum area of the city.

droll (*drōl*) ADJ. queer and amusing. He was a popular guest because his *droll* anecdotes were always amusing.

ā—ale; ă—add; ä—arm; à—ask, ē—eve; ĕ—end; ê—err, her; ə—allow; even; ī—ice; ĭ—ill; ō—oll; ŏ—odd; ô—orb; ōō—food; ŏŏ—foot, put; o—out; th—thin; ū—use; ŭ—up; zh—pleasure

dross (*drŏs*) N. waste matter; worthless impurities. Many methods have been devised to separate the valuable metal from the *dross*.

drudgery N. menial work. Cinderella's fairy godmother rescued her from a life of *drudgery*.

dubious ADJ. doubtful. He has the *dubious* distinction of being the lowest man in his class.

duplicity N. double-dealing; hypocrisy. People were shocked and dismayed when they learned of his *duplicity* in this affair for he had always seemed honest and straightforward.

duress (*-rĕs*) N. forcible restraint, especially unlawfully. The hostages were held under *duress* until the prisoners' demands were met.

earthy ADJ. unrefined; coarse. His *earthy* remarks often embarrassed the women in his audience.

ebullient (*-bŏŏl-*) ADJ. showing excitement; overflowing with enthusiasm. His *ebullient* nature could not be repressed; he was always laughing and gay. ebullience, N.

eccentricity N. oddity; idiosyncrasy. Some of his friends tried to account for his rudeness to strangers as the *eccentricity* of genius. eccentric, ADJ.

ecclesiastic ADJ. pertaining to the church. The minister donned his *ecclesiastic* garb and walked to the pulpit. also N.

ecstasy N. rapture; joy; any overpowering emotion. The announcement that the war had ended brought on an *ecstasy* of joy that resulted in many uncontrolled celebrations.

edify V. instruct; correct morally. Although his purpose was to *edify* and not to entertain his audience, many of his listeners were amused and not enlightened.

educe (*ĭ-dūs*) V. draw forth; elicit. He could not *educe* a principle that would encompass all the data.

eerie (*ĭ-rē*) ADJ. weird. In that *eerie* setting, it was easy to believe in ghosts and other supernatural beings.

efface V. rub out. The coin had been handled so many times that its date had been *effaced*.

effectual ADJ. efficient. If we are to succeed in this endeavor, we must seek *effectual* means of securing our goals.

effeminate ADJ. having womanly traits. His voice was high-pitched and *effeminate*.

effervesce (*-vĕs*) V. bubble over; show excitement. Some of us cannot stand the way she *effervesces* over trifles.

ā—ale; ă—add; ä—arm; à—ask, ē—eve; ĕ—end; ê—err, her; ə—allow; even; ī—ice; ĭ—ill; ō—oll; ŏ—odd; ô—orb; ōō—food; ŏŏ—foot, pŭt; o—oūt; th—thin; ū—use; ŭ—up; zh—pleasure

effete (*ĕ-fēt*) ADJ. worn out; exhausted; barren. The literature of the age reflected the *effete* condition of the writers; no new ideas were forthcoming.

efficacy (*ĕf-*) N. power to produce desired effect. The *efficacy* of this drug depends on the regularity of the dosage.

effigy (*ĕf-ə-jē*) N. dummy. The mob showed its irritation by hanging the judge in *effigy*.

efflorescent ADJ. flowering. Greenhouse gardeners are concerned with the coinciding of the plants' *efflorescent* period with certain holidays.

effrontery N. shameless boldness. He had the *effrontery* to insult the guest.

effulgent (*-fo͝ol-*) ADJ. brilliantly radiant. The *effulgent* rays of the rising sun lit the sky.

effusion N. pouring forth. The critics objected to his literary *effusion* because it was too flowery.

effusive ADJ. pouring forth; gushing. Her *effusive* manner of greeting her friends finally began to irritate them.

egoism N. excessive interest in one's self; belief that one should be interested in one's self rather than in others. His *egoism* prevented him from seeing the needs of his colleagues.

egotism N. conceit; vanity. We found his *egotism* unwarranted and irritating.

egregious (*ĭ-grē-jəs*) ADJ. gross; shocking. He was an *egregious* liar.

egress (*ē-*) N. exit. Barnum's sign "To the *Egress*" fooled many people who thought they were going to see an animal and instead found themselves in the street.

ejaculation N. exclamation. He could not repress an *ejaculation* of surprise when he heard the news.

elation N. a rise in spirits; exaltation. She felt no *elation* at finding the purse.

elegiacal (*ĕl-ə-jī'-*) ADJ. like an elegy; mournful. The essay on the lost crew was *elegiacal* in mood. elegy, N.

elicit (*-lĭs-ət*) V. draw out by discussion. The detectives tried to *elicit* where he had hidden his loot.

elucidate V. explain; enlighten. He was called upon to *elucidate* the disputed points in his article.

elusive ADJ. evasive; baffling; hard to grasp. His *elusive* dreams of wealth were costly to those of his friends who supported him financially.

elusory ADJ. tending to deceive expectations; elusive. He argued that the

ā—ale; ă—add; ä—arm; à—ask, ē—eve; ĕ—end; ê—err, her; ə—allow; even; ī—ice; ĭ—ill; ō—oll; ŏ—odd; ô—orb; o͞o—food; o͝o—foot, put; o—out; th—thin; ū—use; ŭ—up; zh—pleasure

project was an *elusory* one and would bring disappointment to all.

emaciated ADJ. thin and wasted. His long period of starvation had left him wan and *emaciated*.

emanate V. issue forth. A strong odor of sulphur *emanated* from the spring.

emancipate V. set free. At first, the attempts of the Abolitionists to *emancipate* the slaves were unpopular in New England as well as in the South.

embellish V. adorn. His handwriting was *embellished* with flourishes.

embezzlement N. stealing. The bank teller confessed his *embezzlement* of the funds.

emblazon V. deck in brilliant colors. *Emblazoned* on his shield was his family coat of arms.

embroil V. throw into confusion; involve in strife; entangle. He became *embroiled* in the heated discussion when he tried to arbitrate the dispute.

emend V. correct; correct by a critic. The critic *emended* the book by selecting the passages which he thought most appropriate to the text.

emetic (-*mĕt'*-) N. substance causing vomiting. The use of an *emetic* like mustard is useful in cases of poisoning.

eminent ADJ. high; lofty. After his appointment to this *eminent* position, he seldom had time for his former friends.

emolument (-*mŏl'*-) N. salary; compensation. In addition to the *emolument* this position offers, you must consider the social prestige it carries with it.

emulate (*ĕm*-) V. rival; imitate. As long as our political leaders *emulate* the virtues of the great leaders of this country, we shall flourish.

enamored (-*ăm*-) ADJ. in love. Narcissus became *enamored* of his own beauty.

enclave (*ĕn*-*klāv*) N. territory enclosed within an alien land. The Vatican is an independent *enclave* in Italy.

encomiastic ADJ. praising; eulogistic. Some critics believe that his *encomiastic* statements about Napoleon were inspired by his desire for material advancement rather than by an honest belief in the Emperor's genius. encomium, N.

encompass V. surround. Although we were *encompassed* by enemy forces, we were cheerful for we were well stocked and could withstand a siege until our allies joined us.

ā—ale; ă—add; ä—arm; à—ask, ē—eve; ĕ—end; ê—err, her; ə—allow; even; ī—ice; ĭ—ill; ō—oll; ŏ—odd; ô—orb; ōō—food; ŏŏ—foot, put; o—out; th—thin; ū—use; ŭ—up; zh—pleasure

encroachment N. gradual intrusion. The *encroachment* of the factories upon the neighborhood lowered the value of the real estate.

encumber V. burden. Some people *encumber* themselves with too much luggage when they take short trips.

endearment N. fond statement. Your gifts and *endearments* cannot make me forget your earlier insolence.

endive (*ĕn-dīv*) N. species of leafy plant used in salads. The salad contained *endive* in addition to the ingredients she usually used.

endue V. provide with some quality; endow. He was *endued* with a lion's courage.

energize V. invigorate; make forceful and active. We shall have to re-*energize* our activities by getting new members to carry on.

enervate V. weaken. The hot days of August are *enervating*.

engender V. cause; produce. This editorial will *engender* racial intolerance unless it is denounced.

engross V. occupy fully. John was so *engrossed* in his studies that he did not hear his mother call.

enhance V. advance; improve. Your chances for promotion in this department will be *enhanced* if you take some more courses in evening school.

enigma (*-nĭg-*) N. puzzle. Despite all attempts to decipher the code, it remained an *enigma*. enigmatic, ADJ.

ETYMOLOGY 10

DOC, DOCT (to teach)
> **docile**   meek (teachable)
> **document**   something that provides evidence
> **doctor**   learned man (originally, teacher)

DOM, DOMIN (to rule)
> **dominate**   having power over
> **domain**   land under rule
> **dominant**   prevailing

DUC, DUCT (to lead)
> **viaduct**   arched roadway
> **aqueduct**   artificial waterway
> **education**   training (leading out)

DYNAM (power, strength)
> **dynamic**   powerful

ā—ale; ă—add; ä—arm; à—ask; ē—eve; ĕ—end; ê—err, her; ə—allow; even; ī—ice; ĭ—ill; ō—oll; ŏ—odd; ô—orb; ōō—food; oŏ—foot, put; o—out; th—thin; ū—use; ŭ—up; zh—pleasure

dynamite powerful explosive
dynamo engine to make electrical power

EGO (I, self)

egoist person who is self-interested
egotist self-centered person
egocentric revolving about self

TEST—Word List 10—Synonyms

Each of the questions below consists of a word printed in italics, followed by five words or phrases numbered 1 to 5. Choose the numbered word or phrase which is most nearly similar in meaning to the word in italics and write the number of your choice on your answer paper.

181. *elusive* 1 deadly 2 eloping 3 evasive 4 simple 5 petrified
182. *edify* 1 mystify 2 suffice 3 improve 4 erect 5 entertain
183. *dormant* 1 active 2 absurd 3 hibernating 4 unfortunate 5 permanent
184. *egress* 1 entrance 2 bird 3 exit 4 double 5 progress
185. *dubious* 1 external 2 straight 3 sincere 4 doubtful 5 filling in
186. *dogmatic* 1 benign 2 canine 3 impatient 4 petulant 5 arbitrary
187. *elated* 1 debased 2 respectful 3 drooping 4 gay 5 charitable
188. *droll* 1 rotund 2 amusing 3 fearsome 4 tiny 5 strange
189. *doff* 1 withdraw 2 take off 3 remain 4 control 5 start
190. *effigy* 1 requisition 2 organ 3 charge 4 accordion 5 dummy
191. *dour* 1 sullen 2 ornamental 3 grizzled 4 lacking speech 5 international
192. *divulge* 1 look 2 refuse 3 deride 4 reveal 5 harm
193. *efface* 1 countenance 2 encourage 3 recognize 4 blackball 5 rub out
194. *dotage* 1 senility 2 silence 3 sensitivity 4 interest 5 generosity
195. *emaciated* 1 garrulous 2 primeval 3 vigorous 4 disparate 5 thin
196. *enhance* 1 improve 2 doubt 3 scuff 4 gasp 5 agree
197. *embellish* 1 doff 2 don 3 balance 4 adorn 5 equalize
198. *enervate* 1 weaken 2 sputter 3 arrange 4 scrutinize 5 agree
199. *emend* 1 cherish 2 repose 3 correct 4 assure 5 worry
200. *eminent* 1 purposeful 2 high 3 delectable 4 curious 5 urgent

---

ā—ale; ă—add; ä—arm; à—ask, ē—eve; ĕ—end; ê—err, her; ə—allow; even; ī—ice; ĭ—ill; ō—oll; ŏ—odd; ô—orb; ōō—food; ŏŏ—foot, put; o—oüt; th—thin; ū—use; ŭ—up; zh—pleasure

---

Word List 11   ennui - extrovert

ennui (*ŏn-wē*) N. boredom. The monotonous routine of hospital life induced a feeling of *ennui* which made him moody and irritable.

enormity N. hugeness (in a bad sense). He did not realize the *enormity* of his crime until he saw what suffering he had caused.

enrapture V. please intensely. The audience was *enraptured* by the freshness of the voices and the excellent orchestration.

ensconce (*-skŏns*) V. settle comfortably. The parents thought that their children were *ensconced* safely in the private school and decided to leave for Europe.

enthrall V. capture; enslave. From the moment he saw her picture, he was *enthralled* by her beauty.

entity N. real being. As soon as the Charter was adopted, the United Nations became an *entity* and had to be considered as a factor in world diplomacy.

entree (*ŏn-trā*) N. entrance. Because of his wealth and social position, he had *entree* into the most exclusive circles.

entrepreneur (*ăn-trə-prə-nər*) N. businessman; contractor. Opponents of our present tax program argue that it discourages *entrepreneurs* from trying new fields of business activity.

environ (*-vī-*) V. enclose; surround. In medieval days, Paris was *environed* by a wall. environs, N.

ephemeral (*-fĕm-*) ADJ. short-lived; fleeting. The mayfly is an *ephemeral* creature.

epicure N. connoisseur of food and drink. *Epicures* frequent this restaurant because it features exotic wines and dishes.

epicurean N. person who devotes himself to pleasures of the senses, especially to food. This restaurant is famous for its menu, which can cater to the most exotic whim of the *epicurean*. also ADJ.

epigram N. witty thought or saying, usually short. Poor Richard's *epigrams* made Benjamin Franklin famous.

epilogue N. short speech at conclusion of dramatic work. The audience was so disappointed in the play that many did not remain to hear the *epilogue*.

epitaph N. inscription in memory of a dead person. In his will, he dictated the *epitaph* he wanted placed on his tombstone.

epithet N. descriptive word or phrase. Homer's writings were featured by the use of such *epithets* as "rosy-fingered dawn."

ā—ale; ă—add; ä—arm; á—ask; ē—eve; ĕ—end; ê—err, her; ə—allow; even; ī—ice; ĭ—ill; ō—oll; ŏ—odd; ô—orb; ōō—food; ŏŏ—foot, put; o—out; th—thin; ū—use; ŭ—up; zh—pleasure

epitome (*ĭ-pĭt-ə-mē*) N. summary; concise abstract. This final book is the *epitome* of all his previous books. epitomize, V.

epoch N. period of time. The glacial *epoch* lasted for thousands of years.

equable (*ĕk´-*) ADJ. tranquil; steady; uniform. After the hot summers and cold winters of New England, he found the climate of the West Indies *equable* and pleasant.

equanimity N. calmness of temperament. In his later years, he could look upon the foolishness of the world with *equanimity* and humor.

equestrian N. rider on horseback. These paths in the park are reserved for *equestrians* and their steeds. also ADJ.

equinox N. period of equal days and nights; the beginning of Spring and Autumn. The vernal *equinox* is usually marked by heavy rain-storms.

equipage (*ĕk-wə-pĭj*) N. horse-drawn carriage. The *equipage* drew up before the inn.

equity N. fairness; justice. Our courts guarantee *equity* to all.

equivocal (*-kwĭv-*) ADJ. doubtful; ambiguous. Macbeth was misled by the *equivocal* statements of the witches.

equivocate V. lie; mislead; attempt to conceal the truth. The audience saw through his attempts to *equivocate* on the subject under discussion and ridiculed his remarks.

erode V. eat away. The limestone was *eroded* by the dripping water.

errant ADJ. wandering. Many a charming tale has been written about the knights-*errant* who helped the weak and punished the guilty during the Age of Chivalry.

erudite (*ĕr-yə-dīt*) ADJ. learned; scholarly. His *erudite* writing was difficult to read because of the many allusions which were unfamiliar to most readers. erudition, N.

escapade (*ĕs-kə-pād*) N. prank; flighty conduct. The headmaster could not regard this latest *escapade* as a boyish joke and expelled the young man.

eschew (*ĭs-chōō*) V. avoid. He tried to *eschew* all display of temper.

escutcheon (*-kŭch-*) N. shield-shaped surface on which coat of arms is placed. His traitorous acts placed a shameful blot on the family *escutcheon*.

esoteric (*-tĕr-*) ADJ. known only to the chosen few. Those students who had access to his *esoteric* discussions were impressed by the scope of his thinking.

espionage (*ĕs-pē-*) N. spying. In order to maintain its power, the govern-

ā—ale; ă—add; ä—arm; à—ask; ē—eve; ĕ—end; ê—err, her; ə—allow; even; ī—ice; ĭ—ill; ō—oll; ŏ—odd; ô—orb; ōō—food; ŏŏ—foot, put; o—out; th—thin; ū—use; ŭ—up; zh—pleasure

ment developed a system of *espionage* which penetrated every household.

esprit de corps (*ĭs-prēd-ə-kōr*) N. comradeship; spirit. West Point cadets are proud of their *esprit de corps.*

estranged (*-trănj'd*) ADJ. separated. The *estranged* wife sought a divorce.

ethereal ADJ. light; heavenly; fine. Visitors were impressed by her *ethereal* beauty, her delicate charm.

ethnic ADJ. relating to races. Intolerance between *ethnic* groups is deplorable and usually is based on lack of information. ethnology, N.

eulogistic ADJ. praising. To everyone's surprise, the speech was *eulogistic* rather than critical in tone.

eulogy N. praise. All the *eulogies* of his friends could not remove the sting of the calumny heaped upon him by his enemies.

euphemism N. mild expression in place of an unpleasant one. The expression "He passed away" is a *euphemism* for "He died."

euphonious ADJ. pleasing in sound. Italian and Spanish are *euphonious* languages and therefore easily sung.

evanescent ADJ. fleeting; vanishing. For a brief moment, the entire skyline was bathed in an orange-red hue in the *evanescent* rays of the sunset.

evasive ADJ. not frank; eluding. Your *evasive* answers convinced the judge that you were withholding important evidence. evade, V.

evince V. show clearly. When he tried to answer the questions, he *evinced* his ignorance of the subject matter.

evoke V. call forth. He *evoked* much criticism by his hostile manner.

ewer N. water pitcher. The primitive conditions of the period were symbolized by the porcelain *ewer* and basin in the bedroom.

exaction N. exorbitant demand; extortion. The colonies rebelled against the *exactions* of the mother country.

exasperate V. vex. Johnny often *exasperates* his mother with his pranks.

exchequer N. treasury. He had been Chancellor of the *Exchequer* before his promotion to the high office he now holds.

exculpate V. clear from blame. He was *exculpated* of the crime when the real criminal confessed.

execrable (*ĕk-sĭ-*) ADJ. very bad. The anecdote was in *execrable* taste.

exemplary (*-zĕm-*) ADJ. serving as a model; outstanding. Her *exemplary* behavior was praised at Commencement.

exertion N. effort; expenditure of much physical work. The *exertion* spent in unscrewing the rusty bolt left her exhausted.

ā—ale; ă—add; ä—arm; à—ask, ē—eve; ĕ—end; ê—err, her; ə—allow; even; ī—ice; ĭ—ill; ō—oll; ŏ—odd; ô—orb; ōo—food; ŏŏ—foot, put; o—oŭt; th—thin; ū—use; ŭ—up; zh—pleasure

exhort (ĭg-zôrt) v. urge. The evangelist will *exhort* all sinners in his audience to reform.

exhume v. dig out of the ground; remove from a grave. Because of the rumor that he had been poisoned, his body was *exhumed* in order that an autopsy might be performed.

exigency (ĕk-sə-) N. urgent situation. In this *exigency,* we must look for aid from our allies.

exiguous (-zĭg-) ADJ. small; minute. Grass grew there, an *exiguous* out-cropping among the rocks.

exodus N. departure. The *exodus* from the hot and stuffy city was particu-larly noticeable on Friday evenings.

exonerate v. acquit; exculpate. I am sure this letter will *exonerate* you.

exorbitant ADJ. excessive. The people grumbled at his *exorbitant* prices but paid them because he had a monopoly.

exotic ADJ. not native; strange. Because of his *exotic* headdress, he was followed in the streets by small children who laughed at his strange appearance.

expatiate (ĕk-spā-) v. talk at length. At this time, please give us a brief resumé of your work; we shall permit you to *expatiate* later.

expatriate N. exile; someone who has withdrawn from his native land. Henry James was an American *expatriate* who settled in En-gland.

expediency N. that which is advisable or practical. He was guided by *expediency* rather than by ethical considerations.

expeditiously ADV. rapidly and efficiently. Please adjust this matter as *expeditiously* as possible as it is delaying important work.

expiate (ĕk-spē-āt) v. make amends for (a sin). He tried to *expiate* his crimes by a full confession to the authorities.

expostulation N. remonstrance. Despite the teacher's scoldings and *ex-postulations,* the class remained unruly.

expunge v. cancel; remove. If you behave, I will *expunge* this notation from your record.

expurgate v. clean; remove offensive parts of a book. The editors felt that certain passages in the book had to be *expurgated* be-fore it could be used in the classroom.

extant (ĕk-) ADJ. still in existence. Although the authorities suppressed the book, many copies are *extant* and may be purchased at exorbitant prices.

extemporaneous ADJ. not planned; impromptu. Because his *extempo-raneous* remarks were misinterpreted, he decided to write all his speeches in advance.

ā—ale; ă—add; ä—arm; à—ask; ē—eve; ĕ—end; ê—err, her; ə—allow; even; ī—ice; ĭ—ill; ō—oll; ŏ—odd; ô—orb; ōō—food; ŏŏ—foot, put; o—out; th—thin; ū—use; ŭ—up; zh—pleasure

extenuate V. weaken; mitigate. It is easier for us to *extenuate* our own shortcomings than those of others.

extirpate (*ĕk-*) V. root up. We must *extirpate* and destroy this monstrous philosophy.

extol V. praise; glorify. The astronauts were *extolled* as the pioneers of the Space Age.

extort V. wring from; get money by threats, etc. The blackmailer *extorted* money from his victim.

extradition N. surrender of prisoner by one state to another. The lawyers opposed the *extradition* of their client on the grounds that for more than five years he had been a model citizen.

extraneous ADJ. not essential; external. Do not pad your paper with *extraneous* matters; stick to essential items only.

extricate V. free; disentangle. He found that he could not *extricate* himself from the trap.

extrinsic ADJ. external; not inherent; foreign. Do not be fooled by *extrinsic* causes. We must look for the intrinsic reason.

extrovert N. person interested mostly in external objects and actions. A good salesman is usually an *extrovert,* who likes to mingle with people.

ETYMOLOGY 11

ERG, URG (work)
        energy power
        ergatocracy rule of the workers
        metallurgy art of working in metal

ERR (to wander)
        error mistake
        erratic not reliable, not constant
        knight-errant wandering knight

EU (good, well, beautiful) prefix
        eulogize praise
        euphemism substitution of pleasant way of saying something blunt or unpleasant
        eupeptic having good digestion

EX (out) prefix
        expel drive out
        exit way out
        extirpate root out

ā—ale; ă—add; ä—arm; à—ask, ē—eve; ĕ—end; ê—err, her; ə—allow; even; ī—ice; ĭ —ill; ō—oll; ŏ—odd; ô—orb; ōō—food; ŏŏ—foot, put; o—out; th—thin; ū—use; ŭ—up; zh—pleasure

EXTRA (beyond, outside) prefix
> **extraordinary** exceptional
> **extracurricular** beyond the items in the curriculum
> **extraterritorial** beyond the territory of a nation

TEST—Word List 11—Antonyms

Each of the following questions consists of a word printed in italics, followed by five words or phrases numbered 1 to 5. Choose the numbered word or phrase which is most nearly opposite in meaning to the word in italics and write the number of your choice on your answer paper.

201. *exodus* 1 neglect 2 consent 3 entry 4 gain 5 retreat
202. *exasperate* 1 confide 2 formalize 3 placate 4 betray 5 bargain
203. *equivocal* 1 mistaken 2 quaint 3 azure 4 clear 5 universal
204. *exhume* 1 decipher 2 dig 3 integrate 4 admit 5 inter
205. *evasive* 1 frank 2 correct 3 empty 4 fertile 5 watchful
206. *equanimity* 1 agitation 2 stirring 3 volume 4 identity 5 luster
207. *ephemeral* 1 sensuous 2 passing 3 popular 4 distasteful 5 eternal
208. *euphonious* 1 strident 2 lethargic 3 literary 4 significant 5 musical
209. *equable* 1 flat 2 decisive 3 stormy 4 rough 5 scanty
210. *execrable* 1 innumerable 2 philosophic 3 physical 4 excellent 5 meditative
211. *eulogistic* 1 pretty 2 critical 3 brief 4 stern 5 free
212. *ennui* 1 hate 2 excitement 3 seriousness 4 humility 5 kindness
213. *exculpate* 1 accuse 2 prevail 3 acquit 4 ravish 5 accumulate
214. *erudite* 1 professorial 2 stately 3 short 4 unknown 5 ignorant
215. *exonerate* 1 forge 2 accuse 3 record 4 doctor 5 reimburse
216. *extrovert* 1 clown 2 hero 3 ectomorph 4 neurotic 5 introvert
217. *exorbitant* 1 moderate 2 partisan 3 military 4 barbaric 5 expensive
218. *extrinsic* 1 reputable 2 inherent 3 swift 4 ambitious 5 cursory
219. *extraneous* 1 needless 2 decisive 3 essential 4 effective 5 expressive
220. *extemporaneous* 1 rehearsed 2 hybrid 3 humiliating 4 statesmanlike 5 picturesque

ā—ale; ă—add; ä—arm; à—ask, ē—eve; ĕ—end; ê—err, her; ə—allow; even; ī—ice; ĭ —ill; ō—oll; ŏ—odd; ô—orb; o͞o—food; o͝o—foot, put; o—out; th—thin; ū—use; ŭ—up; zh—pleasure

---

Word List 12   extrude - fluster

extrude V. force or push out. Much pressure is required to *extrude* these plastics.

exuberant ADJ. abundant; effusive; lavish. His speeches were famous for his *exuberant* language and vivid imagery.

exude V. discharge; give forth. The maple syrup is obtained from the sap that *exudes* from the trees in early spring. exudation, N.

fabricate V. build; lie. If we pre*fabricate* the buildings in this project, we can reduce the cost considerably.

facade (fə-säd´) N. front of the building. The *facade* of the church had often been photographed by tourists.

facet (făs´-ət) N. small plane surface (of a gem); a side. The stonecutter decided to improve the rough diamond by providing it with several *facets*.

facetious ADJ. humorous; jocular. Your *facetious* remarks are not appropriate at this serious moment.

facile (făs-əl) ADJ. easy; expert. Because he was a *facile* speaker, he never refused a request to address an organization.

facilitate V. make less difficult. He tried to *facilitate* matters at home by getting a part-time job.

faction N. party; clique; dissension. The quarrels and bickering of the two small *factions* within the club disturbed the majority of the members.

factious ADJ. inclined to form factions; causing dissension. Your statement is *factious* and will upset the harmony that now exists.

factitious ADJ. artificial; sham. Hollywood actresses often create *factitious* tears by using glycerine.

factotum (-tōt-) N. handyman; person who does all kinds of work. Although we had hired him as a messenger, we soon began to use him as a general *factotum* around the office.

fain ADV. gladly. The knight said, "I would *fain* be your protector."

fallacious (-lā´-) ADJ. misleading. Your reasoning must be *fallacious* because it leads to a ridiculous answer.

fallible ADJ. liable to err. I know I am *fallible,* but I feel confident that I am right this time.

fallow ADJ. plowed but not sowed; uncultivated. Farmers have learned that it is advisable to permit land to lie *fallow* every few years.

fanaticism N. excessive zeal. The leader of the group was held responsi-

---

ā—ale; ă—add; ä—arm; á—ask; ē—eve; ĕ—end; ê—err, her; ə—allow; even; ī—ice; ĭ—ill; ō—oll; ŏ—odd; ô—orb; ōō—food; ŏŏ—foot, put; o—out; th—thin; ū—use; ù—up; zh—pleasure

ble even though he could not control the *fanaticism* of his followers.

fancied ADJ. imagined; unreal. You are resenting *fancied* insults. No one has ever said such things about you.

fancier N. breeder or dealer of animals. The dog *fancier* exhibited his prize collie at the annual Kennel Club show.

fanciful ADJ. whimsical; visionary. This is a *fanciful* scheme because it does not consider the facts.

fantastic ADJ. unreal; grotesque; whimsical. Your fears are *fantastic* because no such animal as you have described exists.

fastidious ADJ. difficult to please; squeamish. The waitresses disliked serving him dinner because of his very *fastidious* taste.

fatalism N. belief that events are determined by forces beyond one's control. With fatalism, he accepted the hardships which beset him. fatalistic, ADJ.

fatuous ADJ. foolish; inane. He is far too intelligent to utter such *fatuous* remarks.

fauna (*fôn'-*) N. animals of a period or region. The scientist could visualize the *fauna* of the period by examining the skeletal remains and the fossils.

faux pas (*fō-pä*) N. an error or slip (in manners or behavior). Your tactless remarks during dinner were a *faux pas*.

fawning ADJ. courting favor by cringing and flattering. He was constantly surrounded by a group of *fawning* admirers who hoped to win some favor.

fealty (*fē-əl-*) N. loyalty; faithfulness. The feudal lord demanded *fealty* of his vassals.

feasible ADJ. practical. This is an entirely *feasible* proposal. I suggest we adopt it.

fecundity N. fertility; fruitfulness. The *fecundity* of his mind is illustrated by the many vivid images in his poems.

feign (*fān*) V. pretend. Lady Macbeth *feigned* illness in the courtyard.

feint (*fānt*) N. trick; shift; sham blow. The boxer was fooled by his opponent's *feint* and dropped his guard. also V.

felicitous ADJ. apt; suitably expressed; well chosen. He was famous for his *felicitous* remarks and was called upon to serve as master-of-ceremonies at many a banquet.

fell ADJ. cruel; deadly. Henley writes of the "*fell* clutch of circumstance" in his poem "Invictus."

ferment (*fêr-*) N. agitation; commotion. The entire country was in a state of *ferment*.

ā—ale; ă—add; ä—arm; à—ask; ē—eve; ĕ—end; ê—err, her; ə—allow; even; ī—ice; ĭ—ill; ō—oll; ŏ—odd; ô—orb; ōō—food; ȯȯ—foot, put; o—out; th—thin; ū—use; ŭ—up; zh—pleasure

ferret V. drive or hunt out of hiding. He *ferreted* out their secret.

fervent ADJ. ardent; hot. He felt that the *fervent* praise was excessive and somewhat undeserved.

fervid ADJ. ardent. His *fervid* enthusiasm inspired all of us to undertake the dangerous mission.

fervor N. glowing ardor. Their kiss was full of the *fervor* of first love.

fester V. generate pus. When his finger began to *fester,* the doctor lanced it and removed the splinter which had caused the pus to form.

fete (*fāt*) V. honor at a festival. The returning hero was *feted* at a community supper and dance. also N.

fetid (*fĕt-əd*) ADJ. malodorous. The neglected wound became *fetid*.

fetish (*fĕt-*) N. object supposed to possess magical powers; an object of special devotion. The native wore a *fetish* around his neck to ward off evil spirits.

fetter V. shackle. The prisoner was *fettered* to the wall.

fiasco (*fē-ŏs′-kō*) N. total failure. Our ambitious venture ended in a *fiasco*.

fiat (*fē-*) N. command. I cannot accept government by *fiat;* I feel that I must be consulted.

fickle ADJ. changeable; faithless. He discovered she was *fickle*.

fictitious ADJ. imaginary. Although this book purports to be a biography of George Washington, many of the incidents are *fictitious*.

fidelity N. loyalty. A dog's *fidelity* to its owner is one of the reasons why that animal is a favorite household pet.

figment N. invention; imaginary thing. That incident is a *figment* of your imagination.

filch V. steal. The boys *filched* apples from the fruit stand.

filial ADJ. pertaining to a son or daughter. Many children forget their *filial* obligations and disregard the wishes of their parents.

finale (*fə-năl′-ē*) N. conclusion. It is not until we reach the *finale* of this play that we can understand the author's message.

finesse (*fə-nĕs′*) N. delicate skill. The *finesse* and adroitness of the surgeon impressed the observers in the operating room.

finicky ADJ. too particular; fussy. The old lady was *finicky* about her food.

finite (*fī-nīt*) ADJ. limited. It is difficult for humanity with its *finite* existence to grasp the infinite.

fissure (*fĭsh-ər*) N. crevice. The mountain climbers secured footholds in tiny *fissures* in the rock.

fitful ADJ. spasmodic; intermittent. After several *fitful* attempts, he decided to postpone the start of the project until he felt more energetic.

ā—ale; ă—add; ä—arm; à—ask, ē—eve; ĕ—end; ê—err, her; ə—allow; even; ī—ice; ĭ—ill; ō—oll; ŏ—odd; ô—orb; ōō—food; ŏŏ—foot, put; o—out; th—thin; ū—use; ŭ—up; zh—pleasure

flaccid (*flăk-səd*) ADJ. flabby. His sedentary life had left him with *flaccid* muscles.

flagellate (*flăj-ə-*) V. flog; whip. The Romans used to *flagellate* criminals with a whip that had three knotted strands.

flagging ADJ. weak; drooping. The encouraging cheers of the crowd lifted the team's *flagging* spirits.

flagrant (*flā-*) ADJ. conspicuously wicked. We cannot condone such *flagrant* violations of the rules.

flail V. thresh grain by hand; strike or slap. In medieval times, warriors *flailed* their foe with a metal ball attached to a handle.

flair N. talent. He has an uncanny *flair* for discovering new artists before the public has become aware of their existence.

flamboyant (*-bôĩ-*) ADJ. ornate. Modern architecture has discarded the *flamboyant* trimming on buildings and emphasizes simplicity of line.

flaunt V. display ostentatiously. She is not one of those actresses who *flaunt* their physical charms; she can act.

flay V. strip off skin; plunder. The criminal was condemned to be *flayed* alive.

fleck V. spot. Her cheeks, *flecked* with tears, were testimony to the hours of weeping.

fledgling ADJ. inexperienced. While it is necessary to provide these *fledgling* poets with an opportunity to present their work, it is not essential that we admire everything they write. also N.

flick N. light stroke as with a whip. The horse needed no encouragement; only one *flick* of the whip was all the jockey had to apply to get the animal to run at top speed.

flippancy N. trifling gaiety. Your *flippancy* at this serious moment is offensive.

flora N. plants of a region or era. Because she was a botanist, she spent most of her time studying the *flora* of the desert.

florid ADJ. flowery; ruddy. His complexion was even more *florid* than usual because of his anger.

flotilla (*-tĩl-*) N. small fleet. It is always an exciting and interesting moment when the fishing *flotilla* returns to port.

flotsam (*flŏt-*) N. drifting wreckage. Beachcombers eke out a living by salvaging the *flotsam* and jetsam of the sea.

flout V. reject; mock. The headstrong youth *flouted* all authority; he refused to be curbed.

fluctuation N. wavering. Meteorologists watch the *fluctuations* of the barometer in order to predict the weather.

ā—ale; ă—add; ä—arm; à—ask; ē—eve; ĕ—end; ê—err, her; ə—allow; even; ī—ice; ĭ—ill; ō—oll; ŏ—odd; ô—orb; o͞o—food; o͝o—foot, put; o—out; th—thin; ū—use; ŭ—up; zh—pleasure

fluency N. smoothness of speech. He spoke French with *fluency* and ease.

fluster V. confuse. The teacher's sudden question *flustered* him and he stammered his reply.

ETYMOLOGY 12

FAC, FIC, FEC, FECT (to make, to do)
    factory place where things are made
    fiction manufactured story
    affect cause to change

FALL, FALS (to deceive)
    fallacious faulty
    infallible not prone to error, perfect
    falsify lie

FER, LAT (to bring, to bear)
    transfer bring from one place to another
    translate bring from one language to another
    coniferous bearing cones, as pine trees

FIC (making, causing) adjective suffix
    terrific causing fear or awe
    soporific making sleepy

TEST—Word List 12—Synonyms and Antonyms

Each of the questions below consists of a word printed in italics, followed by five words or phrases numbered 1 to 5. Choose the numbered word or phrase which is most nearly the same as or the opposite of the word in italics and write the number of your choice on your answer paper.

221. *finite* 1 bounded 2 established 3 affirmative 4 massive 5 finicky
222. *fiasco* 1 cameo 2 mansion 3 pollution 4 success 5 gamble
223. *flair* 1 conflagration 2 inspiration 3 bent 4 egregiousness 5 magnitude
224. *flamboyant* 1 old-fashioned 2 restrained 3 impulsive 4 cognizant 5 eloquent
225. *fanciful* 1 imaginative 2 knowing 3 elaborate 4 quick 5 lusty
226. *fecundity* 1 prophecy 2 futility 3 fruitfulness 4 need 5 dormancy
227. *fell* 1 propitious 2 illiterate 3 catastrophic 4 futile 5 inherent
228. *fiat* 1 motor 2 degree 3 lesion 4 suture 5 order

ā—ale; ă—add; ä—arm; à—ask, ē—eve; ĕ—end; ê—err, her; ə—allow; even; ī—ice; ĭ—ill; ō—oll; ŏ—odd; ô—orb; o͞o—food; o͝o—foot, put; o—out; th—thin; ū—use; ŭ—up; zh—pleasure

229. *fledgling* 1 weaving 2 bobbing 3 beginning 4 studying 5 flaying
230. *factitious* 1 genuine 2 magnificent 3 polished 4 puny 5 ridiculous
231. *fidelity* 1 brotherhood 2 parentage 3 treachery 4 conscience 5 consistency
232. *flail* 1 succeed 2 harvest 3 knife 4 strike 5 resent
233. *florid* 1 ruddy 2 rusty 3 ruined 4 patient 5 poetic
234. *fatuous* 1 fatal 2 natal 3 terrible 4 sensible 5 tolerable
235. *ferment* 1 stir up 2 fill 3 ferret 4 mutilate 5 banish
236. *fickle* 1 fallacious 2 tolerant 3 loyal 4 hungry 5 stupid
237. *exude* 1 prevent 2 ooze 3 manage 4 protrude 5 insure
238. *feasible* 1 theoretical 2 impatient 3 constant 4 present 5 impractical
239. *feign* 1 deserve 2 condemn 3 condone 4 attend 5 pretend
240. *filch* 1 milk 2 purloin 3 itch 4 cancel 5 resent

Word List 13   flux - gloat

flux N. flowing; series of changes. While conditions are in such a state of *flux,* I do not wish to commit myself too deeply in this affair.

foible N. weakness; slight fault. We can overlook the *foibles* of our friends.

foist V. insert improperly; palm off. I will not permit you to *foist* such ridiculous ideas upon the membership of this group.

foment (-*mĕnt´*) V. stir up; instigate. This report will *foment* dissension in the club.

foolhardy ADJ. rash. Don't be *foolhardy.* Get the advice of experienced people before undertaking this venture.

foppish ADJ. vain about dress and appearance. He tried to imitate the *foppish* manner of the young men of the court.

foray (*fô-*) N. raid. The company staged a midnight *foray* against the enemy outpost.

forbearance N. patience. We must use *forbearance* in dealing with him because he is still weak from his illness.

foreboding N. premonition of evil. Caesar ridiculed his wife's *forebodings* about the Ides of March.

forensic (-*rĕn´-sĭk*) ADJ. suitable to debate or courts of law. In his best *forensic* manner, the lawyer addressed the jury.

formality N. adherence to established rules or procedures. Signing this

---

ā—ale; ă—add; ä—arm; à—ask, ē—eve; ĕ—end; ê—err, her; ə—allow; even; ī—ice; ĭ—ill; ō—oll; ŏ—odd; ô—orb; ōō—food; oò—foot, put; o—oüt; th—thin; ū—use; ŭ—up; zh—pleasure

position is a mere *formality*; it does not obligate you in any way.

formidable (*fôr-*) ADJ. menacing; threatening. We must not treat the battle lightly for we are facing a *formidable* foe.

forte (*fôr-tā*) N. strong point or special talent. I am not eager to play this rather serious role, for my *forte* is comedy.

fortitude N. bravery; courage. He was awarded the medal for his *fortitude* in the battle.

fortuitous ADJ. accidental; by chance. There is no connection between these two events; their timing is extremely *fortuitous*.

foster V. rear; encourage. According to the legend, Romulus and Remus were *fostered* by a she-wolf. also ADJ.

fractious (*frăk-shas*) ADJ. unruly. The *fractious* horse unseated its rider.

frailty N. weakness. Hamlet says, "*Frailty*, thy name is woman."

franchise N. right granted by authority. The city issued a *franchise* to the company to operate surface transit lines on the streets for ninety-nine years. also V.

frantic ADJ. wild. At the time of the collision, many people became *frantic* with fear.

fraudulent ADJ. cheating; deceitful. The government seeks to prevent *fraudulent* and misleading advertising.

fraught (*frôt*) ADJ. filled. Since this enterprise is *fraught* with danger, I will ask for volunteers who are willing to assume the risks.

fray N. brawl. The three musketeers were in the thick of the *fray*.

freebooter N. buccaneer. This town is a rather dangerous place to visit as it is frequented by pirates, *freebooters*, and other plunderers.

frenetic ADJ. frenzied; frantic. His *frenetic* activities convinced us that he had no organized plan of operation.

frenzied ADJ. madly excited. As soon as they smelled smoke, the *frenzied* animals milled about in their cages.

fresco N. painting on plaster (usually fresh). The cathedral is visited by many tourists who wish to admire the *frescoes* by Giotto.

freshet N. sudden flood. Motorists were warned that spring *freshets* had washed away several small bridges and that long detours would be necessary.

fret V. to be annoyed or vexed. To *fret* over your poor grades is foolish; instead, decide to work harder in the future.

friction N. clash in opinion; rubbing against. At this time when harmony is essential, we cannot afford to have any *friction* in our group.

ā—ale; ă—add; ä—arm; à—ask; ē—eve; ĕ—end; ê—err, her; ə—allow; even; ī—ice; ĭ—ill; ō—oll; ŏ—odd; ô—orb; ōō—food; ŏŏ—foot, put; o—out; th—thin; ū—use; ŭ—up; zh—pleasure

frieze (*frēz*) N. ornamental band on a wall. The *frieze* of the church was adorned with sculpture.

frigid ADJ. intensely cold. Alaska is in the *frigid* zone.

fritter V. waste. He could not apply himself to any task and *frittered* away his time in idle conversation.

frolicsome ADJ. prankish; gay. The *frolicsome* puppy tried to lick the face of its master.

froward (*frō* -) ADJ. disobedient; perverse; stubborn. Your *froward* behavior has alienated many of us who might have been your supporters.

frowzy ADJ. slovenly; unkempt; dirty. Her *frowzy* appearance and her cheap decorations made her appear ludicrous in this group.

fructify V. bear fruit. This tree should *fructify* in three years.

frugality N. thrift. In these difficult days, we must live with *frugality*.

fruition (*froō-ĭsh* -) N. bearing of fruit; fulfillment; realization. This building marks the *fruition* of all our aspirations and years of hard work.

frustrate V. thwart; defeat. We must *frustrate* this dictator's plan to seize control of the government.

fulminate V. thunder; explode. The people against whom he *fulminated* were innocent of any wrongdoing.

fulsome ADJ. disgustingly excessive. His *fulsome* praise of the dictator annoyed his listeners.

functionary N. official. As his case was transferred from one *functionary* to another, he began to despair of ever reaching a settlement.

funereal (*-nĭr-ē-əl*) ADJ. sad; solemn. I fail to understand why there is such a *funereal* atmosphere; we have lost a battle, not a war.

furor (*fūr-ôr*) N. frenzy; great excitement. The story of his embezzlement of the funds created a *furor* on the Stock Exchange.

furtive (*fêrt* -) ADJ. stealthy. The boy gave a *furtive* look at his classmate's test paper.

fusion N. union; coalition. The opponents of the political party in power organized a *fusion* of disgruntled groups and became an important element in the election.

fustian (*fŭs* -) ADJ. pompous; bombastic. Several in the audience were deceived by his *fustian* style; they mistook pomposity for erudition.

gadfly N. animal-biting fly; an irritating person. Like a *gadfly,* he irritated all the guests at the hotel; within forty-eight hours, everyone regarded him as an annoying busybody.

gaff N. hook; barbed fishing spear. When he attempted to land the

ā—ale; ă—add; ä—arm; à—ask, ē—eve; ĕ—end; ê—err, her; ə—allow; even; ī—ice; ĭ—ill; ō—oll; ŏ—odd; ô—orb; ōō—food; ŏŏ—foot, put; o—oŭt; th—thin; ū—use; ŭ—up; zh—pleasure

sailfish, he was so nervous that he dropped the *gaff* into the sea. also v.

gainsay (-*sā*) v. deny. He could not *gainsay* the truth of the report.

galleon N. large sailing ship. The Spaniards pinned their hopes on the *galleon,* the large warship; the British, on the smaller and faster pinnace.

galvanize v. stimulate by shock; stir up. The entire nation was *galvanized* into strong military activity by the news of the attack on Pearl Harbor.

gambol v. skip; leap playfully. Watching children *gamboling* in the park is a pleasant experience. also N.

gamely ADV. courageous. Because he had fought *gamely* against a much superior boxer, the crowd gave him a standing ovation when he left the arena.

gamester (*gām-stər*) N. gambler. An inveterate *gamester,* he was willing to wager on the outcome of any event, even one which involved the behavior of insects.

gamut (*găm*-) N. entire range. In this performance, the leading lady was able to demonstrate the complete *gamut* of her acting ability.

gape (*gāp*) v. open widely. The huge pit *gaped* before him; if he stumbled, he would fall in.

garbled ADJ. mixed up; based on false or unfair selection. The *garbled* report confused many readers who were not familiar with the facts. garble, v.

garish (*găr*-) ADJ. gaudy. She wore a *garish* rhinestone necklace.

garner v. gather; store up. He hoped to *garner* the world's literature in one library.

garnish v. decorate. Parsley was used to *garnish* the boiled potato. also N.

garrulity (-*rōō*-) N. talkativeness. The man who married a dumb wife asked the doctor to make him deaf because of his wife's *garrulity* after her cure. garrulous, ADJ.

gauntlet N. leather glove. Now that we have been challenged, we must take up the *gauntlet* and meet our adversary fearlessly.

gazette N. official periodical publication. He read the *gazettes* regularly for the announcement of his promotion.

generality N. vague statement. This report is filled with *generalities;* you must be more specific in your statements.

geniality N. cheerfulness; kindliness; sympathy. This restaurant is famous and popular because of the *geniality* of the proprietor who tries to make everyone happy.

ā—ale; ă—add; ä—arm; à—ask, ê—eve; ĕ—end; ê—err, her; ə—allow; even; ī—ice; ĭ—ill; ō—oll; ŏ—odd; ô—orb; ōō—food; ŏŏ—foot, put; o—out; th—thin; ū—use; ŭ—up; zh—pleasure

genre (zhän-rə) N. style of art illustrating scenes of common life. His painting of fisher folk at their daily tasks is an excellent illustration of *genre* art.

genteel (-tēl) ADJ. well-bred; elegant. We are looking for a man with a *genteel* appearance who can inspire confidence by his cultivated manner.

gentility N. those of gentle birth; refinement. Her family was proud of its *gentility*.

gentry N. people of standing; class of people just below nobility. The local *gentry* did not welcome the visits of the summer tourists and tried to ignore their presence in the community.

germane (-mān) ADJ. pertinent; bearing upon the case at hand. The lawyer objected that the testimony being offered was not *germane* to the case at hand.

gesticulation (jĕ-stĭk-yə-lā-)N. motion; gesture. Operatic performers are trained to make exaggerated *gesticulations* because of the large auditoriums in which they appear.

ghastly ADJ. horrible. The murdered man was a *ghastly* sight.

gibber (jĭb-) V. speak foolishly. The demented man *gibbered* incoherently.

gibbet (jĭb-) N. gallows. The bodies of the highwaymen were left dangling from the *gibbet* as a warning to other would-be transgressors.

gibe (jīb) V. mock. As you *gibe* at their superstitious beliefs, do you realize that you, too, are guilty of similarly foolish thoughts?

gig (gĭg) N. two-wheeled carriage. As they drove down the street in their new *gig,* drawn by the dappled mare, they were cheered by the people who recognized them.

gist (jĭst) N. essence. She was asked to give the *gist* of the essay in two sentences.

glaze V. cover with a thin and shiny surface. The freezing rain *glazed* the streets and made driving hazardous. also N.

glean V. gather leavings. After the crops had been harvested by the machines, the peasants were permitted to *glean* the wheat left in the fields.

glib ADJ. fluent. He is a *glib* speaker.

gloaming N. twilight. The snow began to fall in the *gloaming* and continued all through the night.

gloat V. express evil satisfaction; view malevolently. As you *gloat* over your ill-gotten wealth, do you think of the many victims you have defrauded?

ā—ale; ă—add; ä—arm; à—ask, ē—eve; ĕ—end; ê—err, her; ə—allow; even; ī—ice; ĭ—ill; ō—oll; ŏ—odd; ô—orb; ōō—food; oŏ—foot, put; o—out; th—thin; ū—use; ŭ—up; zh—pleasure

ETYMOLOGY 13

FY (to make) verb suffix

magnify make greater

petrify make into stone

beautify make beautiful

GAM (marriage)

monogamy marriage to one person

bigamy marriage to two people at the same time

polygamy having many spouses at the same time

GEN, GENER (class, race)

genus group of biological species with similar characteristics

generic characteristic of a class

gender class organized according to sex

TEST—Word List 13—Synonyms

Each of the questions below consists of a word printed in italics, followed by five words or phrases numbered 1 to 5. Choose the numbered word or phrase which is most nearly similar in meaning to the word in italics and write the number of your choice on your answer paper.

241. *garnish* 1 paint 2 garner 3 adorn 4 abuse 5 banish
242. *frugality* 1 foolishness 2 extremity 3 indifference 4 enthusiasm 5 economy
243. *foray* 1 excursion 2 contest 3 ranger 4 intuition 5 fish
244. *gadfly* 1 humorist 2 nuisance 3 scholar 4 bum 5 thief
245. *foolhardy* 1 strong 2 unwise 3 brave 4 futile 5 erudite
246. *glib* 1 slippery 2 fashionable 3 antiquated 4 articulate 5 anticlimactic
247. *franchise* 1 subway 2 kiosk 3 license 4 reason 5 fashion
248. *furtive* 1 underhanded 2 coy 3 blatant 4 quick 5 abortive
249. *garner* 1 prevent 2 assist 3 collect 4 compute 5 consult
250. *gist* 1 chaff 2 summary 3 expostulation 4 expiation 5 chore
251. *foster* 1 speed 2 fondle 3 become infected 4 raise 5 roll
252. *foppish* 1 scanty 2 radical 3 orthodox 4 dandyish 5 magnificent
253. *furor* 1 excitement 2 worry 3 flux 4 anteroom 5 lover

ā—ale; ă—add; ä—arm; à—ask; ē—eve; ĕ—end; ê—err, her; ə—allow; even; ī—ice; ĭ—ill; ō—oll; ŏ—odd; ô—orb; o͞o—food; o͝o—foot, put; o—out; th—thin; ū—use; ŭ—up; zh—pleasure

254. *germane*   1 bacteriological 2 middle European 3 prominent 4 warlike 5 relevant
255. *fritter*   1 sour 2 chafe 3 dissipate 4 cancel 5 abuse
256. *garish*   1 sordid 2 flashy 3 prominent 4 lusty 5 thoughtful
257. *formidable*   1 dangerous 2 outlandish 3 grandiloquent 4 impenetrable 5 vulnerable
258. *garrulity*   1 credulity 2 senility 3 loquaciousness 4 speciousness 5 artistry
259. *foment*   1 spoil 2 instigate 3 interrogate 4 settle 5 maintain
260. *galleon*   1 liquid measure 2 ship 3 armada 4 company 5 printer's proof

---

Word List 14   glossy - homily

glossy ADJ. smooth and shining. I want this photograph printed on *glossy* paper.

glut V. overstock; fill to excess. The many manufacturers *glutted* the market and could not find purchasers for the many articles they had produced. also N.

glutinous (*gloot-*) ADJ. sticky; viscous. Molasses is a *glutinous* substance.

gluttonous ADJ. greedy for food. The *gluttonous* boy ate all the cookies.

gnarled (*närld*) ADJ. twisted. The *gnarled* oak tree had been a landmark for years and was mentioned in several deeds.

gnome (*nōm*) N. dwarf; underground spirit. In medieval mythology, *gnomes* were the special guardians and inhabitants of subterranean mines.

goad V. urge on. He was *goaded* by his friends until he yielded to their wishes. also N.

gorge V. stuff oneself. The gluttonous guest *gorged* himself with food as though he had not eaten for days.

gory ADJ. bloody. The audience shuddered as they listened to the details of the *gory* massacre.

gossamer (*gŏs-*) ADJ. sheer; like cobwebs. Nylon can be woven into *gossamer* or thick fabrics. also N.

gouge (*gouj*) V. tear out. In that fight, all the rules were forgotten; the adversaries bit, kicked, and tried to *gouge* each other's eyes out.

ā—ale; ă—add; ä—arm; à—ask, ē—eve; ĕ—end; ê—err, her; ə—allow; even; ī—ice; ĭ—ill; ō—oll; ŏ—odd; ô—orb; ōō—food; ŏŏ—foot, put; o—out; th—thin; ū—use; ŭ—up; zh—pleasure

gourmand (*goŏr-mänd*) N. epicure; person who takes excessive pleasure in food and drink. The *gourmand* liked the French cuisine.

gourmet (*goŏr-mā*) N. connoisseur of food and drink. The *gourmet* stated that this was the best onion soup he had ever tasted.

granary (*grān*-) N. storehouse for grain. We have reason to be thankful, for our crops were good and our *granaries* are full.

grandiloquent ADJ. pompous; bombastic; using high-sounding language. The politician could never speak simply; he was always *grandiloquent.*

grandiose (*grăn*-dē-ōs) ADJ. imposing; impressive. His *grandiose* manner impressed those who met him for the first time.

granulate V. form into grains. Sugar that has been *granulated* dissolves more readily than lump sugar. granule, N.

graphic ADJ. pertaining to the art of delineating; vividly described. I was particularly impressed by the *graphic* presentation of the storm.

gratis (*grăt*-) ADJ. free. The company offered to give one package *gratis* to every purchaser of one of their products. also ADJ.

gratuitous (-tū-) ADJ. given freely; unwarranted. I resent your *gratuitous* remarks because no one asked for them. gratuity, N.

gregarious (*grĭ-gār*-) ADJ. sociable. He was not *gregarious* and preferred to be alone most of the time.

grisly ADJ. ghastly. She shuddered at the *grisly* sight.

grotto N. small cavern. The Blue *Grotto* in Capri can be entered only by small boats rowed by natives through a natural opening in the rocks.

gruel N. liquid food made by boiling oatmeal, etc., in milk or water. Our daily allotment of *gruel* made the meal not only monotonous but also unpalatable.

grueling ADJ. exhausting. The marathon is a *grueling* race.

gruesome ADJ. grisly. People screamed when his *gruesome* appearance was flashed on the screen.

gruff ADJ. rough-mannered. Although he was blunt and *gruff* with most people, he was always gentle with children.

guffaw (*gə-fô*) N. boisterous laughter. The loud *guffaws* that came from the closed room indicated that the members of the committee had not yet settled down to serious business. also V.

guile (*gīl*) N. deceit; duplicity. He achieved his high position by *guile* and treachery.

guileless ADJ. without deceit. He is naive, simple, and *guileless;* he cannot be guilty of fraud.

ā—ale; ă—add; ä—arm; à—ask, ē—eve; ĕ—end; ê—err, her; ə—allow; even; ī—ice; ĭ—ill; ō—oll; ŏ—odd; ô—orb; ōō—food; ŏŏ—foot, put; o—out; th—thin; ū—use; ŭ—up; zh—pleasure

guise N. appearance; costume. In the *guise* of a plumber, the detective investigated the murder case.

gullible ADJ. easily deceived. He preyed upon *gullible* people, who believed his stories of easy wealth.

gustatory ADJ. affecting the sense of taste. This food is particularly *gustatory* because of the spices it contains.

gusto N. enjoyment; enthusiasm. He accepted the assignment with such *gusto* that I feel he would have been satisfied with a smaller salary.

gusty ADJ. windy. The *gusty* weather made sailing precarious.

guttural ADJ. pertaining to the throat. *Guttural* sounds are produced in the throat or in the back of the tongue and palate.

habiliments (-*bĭl-ə-*) N. garb; clothing. Although not a minister, David Belasco used to wear clerical *habiliments*.

hackneyed ADJ. commonplace; trite. The English teacher criticized his story because of its *hackneyed* plot.

haggard ADJ. wasted away; gaunt. After his long illness, he was pale and *haggard*.

haggle V. argue about prices. I prefer to shop in a store that has a one-price policy because, whenever I *haggle* with a shopkeeper, I am never certain that I paid a fair price for the articles I purchased.

halcyon (*hăl-sē-*) ADJ. calm; peaceful. In those *halcyon* days, people were not worried about sneak attacks and bombings.

hallowed ADJ. blessed; consecrated. He was laid to rest in *hallowed* ground.

hallucination N. delusion. I think you were frightened by a *hallucination* which you created in your own mind.

hamper V. obstruct. The minority party agreed not to *hamper* the efforts of the leaders to secure a lasting peace.

hap N. chance; luck. In his poem *Hap*, Thomas Hardy objects to the part chance plays in our lives.

haphazard ADJ. random; by chance. His *haphazard* reading left him unacquainted with authors of the books.

hapless ADJ. unfortunate. This *hapless* creature had never known a moment's pleasure.

harangue (-*răng*) N. noisy speech. In his lengthy *harangue,* the principal berated the offenders. also V.

harass (-*răs*) V. to annoy by repeated attacks. When he could not pay his bills as quickly as he had promised, he was *harassed* by his creditors.

ā—ale; ă—add; ä—arm; à—ask, ê—eve; ĕ—end; ê—err, her; ə—allow; even; ī—ice; ĭ—ill; ō—oll; ŏ—odd; ô—orb; ōō—food; ŏŏ—foot, put; o—out; th—thin; ū—use; ŭ—up; zh—pleasure

harbinger (här-bən-jər) N. forerunner. The crocus is an early *harbinger* of spring.

harping N. tiresome dwelling on a subject. After he had reminded me several times about what he had done for me, I told him to stop *harping* on my indebtedness to him. harp, V.

harridan N. shrewish hag. Most people avoided the *harridan* because they feared her abusive and vicious language.

harrow V. break up ground after plowing; torture. I don't want to *harrow* you at this time by asking you to recall the details of your unpleasant experience.

harry V. raid. The guerrilla band *harried* the enemy nightly.

haughtiness N. pride; arrogance. I resent his *haughtiness* because he is no better than we are.

hauteur (hô-tər) N. haughtiness. His snobbishness is obvious to all who witness his *hauteur* when he talks to those whom he considers his social inferiors.

hawser N. large rope. The ship was tied to the pier by a *hawser*.

hazardous ADJ. dangerous. Your occupation is too *hazzardous* for insurance companies to consider your application.

hazy ADJ. slightly obscure. In *hazy* weather, you cannot see the top of this mountain.

hedonism (hēd-) N. belief that pleasure is the sole aim in life. *Hedonism* and asceticism are opposing philosophies of human behavior.

heedless ADJ. not noticing; disregarding. He drove on, *heedless* of the warnings placed at the side of the road that it was dangerous.

heinous (hā-) ADJ. atrocious; hatefully bad. Hitler's *heinous* crimes will never be forgotten.

heresy N. opinion contrary to popular belief; opinion contrary to accepted religion. He was threatened with excommunication because his remarks were considered to be pure *heresy*.

heretic (hĕr-) N. person who maintains opinions contrary to the doctrines of the church. She was punished by the Spanish Inquisition because she was a *heretic*.

hermitage N. home of a hermit. Even in his remote *hermitage* he could not escape completely from the world.

heterogeneous (-jē-nē-əs) ADJ. dissimilar. In *heterogeneous* groupings, we have an unassorted grouping, while in homogeneous groupings we have people or things which have common traits.

hiatus (hī-āt-) N. gap; pause. There was a *hiatus* of twenty years in the life of Rip van Winkle.

ā—ale; ă—add; ä—arm; à—ask; ē—eve; ĕ—end; ê—err, her; ə—allow; even; ī—ice; ĭ—ill; ō—oll; ŏ—odd; ô—orb; ōō—food; ŏŏ—foot, put; o—oút; th—thin; ū—use; ŭ—up; zh—pleasure

hibernal (*hī-bêrn -*) ADJ. wintry. Bears prepare for their long *hibernal* sleep by overeating.

hibernate V. sleep throughout the winter. Bears are one of the many species of animals that *hibernate*.

hierarchy N. body divided into ranks. It was difficult to step out of one's place in this *hierarchy*.

hieroglyphic N. picture writing. The discovery of the Rosetta Stone enabled scholars to read the ancient Egyptian *hieroglyphics*.

hilarity N. boisterous mirth. This *hilarity* is improper on this solemn day of mourning.

hindmost ADJ. furthest behind. The coward could always be found in the *hindmost* lines whenever a battle was being waged.

hireling N. one who serves for hire [usually contemptuously]. In a matter of such importance, I do not wish to deal with *hirelings;* I must meet with the chief.

hirsute (*hêr-sōō t*) ADJ. hairy. He was a *hirsute* individual with a heavy black beard.

histrionic ADJ. theatrical. He was proud of his *histrionic* ability and wanted to play the role of Hamlet. histrionics, N.

hoary ADJ. white with age. The man was *hoary* and wrinkled.

hogshead N. large barrel. On the trip to England, the ship carried munitions; on its return trip, *hogsheads* filled with French wines and Scotch liquors.

holocaust N. destruction by fire. Citizens of San Francisco remember that the destruction of the city was caused not by the earthquake but by the *holocaust* that followed.

holster N. pistol case. Even when he was not in uniform, he carried a *holster* and pistol under his arm.

homespun ADJ. domestic; made at home. *Homespun* wit like *homespun* cloth was often coarse and plain.

homily (*hŏm -*) N. sermon; serious warning. His speeches were always *homilies,* advising his listeners to repent and reform.

ETYMOLOGY 14

GRAPH, GRAM (writing)

      epigram a pithy statement

      telegram an instantaneous message over great distances (*tele*—far off)

      stenography shorthand (writing narrowly)

GREG (flock, herd)

      gregarious tending to group together as in a herd

ā—ale; ă—add; ä—arm; à—ask; ē—eve; ĕ—end; ê—err, her; ə—allow; even; ī—ice; ĭ—ill; ō—oll; ŏ—odd; ô—orb; ōō—food; oŏ—foot, put; o—oŭt; th—thin; ū—use; ŭ—up; zh—pleasure

aggregate group, total
egregious out of the group; now used in a bad sense as *wicked*

HELI, HELIO (sun)

heliotrope flower that faces the sun
heliograph instrument that uses the sun's rays to send signals
helium element abundant in the sun's atmosphere

TEST—Word List 14—Antonyms

Each of the questions below consists of a word printed in italics, followed by five words or phrases numbered 1 to 5. Choose the numbered word or phrase which is most nearly opposite in meaning to the word in italics and write the number of your choice on your answer paper.

261. *grandiose* 1 false 2 ideal 3 proud 4 simple 5 functional
262. *hibernal* 1 wintry 2 summerlike 3 local 4 seasonal 5 springlike
263. *gregarious* 1 antisocial 2 anticipatory 3 glorious 4 horrendous 5 similar
264. *gratuitous* 1 warranted 2 frank 3 ingenuous 4 frugal 5 pithy
265. *hapless* 1 cheerful 2 consistent 3 fortunate 4 considerate 5 shapely
266. *heterogeneous* 1 orthodox 2 pagan 3 unlike 4 similar 5 banished
267. *gusto* 1 noise 2 panic 3 fancy 4 gloom 5 distaste
268. *gusty* 1 calm 2 noisy 3 fragrant 4 routine 5 gloomy
269. *haphazard* 1 fortuitous 2 indifferent 3 deliberate 4 accidental 5 conspiring
270. *hirsute* 1 scaly 2 bald 3 erudite 4 quiet 5 long
271. *gullible* 1 incredulous 2 fickle 3 tantamount 4 easy 5 stylish
272. *granulate* 1 crystallize 2 store 3 crush 4 magnify 5 sweeten
273. *gourmet* 1 cook 2 maitre d' 3 glutton 4 epicure 5 author
274. *halcyon* 1 pacific 2 prior 3 subsequent 4 puerile 5 martial
275. *gnome* 1 fairy 2 giant 3 pygmy 4 native 5 alien
276. *hilarity* 1 gloom 2 heartiness 3 weakness 4 casualty 5 paucity
277. *hackneyed* 1 carried 2 original 3 banal 4 timely 5 oratorical
278. *heretic* 1 sophist 2 believer 3 interpreter 4 pacifist 5 owner
279. *grisly* 1 unsavory 2 doubtful 3 untidy 4 pleasant 5 bearish
280. *haggard* 1 shrewish 2 inspired 3 plump 4 maidenly 5 vast

ā—ale; ă—add; ä—arm; á—ask, ē—eve; ĕ—end; ê—err, her; ə—allow; even; ī—ice; ĭ —ill; ō—oll; ŏ—odd; ô—orb; ōō—food; ŏŏ—foot, put; o—out; th—thin; ū—use; ŭ—up; zh—pleasure

---

Word List 15   homogeneous - incarnate

homogeneous (-*jē*-*nē*-*əs*) ADJ. of the same kind. Educators try to put pupils of similar abilities into classes because they believe that this *homogeneous* grouping is advisable. homogeneity, N.

horticultural ADJ. pertaining to cultivation of gardens. When he bought his house, he began to look for flowers and decorative shrubs, and began to read books dealing with *horticultural* matters.

hostelry (*hŏs*-) N. inn. Travelers interested in economy should stay at *hostelries* and pensions rather than fashionable hotels.

hubbub N. confused uproar. The marketplace was a scene of *hubbub* and excitement; in all the noise, we could not distinguish particular voices.

humane (-*mān*) ADJ. kind. His *humane* and considerate treatment of the unfortunate endeared him to all.

humdrum ADJ. dull; monotonous. After his years of adventure, he could not settle down to a *humdrum* existence.

humid ADJ. damp. He could not stand the *humid* climate and moved to a drier area.

humility N. humbleness of spirit. He spoke with a *humility* and lack of pride which impressed his listeners.

humus N. substance formed by decaying vegetable matter. In order to improve his garden, he spread *humus* over his lawn and flower beds.

hybrid N. mongrel; mixed breed. Mendel's formula explains the appearance of *hybrids* and pure species in breeding. also ADJ.

hypercritical (*hī*-*pər*-*krĭt*-) ADJ. excessively exacting. You are *hypercritical* in your demands for perfection; we all make mistakes.

hypochondriac (*hī*-*pə*-*kŏn*′-) N. person unduly worried about his health; worrier without cause about illness. The doctor prescribed chocolate pills for his patient who was a *hypochondriac*.

hypocritical (*hĭp*-*ə*-) ADJ. pretending to be virtuous; deceiving. I resent his *hypocritical* posing as a friend for I know he is interested only in his own advancement.

hypothetical (*hī*-*pə*-*thĕt*-) ADJ. based on assumptions or hypotheses. Why do we have to consider *hypothetical* cases when we have actual case histories which we may examine? hypothesis, N.

ā—ale; ă—add; ä—arm; à—ask, ē—eve; ĕ—end; ê—err, her; ə—allow; even; ī—ice; ĭ—ill; ō—oll; ŏ—odd; ô—orb; ōō—food; ŏŏ—foot, put; o—out; th—thin; ū—use; ŭ—up; zh—pleasure

iconoclastic ADJ. attacking cherished traditions. George Bernard Shaw's *iconoclastic* plays often startled people.

ideology N. ideas of a group of people. That *ideology* is dangerous to this country because it embraces undemocratic philosophies.

idiom N. special usage in language. I could not understand their *idiom* because literal translation made no sense.

idiosyncrasy N. peculiarity; eccentricity. One of his personal *idiosyncrasies* was his habit of rinsing all cutlery given him in a restaurant.

idolatry N. worship of idols; excessive admiration. Such *idolatry* of singers of popular ballads is typical of the excessive enthusiasm of youth.

igneous (ĭg-) ADJ. produced by fire; volcanic. Lava, pumice, and other *igneous* rocks are found in great abundance around Mount Vesuvius near Naples.

ignoble (ĭg-nō-) ADJ. of lowly origin; unworthy. This plan is inspired by *ignoble* motives and I must, therefore, oppose it.

ignominious (-mĭn-) ADJ. disgraceful. The country smarted under the *ignominious* defeat and dreamed of the day when it would be victorious. ignominy, N.

illimitable ADJ. infinite. Man, having explored the far corners of the earth, is now reaching out into *illimitable* space.

illusion N. misleading vision. It is easy to create an optical *illusion* in which lines of equal length appear different. illusory, ADJ.

imbecility N. weakness of mind. I am amazed at the *imbecility* of the readers of these trashy magazines.

imbibe V. drink in. The dry soil *imbibed* the rain quickly.

imbroglio (-brōl-yō) N. a complicated situation; perplexity; entanglement. He was called in to settle the *imbroglio* but failed to bring harmony into the situation.

imbue V. saturate, fill. His visits to the famous Gothic cathedrals *imbued* him with feelings of awe and reverence.

immaculate ADJ. pure; spotless. The West Point cadets were *immaculate* as they lined up for inspection.

imminent ADJ. impending; near at hand. The *imminent* battle will determine our success or failure in this conflict.

immobility N. state of being immovable. Modern armies cannot afford the luxury of *immobility,* as they are vulnerable to attack while standing still.

immolate V. offer as a sacrifice. The tribal king offered to *immolate* his daughter to quiet the angry gods.

ā—ale; ă—add; ä—arm; à—ask; ē—eve; ĕ—end; ê—err, her; ə—allow; even; ī—ice; ĭ—ill; ō—oll; ŏ—odd; ô—orb; ōō—food; ŏŏ—foot, put; o—oüt; th—thin; ū—use; ŭ—up; zh—pleasure

immune ADJ. exempt. He was fortunately *immune* from the disease and could take care of the sick.

immutable ADJ. unchangeable. Scientists are constantly seeking to discover the *immutable* laws of nature.

impair V. worsen; diminish in value. This arrest will *impair* his reputation in the community.

impale V. pierce. He was *impaled* by the spear hurled by his adversary.

impasse N. predicament from which there is no escape. In this *impasse,* all turned to prayer as their last hope.

impassive ADJ. without feeling; not affected by pain. The American Indian has been incorrectly depicted as an *impassive* individual, undemonstrative and stoical.

impeach V. charge with crime in office; indict. The angry congressman wanted to *impeach* the President.

impeccable ADJ. faultless. He was proud of his *impeccable* manners.

impecunious ADJ. without money. Now that he was wealthy, he gladly contributed to funds to assist the *impecunious* and the disabled.

impending ADJ. nearing; approaching. The entire country was saddened by the news of his *impending* death.

impenitent ADJ. not repentant. We could see by his brazen attitude that he was *impenitent.*

imperious ADJ. domineering. His *imperious* manner indicated that he had long been accustomed to assuming command.

impermeable ADJ. impervious; not permitting passage through its substance. This new material is *impermeable* to liquids.

impertinent ADJ. insolent. I regard your remarks as *impertinent* and resent them.

imperturbability N. calmness. We are impressed by his *imperturbability* in this critical moment and are calmed by it.

impervious ADJ. not penetrable; not permitting passage through. You cannot change their habits for their minds are *impervious* to reasoning.

impetuous ADJ. violent; hasty; rash. We tried to curb his *impetuous* behavior because we felt that in his haste he might offend some people.

impetus (*im -*) N. moving force. It is a miracle that there were any survivors since the two automobiles that collided were traveling with great *impetus.*

impiety (*-pī -ət-ē*) N. irreverence; wickedness. We must regard your blasphemy as an act of *impiety.*

ā—ale; ă—add; ä—arm; à—ask, ē—eve; ĕ—end; ê—err, her; ə—allow; evĕn; ī—ice; ĭ —ill; ō—oll; ŏ—odd; ô—orb; ōō—food; ŏŏ—foot, put; o—out; th—thin; ū—use; ŭ—up; zh—pleasure

impious (*im-pē-əs*) ADJ. irreverent. The congregation was offended by his *impious* remarks.

implacable (*-plăk-*) ADJ. incapable of being pacified. Madame Defarge was the *implacable* enemy of the Evremonde family.

implication N. that which is hinted at or suggested. If I understand the *implications* of your remark, you do not trust our captain.

implicit ADJ. understood but not stated. It is *implicit* that you will come to our aid if we are attacked.

impolitic (*-pŏl-*) ADJ. not wise. I think it is *impolitic* to raise this issue at the present time because the public is too angry.

import (*im-*) N. significance. I feel that you have not grasped the full *import* of the message sent to us by the enemy.

importune V. beg earnestly. I must *importune* you to work for peace at this time. importunate, ADJ.

imprecate (*ĭm'-*) V. curse; pray that evil will befall. To *imprecate* Hitler's atrocities is not enough; we must insure against any future practice of genocide.

impregnable (*-prĕg-nə-*) ADJ. invulnerable. Until the development of the airplane as a military weapon, the fort was considered *impregnable*.

impromptu (*-prŏmp'-*) ADJ. without previous preparation. His listeners were amazed that such a thorough presentation could be made in an *impromptu* speech.

impropriety (*-prī-*) N. state of being inappropriate. Because of the *impropriety* of his costume, he was denied entrance into the dining room.

improvident ADJ. thriftless. He was constantly being warned to mend his *improvident* ways and begin to "save for a rainy day."

improvise V. compose on the spur of the moment. He would sit at the piano and *improvise* for hours on themes from Bach and Handel.

impugn (*-pūn*) V. doubt; challenge; gainsay. I cannot *impugn* your honesty without evidence.

impunity N. freedom from punishment. The bully mistreated everyone in the class with *impunity* for he felt that no one would dare retaliate.

imputation N. charge; reproach. You cannot ignore the *imputations* in his speech that you are the guilty party.

inadvertence N. oversight; carelessness. By *inadvertence*, he omitted two questions on the examination.

inalienable ADJ. not to be taken away; nontransferable. The Declaration

ā—ale; ă—add; ä—arm; à—ask, ē—eve; ĕ—end; ê—err, her; ə—allow; even; ī—ice; ĭ—ill; ō—oll; ŏ—odd; ô—orb; o͞o—food; o͝o—foot, put; o—out; th—thin; ū—use; ŭ—up; zh—pleasure

of Independence mentions the *inalienable* rights that all of us possess.

inane (*ĭn-ān*) ADJ. silly; senseless. Such comments are *inane* because they do not help us solve our problem. inanity, N.

inanimate ADJ. lifeless. She was asked to identify the still and *inanimate* body.

inarticulate ADJ. speechless; producing indistinct speech. He became *inarticulate* with rage and uttered sounds without meaning.

incapacitate V. disable. During the winter, many people were *incapacitated* by respiratory ailments.

incarcerate V. imprison. The warden will *incarcerate* the felon.

incarnate ADJ. endowed with flesh; personified. Your attitude is so fiendish that you must be a devil *incarnate*.

ETYMOLOGY 15

IL, ILE (pertaining to, capable of) adjective suffix
   puerile pertaining to a child
   ductile capable of being led
   civil pertaining to a citizen

TEST—Word List 15—Synonyms and Antonyms

Each of the questions below consists of a word printed in italics, followed by five words or phrases numbered 1 to 5. Choose the numbered word or phrase which is most nearly the same as or the opposite of the word in italics and write the number of your choice on your answer paper.

281. *immutable*   1 silent 2 changeable 3 articulate 4 loyal 5 varied
282. *incarcerate*   1 inhibit 2 acquit 3 account 4 imprison 5 force
283. *importune*   1 export 2 plead 3 exhibit 4 account 5 visit
284. *inalienable*   1 inherent 2 repugnant 3 closed to immigration 4 full 5 accountable
285. *impetuous*   1 rash 2 inane 3 just 4 flagrant 5 redolent
286. *impromptu*   1 prompted 2 appropriate 3 rehearsed 4 foolish 5 vast
287. *immolate*   1 debate 2 scour 3 sacrifice 4 sanctify 5 ratify
288. *impervious*   1 impenetrable 2 vulnerable 3 chaotic 4 cool 5 perfect

ā—ale; ă—add; ä—arm; à—ask, ē—eve; ĕ—end; ê—err, her; ə—allow; ev_en; ī—ice; ĭ—ill; ō—oll; ŏ—odd; ô—orb; o͞o—food; o͝o—foot; put; o—out; th—thin; ū—use; ŭ—up; zh—pleasure

289. *impeccable*   1 unmentionable 2 quotable 3 blinding 4 faulty 5 hampering

290. *hypercritical*   1 intolerant 2 false 3 extreme 4 inarticulate 5 cautious

291. *impassive*   1 active 2 demonstrative 3 perfect 4 anxious 5 irritated

292. *impair*   1 separate 2 make amends 3 make worse 4 falsify 5 cancel

293. *immaculate*   1 chastened 2 chewed 3 sullied 4 angered 5 beaten

294. *impolitic*   1 campaigning 2 advisable 3 appropriate 4 legal 5 fortunate

295. *hubbub*   1 bedlam 2 fury 3 cap 4 axle 5 wax

296. *impecunious*   1 affluent 2 afflicted 3 affectionate 4 affable 5 afraid

297. *hypothetical*   1 logical 2 fantastic 3 wizened 4 assumed 5 axiomatic

298. *hybrid*   1 product 2 species 3 mixture 4 fish 5 genus

299. *impunity*   1 violation 2 liability 3 joke 4 play on words 5 canard

300. *inane*   1 passive 2 wise 3 intoxicated 4 mellow 5 silent

---

Word List 16   incendiary - intellect

incendiary N. arsonist. The fire spread in such an unusual manner that the fire department chiefs were certain that it had been set by an *incendiary*. also ADJ.

incentive N. spur; motive. Students who dislike school must be given an *incentive* to learn.

incessant ADJ. uninterrupted. The crickets kept up an *incessant* chirping which disturbed our attempts to fall asleep.

inchoate (ĭn-kō-) ADJ. recently begun; rudimentary; elementary. Before the Creation, the world was an *inchoate* mass.

incipient ADJ. beginning; in an early stage. I will go to sleep early for I want to break an *incipient* cold.

incisive (-sī-) ADJ. cutting; sharp. His *incisive* remarks made us see the fallacy in our plans.

incite V. arouse to action. The demagogue *incited* the mob to take action into its own hands.

inclement ADJ. stormy; unkind. I like to read a good book in *inclement* weather.

ā—ale; ă—add; ä—arm; à—ask, ē—eve; ĕ—end; ê—err, her; ə—allow;
even; ī—ice; ĭ—ill; ō—oll; ŏ—odd; ô—orb; o͞o—food; o͝o—foot, pu̇t;
o—ou̇t; th—thin; ū—use; ŭ—up; zh—pleasure

inclusive ADJ. tending to include all. This meeting will run from January 10 to February 15 *inclusive*.

incognito (-*nēt*-) ADV. with identity concealed; using an assumed name. The monarch enjoyed traveling through the town *incognito* and mingling with the populace. also ADJ.

incoherence N. lack of relevance; lack of intelligibility. The bereaved father sobbed and stammered, caught up in the *incoherence* of his grief.

incommodious (-*mōd*-) ADJ. not spacious. In their *incommodious* quarters, they had to improvise for closet space.

incompatible ADJ. inharmonious. The married couple argued incessantly and finally decided to separate because they were *incompatible*.

incongruity (-*groō ′*-) N. lack of harmony; absurdity. The *incongruity* of his wearing sneakers with formal attire amused the observers.

inconsequential (-*kwĕn*-) ADJ. of trifling significance. Your objections are *inconsequential* and may be disregarded.

incontrovertible (-*vêrt*-) ADJ. indisputable. We must yield to the *incontrovertible* evidence which you have presented and free your client.

incorporeal (-*pôr-ē*-) ADJ. immaterial; without a material body. We must devote time to the needs of our *incorporeal* mind as well as our corporeal body.

incorrigible (-*kôr*-) ADJ. uncorrectable. Because he was an *incorrigible* criminal, he was sentenced to life imprisonment.

incredulity (-*dū*-) N. a tendency to disbelief. Your *incredulity* in the face of all the evidence is hard to understand.

increment N. increase. The new contract calls for a 10 percent *increment* in salary for each employee for the next two years.

incriminate V. accuse. The evidence gathered against the racketeers *incriminates* some high public officials as well.

incubate V. hatch; scheme. Inasmuch as our supply of electricity is cut off, we shall have to rely on the hens to *incubate* these eggs.

incubus N. burden; mental care; nightmare. The *incubus* of financial worry helped bring on his nervous breakdown.

inculcate V. teach. In an effort to *inculcate* religious devotion, the officials ordered that the school day begin with the singing of a hymn.

incumbent N. officeholder. The newly elected public official received valuable advice from the present *incumbent*. also ADJ.

incursion N. temporary invasion. The nightly *incursions* and hit-and-run

ā—ale; ă—add; ä—arm; à—ask, ē—eve; ĕ—end; ê—err, her; ə—allow; even; ī—ice; ĭ—ill; ō—oll; ŏ—odd; ô—orb; ōō—food; ŏŏ—foot, put; o—out; th—thin; ū—use; ŭ—up; zh—pleasure

raids of our neighbors across the border tried the patience of the country to the point where we decided to retaliate in force.

indefatigable (-*făt*-) ADJ. tireless. He was *indefatigable* in his constant efforts to raise funds for the Red Cross.

indemnify V. make secure against loss; compensate for loss. The city will *indemnify* all home owners whose property is spoiled by this project.

indenture V. bind as servant or apprentice to master. Many immigrants could come to America only after they had *indentured* themselves for several years. also N.

indict (-*dīt*) V. charge. If the grand jury *indicts* the suspect, he will go to trial.

indigenous (-*dĭj-ə*-) ADJ. native. Tobacco is one of the *indigenous* plants which the early explorers found in this country.

indigent (*ĭn*-) ADJ. poor. Because he was *indigent,* he was sent to the welfare office.

indignity N. offensive or insulting treatment. Although he seemed to accept cheerfully the *indignities* heaped upon him, he was inwardly very angry.

indisputable (-*pūt*-) ADJ. too certain to be disputed. In the face of these *indisputable* statements, I withdraw my complaint.

indite V. write; compose. Cyrano *indited* many letters for Christian.

indolence (*ĭn*-) N. laziness. The sultry weather in the tropics encourages a life of *indolence.*

indomitable ADJ. unconquerable. The founders of our country had *indomitable* willpower.

indubitably ADV. beyond a doubt. Because his argument was *indubitably* valid, the judge accepted it.

indulgent ADJ. humoring; yielding; lenient. An *indulgent* parent may spoil a child by creating an artificial atmosphere of leniency.

ineffable ADJ. unutterable; cannot be expressed in speech. Such *ineffable* joy must be experienced; it cannot be described.

inept ADJ. unsuited; absurd; incompetent. The constant turmoil in the office proved that he was an *inept* administrator.

inexorable (-*ĕks*-) ADJ. relentless; unyielding; implacable. After listening to the pleas for clemency, the judge was *inexorable* and gave the convicted man the maximum punishment allowed by law.

infallible ADJ. unerring. We must remember that none of us is *infallible.*

infamous (*ĭn*-) ADJ. notoriously bad. Jesse James was an *infamous* outlaw.

ā—ale; ă—add; ä—arm; à—ask, ē—eve; ĕ—end; ê—err, her; ə—allow; even; ī—ice; ĭ —ill; ō—oll; ŏ—odd; ô—orb; ōō—food; ŏŏ—foot, put; o—oüt; th—thin; ū—use; ŭ—up; zh—pleasure

inference N. conclusion drawn from data. I want you to check this *inference* because it may have been based on insufficient information.

infinitesimal ADJ. very small. In the twentieth century, physicists have made their greatest discoveries about the characteristics of *infinitesimal* objects like the atom and its parts.

infirmity N. weakness. His greatest *infirmity* was lack of willpower.

inflated ADJ. enlarged (with air or gas). After the balloons were *inflated,* they were distributed among the children.

influx N. flowing into. The *influx* of refugees into the country has taxed the relief agencies severely.

infraction N. violation. Because of his many *infractions* of school regulations, he was suspended by the dean.

infringe V. violate; encroach. I think your machine *infringes* on my patent.

ingenuous (-*jĕn-ū-*) ADJ. naive; young; unsophisticated. These remarks indicate that you are *ingenuous* and unaware of life's harsher realities.

ingrate N. ungrateful person. You are an *ingrate* since you have treated my gifts with scorn.

ingratiate (-*grā-*) V. become popular with. He tried to *ingratiate* himself into her parents' good graces.

inherent (-*hĩr-*) ADJ. firmly established by nature or habit. His *inherent* love of justice compelled him to come to their aid.

inhibit V. prohibit; restrain. The child was not *inhibited* in his responses. inhibition, N.

inimical (*ĭn-ĩm'-*) ADJ. unfriendly; hostile. She felt that they were *inimical* and were hoping for her downfall.

iniquitous ADJ. unjust; wicked. I cannot approve of the *iniquitous* methods you used to gain your present position. iniquity, N.

inkling N. hint. This came as a complete surprise to me as I did not have the slightest *inkling* of your plans.

innate ADJ. inborn. His *innate* talent for music was soon recognized by his parents.

innocuous ADJ. harmless. Let him drink it; it is *innocuous.*

innovation N. change; introduction of something new. He loved *innovations* just because they were new.

innuendo (*ĭn-ū-ĕn-*) N. hint; insinuation. I resent the *innuendos* in your statement more than the statement itself.

inordinate ADJ. unrestrained; excessive. She had an *inordinate* fondness for candy.

ā—ale; ă—add; ä—arm; à—ask, ē—eve; ĕ—end; ê—err, her; ə—allow;
even; ī—ice; ĭ—ill; ō—oll; ŏ—odd; ô—orb; ōō—food; oŏ—foot, put;
o—out; th—thin; ū—use; ŭ—up; zh—pleasure

insatiable ADJ. not easily satisfied; greedy. His thirst for knowledge was *insatiable;* he was always in the library.

inscrutable ADJ. incomprehensible; not to be discovered. I fail to understand the reasons for your outlandish behavior; your motives are *inscrutable.*

insensate (-sĕn´-) ADJ. without feeling. He lay there as *insensate* as a log.

insidious ADJ. treacherous; stealthy; sly. The fifth column is *insidious* because it works secretly within our territory for our defeat.

insinuate V. hint; imply. What are you trying to *insinuate* by that remark?

insipid ADJ. tasteless; dull. I am bored by your *insipid* talk.

insolent ADJ. haughty and contemptuous. I resent your *insolent* manner.

insolvency N. bankruptcy; lack of ability to repay debts. When rumors of his *insolvency* reached his creditors, they began to press him for payment of the money due them.

insomnia N. wakefulness; inability to sleep. He refused to join us in a midnight cup of coffee because he claimed it gave him *insomnia.*

instigate V. urge; start; provoke. I am afraid that this statement will *instigate* a revolt.

insular ADJ. like an island; narrow-minded. In an age of such rapid means of communication, we cannot afford to be hemmed in by such *insular* ideas.

insuperable ADJ. insurmountable; invincible. In the face of *insuperable* difficulties they maintained their courage and will to resist.

insurgent ADJ. rebellious. We will not discuss reforms until the *insurgent* troops have returned to their homes. also N.

integrate V. make whole; combine; make into one unit. He tried to *integrate* all their activities into one program.

integrity N. wholeness; purity; uprightness. He was a man of great *integrity.*

intellect N. higher mental powers. He thought college would develop his *intellect.*

ETYMOLOGY 16

IN (in, into, upon, toward) prefix
        incursion invasion
        insidious treacherous
IN (not, without) prefix
        inconsequential not significant

ā—ale; ă—add; ä—arm; à—ask, ē—eve; ĕ—end; ê—err, her; ə—allow; even; ī—ice; ĭ—ill; ō—oll; ŏ—odd; ô—orb; ōō—food; ŏŏ—foot, put; o—oŭt; th—thin; ū—use; ŭ—up; zh—pleasure

inimical hostile, not friendly
insipid tasteless

TEST—Word List 16—Synonyms

Each of the questions below consists of a word printed in
italics, followed by five words or phrases numbered 1 to 5.
Choose the numbered word or phrase which is most nearly
similar in meaning to the word in italics and write the number
of your choice on your answer paper.

301. *incentive* 1 objective 2 goad 3 stimulation 4 beginning 5 simulation
302. *indubitably* 1 flagrantly 2 doubtfully 3 carefully 4 carelessly 5 certainly
303. *inconsequential* 1 disorderly 2 insignificant 3 subsequent 4 insufficient 5 preceding
304. *insinuate* 1 resist 2 suggest 3 report 4 rectify 5 lecture
305. *incorrigible* 1 narrow 2 straight 3 inconceivable 4 unreliable 5 unreformable
306. *ingenuous* 1 clever 2 stimulating 3 naive 4 wily 5 cautious
307. *indolence* 1 sloth 2 poverty 3 latitude 4 aptitude 5 anger
308. *innocuous* 1 not capable 2 not dangerous 3 not eager 4 not frank 5 not peaceful
309. *insipid* 1 witty 2 flat 3 wily 4 talkative 5 lucid
310. *incompatible* 1 capable 2 reasonable 3 faulty 4 indifferent 5 alienated
311. *incriminate* 1 exacerbate 2 involve 3 intimidate 4 lacerate 5 prevaricate
312. *infirmity* 1 disability 2 age 3 inoculation 4 hospital 5 unity
313. *infallible* 1 final 2 unbelievable 3 perfect 4 inaccurate 5 inquisitive
314. *indigent* 1 lazy 2 pusillanimous 3 penurious 4 affluent 5 contrary
315. *inclement* 1 unfavorable 2 abandoned 3 kindly 4 selfish 5 active
316. *integrate* 1 tolerate 2 unite 3 flow 4 copy 5 assume
317. *inimical* 1 antagonistic 2 anonymous 3 fanciful 4 accurate 5 seldom
318. *inculcate* 1 exculpate 2 educate 3 exonerate 4 prepare 5 embarrass
319. *indignity* 1 pomposity 2 bombast 3 obeisance 4 insult 5 message

ā—ale; ă—add; ä—arm; à—ask, ê—eve; ĕ—end; ê—err, her; ə—allow;
even; ī—ice; ĭ—ill; ō—oll; ŏ—odd; ô—orb; ōō—food; ŏŏ—foot, put;
o—out; th—thin; ū—use; ŭ—up; zh—pleasure

320. *insensate* 1 aggrieved 2 unconcerned 3 angered 4 patent 5 prehensile

---

Word List 17   intelligentsia - levity

intelligentsia N. the intelligent and educated classes [often used derogatorily]. He preferred discussions about sports and politics to the literary conversations of the *intelligentsia.*

inter (*-têr*) V. bury. They are going to *inter* the body tomorrow.

interim N. meantime. The company will not consider our proposal until next week; in the *interim,* let us proceed as we have in the past.

interment (*-têr-*) N. burial. *Interment* will take place in the church cemetery at 2 P.M. Wednesday.

interminable ADJ. endless. Although his speech lasted for only twenty minutes, it seemed *interminable* to his bored audience.

intermittent ADJ. periodic; on and off. Our picnic was marred by *intermittent* rains.

intimate V. hint. She *intimated* rather than stated her preferences.

intimidation (*-dā-*) N. fear. A ruler who maintains his power by *intimidation* is bound to develop clandestine resistance.

intransigent (*-jənt*) ADJ. refusing any compromise. The strike settlement has collapsed because both sides are *intransigent.*

intrepid (*-trĕp-*) ADJ. fearless. For his *intrepid* conduct in battle, he was promoted.

intrinsic ADJ. belonging to a thing in itself; inherent. Although the *intrinsic* value of this award is small, I shall always cherish it.

introvert N. one who is introspective; inclined to think more about oneself. In his poetry, he reveals that he is an *introvert* by his intense interest in his own problems. also V.

intrude V. trespass; enter as an uninvited person. He hesitated to *intrude* on their conversation.

intuition N. power of knowing without reasoning. She claimed to know the truth by *intuition.* intuitive, ADJ.

inundate V. overflow; flood. The tremendous waves *inundated* the town.

inured ADJ. accustomed; hardened. He became *inured* to the Alaskan cold.

invective N. abuse. He had expected criticism but not the *invective* which greeted his proposal.

ā—ale; ă—add; ä—arm; à—ask, ē—eve; ĕ—end; ê—err, her; ə—allow; even; ī—ice; ĭ —ill; ō—oll; ŏ—odd; ô—orb; ōō—food; ŏŏ—foot, put; o—out; th—thin; ū—use; ŭ—up; zh—pleasure

inveigle (-*vā*-) v. lead astray; wheedle. He was *inveigled* into joining the club.

inverse ADJ. opposite. There is an *inverse* ratio between the strength of light and its distance.

inveterate ADJ. deep-rooted; habitual. He is an *inveterate* smoker.

invidious ADJ. designed to create ill will or envy. We disregarded her *invidious* remarks because we realized how jealous she was.

inviolability (-*vī-ə-lə-bĭl*-) N. security from being destroyed, corrupted or profaned. They respected the *inviolability* of her faith and did not try to change her manner of living.

invulnerable ADJ. incapable of injury. Achilles was *invulnerable* except in his heel.

iota (ī-*ōt*-ə) N. very small quantity. He hadn't an *iota* of common sense.

irascible (ĭr-*ăs*-ə-bəl) ADJ. irritable; easily angered. His *irascible* temper frightened me.

iridescent (-*dĕs*-) ADJ. exhibiting rainbowlike colors. He admired the *iridescent* hues of the oil that floated on the surface of the water.

ironical (-*rŏn*-) ADJ. resulting in an unexpected and contrary manner. It is *ironical* that his success came when he least wanted it. irony, N.

irreconcilable ADJ. incompatible; not able to be resolved. Because the separated couple were *irreconcilable,* the marriage counselor recommended a divorce.

irrelevant (-*rĕl*-) ADJ. not applicable; unrelated. This statement is *irrelevant* and should be disregarded by the jury.

irremediable (-*mēd*-) ADJ. incurable; uncorrectable. The error he made was *irremediable.*

irreparable (-*rĕp*-) ADJ. not able to be corrected or repaired. Your apology cannot atone for the *irreparable* damage you have done to his reputation.

irreverent ADJ. lacking proper respect. The worshippers resented his *irreverent* remarks about their faith.

irrevocable (-*rĕv*-) ADJ. unalterable. Let us not brood over past mistakes since they are *irrevocable.*

iterate (*ĭt*-) v. utter a second time; repeat. I will *iterate* the warning I have previously given to you.

itinerant (ī-*tĭn*-) ADJ. wandering; traveling. He was an *itinerant* peddler and traveled through Pennsylvania and Virginia selling his wares. also N.

ā—ale; ă—add; ä—arm; à—ask; ē—eve; ĕ—end; ê—err, her; ə—allow; even; ī—ice; ĭ—ill; ō—oll; ŏ—odd; ô—orb; ōō—food; ŏŏ—foot, put; o—out; th—thin; ū—use; ŭ—up; zh—pleasure

jaded ADJ. fatigued; surfeited. He looked for exotic foods to stimulate his *jaded* appetite.

jargon N. language used by special group; gibberish. We tried to understand the *jargon* of the peddlers in the market-place but could not find any basis for comprehension.

jaundiced ADJ. yellowed; prejudiced; envious. He gazed at the painting with *jaundiced* eyes.

jeopardy (*jĕp* -) N. exposure to death or danger. He cannot be placed in double *jeopardy.*

jettison V. throw overboard. In order to enable the ship to ride safely through the storm, the captain had to *jettison* much of his cargo.

jingoism N. extremely aggressive and militant patriotism. We must be careful to prevent a spirit of *jingoism* from spreading at this time; the danger of a disastrous war is too great.

jocose (*jō-kōs*) ADJ. giving to joking. The salesman was so *jocose* that many of his customers suggested that he become a "stand-up" comic.

jocular (*jŏk* -) ADJ. said or done in jest. Do not take my *jocular* remarks seriously.

jocund ADJ. merry. Santa Claus is always vivacious and *jocund.*

jollitiy N. gaiety; cheerfulness. The festive Christmas dinner was a merry one, and old and young alike joined in the general *jollity.*

jubilation N. rejoicing. There was great *jubilation* when the armistice was announced.

judicious ADJ. wise; determined by sound judgment. I believe that this plan is not *judicious;* it is too risky.

junket N. a merry feast or picnic. The opposition claimed that his trip to Europe was merely a political *junket.*

junta (*hoŏn'-tə*) N. group of men joined in political intrigue; cabal. As soon as he learned of its existence, the dictator ordered the execution of all of the members of the *junta.*

ken N. range of knowledge. I cannot answer your question since this matter is beyond my *ken.*

kiosk (*kē-ŏsk*) N. summerhouse; open pavilion. She waited at the subway *kiosk.*

kismet N. fate. *Kismet* is the Arabic word for "fate."

kith N. familiar friends. He always helped both his *kith* and kin.

kleptomaniac N. person who has a compulsive desire to steal. They discovered that the wealthy customer was a *kleptomaniac* when they caught her stealing some cheap trinkets.

ā—ale; ă—add; ä—arm; à—ask, ē—eve; ĕ—end; ê—err, her; ə—allow; even; ī—ice; ĭ —ill; ō—oll; ŏ—odd; ô—orb; ōō—food; ŏŏ—foot, put; o—oŭt; th—thin; ū—use; ŭ—up; zh—pleasure

knavery N. rascality. We cannot condone such *knavery* in public officials.

knell N. tolling of a bell at a funeral; sound of the funeral bell. "The curfew tolls the *knell* of parting day."

knoll N. little round hill. Robert Louis Stevenson's grave is on a *knoll* in Samoa.

labyrinth N. maze. Tom and Betty were lost in the *labyrinth* of secret caves.

lacerate (*lăs-ə-*) V. mangle; tear. Her body was *lacerated* in the automobile crash.

lackadaisical ADJ. affectedly languid. He was *lackadaisical* and indifferent about his part in the affair.

lackey N. footman; toady. The duke was followed by his *lackeys*.

laconic ADJ. brief and to the point. Will Rogers' *laconic* comments on the news made him world famous.

laggard ADJ. slow; sluggish. The sailor had been taught not to be *laggard* in carrying out orders.

lagniappe (*lăn-yăp*) N. trifling present given to a customer. The butcher threw in some bones for the dog as a *lagniappe*.

lagoon N. shallow body of water near a sea; lake. They enjoyed their swim in the calm *lagoon*.

laity (*lā-ĭ-tē*) N. laymen; persons not connected with the clergy. The *laity* does not always understand the clergy's problems.

lambent ADJ. flickering; softly radiant. They sat quietly before the *lambent* glow of the fireplace.

laminated ADJ. made of thin plates or scales. Banded gneiss is a *laminated* rock.

lampoon V. ridicule. This article *lampoons* the pretensions of some movie moguls. also N.

languid ADJ. weary; sluggish; listless. Her siege of illness left her *languid* and pallid.

languish V. lose animation; lose strength. In stories, lovelorn damsels used to *languish* and pine away.

lapidary N. worker in precious stones. He employed a *lapidary* to cut the large diamond.

largess (*lär-zhĕs*) N. generous gift. Lady Bountiful distributed *largess* to the poor.

lascivious ADJ. lustful. The *lascivious* books were confiscated and destroyed.

lassitude N. languor; weariness. The hot, tropical weather created a feeling of *lassitude* and encouraged drowsiness.

ā—ale; ă—add; ä—arm; à—ask; ē—eve; ĕ—end; ê—err, her; ə—allow;
even; ī—ice; ĭ—ill; ō—oll; ŏ—odd; ô—orb; ōō—food; ŏŏ—foot, put;
o—out; th—thin; ū—use; ŭ—up; zh—pleasure

latent (/lāt-/) ADJ. dormant; hidden. His *latent* talent was discovered by accident.

lateral ADJ. coming from the side. In order to get good plant growth, the gardener must pinch off all *lateral* shoots.

latitude N. freedom from narrow limitations. I think you have permitted your son too much *latitude* in this matter.

laudatory ADJ. expressing praise. The critics' *laudatory* comments helped to make her a star.

lave (/lāv/) V. wash. The running water will *lave* away all stains.

lavish ADJ. liberal; wasteful. The actor's *lavish* gifts pleased her. also V.

lecherous ADJ. impure in thought and act; lustful; unchaste. He is a *lecherous* and wicked old man.

lesion N. unhealthy change in structure; injury. Many *lesions* are the result of disease.

lethal ADJ. deadly. It is unwise to leave *lethal* weapons where children may find them.

lethargic (/lə-thär-/) ADJ. drowsy; dull. The stuffy room made him *lethargic*.

levity N. lightness. Such *levity* is improper on this serious occasion.

ETYMOLOGY 17

INTER (between, among) prefix
        intervene come between
        international between nations
        interjection a statement thrown in

IST (one who practices) noun suffix
        humorist one who provides humor
        specialist one who engages in a specialty
        optimist one who is hopeful

IT, ITINER (journey, road)
        exit way out
        itinerary plan of journey
        itinerant traveling from place to place

ITY (state of being) noun suffix
        annuity state of being paid yearly
        credulity state of being gullible
        sagacity wisdom

IZE, ISE (to make) verb suffix
        victimize make a victim
        rationalize reason
        harmonize make peaceful

ā—ale; ă—add; ä—arm; à—ask; ē—eve; ĕ—end; ê—err, her; ə—allow; even; ī—ice; ĭ—ill; ō—oll; ŏ—odd; ô—orb; o͞o—food; o͝o—foot, put; o—out; th—thin; ū—use; ŭ—up; zh—pleasure

JAC, JACT, JEC (to throw)
>   **projectile** missile; something thrown forward
>   **trajectory** path taken by thrown object
>   **reject** throw back

JUR, JURAT (to swear)
>   **abjure** renounce
>   **perjure** testify falsely
>   **jury** group of men sworn to seek the truth

LABOR, LABORAT (to work)
>   **laboratory** place where work is done
>   **collaborate** work together with others
>   **laborious** difficult

LEG, LECT (to choose, to read)
>   **election** choice
>   **legible** able to be read
>   **eligible** able to be selected

LEG (law)
>   **legislature** law-making body
>   **legitimate** lawful
>   **legal** lawful

TEST—Word List 17—Antonyms

Each of the questions below consists of a word printed in italics, followed by five words or phrases numbered 1 to 5. Choose the numbered word or phrase which is most nearly opposite in meaning to the word in italics and write the number of your choice on your answer paper.

321. *intermittent* 1 heavy 2 fleeting 3 constant 4 fearless 5 responding
322. *irreverent* 1 related 2 mischievous 3 respecting 4 pious 5 violent
323. *inundate* 1 abuse 2 deny 3 swallow 4 treat 5 drain
324. *laconic* 1 milky 2 verbose 3 wicked 4 flagrant 5 derelict
325. *inter* 1 exhume 2 amuse 3 relate 4 frequent 5 abandon
326. *latent* 1 hidden 2 forbidding 3 execrable 4 early 5 obvious
327. *intransigent* 1 stationary 2 yielding 3 incorruptible 4 magnificent 5 grandiose
328. *jaded* 1 upright 2 stimulated 3 aspiring 4 applied 5 void
329. *levity* 1 bridge 2 dam 3 praise 4 blame 5 solemnity

ā—ale; ă—add; ä—arm; à—ask, ē—eve; ĕ—end; ê—err, her; ə—allow; even; ī—ice; ĭ—ill; ō—oll; ŏ—odd; ô—orb; ōō—food; ŏŏ—foot; put; o—out; th—thin; ū—use; ŭ—up; zh—pleasure

330. *inveterate* 1 inexperienced 2 sophisticated 3 professional 4 wicked 5 ascetic
331. *lampoon* 1 darken 2 praise 3 abandon 4 sail 5 fly
332. *irrelevant* 1 lacking piety 2 fragile 3 congruent 4 pertinent 5 varied
333. *intrepid* 1 cold 2 hot 3 understood 4 callow 5 craven
334. *intrinsic* 1 extrinsic 2 abnormal 3 above 4 abandoned 5 basic
335. *lackadaisical* 1 monthly 2 possessing time 3 ambitious 4 pusillanimous 5 intelligent
336. *lethargic* 1 convalescent 2 beautiful 3 enervating 4 invigorating 5 interrogating
337. *inured* 1 accustomed 2 fitted 3 intestate 4 futile 5 inexperienced
338. *jaundiced* 1 whitened 2 inflamed 3 quickened 4 aged 5 unbiased
339. *kith* 1 outfit 2 strangers 3 brothers 4 ceramics tool 5 quality
340. *laudatory* 1 dirtying 2 disclaiming 3 defamatory 4 inflammatory 5 debased

---

Word List 18   lewd - mendicant

lewd ADJ. lustful. They found his *lewd* stories objectionable.

lexicon N. dictionary. I cannot find this word in any *lexicon* in the library. lexicographer, N.

liaison (*lē -ə-zän*) N. officer who acts as go-between for two armies. As the *liaison,* he had to avoid offending the leaders of the two armies. also ADJ.

libelous ADJ. defamatory; injurious to the good name of a person. He sued the newspaper because of its *libelous* story.

libertine N. debauched person, roué. Although she was aware of his reputation as a *libertine,* she felt she could reform him and help him break his dissolute way of life.

libidinous (*-bĭd-*) ADJ. lustful. They objected to his *libidinous* behavior.

libretto N. text of an opera. The composer of an opera's music is remembered more frequently than the author of its *libretto.*

licentious ADJ. wanton; lewd; dissolute. The *licentious* monarch helped bring about his country's downfall.

lieu (*lōō*) N. instead of. They accepted his check in *lieu* of cash.

limn (*lĭm*) V. portray; describe vividly. He was never satisfied with his attempts to *limn* her beauty on canvas.

limpid ADJ. clear. A *limpid* stream ran through his property.

linguistic ADJ. pertaining to language. The modern tourist will encounter

ā—ale; ă—add; ä—arm; ȧ—ask, ē—eve; ĕ—end; ê—err, hẹr; ə—allow; evẹn; ī—ice; ĭ—ill; ō—oll; ŏ—odd; ô—orb; ōō—food; ŏŏ—foot, put; o—out; th—thin; ū—use; ŭ—up; zh—pleasure

very little *linguistic* difficulty as English has become an almost universal language.

liquidate v. settle accounts; clear up. He was able to *liquidate* all his debts in a short period of time.

listless ADJ. lacking in spirit or energy. We had expected him to be full of enthusiasm and were surprised by his *listless* attitude.

lithe (*līth*) ADJ. flexible; supple. Her figure was *lithe* and willowy.

litigation N. lawsuit. Try to settle this amicably; I do not want to start *litigation*.

livid ADJ. lead-colored; black and blue; enraged. His face was so *livid* with rage that we were afraid that he might have an attack of apoplexy.

loath (*lōth*) ADJ. averse; reluctant. They were both *loath* for him to go.

loathe v. detest. We *loathed* the wicked villain.

lode N. metal-bearing vein. If this *lode* which we have discovered extends for any distance, we have found a fortune.

longevity (-*jĕv*-) N. long life. The old man was proud of his *longevity*.

lope v. gallop slowly. As the horses *loped* along, we had an opportunity to admire the ever-changing scenery.

loquacious ADJ. talkative. She is very *loquacious* and can speak on the telephone for hours.

lout N. clumsy person. The delivery boy is an awkward *lout*.

lucent ADJ. shining. The moon's *lucent* rays silvered the river.

lucid ADJ. bright; easily understood. His explanation was *lucid* and to the point.

lucrative ADJ. profitable. He turned his hobby into a *lucrative* profession.

lucre N. money. Preferring *lucre* to fame, he wrote stories of popular appeal.

lugubrious ADJ. mournful. The *lugubrious* howling of the dogs added to our sadness.

luminous ADJ. shining; issuing light. The sun is a *luminous* body.

lunar ADJ. pertaining to the moon. *Lunar* craters can be plainly seen with the aid of a small telescope.

lurid ADJ. wild; sensational. The *lurid* stories he told shocked his listeners.

luscious ADJ. pleasing to taste or smell. The ripe peach was *luscious*.

luster N. shine; gloss. The soft *luster* of the silk in the dim light was pleasing.

lustrous ADJ. shining. Her large and *lustrous* eyes gave a touch of beauty to an otherwise drab face.

ā—ale; ǎ—add; ä—arm; à—ask; ē—eve; ĕ—end; ê—err, her; ə—allow; evĕn; ī—ice; ĭ—ill; ō—oll; ŏ—odd; ô—orb; ōō—food; ŏŏ—foot, put; o—out; th—thin; ū—use; ŭ—up; zh—pleasure

luxuriant ADJ. fertile; abundant; ornate. Farming was easy in this *luxuriant* soil.

macabre (-*kăb*-) ADJ. gruesome; grisly. The city morgue is a *macabre* spot for the uninitiated.

macerate (*măs*-) V. waste away. Cancer *macerated* his body.

Machiavellian (*măk-ē-ə-věl*-) ADJ. crafty; double-dealing. I do not think he will be a good ambassador because he is not accustomed to the *Machiavellian* maneuverings of foreign diplomats.

machinations (*măk-ə-nā*-) N. schemes. I can see through your wily *machinations*.

madrigal N. pastoral song. His program of folk songs included several *madrigals* which he sang to the accompaniment of a lute.

maelstrom (*māl*-) N. whirlpool. The canoe was tossed about in the *maelstrom*.

magnanimous ADJ. generous. The philanthropist was most *magnanimous*.

magnate N. person of prominence or influence. The steel *magnate* decided to devote more time to city politics.

magniloquent ADJ. boastful, pompous. In their stories of the trial, the reporters ridiculed the *magniloquent* speeches of the defense attorney.

magnitude N. greatness; extent. It is difficult to comprehend the *magnitude* of his crime.

maim V. mutilate; injure. The hospital could not take care of all who had been wounded or *maimed* in the railroad accident.

malediction N. curse. The witch uttered *maledictions* against her captors.

malefactor N. criminal. We must try to bring these *malefactors* to justice.

malevolent ADJ. wishing evil. We must thwart his *malevolent* schemes.

malicious ADJ. dictated by hatred or spite. The *malicious* neighbor spread the gossip.

malign (-*līn*) V. speak evil of; defame. Because of her hatred of the family, she *maligns* all who are friendly to them.

malignant (-*lĭg*-) ADJ. having an evil influence; virulent. This is a *malignant* disease; we may have to use drastic measures to stop its spread.

malingerer (-*lĭng*-*gər*-) N. one who feigns illness to escape duty. The captain ordered the sergeant to punish all *malingerers*.

mall N. public walk. The *Mall* in Central Park has always been a favorite spot for Sunday strollers.

malleable (*măl*-) ADJ. capable of being shaped by pounding. Gold is a *malleable* metal.

ā—ale; ă—add; ä—arm; à—ask; ē—eve; ĕ—end; ê—err, her; ə—allow; even; ī—ice; ĭ—ill; ō—oll; ŏ—odd; ô—orb; ōō—food; ŏŏ—foot; put; o—out; th—thin; ū—use; ŭ—up; zh—pleasure

mammoth ADJ. gigantic. The *mammoth* corporations of the twentieth century are a mixed blessing.

mandatory ADJ. obligatory. These instructions are *mandatory;* any violation will be severely punished.

maniacal (-*nī*-) ADJ. raving mad. His *maniacal* laughter frightened us.

manifest ADJ. understandable; clear. His evil intentions were *manifest* and yet we could not stop him. also V.

manifesto N. declaration; statement of policy. This statement may be regarded as the *manifesto* of the party's policy.

manipulate V. operate with the hands. How do you *manipulate* these puppets?

marauder N. raider; intruder. The sounding of the alarm frightened the *marauders.*

marital ADJ. pertaining to marriage. After the publication of his book on *marital* affairs, he was often consulted by married people on the verge of divorce.

maritime ADJ. bordering on the sea; nautical. The *Maritime* Provinces depend on the sea for their wealth.

marrow N. soft tissue filling the bones. The frigid cold chilled the traveler to the *marrow.*

martial ADJ. warlike. The sound of *martial* music is always inspiring.

martinet N. strict disciplinarian. The commanding officer was a *martinet* who observed each regulation to the letter.

masticate V. chew. We must *masticate* our food carefully and slowly in order to avoid stomach disorders.

maternal ADJ. motherly. Many animals display *maternal* instincts only while their offspring are young and helpless.

matricide N. murder of a mother by a child. A crime such as *matricide* is inconceivable.

matrix (*mā*-) N. mold or die. The cast around the *matrix* was cracked.

maudlin ADJ. effusively sentimental. I do not like such *maudlin* pictures. I call them tearjerkers.

mausoleum (-*lē*-) N. monumental tomb. His body was placed in the family *mausoleum.*

mauve (*mōv*) ADJ. pale purple. The *mauve* tint in the lilac bush was another indication that Spring had finally arrived.

maxim N. proverb; a truth pithily stated. Aesop's fables illustrate moral *maxims.*

meander V. to wind or turn in its course. It is difficult to sail up this stream because of the way it *meanders* through the countryside.

meddlesome ADJ. interfering. He felt his marriage was suffering because of his *meddlesome* mother-in-law.

ā—ale; ă—add; ä—arm; à—ask; ē—eve; ĕ—end; ê—err, her; ə—allow; even; ī—ice; ĭ—ill; ō—oll; ŏ—odd; ô—orb; ōō—food; ŏŏ—foot, pu̱t; o—oút; th—thin; ū—use; ŭ—up; zh—pleasure

mediate V. settle a dispute through the services of an outsider. Let us *mediate* our differences rather than engage in a costly strike.

mediocre ADJ. ordinary; commonplace. We were disappointed because he gave a rather *mediocre* performance in this role.

meditation N. reflection; thought. She reached her decision only after much *meditation*.

medley N. mixture. The band played a *medley* of Gershwin tunes.

melee (*mā-lā*) N. fight. The captain tried to ascertain the cause of the *melee* which had broken out among the crew members.

mellifluous ADJ. flowing smoothly; smooth. Italian is a *mellifluous* language.

memento N. token; reminder. Take this book as a *memento* of your visit.

memorialize V. commemorate. Let us *memorialize* his great contribution by dedicating this library in his honor.

mendacious (*-dā-*) ADJ. lying; false. He was a pathological liar, and his friends learned to discount his *mendacious* stories.

mendicant N. beggar. From the moment we left the ship, we were surrounded by *mendicants* and peddlers.

ETYMOLOGY 18

LIB, LIBR, LIBER (book)
      library collection of books
      libretto the "book" of a musical play
      libel slander (originally found in a little book)

LOQU, LOCUT (to talk)
      soliloquy speech by one individual
      loquacious talkative
      elocution speech

LUC (light)
      elucidate enlighten
      lucid clear
      translucent allowing some light to pass through

MAL (bad) prefix
      malevolent evil (wishing bad)
      malediction curse (state of saying evil)
      malefactor evildoer

MAN (hand)
      manufacture create (make by hand)
      manuscript writing by hand
      emancipate free (to let go from the hand)

ā—ale; ă—add; ä—arm; à—ask; ē—eve; ĕ—end; ê—err, her; ə—allow; even; ī—ice; ĭ—ill; ō—oll; ŏ—odd; ô—orb; o͞o—food; o͝o—foot, put; o—out; th—thin; ū—use; ŭ—up; zh—pleasure

MAR (sea)

> **maritime** connected with seafaring
> **submarine** undersea craft
> **mariner** seaman

TEST—Word List 18—Synonyms and Antonyms

Each of the questions below consists of a word printed in italics, followed by five words or phrases numbered 1 to 5. Choose the numbered word or phrase which is most nearly the same as or the opposite of the word in italics and write the number of your choice on your answer paper.

341. *magnitude* 1 realization 2 fascination 3 enormity 4 gratitude 5 interference
342. *maniacal* 1 demoniac 2 saturated 3 sane 4 sanitary 5 handcuffed
343. *loquacious* 1 taciturn 2 sentimental 3 soporific 4 soothing 5 sedate
344. *malefactor* 1 quail 2 lawbreaker 3 beneficiary 4 banker 5 female agent
345. *mellifluous* 1 porous 2 honeycombed 3 strong 4 strident 5 viscous
346. *limpid* 1 erect 2 turbid 3 tangential 4 timid 5 weary
347. *mediocre* 1 average 2 bitter 3 medieval 4 industrial 5 agricultural
348. *macabre* 1 musical 2 frightening 3 chewed 4 wicked 5 exceptional
349. *malign* 1 intersperse 2 vary 3 emphasize 4 frighten 5 eulogize
350. *lithe* 1 stiff 2 limpid 3 facetious 4 insipid 5 vast
351. *lurid* 1 dull 2 duplicate 3 heavy 4 grotesque 5 intelligent
352. *malevolent* 1 kindly 2 vacuous 3 ambivalent 4 volatile 5 primitive
353. *manifest* 1 limited 2 obscure 3 faulty 4 varied 5 vital
354. *loath* 1 loose 2 evident 3 deliberate 4 eager 5 tiny
355. *malediction* 1 misfortune 2 hap 3 fruition 4 correct pronunciation 5 benediction
356. *magniloquent* 1 loquacious 2 bombastic 3 rudimentary 4 qualitative 5 minimizing
357. *lugubrious* 1 frantic 2 cheerful 3 burdensome 4 oily 5 militant
358. *malleable* 1 brittle 2 blatant 3 brilliant 4 brownish 5 basking
359. *martial* 1 bellicose 2 celibate 3 divorced 4 quiescent 5 planetary
360. *livid* 1 alive 2 mundane 3 positive 4 purplish 5 vast

ā—ale; ă—add; ä—arm; à—ask, ē—eve; ĕ—end; ê—err, her; ə—allow; even; ī—ice; ĭ—ill; ō—oll; ŏ—odd; ô—orb; o͞o—food; o͝o—foot, put; o—out; th—thin; ū—use; ŭ—up; zh—pleasure

Word List 19   menial - nadir

menial ADJ. suitable for servants; low. I cannot understand why a person of your ability and talent should engage in such *menial* activities. also N.

mentor N. teacher. During this very trying period, he could not have had a better *mentor,* for the teacher was sympathetic and understanding.

mercantile ADJ. concerning trade. I am more interested in the opportunities available in the *mercantile* field than I am in those in the legal profession.

mercenary ADJ. interested in money or gain. I am certain that your action was prompted by *mercenary* motives. also N.

mercurial ADJ. fickle; changing. He was of a *mercurial* temperament and therefore unpredictable.

meretricious (*měr-ə-trĭsh´-*) ADJ. flashy; tawdry. Her jewels were inexpensive but not *meretricious.*

meringue (*mə-rǎng*) N. a pastry decoration made of white of eggs. The lemon *meringue* pie is one of our specialties.

mesa (*mā-sə*) N. high, flat-topped hill. The *mesa,* rising above the surrounding countryside, was the most conspicuous feature of the area.

metallurgical ADJ. pertaining to the art of removing metals from ores. During the course of his *metallurgical* research, the scientist developed a steel alloy of tremendous strength.

metamorphosis N. change of form. The *metamorphosis* of caterpillar to butterfly is typical of many such changes in animal life.

metaphysical ADJ. pertaining to speculative philosophy. The modern poets have gone back to the fanciful poems of the *metaphysical* poets of the seventeenth century for many of their images. metaphysics, N.

mete (*mēt*) V. measure; distribute. He tried to be impartial in his efforts to *mete* out justice.

meticulous ADJ. excessively careful. He was *meticulous* in checking his accounts.

metropolis N. large city. Every evening this terminal is filled with the thousands of commuters who are going from this *metropolis* to their homes in the suburbs.

mettle N. courage; spirit. When challenged by the other horses in the race, the thoroughbred proved its *mettle* by its determination to hold the lead.

ā—ale; ă—add; ä—arm; à—ask, ē—eve; ĕ—end; ê—err, her; ə—allow; even; ī—ice; ĭ —ill; ō—oll; ŏ—odd; ô—orb; ōō—food; ŏŏ—foot, put; o—out; th—thin; ū—use; ŭ—up; zh—pleasure

mews N. group of stables built around a courtyard. Let us visit the *mews* to inspect the newly purchased horse.

mien (*mēn*) N. demeanor; bearing. She had the gracious *mien* of a queen.

migrant ADJ. changing its habitat; wandering. These *migrant* birds return every spring. also N.

migratory ADJ. wandering. The return of the *migratory* birds to the northern sections of this country is a harbinger of spring.

militate V. work against. Your record of lateness and absence will *militate* against your chances of promotion.

mincing ADJ. affectedly dainty. Yum-Yum walked across the stage with *mincing* steps.

mirage (*-räzh´*) N. unreal reflection; optical illusion. The lost prospector was fooled by a *mirage* in the desert.

misadventure N. mischance; ill luck. The young explorer met death by *misadventure*.

misanthrope N. one who hates mankind. We thought the hermit was a *misanthrope* because he shunned our society.

misapprehension N. error; misunderstanding. To avoid *misapprehension,* I am going to ask all of you to repeat the instructions I have given.

miscegenation N. intermarriage between races. Some states passed laws against *miscegenation*.

miscellany N. mixture of writings on various subjects. This is an interesting *miscellany* of nineteenth-century prose.

mischance N. ill luck. By *mischance,* he lost his week's salary.

miscreant N. wretch; villain. His kindness to the *miscreant* amazed all of us who had expected to hear severe punishment pronounced.

misdemeanor N. minor crime. The culprit pleaded guilty to a *misdemeanor* rather than face trial for a felony.

misgivings N. doubts. Hamlet described his *misgivings* to Horatio but decided to fence with Laertes despite his foreboding of evil.

mishap (*mĭs´-*) N. accident. With a little care you could have avoided this *mishap*.

misnomer N. wrong name; incorrect designation. His tyrannical conduct proved to all that his nickname, King Eric the Just, was a *misnomer*.

misogynist N. hater of women. She accused him of being a *misogynist* because he had been a bachelor all his life.

missile N. object to be thrown or projected. Scientists are experimenting with guided *missiles.*

ā—ale; ă—add; ä—arm; à—ask, ē—eve; ĕ—end; ê—err, her; ə—allow; even; ī—ice; ĭ—ill; ō—oll; ŏ—odd; ô—orb; ōō—food; ŏŏ—foot, put; o—out; th—thin; ū—use; ŭ—up; zh—pleasure

mite N. very small object or creature; small coin. The criminal was so heartless that he even stole the widow's *mite*.

mitigate V. appease. Nothing he did could *mitigate* her wrath; she was unforgiving.

mobile ADJ. movable; not fixed. The *mobile* blood bank operated by the Red Cross visited our neighborhood today. mobility, N.

mode (mōd) N. prevailing style. She was not used to their lavish *mode* of living.

modicum (mŏd-) N. limited quantity. Although his story is based on a *modicum* of truth, most of the events he describes are fictitious.

modish ADJ. fashionable. She always discarded all garments which were no longer *modish*.

modulation N. toning down; changing from one key to another. When she spoke, it was with quiet *modulation* of voice.

moiety (môî-ət-ē) N. half; part. There is a slight *moiety* of the savage in her personality which is not easily perceived by those who do not know her well.

mollify V. soothe. We tried to *mollify* the hysterical child by promising her many gifts.

molt V. shed or cast off hair or feathers. The male robin *molted* in the spring.

molten ADJ. melted. The city of Pompeii was destroyed by volcanic ash rather than by *molten* lava flowing from Mount Vesuvius.

momentous ADJ. very important. On this *momentous* occasion, we must be very solemn.

monetary ADJ. pertaining to money. She was in complete charge of all *monetary* matters affecting the household.

monotheism (mŏn-) N. belief in one God. Abraham was the first to proclaim his belief in *monotheism*.

moodiness N. fits of depression or gloom. We could not discover the cause of his recurrent *moodiness*.

moot (mōot) ADJ. debatable. Our tariff policy is a *moot* subject.

morbid ADJ. given to unwholesome thought; gloomy. These *morbid* speculations are dangerous; we must lighten our thinking by emphasis on more pleasant matters.

mordant ADJ. biting; sarcastic; stinging. Actors feared the critic's *mordant* pen.

mores (môr'-āz) N. customs. The *mores* of Mexico are those of Spain with some modifications.

moribund ADJ. at the point of death. The doctors called the family to the bedside of the *moribund* patient.

ā—ale; ă—add; ä—arm; à—ask, ē—eve; ĕ—end; ê—err, her; ə—allow; even; ī—ice; ĭ—ill; ō—oll; ŏ—odd; ô—orb; ōō—food; ŏŏ—foot, put; o—out; th—thin; ū—use; ŭ—up; zh—pleasure

morose (-*rōs*) ADJ. ill-humored; sullen. When we first meet Hamlet, we find him *morose* and depressed.

mortician N. undertaker. The *mortician* prepared the corpse for burial.

mortify V. humiliate; punish the flesh. She was so *mortified* by her blunder that she ran to her room in tears.

mote N. small speck. The tiniest *mote* in the eye is very painful.

motif (*mō-tēf*) N. theme. This simple *motif* runs throughout the entire score.

motley ADJ. parti-colored; mixed. The captain had gathered a *motley* crew to sail the vessel.

mountebank N. charlatan; boastful pretender. The patent medicine man was a *mountebank*.

muddle V. confuse; mix up. His thoughts were *muddled* and chaotic. also N.

muggy ADJ. warm and damp. August in New York City is often *muggy*.

mulct (*mŭlkt*) V. defraud a person of something. The lawyer was accused of trying to *mulct* the boy of his legacy.

multiform ADJ. having many forms. Snowflakes are *multiform* but always hexagonal.

multilingual ADJ. having many languages. Because they are bordered by so many countries, the Swiss people are *multilingual*.

multiplicity N. state of being numerous. He was appalled by the *multiplicity* of details he had to complete before setting out on his mission.

mundane ADJ. worldly as opposed to spiritual. He was concerned only with *mundane* matters, especially the daily stock market quotations.

munificent ADJ. very generous. The *munificent* gift was presented to the bride.

murkiness N. darkness; gloom. The *murkiness* and fog of the waterfront that evening depressed me.

muse V. ponder. For a moment he *mused* about the beauty of the scene, but his thoughts soon changed as he recalled his own personal problems. also N.

musky ADJ. having the odor of musk. She left a trace of *musky* perfume behind her.

musty ADJ. stale; spoiled by age. The attic was dark and *musty*.

mutable ADJ. changing in form; fickle. His opinions were *mutable* and easily influenced by anyone who had any powers of persuasion.

mutilate V. maim. The torturer threatened to *mutilate* his victim.

ā—ale; ă—add; ä—arm; à—ask, ê—eve; ĕ—end; ê—err, her; ə—allow; even; ī—ice; ĭ—ill; ō—oll; ŏ—odd; ô—orb; o͞o—food; o͝o—foot, put; o—out; th—thin; ū—use; ŭ—up; zh—pleasure

mutinous ADJ. unruly; rebellious. The captain had to use force to quiet his *mutinous* crew.

myriad N. very large number. *Myriads* of mosquitoes from the swamps invaded our village every twilight. also ADJ.

nadir (nā-) N. lowest point. Although few people realized it, the Dow-Jones averages had reached their *nadir* and would soon begin an upward surge.

ETYMOLOGY 19

MITT, MISS (to send)
  missile projectile
  admit allow in
  dismiss send away
  transmit send across

MON, MONIT (to warn)
  admonish warn
  premonition foreboding
  monitor watcher (warner)

MORI, MORT (to die)
  mortuary funeral parlor
  moribund dying
  immortal not dying

TEST—Word List 19—Synonyms

Each of the questions below consists of a word printed in italics, followed by five words or phrases numbered 1 to 5. Choose the numbered word or phrase which is most nearly similar in meaning to the word in italics and write the number of your choice on your answer paper.

361. *modish*   1 sentimental   2 stylish   3 vacillating   4 contrary   5 adorned
362. *mordant*   1 dying   2 trenchant   3 fabricating   4 controlling   5 avenging
363. *mollify*   1 avenge   2 attenuate   3 attribute   4 mortify   5 appease
364. *menial*   1 intellectual   2 clairvoyant   3 servile   4 arrogant   5 laudatory
365. *moribund*   1 dying   2 appropriate   3 leather bound   4 answering   5 undertaking
366. *mirage*   1 dessert   2 illusion   3 water   4 mirror   5 statement

---

ā—ale; ă—add; ä—arm; à—ask; ē—eve; ĕ—end; ê—err, her; ə—allow; evēn; ī—ice; ĭ—ill; ō—oll; ŏ—odd; ô—orb; ōō—food; ŏŏ—foot, put; o—out; th—thin; ū—use; ŭ—up; zh—pleasure

367. *mischance* 1 opportunity 2 ordinance 3 aperture 4 anecdote 5 adversity
368. *mundane* 1 global 2 futile 3 spiritual 4 heretic 5 worldly
369. *multilingual* 1 variegated 2 polyglot 3 multilateral 4 polyandrous 5 multiplied
370. *moot* 1 visual 2 invisible 3 controversial 4 anticipatory 5 obsequious
371. *motley* 1 active 2 disguised 3 variegated 4 somber 5 sick
372. *mulct* 1 swindle 2 hold 3 record 4 print 5 fertilize
373. *munificent* 1 grandiose 2 puny 3 philanthropic 4 poor 5 gracious
374. *monetary* 1 boring 2 fascinating 3 fiscal 4 stationary 5 stationery
375. *misanthrope* 1 benefactor 2 philanderer 3 hermit 4 aesthete 5 epicure
376. *mentor* 1 guide 2 genius 3 talker 4 philosopher 5 stylist
377. *meticulous* 1 steadfast 2 remiss 3 quaint 4 painstaking 5 overt
378. *muggy* 1 attacking 2 fascinating 3 humid 4 characteristic 5 gelid
379. *musty* 1 flat 2 necessary 3 indifferent 4 nonchalant 5 vivid
380. *misdemeanor* 1 felony 2 peccadillo 3 indignity 4 fiat 5 illiteracy

---

Word List 20   naiveté - optometrist

naiveté (*nä-ē-və-tā*) N. quality of being unsophisticated. I cannot believe that such *naiveté* is unassumed in a person of her age and experience.

natal (*nāt-*) ADJ. pertaining to birth. He refused to celebrate his *natal* day because it reminded him of the few years he could look forward to.

natation N. swimming. The Red Cross emphasizes the need for courses in *natation.*

nauseate V. cause to become sick; fill with disgust. The foul smells began to *nauseate* him.

nave N. main body of a church. The *nave* of the cathedral was empty at this hour.

nebulous ADJ. cloudy; hazy. Your theories are too *nebulous;* please clarify them.

necrology N. obituary notice; list of the dead. The *necrology* of those buried in this cemetery is available in the office.

necromancy N. black magic; dealings with the dead. Because he was able to perform feats of *necromancy,* the natives thought he was in league with the devil.

ā—ale; ă—add; ä—arm; à—ask, ê—eve; ĕ—end; ê—err, her; ə—allow; even; ī—ice; ĭ—ill; ō—oll; ŏ—odd; ô—orb; ōō—food; ŏŏ—foot, put; o—out; th—thin; ū—use; ŭ—up; zh—pleasure

nefarious ADJ. very wicked. He was universally feared because of his many *nefarious* deeds.

negation N. denial. I must accept his argument since you have been unable to present any *negation* of his evidence.

nemesis (něm´-) N. revenging agent. Captain Bligh vowed to be Christian's *nemesis*.

neophyte N. recent convert; beginner. This mountain slope contains slides that will challenge experts as well as *neophytes*.

nepotism N. favoritism (to a relative). John left his position with the company because he felt that advancement was based on *nepotism* rather than ability.

nettle V. annoy; vex. Do not let him *nettle* you with his sarcastic remarks.

nexus N. connection. I fail to see the *nexus* which binds these two widely separated events.

nib N. beak; pen point. The *nibs* of fountain pens often became clotted and corroded.

nicety (nī-sət-ē) N. precision; minute distinction. I cannot distinguish between such *niceties* of reasoning.

niggardly (nĭg´-) ADJ. meanly stingy; parsimonious. The *niggardly* pittance the widow receives from the government cannot keep her from poverty.

nocturnal ADJ. done at night. Mr. Jones obtained a watchdog to prevent the *nocturnal* raids on his chicken coops.

noisome ADJ. foul smelling; unwholesome. I never could stand the *noisome* atmosphere surrounding the slaughter houses.

nomadic ADJ. wandering. Several *nomadic* tribes of Indians would hunt in this area each year.

nonchalance N. indifference; lack of interest. Few people could understand how he could listen to the news of the tragedy with such *nonchalance;* the majority regarded him as callous and unsympathetic.

noncommittal ADJ. neutral; unpledged; undecided. We were annoyed by his *noncommittal* reply for we had been led to expect definite assurances of his approval.

nonentity N. nonexistence; person of no importance. Of course you are a *nonentity;* you will continue to be one until you prove your value to the community.

non sequitur N. a conclusion that does not follow from the facts stated. Your term paper is full of *non sequiturs;* I cannot see how you reached the conclusions you state.

nosegay N. fragrant bouquet. These spring flowers will make an attractive *nosegay*.

ā—ale; ă—add; ä—arm; à—ask, ē—eve; ĕ—end; ê—err, her; ə—allow; even; ī—ice; ĭ—ill; ō—oll; ŏ—odd; ô—orb; ōō—food; ŏŏ—foot, put; o—out; th—thin; ū—use; ŭ—up; zh—pleasure

nostalgia N. homesickness; longing for the past. The first settlers found so much work to do that they had little time for *nostalgia.*

notorious ADJ. outstandingly bad; unfavorably known. Captain Kidd was a *notorious* pirate.

novice N. beginner. Even a *novice* can do good work if he follows these simple directions.

noxious ADJ. harmful. We must trace the source of these *noxious* gases before they asphyxiate us.

nugatory ADJ. futile; worthless. This agreement is *nugatory* for no court will enforce it.

nullify V. to make invalid. Once the contract was *nullified,* it no longer had any legal force.

numismatist (-*mĭz*-) N. person who collects coins. The *numismatist* had a splendid collection of antique coins.

nurture V. bring up; feed; educate. We must *nurture* the young so that they will develop into good citizens.

nutrient ADJ. providing nourishment. During the convalescent period, the patient must be provided with *nutrient* foods. also N.

oaf N. stupid, awkward person. He called the unfortunate waiter a clumsy *oaf.*

obdurate ADJ. stubborn. He was *obdurate* in his refusal to listen to our complaints.

obeisance (ō-*bās*-) N. bow. She made an *obeisance* as the king and queen entered the room.

obelisk N. tall column tapering and ending in a pyramid. Cleopatra's Needle is an *obelisk* in Central Park, New York City.

obese (-*bēs*) ADJ. fat. It is advisable that *obese* people try to lose weight.

obfuscate V. confuse; muddle. Do not *obfuscate* the issues by dragging in irrelevant arguments.

obituary ADJ. death notice. I first learned of his death when I read the *obituary* column in the newspaper. also N.

objurgate V. scold; rebuke severely. I am afraid he will *objurgate* us publicly for this offense.

oblique ADJ. slanting; deviating from the perpendicular or from a straight line. The sergeant ordered the men to march *"Oblique* Right."

obliquity N. departure from right principles; perversity. His moral decadence was marked by his *obliquity* from the ways of integrity and honesty.

obliterate V. destroy completely. The tidal wave *obliterated* several island villages.

oblivion N. forgetfulness. His works had fallen into a state of *oblivion;* no one bothered to read them.

ā—ale; ă—add; ä—arm; à—ask; ē—eve; ĕ—end; ê—err, her; ə—allow; even; ī—ice; ĭ—ill; ō—oll; ŏ—odd; ô—orb; o͞o—food; o͝o—foot, put; o—out; th—thin; ū—use; ŭ—up; zh—pleasure

obloquy (ŏb-lə-kwē) N. slander; disgrace; infamy. I resent the *obloquy* that you are casting upon my reputation.

obnoxious ADJ. offensive. I find your behavior *obnoxious;* please amend your ways.

obsequious (-sē-) ADJ. slavishly attentive; servile; sycophantic. Nothing is more disgusting to me than the *obsequious* demeanor of the people who wait upon you.

obsession N. fixed idea; continued brooding. This *obsession* with the supernatural has made him unpopular with his neighbors.

obsolete ADJ. outmoded. That word is *obsolete;* do not use it.

obtrude V. push into prominence. The other members of the group object to the manner in which you *obtrude* your opinions into matters of no concern to you.

obtrusive ADJ. pushing forward. I found him a very *obtrusive* person, constantly seeking the center of the stage.

obtuse ADJ. blunt; stupid. Because he was so *obtuse,* he could not follow the teacher's reasoning and asked foolish questions.

obviate V. make unnecessary; get rid of. I hope this contribution will *obviate* any need for further collections of funds.

occult (-kŭlt) ADJ. mysterious; secret; supernatural. The *occult* rites of the organization were revealed only to members. also N.

oculist N. physician who specializes in treatment of the eyes. In many states, an *oculist* is the only one who may apply medicinal drops to the eyes for the purpose of examining them.

odious ADJ. hateful. I find the task of punishing you most *odious.* odium, N.

odoriferous ADJ. giving off an odor. The *odoriferous* spices stimulated his jaded appetite.

odorous ADJ. having an odor. This variety of hybrid tea rose is more *odorous* than the one you have in your garden.

officious ADJ. meddlesome; excessively trying to please. Browning informs us that the Duke resented the bough of cherries some *officious* fool brought to the Duchess.

ogle (ōg-əl) V. glance coquettishly at; make eyes at. Sitting for hours at the sidewalk cafe, the old gentleman would *ogle* the young girls and recall his youthful romances.

olfactory ADJ. concerning the sense of smell. The *olfactory* organ is the nose.

oligarchy N. government by a few. The feudal *oligarchy* was supplanted by an autocracy.

ā—ale; ǎ—add; ä—arm; à—ask, ē—eve; ĕ—end; ê—err, her; ə—allow; even; ī—ice; ǐ—ill; ō—oll; ŏ—odd; ô—orb; oo—food; oŏ—foot, put; o—out; th—thin; ū—use; ŭ—up; zh—pleasure

ominous ADJ. threatening. These clouds are *ominous;* they portend a severe storm.

omnipotent (-*nĭp*-) ADJ. all-powerful. The monarch regarded himself as *omnipotent* and responsible to no one for his acts.

omniscient (-*nĭsh -ənt*) ADJ. all-knowing. I do not pretend to be *omniscient,* but I am positive about this item.

omnivorous (-*nĭv*-) ADJ. eating both plant and animal food; devouring everything. Some animals, including man, are *omnivorous* and eat both meat and vegetables; others are either carnivorous or herbivorous.

onerous (*ŏn*-) ADJ. burdensome. He asked for an assistant because his work load was too *onerous*. onus, N.

onomatopoeia (-*pē -yə*) N. words formed in imitation of natural sounds. Words like "rustle" and "gargle" are illustrations of *onomatopoeia*.

onslaught N. vicious assault. We suffered many casualties during the unexpected *onslaught* of the enemy troops.

opalescent ADJ. iridescent. The Ancient Mariner admired the *opalescent* sheen on the water.

opaque ADJ. dark; not transparent. I want something *opaque* placed in this window so that no one will be able to watch me.

opiate N. sleep producer; deadener of pain. By such *opiates,* he made the people forget their difficulties and accept their unpleasant circumstances.

opportune ADJ. timely; well chosen. You have come at an *opportune* moment for I need a new secretary.

opprobrious ADJ. disgraceful. I find your conduct so *opprobrious* that I must exclude you from classes.

optician N. maker and seller of eyeglasses. The patient took the prescription given him by his oculist to the *optician*.

optometrist N. one who fits glasses to remedy visual defects. Although an *optometrist* is qualified to treat many eye disorders, he may not use medicines or surgery in his examinations.

ETYMOLOGY 20

NAV (ship)

> **navigate** sail a ship
> **circumnavigate** sail around the world
> **naval** pertaining to ships

ā—ale; ă—add; ä—arm; à—ask, ē—eve; ĕ—end; ê—err, her; ə—allow; even; ī—ice; ĭ—ill; ō—oll; ŏ—odd; ô—orb; ōō—food; ŏŏ—foot, put; o—out; th—thin; ū—use; ŭ—up; zh—pleasure

OMNI (all)
>   **omniscient** all knowing
>   **omnipotent** all powerful
>   **omnivorous** eating everything

OPER (to work)
>   **operate** work
>   **cooperation** working together
>   **opera** musical drama (specialized kind of work)

TEST—Word List 20—Antonyms

Each of the questions below consists of a word printed in italics, followed by five words or phrases numbered 1 to 5. Choose the numbered word or phrase which is most nearly opposite in meaning to the word in italics and write the number of your choice on your answer paper.

381. *obsession* 1 whim 2 loss 3 phobia 4 delusion 5 feud
382. *nefarious* 1 wanton 2 lacking 3 benign 4 impious 5 futile
383. *obdurate* 1 yielding 2 fleeting 3 finite 4 fascinating 5 permanent
384. *obtuse* 1 sheer 2 transparent 3 tranquil 4 timid 5 shrewd
385. *nocturnal* 1 harsh 2 marauding 3 patrolling 4 daily 5 fallow
386. *obloquy* 1 praise 2 rectangle 3 circle 4 dialogue 5 cure
387. *neophyte* 1 veteran 2 satellite 3 aspirant 4 handwriting 5 violence
388. *opportune* 1 occasional 2 fragrant 3 fragile 4 awkward 5 neglected
389. *obese* 1 skillful 2 cadaverous 3 clever 4 unpredictable 5 lucid
390. *opiate* 1 distress 2 sleep 3 stimulant 4 laziness 5 despair
391. *notorious* 1 fashionable 2 renowned 3 infamous 4 intrepid 5 invincible
392. *odious* 1 fragrant 2 redolent 3 fetid 4 delightful 5 puny
393. *nebulous* 1 starry 2 clear 3 cold 4 fundamental 5 porous
394. *omniscient* 1 sophisticated 2 ignorant 3 essential 4 trivial 5 isolated
395. *obsolete* 1 heated 2 desolate 3 renovated 4 frightful 5 automatic
396. *niggardly* 1 protected 2 biased 3 prodigal 4 bankrupt 5 placated
397. *omnipotent* 1 weak 2 democratic 3 despotic 4 passionate 5 late
398. *negation* 1 postulation 2 hypothecation 3 affirmation 4 violation 5 anticipation

ā—ale; ă—add; ä—arm; á—ask, ē—eve; ĕ—end; ê—err, her; ə—allow; even; ī—ice; ĭ—ill; ō—oll; ŏ—odd; ô—orb; o͞o—food; o͝o—foot, put; o—out; th—thin; ū—use; ŭ—up; zh—pleasure

399. *noisome* 1 quiet 2 dismayed 3 fragrant 4 sleepy 5 inquisitive
400. *obsequious* 1 successful 2 democratic 3 supercilious 4 ambitious 5 lamentable

---

Word List 21   opulence - perfunctory

opulence (ŏp-yə-) N. wealth. Visitors from Europe are amazed at the *opulence* of this country.

oratorio N. dramatic poem set to music. The Glee Club decided to present an *oratorio* during their recital.

ordinance N. decree. Passing a red light is a violation of a city *ordinance*.

orifice (ôr-) N. mouthlike opening; small opening. The Howe Caverns were discovered when someone observed that a cold wind was issuing from an *orifice* in the hillside.

ornate (-nāt'-) ADJ. excessively decorated; highly decorated. Furniture of the Baroque period can be recognized by its *ornate* carvings.

ornithologist N. scientific student of birds. Audubon's drawings of American bird life have been of interest not only to the *ornithologists* but also to the general public.

oscillate (ŏs-ə-) V. vibrate pendulumlike; waver. It is interesting to note how public opinion *oscillates* between the extremes of optimism and pessimism.

ossify V. change or harden into bone. When he called, his opponent a "bonehead," he implied that his adversary's brain had *ossified* and that he was not capable of clear thinking.

ostensible ADJ. apparent; professed; pretended. Although the *ostensible* purpose of this expedition is to discover new lands, we are really interested in finding new markets for our products.

ostentatious ADJ. showy; pretentious. The real hero is never *ostentatious*.

ostracize V. exclude from public favor; ban. As soon as the newspapers carried the story of his connection with the criminals, his friends began to *ostracize* him. ostracism, N.

overt (-vêrt) ADJ. open to view. According to the United States Constitution, a person must commit an *overt* act before he may be tried for treason.

pacifist N. one opposed to force; antimilitarist. The *pacifists* urged that we reduce our military budget and recall our troops stationed overseas.

ā—ale; ă—add; ä—arm; à—ask, ē—eve; ĕ—end; ê—err, her; ə—allow; even; ī—ice; ĭ—ill; ō—oll; ŏ—odd; ô—orb; ōō—food; ŏŏ—foot; pu̇t; o—out; th—thin; ū—use; ŭ—up; zh—pleasure

paean (pē-) N. song of praise or joy. They sang *paeans* of praise.

palatable ADJ. agreeable; pleasing to the taste. Paying taxes can never be made *palatable*.

palatial ADJ. magnificent. He proudly showed us through his *palatial* home.

palaver (-lăv′-) N. discussion; misleading speech; chatter. In spite of all the *palaver* before the meeting, the delegates were able to conduct serious negotiations when they sat down at the conference table. also V.

palette N. board on which painter mixes pigments. At the present time, art supply stores are selling a paper *palette* which may be discarded after use.

pallet N. small, poor bed. The weary traveler went to sleep on his straw *pallet*.

palliate V. ease pain; make less guilty or offensive. Doctors must *palliate* that which they cannot cure.

pallid ADJ. pale; wan. Because his occupation required that he work at night and sleep during the day, he had an exceptionally *pallid* complexion.

palpable ADJ. tangible; easily perceptible. I cannot understand how you could overlook such a *palpable* blunder.

palpitate V. throb; flutter. As he became excited, his heart began to *palpitate* more and more erratically.

paltry (pôl-) ADJ. insignificant; petty. This is a *paltry* sum to pay for such a masterpiece.

panacea (păn-ə-sē-ə) N. cure-all; remedy for all diseases. There is no easy *panacea* that will solve our complicated international situation.

pandemonium N. wild tumult. When the ships collided in the harbor, *pandemonium* broke out among the passengers.

pander V. cater to the low desires of others. Books which *pander* to man's lowest instincts should be banned.

panegyric (-jĭr-) N. formal praise. The modest hero blushed as he listened to the *panegyrics* uttered by the speakers about his valorous act.

panorama N. comprehensive view; unobstructed view in all directions. Tourists never forget the impact of their first *panorama* of the Grand Canyon.

pantomime N. acting without dialogue. Because he worked in *pantomime,* the clown could be understood wherever he appeared. also V.

ā—ale; ă—add; ä—arm; à—ask; ē—eve; ĕ—end; ê—err, her; ə—allow; even; ī—ice; ĭ—ill; ō—oll; ŏ—odd; ô—orb; ōō—food; ŏŏ—foot, put; o—out; th—thin; ū—use; ŭ—up; zh—pleasure

papyrus (*-pī-*) N. ancient paper made from stem of papyrus plant. The ancient Egyptians were among the first to write on *papyrus*.

parable N. short, simple story teaching a moral. Let us apply to our own conduct the lesson that this *parable* teaches.

paradox N. statement that looks false but is actually correct; a contradictory statement. Wordsworth's "The child is father to the man" is an example of *paradox*.

paragon N. model of perfection. The class disliked him because the teacher was always pointing to him as a *paragon* of virtue.

parallelism N. state of being parallel; similarity. There is a striking *parallelism* between the two ages.

paranoia (*-nôĭ -ə*) N. chronic form of insanity marked by delusions of grandeur or persecution. The psychiatrists analyzed his ailment as *paranoia*.

paraphernalia (*-nāl'-*) N. equipment; odds and ends. His desk was cluttered with paper, pen, ink, dictionary and other *paraphernalia* of the writing craft.

paraphrase V. restate a passage in one's own words while retaining thought of author. In 250 words or less, *paraphrase* this article. also N.

parasite N. animal or plant living on another; toady; sycophant. The tapeworm is an example of the kind of *parasite* that may infest the human body.

paregoric N. medicine that eases pain. The doctor prescribed a *paregoric* to alleviate his suffering.

pariah (*-rī-*) N. social outcast. I am not a *pariah* to be shunned and ostracized.

parlance N. language; idiom. All this legal *parlance* confuses me; I need an interpreter.

parley N. conference. The peace *parley* has not produced the anticipated truce. also V.

parody N. humorous imitation; travesty. We enjoyed the clever *parodies* of popular songs which the chorus sang.

paroxysm N. fit or attack of pain, laughter, rage. When he heard of his son's misdeeds, he was seized by a *paroxysm* of rage.

parricide N. person who murders his own father; murder of a father. The jury was shocked by the details of this vicious *parricide* and found the man who had killed his father guilty of murder in the first degree.

parry V. ward off a blow. He was content to wage a defensive battle and tried to *parry* his opponent's thrusts.

ā—ale; ă—add; ä—arm; à—ask; ē—eve; ĕ—end; ê—err, her; ə—allow; evĕn; ī—ice; ĭ—ill; ō—oll; ŏ—odd; ô—orb; ōō—food; ŏŏ—foot, put; o—out; th—thin; ū—use; ŭ—up; zh—pleasure

parsimonious ADJ. stingy; excessively frugal. His *parsimonious* nature did not permit him to enjoy any luxuries.

partiality N. inclination; bias. As a judge, not only must I be unbiased, but I must also avoid any evidence of *partiality* when I award the prize.

parvenu N. upstart; newly rich person. Although extremely wealthy, he was regarded as a *parvenu* by the aristocratic members of society.

passive ADJ. not active; acted upon. Mahatma Gandhi urged his followers to pursue a program of *passive* resistance as he felt that it was more effective than violence and acts of terrorism.

pastoral ADJ. rural. In these stories of *pastoral* life, we find an understanding of the daily tasks of country folk.

patent ADJ. open for the public to read; obvious. It was *patent* to everyone that the witness spoke the truth. also N.

pathetic ADJ. causing sadness, compassion, pity; touching. Everyone in the auditorium was weeping by the time he finished his *pathetic* tale about the orphaned boy.

pathos (*pā-thŏs*) N. tender sorrow; pity; quality in art or literature that produces these feelings. The quiet tone of *pathos* that ran through the novel never degenerated into the maudlin or the overly sentimental.

patriarch (*pā-*) N. father and ruler of a family or tribe. In many primitive tribes, the leader and lawmaker was the *patriarch*.

patricide N. person who murders his father; murder of a father. The words parricide and *patricide* have exactly the same meaning.

patrimony N. inheritance from father. As predicted by his critics, he spent his *patrimony* within two years of his father's death.

paucity N. scarcity. The poor test papers indicate that the members of this class have a *paucity* of intelligence.

peccadillo N. slight offense. If we examine these escapades carefully, we will realize that they are mere *peccadilloes* rather than major crimes.

peculate V. steal; embezzle. His crime of *peculating* public funds entrusted to his care is especially damnable.

pecuniary ADJ. pertaining to money. I never expected a *pecuniary* reward for my work in this activity.

pedagogue N. teacher; dull and formal teacher. He could never be a stuffy *pedagogue;* his classes were always lively and filled with humor.

ā—ale; ă—add; ä—arm; à—ask, ē—eve; ĕ—end; ê—err, her; ə—allow; even; ī—ice; ĭ—ill; ō—oll; ŏ—odd; ô—orb; ōō—food; ŏŏ—foot, put; o—out; th—thin; ū—use; ŭ—up; zh—pleasure

pedantic ADJ. showing off learning; bookish. What you say is *pedantic* and reveals an unfamiliarity with the realities of life. pedant, N.

pediatrician N. expert in children's diseases. The family doctor advised the parents to consult a *pediatrician* about their child's ailment.

pelf N. stolen property; money or wealth [in a contemptuous sense]. Your possessions are only *pelf;* they will give you no lasting pleasure.

pell-mell ADV. in confusion; disorderly. The excited students dashed *pell-mell* into the stadium to celebrate the victory.

pellucid (*-lōō-səd*) ADJ. transparent; limpid; easy to understand. After reading these stodgy philosophers, I find his *pellucid* style very enjoyable.

penance N. self-imposed punishment for sin. The Ancient Mariner said, "I have *penance* done and *penance* more will do," to atone for the sin of killing the albatross.

penchant (*pĕn'-chänt*) N. strong inclination; liking. He had a strong *penchant* for sculpture.

pendant ADJ. hanging down from something. Her *pendant* earrings glistened in the light.

pendent ADJ. suspended; jutting; pending. The *pendent* rock hid the entrance to the cave.

penitent ADJ. repentant. When he realized the enormity of his crime, he became remorseful and *penitent.* also N.

pensive ADJ. dreamily thoughtful; thoughtful with a hint of sadness. The *pensive* youth gazed at the painting for a long time and then sighed.

penumbra (*-nŭm-*) N. partial shadow (in an eclipse). During an eclipse, we can see an area of total darkness and a lighter area which is the *penumbra.*

penurious (*-yoŏr-*) ADJ. stingy; parsimonious. He was a *penurious* man, averse to spending money even for the necessities of life.

penury (*pĕn-*) N. extreme poverty. We find much *penury* and suffering in this slum area.

percussion ADJ. striking one object against another sharply. The drum is a *percussion* instrument.

perdition N. damnation; complete ruin. He was damned to eternal *perdition.*

peremptory (*pə-rĕmp-*) ADJ. demanding and leaving no choice. I resent your *peremptory* attitude.

ā—ale; ă—add; ä—arm; à—ask, ē—eve; ĕ—end; ê—err, her; ə—allow; even; ī—ice; ĭ—ill; ō—oll; ŏ—odd; ô—orb; ōō—food; ŏŏ—foot, put; o—out; th—thin; ū—use; ŭ—up; zh—pleasure

perennial (-*rĕn*-) N. lasting. These plants are hardy *perennials* and will bloom for many years. also ADJ.

perfidious (-*fĭd*-) ADJ. basely false. Your *perfidious* gossip is malicious and dangerous.

perfidy (*pĕr*-) N. violation of a trust. When we learned of his *perfidy*, we were shocked and dismayed.

perforce (-*fôrs*) ADV. of necessity. I must *perforce* leave, as my train is about to start.

perfunctory ADJ. superficial; listless; not thorough. He overlooked many weaknesses when he inspected the factory in his *perfunctory* manner.

ETYMOLOGY 21

PAC (peace)
        pacify make peaceful
        pacific peaceful
        pacifist person opposed to war
PEL, PULS (to drive)
        compulsion a forcing to do
        repel drive back
        expel drive out, banish

TEST—Word List 21—Synonyms and Antonyms

Each of the following questions consists of a word printed in italics, followed by five words or phrases numbered 1 to 5. Choose the numbered word or phrase which is most nearly the same as or the opposite of the word in italics and write the number of your choice on your answer paper.

401. *ostentatious* 1 occasional 2 flashy 3 intermittent 4 authentic 5 hospitable
402. *palliate* 1 smoke 2 quicken 3 substitute 4 alleviate 5 sadden
403. *pandemonium* 1 calm 2 frustration 3 efficiency 4 impishness 5 sophistication
404. *pariah* 1 village 2 suburb 3 outcast 4 disease 5 benefactor
405. *papyrus* 1 mountain 2 peninsula 3 paper 4 animal 5 pyramid
406. *penchant* 1 distance 2 imminence 3 dislike 4 attitude 5 void
407. *perennial* 1 flowering 2 recurring 3 centennial 4 partial 5 deciduous

ā—ale; ă—add; ä—arm; à—ask, ē—eve; ĕ—end; ê—err, her; ə—allow; even; ī—ice; ĭ—ill; ō—oll; ŏ—odd; ô—orb; o͞o—food; o͝o—foot, put; o—out; th—thin; ū—use; ŭ—up; zh—pleasure

408. *pellucid* 1 logistical 2 philandering 3 limpid 4 vagrant 5 warranted
409. *paucity* 1 pouch 2 peace 3 quickness 4 abundance 5 nuisance
410. *panegyric* 1 medication 2 panacea 3 rotation 4 vacillation 5 praise
411. *paean* 1 serf 2 pealing 3 lien 4 lament 5 folly
412. *opulence* 1 pessimism 2 patriotism 3 potency 4 passion 5 poverty
413. *pallet* 1 bed 2 pigment board 3 bench 4 spectrum 5 quality
414. *parable* 1 equality 2 allegory 3 frenzy 4 folly 5 cuticle
415. *paranoia* 1 fracture 2 statement 3 quantity 4 benefaction 5 sanity
416. *parsimonious* 1 grammatical 2 syntactical 3 effective 4 extravagant 5 esoteric
417. *penurious* 1 imprisoned 2 captivated 3 parsimonious 4 vacant 5 abolished
418. *perfunctory* 1 official 2 thorough 3 insipid 4 vicarious 5 distinctive
419. *orifice* 1 altar 2 gun 3 guitar 4 device 5 opening
420. *paradox* 1 exaggeration 2 contradiction 3 hyperbole 4 invective 5 poetic device

---

Word List 22   perimeter - precedent (n)

perimeter N. outer boundary. To find the *perimeter* of any quadrilateral, we add the four sides.

peripatetic (-*tĕt*-) ADJ. walking about; moving. The *peripatetic* school of philosophy derives its name from the fact that Aristotle walked with his pupils while discussing philosophy with them.

periphery (-*rĭf*-) N. edge, especially of a round surface. He sensed that there was something just beyond the *periphery* of his vision.

perjury N. false testimony while under oath. When several witnesses appeared to challenge his story, he was indicted for *perjury*.

permeable (*pêr*-) ADJ. porous; allowing passage through. Glass is *permeable* to light.

permeate V. pass through; spread. The odor of frying onions *permeated* the air.

pernicious ADJ. very destructive. He argued that these books had a *pernicious* effect on young and susceptible minds.

ā—ale; ă—add; ä—arm; à—ask, ē—eve; ĕ—end; ê—err, her; ə—allow; even; ī—ice; ĭ—ill; ō—oll; ŏ—odd; ô—orb; o͞o—food; o͝o—foot; put; o—out; th—thin; ū—use; ŭ—up; zh—pleasure

perpetrate V. commit an offense. Only an insane person could *perpetrate* such a horrible crime.

perpetual ADJ. everlasting. Ponce de Leon hoped to find *perpetual* youth.

persiflage (*pêr-sĭ-fläzh*) N. flippant conversation; banter. This *persiflage* is not appropriate when we have such serious problems to discuss.

perspicacious ADJ. having insight; penetrating; astute. We admired his *perspicacious* wisdom and sagacity.

pert ADJ. impertinent; forward. I think your *pert* and impudent remarks call for an apology.

pertinacious ADJ. stubborn; persistent. He is bound to succeed because his *pertinacious* nature will not permit him to quit.

pertinent ADJ. suitable; to the point. The lawyer wanted to know all the *pertinent* details.

perturb V. disturb greatly. I am afraid this news will *perturb* him.

perturbation N. agitation. I fail to understand why such an innocent remark should create such *perturbation*.

perusal (*-roō* -) N. reading. I am certain that you have missed important details in your rapid *perusal* of this document. peruse, V.

pervade V. spread throughout. As the news of the defeat *pervaded* the country, a feeling of anger directed at the rulers who had been the cause of the disaster grew.

perverse ADJ. stubborn; intractable. Because of your *perverse* attitude, I must rate you as deficient in cooperation.

perversion N. corruption; turning from right to wrong. Inasmuch as he had no motive for his crimes, we could not understand his *perversion*.

perversity N. stubborn maintenance of a wrong cause. I cannot forgive your *perversity* in repeating such an impossible story.

pervious ADJ. penetrable. He has a *pervious* mind and readily accepts new ideas.

pessimism N. belief that life is basically bad or evil; gloominess. The good news we have been receiving lately indicates that there is little reason for your *pessimism*.

pestilential ADJ. causing plague; baneful. People were afraid to explore the *pestilential* swamp. pestilence, N.

petrify V. turn to stone. His sudden and unexpected appearance seemed to *petrify* her.

petulant (*pĕch-ə-*) ADJ. touchy; peevish. The feverish patient was *petulant* and restless.

ā—ale; ă—add; ä—arm; à—ask, ē—eve; ĕ—end; ê—err, her; ə—allow; even; ī—ice; ĭ—ill; ō—oll; ŏ—odd; ô—orb; ōō—food; ŏŏ—foot, put; o—oŭt; th—thin; ū—use; ŭ—up; zh—pleasure

phial N. small bottle. Even though it is small, this *phial* of perfume is expensive.

philander V. make love lightly; flirt. Do not *philander* with my affections because love is too serious.

philanthropist N. lover of mankind; doer of good. As he grew older, he became famous as a *philanthropist* and benefactor of the needy.

philistine (*fǐl-ə-*) N. narrow-minded person, uncultured and exclusively interested in material gain. We need more men of culture and enlightenment; we have too many *philistines* among us.

philology N. study of language. The professor of *philology* advocated the use of Esperanto as an international language.

phlegmatic (*flĕg-măt-*) ADJ. calm; not easily disturbed. The nurse was a cheerful but *phlegmatic* person.

physiognomy N. face. He prided himself on his ability to analyze a person's character by studying his *physiognomy*.

pied (*pīd*) ADJ. variegated; multicolored. The *Pied* Piper of Hamelin got his name from the multicolored clothing he wore.

pillage (*pǐl-ǐj*) V. plunder. The enemy *pillaged* the quiet village and left it in ruins.

pillory V. punish by placing in a wooden frame and subjecting to ridicule. Even though he was mocked and *pilloried,* he maintained that he was correct in his beliefs. also N.

pinion V. restrain. They *pinioned* his arms against his body but left his legs free so that he could move about. also N.

pinnacle N. peak. We could see the morning sunlight illuminate the *pinnacle* while the rest of the mountain lay in shadow.

pious ADJ. devout. The *pious* parents gave their children a religious upbringing.

piquant (*pē-kənt*) ADJ. pleasantly tart-tasting; stimulating. The *piquant* sauce added to our enjoyment of the meal. piquancy, N.

pique (*pēk*) N. irritation; resentment. She showed her *pique* by her refusal to appear with the other contestants at the end of the contest.

piscatorial ADJ. pertaining to fishing. He spent many happy hours in his *piscatorial* activities.

pithy ADJ. concise; meaty. I enjoy reading his essays because they are always compact and *pithy*.

pittance N. a small allowance or wage. He could not live on the *pittance* he received as a pension and had to look for an additional source of revenue.

ā—ale; ă—add; ä—arm; à—ask, ē—eve; ĕ—end; ê—err, her; ə—allow; even; ī—ice; ǐ —ill; ō—oll; ŏ—odd; ô—orb; o͞o—food; o͝o—foot, put; o—out; th—thin; ū—use; ŭ—up; zh—pleasure

placate V. pacify; conciliate. The teacher tried to *placate* the angry mother.

placid ADJ. peaceful; calm. After his vacation in this *placid* section, he felt soothed and rested.

plagiarism N. theft of another's ideas or writings passed off as original. The editor recognized the *plagiarism* and rebuked the culprit who had presented the manuscript as original.

plaintive ADJ. mournful. The dove has a *plaintive* and melancholy call.

platitude N. trite remark; commonplace statement. The *platitudes* in his speech were applauded by the vast majority in his audience; only a few people perceived how trite his remarks were.

plauditory ADJ. approving; applauding. The theatrical company reprinted the *plauditory* comments of the critics in its advertisement.

plebeian (*-bē-*) ADJ. common; pertaining to the common people. His speeches were aimed at the *plebeian* minds and emotions; they disgusted the more refined.

plenary (*plē-*) ADJ. complete; full. The union leader was given *plenary* power to negotiate a new contract with the employers.

plenipotentiary ADJ. fully empowered. Since he was not given *plenipotentiary* powers by his government, he could not commit his country without consulting his superiors. also N.

plethora (*plĕth-*) N. excess; overabundance. She offered a *plethora* of reasons for her shortcomings.

plumb ADJ. checking perpendicularity; vertical. Before hanging wallpaper it is advisable to drop a *plumb* line from the ceiling as a guide. also N. and V.

podiatrist (*-dī-*) N. doctor who treats ailments of the feet. He consulted a *podiatrist* about his fallen arches.

podium N. pedestal; raised platform. The audience applauded as the conductor made his way to the *podium*.

poignant (*pôĭ-nyənt*) ADJ. keen; piercing; severe. Her *poignant* grief left her pale and weak.

politic ADJ. expedient; prudent; well devised. Even though he was disappointed, he did not think it *politic* to refuse this offer.

poltroon (*-troōn ′*) N. coward. Only a *poltroon* would so betray his comrades at such a dangerous time.

polygamist (*-lĭg-*) N. one who has more than one spouse at a time. He was arrested as a *polygamist* when his two wives filed complaints about him.

polyglot ADJ. speaking several languages. New York City is a *polyglot*

ā—ale; ă—add; ä—arm; à—ask, ē—eve; ĕ—end; ê—err, her; ə—allow; even; ī—ice; ĭ—ill; ō—oll; ŏ—odd; ô—orb; ōō—food; ŏŏ—foot, put; o—out; th—thin; ū—use; ŭ—up; zh—pleasure

community because of the thousands of immigrants who settle there.

pommel V. beat. The severity with which he was *pommeled* was indicated by the bruises he displayed on his head and face.

ponderous ADJ. weighty; unwieldly. His humor lacked the light touch; his jokes were always *ponderous*.

portend V. foretell; presage. The king did not know what these omens might *portend* and asked his soothsayers to interpret them.

portent N. sign; omen; forewarning. He regarded the black cloud as a *portent* of evil.

portentous (-*tĕnt*-) ADJ. ominous; serious. I regard our present difficulties and dissatisfactions as *portentous* omens of future disaster.

portly ADJ. stately; stout. The overweight gentleman was shown a size 44 *portly* suit.

posterity N. descendants; future generations. We hope to leave a better world to *posterity*.

posthumous (*pŏs-chə*-) ADJ. after death (as of child born after father's death or book published after author's death). The critics ignored his works during his lifetime; it was only after the *posthumous* publication of his last novel that they recognized his great talent.

postulate N. self-evident truth. We must accept these statements as *postulates* before pursuing our discussions any further. also V.

potentate (*pō̆t*-) N. monarch; sovereign. The *potentate* spent more time at Monte Carlo than he did at home with his people.

potential ADJ. expressing possibility; latent. This juvenile delinquent is a *potential* murderer. also N.

potion N. dose (of liquid). Tristan and Isolde drink a love *potion* in the first act of the opera.

potpourri (*pō-poŏ-rē* ʹ) N. heterogeneous mixture; medley. He offered a *potpourri* of folk songs from many lands.

poultice (*pōl*/-) N. soothing application applied to sore and inflamed portions of the body. He was advised to apply a flaxseed *poultice* to the inflammation.

practicable ADJ. feasible. The board of directors decided that the plan was *practicable* and agreed to undertake the project.

practical ADJ. based on experience; useful. He was a *practical* man, opposed to theory.

pragmatic ADJ. practical; concerned with practical values. This test

---

ā—ale; ă—add; ä—arm; á—ask, ē—eve; ĕ—end; ê—err, her; ə—allow; even; ī—ice; ĭ—ill; ō—oll; ŏ—odd; ô—orb; o͞o—food; o͝o—foot, pŭt; o—oŭt; th—thin; ū—use; ŭ—up; zh—pleasure

should provide us with a *pragmatic* analysis of the value of this course.

prate V. speak foolishly; boast idly. Let us not *prate* about our qualities; rather, let our virtues speak for themselves.

prattle V. babble. The little girl *prattled* endlessly about her dolls. also N.

preamble N. introductory statement. In the *Preamble* to the Constitution, the purpose of the document is set forth.

precarious ADJ. uncertain; risky. I think this stock is a *precarious* investment and advise against its purchase.

precedent (*prĕs* -) N. something preceding in time which may be used as an authority or guide for future action. This decision sets a *precedent* for future cases of a similar nature.

ETYMOLOGY 22

PET, PETIT (to seek)
> **petition** request
> **appetite** craving, desire
> **compete** vie with others

PON, POSIT (to place)
> **postpone** place after
> **preposition** that which goes before
> **positive** definite, unquestioned (definitely placed)

PORT, PORTAT (to carry)
> **portable** able to be carried
> **transport** carry across
> **export** carry out (of country)

TEST—Word List 22—Synonyms

Each of the questions below consists of a word printed in italics, followed by five words or phrases numbered 1 to 5. Choose the numbered word or phrase which is most nearly similar in meaning to the word in italics and write the number of your choice on your answer paper.

421. *pillage* 1 hoard 2 plunder 3 versify 4 denigrate 5 confide
422. *petrify* 1 turn to water 2 refine 3 turn to stone 4 turn to gas 5 repeat

---

ā—ale; ă—add; ä—arm; á—ask, ē—eve; ĕ—end; ê—err, her; ə—allow; even; ī—ice; ĭ—ill; ō—oll; ŏ—odd; ô—orb; ōō—food; ŏŏ—foot, put; o—out; th—thin; ū—use; ŭ—up; zh—pleasure

423. *pernicious* 1 practical 2 comparative 3 destructive 4 tangible 5 detailed
424. *physiognomy* 1 posture 2 head 3 physique 4 face 5 size
425. *pertinent* 1 understood 2 living 3 discontented 4 puzzling 5 relevant
426. *permeate* 1 enlarge 2 produce 3 prod 4 disfigure 5 spread
427. *phlegmatic* 1 calm 2 cryptic 3 practical 4 salivary 5 dishonest
428. *pertinacious* 1 sticking 2 consumptive 3 superficial 4 skilled 5 advertised
429. *permeable* 1 perishable 2 effective 3 plodding 4 porous 5 lasting
430. *philander* 1 flirt 2 quiz 3 decline 4 profit 5 quarrel
431. *pert* 1 impertinent 2 perishable 3 moral 4 deliberate 5 stubborn
432. *peripatetic* 1 worldly 2 moving 3 disarming 4 seeking 5 inherent
433. *petulant* 1 angry 2 moral 3 declining 4 underhanded 5 touchy
434. *perpetual* 1 eternal 2 standard 3 serious 4 industrial 5 interpretive
435. *plaintive* 1 mournful 2 senseless 3 persistent 4 rural 5 evasive
436. *pinion* 1 express 2 report 3 reveal 4 submit 5 restrain
437. *placate* 1 determine 2 transmit 3 pacify 4 allow 5 define
438. *pinnacle* 1 foothills 2 card game 3 pass 4 taunt 5 peak
439. *pique* 1 pyramid 2 revolt 3 resentment 4 struggle 5 inventory
440. *pious* 1 historic 2 devout 3 multiple 4 fortunate 5 authoritative

---

Word List 23   precedent (adj.) - purview

precedent (*-sēd-*) ADJ. preceding in time, rank, etc. Our discussions, *precedent* to this event, certainly did not give you any reason to believe that we would adopt your proposal.

precept N. practical rule guiding conduct. "Love thy neighbor as thyself" is a worthwhile *precept.*

precipitate (*-sĭp -ət-ət*) ADJ. headlong; rash. Do not be *precipitate* in this matter; investigate further.

precipitate (*-sĭp -ə-tāt*) V. throw headlong; hasten. We must be patient as we cannot *precipitate* these results.

precipitous ADJ. steep. This hill is difficult to climb because it is so *precipitous.*

precise ADJ. exact. If you don't give me *precise* directions and a map, I'll never find your place.

ā—ale; ă—add; ä—arm; à—ask, ē—eve; ĕ—end; ê—err, her; ə—allow; even, ī—ice; ĭ —ill; ō—oll; ŏ—odd; ô—orb; ōō—food; oŏ—foot, put; o—oūt; th—thin; ū—use; ŭ—up; zh—pleasure

preclude V. make impossible; eliminate. This contract does not *preclude* my being employed by others at the same time that I am working for you.

precocious ADJ. developed ahead of time. By his rather adult manner of discussing serious topics, the child demonstrated that he was *precocious*.

precursor N. forerunner. Gray and Burns were *precursors* of the Romantic Movement in English literature.

predatory ADJ. plundering. The hawk is a *predatory* bird.

predilection (-*ĕk*-) N. partiality; preference. Although the artist used various media from time to time, he had a *predilection* for watercolor.

preeminent (*prē-ĕm*-) ADJ. outstanding; superior. The king traveled to Boston because he wanted the *preeminent* surgeon in the field to perform the operation.

prefatory (*prĕf*-) ADJ. introductory. The chairman made a few *prefatory* remarks before he called on the first speaker.

prelude N. introduction; forerunner. I am afraid that this border raid is the *prelude* to more serious attacks.

premeditate V. plan in advance. He had *premeditated* the murder for months, reading about common poisons and buying weed-killer that contained arsenic.

premonition N. forewarning. We ignored these *premonitions* of disaster because they appeared to be based on childish fears.

preponderate V. be superior in power; outweigh. I feel confident that the forces of justice will *preponderate* eventually in this dispute.

preposterous ADJ. absurd; ridiculous. The excuse he gave for his lateness was so *preposterous* that everyone laughed.

presage (*prĕs*-) V. foretell. The vultures flying overhead *presaged* the discovery of the corpse in the desert.

presentiment (-*zĕnt*-) N. premonition; foreboding. Hamlet felt a *presentiment* about his meeting with Laertes.

presumption N. arrogance; effrontery. She had the *presumption* to disregard our advice.

pretentious ADJ. ostentatious; ambitious. I do not feel that your limited resources will permit you to carry out such a *pretentious* program.

prevaricate V. lie. Some people believe that to *prevaricate* in a good cause is justifiable and regard the statement as a "white lie."

prim ADJ. very precise and formal; exceedingly proper. Many people

---

ā—ale; ă—add; ä—arm; à—ask, ē—eve; ĕ—end; ê—err, her; ə—allow; even; ī—ice; ĭ—ill; ō—oll; ŏ—odd; ô—orb; ōō—food; ŏŏ—foot, put; o—out; th—thin; ū—use; ŭ—up; zh—pleasure

commented on the contrast between the *prim* attire of the young lady and the inappropriate clothing worn by her escort.

primordial (*prī-môrd*-) ADJ. existing at the beginning (of time); rudimentary. The Neanderthal Man is one of our *primordial* ancestors.

pristine ADJ. characteristic of earlier times; primitive; unspoiled. This area has been preserved in all its *pristine* wildness.

privy ADJ. secret; hidden; not public. We do not care for *privy* chamber government.

probity N. uprightness; incorruptibility. Everyone took his *probity* for granted; his defalcations, therefore, shocked us all.

proboscis (*-bŏs* *-əs*) N. long snout; nose. The elephant uses his *proboscis* to handle things and carry them from place to place.

proclivity N. inclination; natural tendency. He has a *proclivity* to grumble.

procrastinate V. postpone; delay. It is wise not to *procrastinate;* otherwise, we find ourselves bogged down in a mass of work which should have been finished long ago.

prodigal ADJ. wasteful; reckless with money. The *prodigal* son squandered his inheritance. also N.

prodigious ADJ. marvelous; enormous. He marveled at her *prodigious* appetite.

profane V. violate; desecrate. Tourists are urged not to *profane* the sanctity of holy places by wearing improper garb. also ADJ.

profligate ADJ. dissipated; wasteful; licentious. In this *profligate* company, he lost all sense of decency. also N.

profusion N. lavish expenditure; overabundant condition. Seldom have I seen food and drink served in such *profusion.*

progenitor N. ancestor. We must not forget the teachings of our *progenitors* in our desire to appear modern.

progeny N. children; offspring. He was proud of his *progeny* but regarded George as the most promising of all his children.

prognosis N. forecasted course of a disease; prediction. If the doctor's *prognosis* is correct, the patient will be in a coma for at least twenty-four hours.

prognosticate V. predict. I *prognosticate* disaster unless we change our wasteful ways.

prolific ADJ. abundantly fruitful. He was a *prolific* writer and wrote as many as three books a year.

prolix ADJ. verbose; drawn out. His *prolix* arguments irritated the jury. prolixity, N.

promiscuous ADJ. mixed indiscriminately; haphazard; irregular. In the

ā—ale; ă—add; ä—arm; à—ask, ē—eve; ĕ—end; ê—err, her; ə—allow; even; ī—ice; ĭ—ill; ō—oll; ŏ—odd; ô—orb; ōō—food; ŏŏ—foot, put; o—out; th—thin; ū—use; ŭ—up; zh—pleasure

opera *La Boheme,* we get a picture of the *promiscuous* life led by the young artists of Paris.

promontory N. headland. They erected a lighthouse on the *promontory* to warn approaching ships of their nearness to the shore.

promulgate V. make known by official proclamation or publication. As soon as the Civil Service Commission *promulgates* the names of the successful candidates, we shall begin to hire members of our staff.

prone ADJ. inclined to; prostrate. She was *prone* to sudden fits of anger.

propagate V. multiply; spread. I am sure disease must *propagate* in such unsanitary and crowded areas.

propensity N. natural inclination. I dislike your *propensity* to belittle every contribution he makes to our organization.

propitiate V. appease. The natives offered sacrifices to *propitiate* the gods.

propitious ADJ. favorable; kindly. I think it is advisable that we wait for a more *propitious* occasion to announce our plans.

propound V. put forth for analysis. In your discussion, you have *propounded* several questions; let us consider each one separately.

propriety N. fitness; correct conduct. I want you to behave at this dinner with *propriety;* don't embarrass me.

propulsive ADJ. driving forward. The jet plane has a greater *propulsive* power than the engine-driven plane.

prorogue (*prə-rōg*) V. dismiss parliament; end officially. It was agreed that the king could not *prorogue* parliament until it had been in session for at least fifty days.

prosaic (*prō-zā -ĭk*) ADJ. commonplace; dull. I do not like this author because he is so unimaginative and *prosaic.*

proscribe V. ostracize; banish; outlaw. Antony, Octavius, and Lepidus *proscribed* all those who had conspired against Julius Caesar.

prosody (*prŏs -*) N. the art of versification. This book on *prosody* contains a rhyming dictionary as well as samples of the various verse forms.

prostrate V. stretch out full on ground. He *prostrated* himself before the idol. also ADJ.

protégé (*prōt -ə-zhā*) N. person under the protection and support of a patron. Cyrano de Bergerac refused to be a *protégé* of Cardinal Richelieu.

ā—ale; ă—add; ä—arm; à—ask, ē—eve; ĕ—end; ê—err, her; ə—allow; even; ī—ice; ĭ—ill; ō—oll; ŏ—odd; ô—orb; ōō—food; ŏŏ—foot, put; o—out; th—thin; ū—use; ŭ—up; zh—pleasure

protocol N. diplomatic etiquette. We must run this state dinner according to *protocol* if we are to avoid offending any of our guests.

protract V. prolong. Do not *protract* this phone conversation as I expect an important business call within the next few minutes.

protrude V. stick out. His fingers *protruded* from the holes in his gloves.

provender (*prŏv*-) N. dry food; fodder. I am not afraid of a severe winter because I have stored a large quantity of *provender* for the cattle.

provident ADJ. displaying foresight; thrifty; preparing for emergencies. In his usual *provident* manner, he had insured himself against this type of loss.

proviso (-*vī-zō*) N. stipulation. I am ready to accept your proposal with the *proviso* that you meet your obligations within the next two weeks.

provocation N. cause for anger or retaliation. In order to prevent a sudden outbreak of hostilities, we must give our foe no *provocation*.

proximity N. nearness. The deer sensed the hunter's *proximity* and bounded away.

proxy N. authorized agent. Please act as my *proxy* and vote for this slate of candidates.

prurient ADJ. based on lascivious thoughts. The police attempted to close the theater where the *prurient* film was being presented.

pseudonym N. pen name. Samuel Clemens' *pseudonym* was Mark Twain.

psyche (*sī-kē*) N. soul; mind. It is difficult to delve into the *psyche* of a human being.

psychiatrist N. a doctor who treats mental diseases. A *psychiatrist* often needs long conferences with his patient before a diagnosis can be made.

puerile (*pūr-əl*) ADJ. childish. His *puerile* pranks sometimes offended his serious-minded friends.

pugnacious ADJ. combative; disposed to fight. As a child he was *pugnacious* and fought with everyone.

puissant (*pwĭs*-) ADJ. powerful; strong; potent. We must keep his friendship for he will make a *puissant* ally.

pulchritude N. beauty; comeliness. I do not envy the judges who have to select this year's Miss America from this collection of female *pulchritude*.

ā—ale; ă—add; ä—arm; à—ask, ē—eve; ĕ—end; ê—err, her; ə—allow; even; ī—ice; ĭ—ill; ō—oll; ŏ—odd; ô—orb; ōō—food; ŏŏ—foot, p<u>u</u>t; o—o<u>u</u>t; th—<u>th</u>in; ū—use; ŭ—<u>u</u>p; zh—plea<u>s</u>ure

pulmonary ADJ. pertaining to the lungs. In his researches on *pulmonary* diseases, he discovered many facts about the lungs of animals and human beings.

pulsate V. throb. We could see the blood vessels in his temple *pulsate* as he became more angry.

punctilious ADJ. laying stress on niceties of conduct, form; precise. We must be *punctilious* in our planning of this affair, for any error may be regarded as a personal affront.

pungent (*pŭn-jənt*) ADJ. stinging; caustic. The *pungent* aroma of the smoke made me cough.

punitive (*pū-*) ADJ. punishing. He asked for *punitive* measures against the offender.

puny ADJ. insignificant; tiny; weak. Our *puny* efforts to stop the flood were futile.

purgatory N. place of spiritual expiation. In this *purgatory,* he could expect no help from his comrades.

purge V. clean by removing impurities; to clear of charges. If you are to be *purged* of the charge of contempt of Congress, you must be willing to answer the questions previously asked. also N.

purloin V. steal. In the story, "The *Purloined* Letter," Poe points out that the best hiding place is often the most obvious place.

purport N. intention; meaning. If the *purport* of your speech was to arouse the rabble, you succeeded admirably. also V.

purveyor N. furnisher of foodstuffs; caterer. As *purveyor* of rare wines and viands, he traveled through France and Italy every year in search of new products to sell.

purview N. scope. The sociological implications of these inventions are beyond the *purview* of this book.

ETYMOLOGY 23

PRAEDO, PREDA (prey)
  predacious living by prey
  predatory pillaging, plundering
PRE (before) prefix
  precocious ahead of time
  precursor forerunner
PRO (before, toward) prefix
  prognosticate foretell
  propulsive driving forward

ā—ale; ă—add; ä—arm; à—ask, ē—eve; ĕ—end; ê—err, her; ə—allow;
even; ī—ice; ĭ—ill; ō—oll; ŏ—odd; ô—orb; ōō—food; ŏŏ—foot, put;
o—oŭt; th—thin; ū—use; ŭ—up; zh—pleasure

TEST—Word List 23—Antonyms

Each of the questions below consists of a word printed in italics, followed by five words or phrases numbered 1 to 5. Choose the numbered word or phrase which is most nearly opposite in meaning to the word in italics and write the number of your choice on your answer paper.

441. *precipitate* 1 fast 2 anticipatory 3 cautious 4 considerate 5 dry
442. *prim* 1 informal 2 prior 3 exterior 4 private 5 cautious
443. *protract* 1 make circular 2 shorten 3 further 4 retrace 5 involve
444. *prelude* 1 intermezzo 2 overture 3 aria 4 aftermath 5 duplication
445. *probity* 1 regret 2 assumption 3 corruptibility 4 extent 5 upswing
446. *pretentious* 1 ominous 2 calm 3 unassuming 4 futile 5 volatile
447. *prodigal* 1 wandering 2 thrifty 3 consistent 4 compatible 5 errant
448. *prosaic* 1 pacified 2 reprieved 3 pensive 4 imaginative 5 rhetorical
449. *propitious* 1 rich 2 induced 3 promoted 4 indicative 5 unfavorable
450. *puerile* 1 fragrant 2 adult 3 lonely 4 feminine 5 masterly
451. *pulchritude* 1 ugliness 2 notoriety 3 bestiality 4 masculinity 5 servitude
452. *prefatory* 1 outstanding 2 magnificent 3 conclusive 4 intelligent 5 predatory
453. *punctilious* 1 happy 2 active 3 vivid 4 careless 5 futile
454. *puissant* 1 pouring 2 fashionable 3 articulate 4 healthy 5 weak
455. *prolix* 1 stupid 2 indifferent 3 redundant 4 livid 5 pithy
456. *profane* 1 sanctify 2 desecrate 3 define 4 manifest 5 urge
457. *presumption* 1 assertion 2 activation 3 motivation 4 proposition 5 humility
458. *pristine* 1 cultivated 2 condemned 3 crude 4 cautious 5 critical
459. *prodigious* 1 infinitesimal 2 indignant 3 indifferent 4 indisposed 5 insufficient
460. *punitive* 1 large 2 vindictive 3 rewarding 4 restive 5 languishing

---

Word List 24   pusillanimous - reiterate

pusillanimous ADJ. cowardly; fainthearted. You should be ashamed of your *pusillanimous* conduct during this dispute.

ā—ale; ă—add; ä—arm; à—ask, ē—eve; ĕ—end; ê—err, her; ə—allow; even; ī—ice; ĭ—ill; ō—oll; ŏ—odd; ô—orb; ōō—food; ŏŏ—foot, put; o—out; th—thin; ū—use; ŭ—up; zh—pleasure

putrid ADJ. foul; rotten; decayed. The gangrenous condition of the wound was indicated by the *putrid* smell when the bandages were removed. putrescence, N.

pyromaniac N. person with an insane desire to set things on fire. The detectives searched the area for the *pyromaniac* who had set these costly fires.

quack N. charlatan; impostor. Do not be misled by the exorbitant claims of this *quack*.

quaff (kwäf) V. drink with relish. As we *quaffed* our ale, we listened to the gay songs of the students in the tavern.

quail V. cower; lose heart. He was afraid that he would *quail* in the face of danger.

qualms N. misgivings. His *qualms* of conscience had become so great that he decided to abandon his plans.

quandary N. dilemma. When the two colleges to which he had applied accepted him, he was in a *quandary* as to which one he should attend.

quay (kē) N. dock; landing place. Because of the captain's carelessness, the ship crashed into the *quay*.

quell V. put down; quiet. The police used fire hoses and tear gas to *quell* the rioters.

querulous ADJ. fretful; whining. His classmates were repelled by his *querulous* and complaining statements.

quibble V. equivocate; play on words. Do not *quibble;* I want a straightforward and definite answer. also N.

quiescent (kwī'-ēs'-) ADJ. at rest; dormant. After this geyser erupts, it will remain *quiescent* for twenty-four hours.

quietude (kwī-ə-tūd') N. tranquillity. He was impressed by the air of *quietude* and peace that pervaded the valley.

quintessence N. purest and highest embodiment. These books display the *quintessence* of wit.

quip N. taunt. You are unpopular because you are too free with your *quips* and sarcastic comments. also V.

quirk N. startling twist; caprice. By a *quirk* of fate, he found himself working for the man whom he had discharged years before.

qui vive (kē-vēv) N. wide awake; expectant. Let us be on the *qui vive*.

quixotic (kwĭk-sŏt'-) ADJ. idealistic but impractical. He is constantly presenting these *quixotic* schemes.

quizzical ADJ. bantering; comical; humorously serious. Will Rogers' *quizzical* remarks endeared him to his audiences.

rabid (răb'-) ADJ. like a fanatic; furious. He was a *rabid* follower of the

ā—ale; ă—add; ä—arm; à—ask, ē—eve; ĕ—end; ê—err, her; ə—allow; even; ī—ice; ĭ—ill; ō—oll; ŏ—odd; ô—orb; ōō—food; ŏŏ—foot, put; o—out; th—thin; ū—use; ŭ—up; zh—pleasure

Dodgers and watched them play whenever he could go to the ball park.

ragamuffin N. person wearing tattered clothes. He felt sorry for the *ragamuffin* who was begging for food and gave him money to buy a meal.

ramification N. branching out; subdivision. We must examine all the *ramifications* of this problem.

ramp N. slope; inclined plane. The house was built with *ramps* instead of stairs in order to enable the man in the wheelchair to move easily from room to room and floor to floor.

rampant ADJ. rearing up on hind legs; unrestrained. The *rampant* weeds in the garden killed all the flowers which had been planted in the spring.

rancid ADJ. having the odor of stale fat. A *rancid* odor filled the ship's galley.

rancor N. bitterness; hatred. Let us forget our *rancor* and cooperate in this new endeavor.

rant V. rave; speak bombastically. As we heard him *rant* on the platform, we could not understand his strange popularity with many people.

rapacious ADJ. excessively grasping; plundering. Hawks and other *rapacious* birds may be killed at any time.

rapprochement (răp-rō sh-mǎn) N. reconciliation. Both sides were eager to effect a *rapprochement* but did not know how to undertake a program designed to bring about harmony.

rarefied ADJ. made less dense [of a gas]. The mountain climbers had difficulty breathing in the *rarefied* atmosphere.

ratiocination N. reasoning; act of drawing conclusions from premises. Poe's "The Gold Bug" is a splendid example of the author's use of *ratiocination*.

rationalize V. reason; justify an improper act. Do not try to *rationalize* your behavior by blaming your companions.

raucous ADJ. harsh and shrill. His *raucous* laughter irritated me.

ravage (răv-) V. plunder; despoil. The marauding army *ravaged* the countryside.

ravening (răv-) ADJ. rapacious; seeking prey. We kept our fires burning all night to frighten the *ravening* wolves.

ravenous (răv-) ADJ. extremely hungry. The *ravenous* dog upset several garbage pails in its search for food.

raze (rāz) V. destroy completely. The owners intend to *raze* the hotel and erect an office building on the site.

ā—ale; ă—add; ä—arm; à—ask, ē—eve; ĕ—end; ê—err, her; ə—allow; even; ī—ice; ĭ—ill; ō—oll; ŏ—odd; ô—orb; ōo—food; oŏ—foot, put; o—out; th—thin; ū—use; ŭ—up; zh—pleasure

realm N. kingdom; sphere. The *realm* of possibilities for the new invention was endless.

rebate N. discount. We offer a *rebate* of ten percent to those who pay cash.

recalcitrant ADJ. obstinately stubborn. Donkeys are reputed to be the most *recalcitrant* of animals.

recant V. repudiate; withdraw previous statement. Unless you *recant* your confession, you will be punished severely.

recapitulate V. summarize. Let us *recapitulate* what has been said thus far before going ahead.

recession N. withdrawal; retreat. The *recession* of the troops from the combat area was completed in an orderly manner.

recipient N. receiver. Although he had been the *recipient* of many favors, he was not grateful to his benefactor.

reciprocal ADJ. mutual; exchangeable; interacting. The two nations signed a *reciprocal* trade agreement.

reciprocate V. repay in kind. If they attack us, we shall be compelled to *reciprocate* and bomb their territory.

recluse (*rĕk-lōōs*) N. hermit. The *recluse* lived in a hut in the forest.

reconcile V. make friendly after quarrel; correct inconsistencies. Each month we *reconcile* our checkbook with the bank statement.

recondite ADJ. abstruse; profound; secret. He read many *recondite* books in order to obtain the material for his scholarly thesis.

reconnaissance N. survey of enemy by soldiers; reconnoitering. If you encounter any enemy soldiers during your *reconnaissance*, capture them for questioning.

recourse N. resorting to help when in trouble. The boy's only *recourse* was to appeal to his father for aid.

recreant (*rĕk'-*) N. coward; betrayer of faith. The religious people ostracized the *recreant* who had abandoned their faith.

recrimination N. countercharges. Loud and angry *recriminations* were her answer to his accusations.

rectify V. correct. I want to *rectify* my error before it is too late.

rectitude N. uprightness. He was renowned for his *rectitude* and integrity.

recumbent ADJ. reclining; lying down completely or in part. The command "AT EASE" does not permit you to take a *recumbent* position.

recuperate (*rĭ-kū-*) V. recover. The doctors were worried because the patient did not *recuperate* as rapidly as they had expected.

ā—ale; ă—add; ä—arm; à—ask, ē—eve; ĕ—end; ê—err, hêr; ə—allow; ēven; ī—ice; ĭ—ill; ō—oll; ŏ—odd; ô—orb; ōō—food; ŏŏ—foot; put; o—out; th—thin; ū—use; ŭ—up; zh—pleasure

recurrent ADJ. occurring again and again. These *recurrent* attacks disturbed us and we consulted a physician.

redolent (*rĕd-*) ADJ. fragrant; odorous; suggestive of an odor. Even though it is February, the air is *redolent* of spring.

redoubtable ADJ. formidable; causing fear. The neighboring countries tried not to offend the Russians because they could be *redoubtable* foes.

redress (*-drĕs*) N. remedy; compensation. Do you mean to tell me that I can get no *redress* for my injuries? also V.

redundant ADJ. superfluous; excessively wordy; repetitious. Your composition is *redundant;* you can easily reduce its length.

reek V. emit (odor). The room *reeked* with stale tobacco smoke. also N.

refection N. slight refreshment. In our anxiety to reach our destination as rapidly as possible, we stopped on the road for only a quick *refection.*

refectory N. dining hall. In this huge *refectory,* we can feed the entire student body at one sitting.

refraction N. bending of a ray of light. When you look at a stick inserted in water, it looks bent because of the *refraction* of the light by the water.

refractory ADJ. stubborn; unmanageable. The *refractory* horse was eliminated from the race.

refulgent ADJ. radiant. We admired the *refulgent* moon and watched it for a while.

refutation N. disproof of opponents' arguments. I will wait until I hear the *refutation* before deciding whom to favor.

regal ADJ. royal. He has a *regal* manner.

regale (*-gāl*) V. entertain. John *regaled* us with tales of his adventures in Africa.

regatta (*-găt'-*) N. boat or yacht race. Many boating enthusiasts followed the *regatta* in their own yachts.

regeneration N. spiritual rebirth. Modern penologists strive for the *regeneration* of the prisoners.

regime (*rā-zhēm*) N. method or system of government. When a Frenchman mentions the Old *Regime,* he refers to the government existing before the revolution.

regimen (*rĕj-*) N. prescribed diet and habits. I doubt whether the results warrant our living under such a strict and inflexible *regimen.*

rehabilitate V. restore to proper condition. We must *rehabilitate* those whom we send to prison.

ā—ale; ă—add; ä—arm; à—ask, ē—eve; ĕ—end; ê—err, her; ə—allow; even; ī—ice; ĭ —ill; ō—oll; ŏ—odd; ô—orb; ōō—food; oŏ—foot, pŭt; o—oūt; th—thin; ū—use; ŭ—up; zh—pleasure

reimburse v. repay. Let me know what you have spent and I will *reimburse* you.

reiterate v. repeat. I shall *reiterate* this message until all have understood it.

ETYMOLOGY 24

PUT, PUTAT (to trim, to calculate)
        computation a reckoning
        amputate cut off
        putative supposed (calculated)
QUAER, QUAESIT (to ask)
        inquiry investigation
        inquisitive questioning
        query question

TEST—Word List 24—Synonyms and Antonyms

Each of the questions below consists of a word printed in italics, followed by five words or phrases numbered 1 to 5. Choose the numbered word or phrase which is most nearly the same as or the opposite of the word in italics and write the number of your choice on your answer paper.

461. *regal* 1 oppressive 2 common 3 major 4 basic 5 entertaining
462. *rebate* 1 relinquish 2 settle 3 discount 4 cancel 5 elicit
463. *quandary* 1 quagmire 2 dilemma 3 epigram 4 enemy 5 finish
464. *refractory* 1 articulate 2 sinkable 3 vaunted 4 useless 5 manageable
465. *raze* 1 shave 2 heckle 3 finish 4 tear down 5 write
466. *putrid* 1 sick 2 lovely 3 aromatic 4 arrogant 5 humid
467. *recuperate* 1 reenact 2 engage 3 recapitulate 4 recover 5 encounter
468. *ravage* 1 rank 2 revive 3 plunder 4 pillory 5 age
469. *quaff* 1 drug 2 imbibe 3 seal 4 scale 5 joke
470. *rectify* 1 remedy 2 avenge 3 create 4 assemble 5 attribute
471. *raucous* 1 mellifluous 2 uncooked 3 realistic 4 veracious 5 anticipating
472. *pusillanimous* 1 poverty-stricken 2 chained 3 posthumous 4 cowardly 5 strident

---

ā—ale; ă—add; ä—arm; à—ask, ē—eve; ĕ—end; ê—err, her; ə—allow; even; ī—ice; ĭ—ill; ō—oll; ŏ—odd; ô—orb; ōō—food; ŏŏ—foot, put; o—out; th—thin; ū—use; ŭ—up; zh—pleasure

473. *recreant* 1 vacationing 2 faithful 3 indifferent 4 obliged 5 reviving
474. *quixotic* 1 rapid 2 exotic 3 longing 4 timid 5 idealistic
475. *rehabilitate* 1 clothe 2 destroy 3 avenge 4 vanish 5 embarrass
476. *qui vive* 1 alive 2 fast 3 gloomy 4 vivid 5 awake
477. *reimburse* 1 remunerate 2 constitute 3 dip 4 demolish 5 patronize
478. *regatta* 1 impertinence 2 boat race 3 satisfaction 4 saturation 5 quiz
479. *reiterate* 1 gainsay 2 revive 3 revenge 4 repeat 5 return
480. *refulgent* 1 overflowing 2 effortless 3 dim 4 noisy 5 snoring

---

Word List 25   rejuvenate - rostrum

rejuvenate V. make young again. The charlatan claimed that his elixir would *rejuvenate* the aged and weary.

relegate V. banish; consign to inferior position. If we *relegate* these experienced people to positions of unimportance because of their political persuasions, we shall lose the services of valuably trained personnel.

relevancy N. pertinence; reference to the case in hand. I was impressed by the *relevancy* of your remarks. relevant, ADJ.

relinquish V. abandon. I will *relinquish* my claims to this property if you promise to retain my employees.

relish V. savor; enjoy. I *relish* a good joke as much as anyone else. also N.

remediable (-*mēd*-) ADJ. reparable. Let us be grateful that the damage is *remediable*.

remedial ADJ. curative; corrective. Because he was a slow reader, he decided to take a course in *remedial* reading.

reminiscence N. recollection. Her *reminiscences* of her experiences are so fascinating that she ought to write a book.

remiss ADJ. negligent. He was accused of being *remiss* in his duty.

remnant N. remainder. I suggest that you wait until the store places the *remnants* of these goods on sale.

remonstrate (-*mŏn*-) V. protest. I must *remonstrate* about the lack of police protection in this area.

remunerative ADJ. compensating; rewarding. I find my new work so

---

ā—ale; ă—add; ä—arm; à—ask, ē—eve; ĕ—end; ê—err, her; ə—allow; even; ī—ice; ĭ—ill; ō—oll; ŏ—odd; ô—orb; ōō—food; ŏŏ—foot, put; o—oūt; th—thin; ū—use; ŭ—up; zh—pleasure

remunerative that I may not return to my previous employment. remuneration, N.

rend V. split; tear apart. In his grief, he tried to *rend* his garments.

render V. deliver; provide; represent. He *rendered* aid to the needy and indigent.

rendezvous (rŏn-dĭ-vōō) N. meeting place. The two fleets met at the *rendezvous* at the appointed time. also V.

renegade N. deserter; apostate. Because he refused to support his fellow members in their drive, he was shunned as a *renegade*.

renounce V. abandon; discontinue; disown; repudiate. Joan of Arc refused to *renounce* her statements even though she knew she would be burned at the stake as a witch.

renovate V. restore to good condition; renew. They claim that they can *renovate* worn shoes so that they look like new ones.

renunciation N. giving up; renouncing. Do not sign this *renunciation* of your right to sue until you have consulted a lawyer.

reparable (rĕp-) ADJ. capable of being repaired. Fortunately, the damages we suffered in the accident were *reparable*.

reparation N. amends; compensation. At the peace conference, the defeated country promised to pay *reparations* to the victors.

repartee (rĕp-ər-tē) N. clever reply. He was famous for his witty *repartee* and his sarcasm.

repellent ADJ. driving away; unattractive. Mosquitoes find the odor so *repellent* that they leave any spot where this liquid has been sprayed. also N.

repercussion N. rebound; reverberation; reaction. I am afraid that this event will have serious *repercussions*.

repertoire N. list of works of music, drama, etc., a performer is prepared to present. The opera company decided to include *Madame Butterfly* in its *repertoire* for the following season.

replenish V. fill up again. The end of rationing enabled us to *replenish* our supply of canned food.

replete (-plēt) ADJ. filled to capacity; abundantly supplied. This book is *replete* with humorous situations.

replica N. copy. Are you going to hang this *replica* of the Declaration of Independence in the classroom or in the auditorium?

repository N. storehouse. Libraries are *repositories* of the world's best thoughts.

reprehensible ADJ. deserving blame. Your vicious conduct in this situation is *reprehensible*.

ā—ale; ă—add; ä—arm; à—ask, ē—eve; ĕ—end; ê—err, her; ə—allow; even; ī—ice; i—ill; ō—oll; ŏ—odd; ô—orb; ōo—food; oŏ—foot, put; o—out; th—thin; ū—use; ŭ—up; zh—pleasure

reprieve N. temporary stay. During the twenty-four-hour *reprieve,* the lawyers sought to make the stay of execution permanent. also V.

reprimand V. reprove severely. I am afraid that my parents will *reprimand* me when I show them my report card. also N.

reprisal N. retaliation. I am confident that we are ready for any *reprisals* the enemy may undertake.

reprobation N. severe disapproval. The students showed their *reprobation* of his act by refusing to talk with him.

repudiate V. disown; disavow. He announced that he would *repudiate* all debts incurred by his wife.

repugnance N. loathing. She looked at the snake with *repugnance.*

requiem N. mass for the dead; dirge. They played Mozart's *Requiem* at the funeral.

requisite N. necessary requirement. Many colleges state that a student must offer three years of a language as a *requisite* for admission.

requite V. repay; revenge. The wretch *requited* his benefactors by betraying them.

rescind V. cancel. Because of public resentment, the king had to *rescind* his order.

rescission N. abrogation; annulment. The *rescission* of the unpopular law was urged by all political parties.

resonant (*rĕz -*) ADJ. echoing; resounding; possessing resonance. His *resonant* voice was particularly pleasing.

respite (*rĕs -pət*) N. delay in punishment; interval of relief; rest. The judge granted the condemned man a *respite* to enable his attorneys to file an appeal.

resplendent ADJ. brilliant; lustrous. The toreador wore a *resplendent* costume.

responsiveness N. state of reacting readily to appeals, orders, etc. The audience cheered and applauded, delighting the performers by its *responsiveness.*

restitution N. reparation; indemnification. He offered to make *restitution* for the window broken by his son.

restive ADJ. unmanageable; fretting under control. We must quiet the *restive* animals.

resuscitate V. revive. The lifeguard tried to *resuscitate* the drowned child by applying artificial respiration.

retaliate V. repay in kind (usually for bad treatment). Fear that we will *retaliate* immediately deters our foe from attacking us.

ā—ale; ă—add; ä—arm; ä—ask, ē—eve; ĕ—end; ê—err, her; ə—allow; even; ī—ice; ĭ—ill; ō—oll; ŏ—odd; ô—orb; o͞o—food; o͝o—foot, put; o—out; th—thin; ū—use; ŭ—up; zh—pleasure

retentive ADJ. holding; having a good memory. The pupil did not need to spend much time in study as he had a *retentive* mind.

reticence N. reserve; uncommunicativeness; inclination to be silent. Because of the *reticence* of the key witness, the case against the defendant collapsed.

retinue N. following; attendants. The queen's *retinue* followed her down the aisle.

retraction N. withdrawal. He dropped his libel suit after the newspaper published a *retraction* of its statement.

retribution N. vengeance; compensation; punishment for offenses. The evangelist maintained that an angry Deity would exact *retribution* from the sinners.

retrieve V. recover; find and bring in. The dog was intelligent and quickly learned to *retrieve* the game killed by the hunter.

retroactive ADJ. of a law which dates back to a period before its enactment. Because the law was *retroactive* to the first of the year, we found he was eligible for the pension.

retrograde V. going backwards; degenerating. Instead of advancing, our civilization seems to have *retrograded* in ethics and culture.

retrospective ADJ. looking back on the past. It is only when we become *retrospective* that we can appreciate the tremendous advances made during this century.

revelry N. boisterous merrymaking. New Year's Eve is a night of *revelry*.

reverberate V. echo; resound. The entire valley *reverberated* with the sound of the church bells.

reverie N. daydream; musing. He was awakened from his *reverie* by the teacher's question.

revile V. slander; vilify. He was avoided by all who feared that he would *revile* and abuse them if they displeased him.

revulsion N. sudden violent change of feeling; reaction. Many people in this country who admired dictatorships underwent a *revulsion* when they realized what Hitler and Mussolini were trying to do.

rhapsodize V. to speak or write in an exaggeratedly enthusiastic manner. She greatly enjoyed her Hawaiian vacation and *rhapsodized* about it for weeks.

rhetoric N. art of effective communication; insincere language. All writers, by necessity, must be skilled in *rhetoric*. rhetorical, ADJ.

rheumy (*roo̅ -me̅*) ADJ. pertaining to a discharge from nose and eyes. His *rheumy* eyes warned us that he was coming down with a cold.

ā—ale; ă—add; ä—arm; à—ask, ē—eve; ĕ—end; ê—err, her; ə—allow; even; ī—ice; ĭ—ill; ō—oll; ŏ—odd; ô—orb; o̅o̅—food; o͝o—foot, put; o—out; th—thin; ū—use; ŭ—up; zh—pleasure

ribald (rĭb-) ADJ. wanton; profane. He sang a *ribald* song which offended many of us.

rife ADJ. abundant; current. In the face of the many rumors of scandal, which are *rife* at the moment, it is best to remain silent.

rift N. opening; break. The plane was lost in the stormy sky until the pilot saw the city through a *rift* in the clouds.

rigor N. severity. Many settlers could not stand the *rigors* of the New England winters.

rime N. white frost. The early morning dew had frozen and everything was covered with a thin coat of *rime*.

risible (rĭz-) ADJ. inclined to laugh; ludicrous. His remarks were so *risible* that the audience howled with laughter. risibility, N.

risqué (rĭ-skā) ADJ. verging upon the improper; offcolor. Please do not tell your *risqué* anecdotes at this party.

roan ADJ. brown mixed with gray or white. You can distinguish this horse in a race because it is *roan* while all the others are bay or chestnut.

robust (-bŭst) ADJ. vigorous; strong. The candidate for the football team had a *robust* physique.

rococo (rə-kō -kō) ADJ. ornate; highly decorated. The *rococo* style in furniture and architecture, marked by scrollwork and excessive decoration, flourished during the middle of the eighteenth century.

roil V. to make liquids murky by stirring up sediment. Be careful when you pour not to *roil* the wine; if you stir up the sediment you'll destroy the flavor.

roseate (rō ´-zē-ət) ADJ. rosy; optimistic. I am afraid you will have to alter your *roseate* views in the light of the distressing news that has just arrived.

rostrum N. platform for speech-making; pulpit. The crowd murmured angrily and indicated that they did not care to listen to the speaker who was approaching the *rostrum*.

ETYMOLOGY 25

RID, RIS (to laugh)

        derision scorn

        risibility inclination to laughter

        ridiculous deserving to be laughed at

ROG, ROGAT (to ask)

        interrogate to question

ā—ale; ă—add; ä—arm; à—ask, ē—eve; ĕ—end; ê—err, her; ə—allow; even; ī—ice; ĭ—ill; ō—oll; ŏ—odd; ô—orb; ōō—food; ŏŏ—foot, put; o—out; th—thin; ū—use; ŭ—up; zh—pleasure

prerogative privilege
derogatory disparaging (asking a question to belittle)

TEST—Word List 25—*Synonyms*

Each of the questions below consists of a word printed in italics, followed by five words or phrases numbered 1 to 5. Choose the numbered word or phrase which is most nearly similar in meaning to the word in italics and write the number of your choice on your answer paper.

481. *restive* 1 buoyant 2 restless 3 remorseful 4 resistant 5 retiring
482. *replenish* 1 polish 2 repeat 3 reinstate 4 refill 5 refuse
483. *remonstrate* 1 display 2 restate 3 protest 4 resign 5 reiterate
484. *repugnance* 1 belligerence 2 tenacity 3 renewal 4 pity 5 loathing
485. *repercussion* 1 reverberation 2 restitution 3 resistance 4 magnificence 5 acceptance
486. *remiss* 1 lax 2 lost 3 foolish 4 violating 5 ambitious
487. *repudiate* 1 besmirch 2 appropriate 3 annoy 4 reject 5 avow
488. *repellent* 1 propulsive 2 unattractive 3 porous 4 stiff 5 elastic
489. *remedial* 1 therapeutic 2 corrective 3 traumatic 4 philandering 5 psychotic
490. *reprisal* 1 reevaluation 2 assessment 3 loss 4 retaliation 5 nonsense
491. *repartee* 1 witty retort 2 willful departure 3 spectator 4 monologue 5 sacrifice
492. *relish* 1 desire 2 nibble 3 savor 4 vindicate 5 avail
493. *replica* 1 museum piece 2 famous site 3 battle emblem 4 facsimile 5 replacement
494. *reparation* 1 result 2 compensation 3 alteration 4 retaliation 5 resistance
495. *robust* 1 vigorous 2 violent 3 vicious 4 villainous 5 voracious
496. *retinue* 1 continuation 2 attendants 3 application 4 beleaguer 5 assessment
497. *rife* 1 direct 2 scant 3 abundant 4 grim 5 mature
498. *reticence* 1 reserve 2 fashion 3 treachery 4 loquaciousness 5 magnanimity
499. *retrograde* 1 receding 2 inclining 3 evaluating 4 concentrating 5 directing
500. *retentive* 1 grasping 2 accepting 3 repetitive 4 avoiding 5 fascinating

ā—ale; ă—add; ä—arm; à—ask; ē—eve; ĕ—end; ê—err, her; ə—allow; even; ī—ice; ĭ—ill; ō—oll; ŏ—odd; ô—orb; ōō—food; ŏŏ—foot, pŭt; o—oŭt; th—thin; ū—use; ŭ—up; zh—pleasure

Word List 26   rote - silt

rote N. repetition. He recited the passage by *rote* and gave no indication he understood what he was saying.

rotundity N. roundness; sonorousness of speech. Washington Irving emphasized the *rotundity* of the governor by describing his height and circumference.

rubble N. fragments. Ten years after World War II, some of the *rubble* left by enemy bombings could still be seen.

rubicund (*rōō* -) ADJ. having a healthy reddish color; ruddy; florid. His *rubicund* complexion was the result of an active outdoor life.

ruddy ADJ. reddish; healthy-looking. His *ruddy* features indicated that he had spent much time in the open.

rudimentary ADJ. not developed; elementary. His dancing was limited to a few *rudimentary* steps.

rueful ADJ. regretful; sorrowful; dejected. The artist has captured the sadness of childhood in his portrait of the boy with the *rueful* countenance.

ruminate V. chew the cud; ponder. We cannot afford to wait while you *ruminate* upon these plans.

rummage V. ransack; thoroughly search. When we *rummaged* through the trunks in the attic, we found many souvenirs of our childhood days. also N.

ruse N. trick; stratagem. You will not be able to fool your friends with such an obvious *ruse*.

rusticate V. banish to the country; dwell in the country. I like city life so much that I can never understand how people can *rusticate* in the suburbs.

ruthless ADJ. pitiless. The escaped convict was a dangerous and *ruthless* murderer.

saccharine ADJ. cloyingly sweet. She tried to ingratiate herself, speaking sweetly and smiling a *saccharine* smile.

sacerdotal (*săs-ər-dōt'*-) ADJ. priestly. The priest decided to abandon his *sacerdotal* duties and enter the field of politics.

sacrilegious (-*lĭj*-) ADJ. desecrating; profane. His stealing of the altar cloth was a very *sacrilegious* act.

sacrosanct (*săk*-) ADJ. most sacred; inviolable. The brash insurance salesman invaded the *sacrosanct* privacy of the office of the president of the company.

sadistic (-*dĭs*-) ADJ. inclined to cruelty. If we are to improve conditions in this prison, we must first get rid of the *sadistic* warden.

ā—ale; ă—add; ä—arm; à—ask; ē—eve; ĕ—end; ê—err, her; ə—allow; even; ī—ice; ĭ—ill; ō—oll; ŏ—odd; ô—orb; ōō—food; oŏ—foot, put; o—oŭt; th—thin; ū—use; ŭ—up; zh—pleasure

saffron ADJ. orange-colored; colored like the autumn crocus. The Hallow-
      een cake was decorated with *saffron*-colored icing.
saga (*săg* -) N. Scandinavian myth; any legend. This is a *saga* of the sea
      and the men who risk their lives on it.
sagacious ADJ. keen; shrewd; having insight. He is much too *sagacious*
      to be fooled by a trick like that.
salient (*sā* -*lyənt*) ADJ. prominent. One of the *salient* features of that news-
      paper is its excellent editorial page.
saline (*sā* -*lēn*) ADJ. salty. The slightly *saline* taste of this mineral water is
      pleasant.
sallow ADJ. yellowish; sickly in color. We were disturbed by his *sallow*
      complexion.
salubrious (-*loō* -) ADJ. healthful. Many people with hay fever move to
      more *salubrious* sections of the country during the months of
      August and September.
salutary ADJ. tending to improve; beneficial; wholesome. The punish-
      ment had a *salutary* effect on the boy, as he became a model
      student.
salvage V. rescue from loss. All attempts to *salvage* the wrecked ship
      failed. also N.
sangfroid (*sän* -*frwä*) N. coolness in a trying situation. The captain's
      sangfroid helped to allay the fears of the passengers.
sanguinary ADJ. bloody. The battle of Iwo Jima was unexpectedly *san-
      guinary*.
sanguine ADJ. cheerful; hopeful. Let us not be too *sanguine* about the
      outcome.
sapid (*săp* -) ADJ. savory; tasty; relishable. This chef has the knack of
      making most foods more *sapid* and appealing.
sapient (*sā* -) ADJ. wise; shrewd. The students enjoyed the professor's
      sapient digressions more than his formal lectures.
sardonic ADJ. disdainful; sarcastic; cynical. The *sardonic* humor of
      nightclub comedians who satirize or ridicule patrons in the
      audience strikes some people as amusing and others as
      rude.
sate V. satisfy to the full; cloy. Its hunger *sated,* the lion dozed.
satiate V. surfeit; satisfy fully. The guests, having eaten until they were
      satiated, now listened inattentively to the speakers.
satiety (-*tī* -*ət-ē*) N. condition of being crammed full; glutted state; reple-
      tion. The *satiety* of the guests at the sumptuous feast became
      apparent when they refused the delicious dessert.
saturate V. soak. Their clothes were *saturated* by the rain.

a—ale; ã—add; ä—arm; à—ask, ē—eve; ĕ—end; ê—err, her; ə—allow;
even; ī—ice; ĭ—ill; ō—oll; ŏ—odd; ô—orb; ōō—food; ŏŏ—foot, put;
o—out; th—thin; ū—use; ŭ—up; zh—pleasure

saturnine (*săt-ər-nīn*) ADJ. gloomy. Do not be misled by his *saturnine* countenance; he is not as gloomy as he looks.

saunter V. stroll slowly. As we *sauntered* through the park, we stopped frequently to admire the spring flowers.

savant (*să-vänt*) N. scholar. Our faculty includes many world-famous *savants*.

savoir faire (*săv-wär-făr*) N. tact; poise; sophistication. I envy his *savoir faire;* he always knows exactly what to do and say.

savor V. have a distinctive flavor, smell, or quality. I think your choice of a successor *savors* of favoritism.

scavenger N. collector and disposer of refuse; animal that devours refuse and carrion. The Oakland *Scavenger* Company is responsible for the collection and disposal of the community's garbage.

schism (*sĭz-əm*) N. division; split. Let us not widen the *schism* by further bickering.

scintilla N. shred; least bit. You have not produced a *scintilla* of evidence to support your argument.

scintillate V. sparkle; flash. I enjoy her dinner parties because the food is excellent and the conversation *scintillates*.

scion (*sī-ən*) N. offspring. The farm boy felt out of place in the school attended by the *scions* of the wealthy and noble families.

scourge (*skêrj*) N. lash; whip; severe punishment. They feared the plague and regarded it as a deadly *scourge*. also V.

scrupulous ADJ. conscientious; extremely thorough. I can recommend him for a position of responsibility for I have found him a very *scrupulous* young man.

scullion N. menial kitchen worker. Lynette was angry because she thought she had been given a *scullion* to act as her defender.

scurrilous ADJ. obscene; indecent. Your *scurrilous* remarks are especially offensive because they are untrue.

scuttle V. sink. The sailors decided to *scuttle* their vessel rather than surrender it to the enemy.

sebaceous (*-bā-*) ADJ. oily; fatty. The *sebaceous* glands secrete oil to the hair follicles.

secession N. withdrawal. The *secession* of the Southern states provided Lincoln with his first major problem after his inauguration.

secular (*sĕk-*) ADJ. worldly; not pertaining to church matters; temporal. The church leaders decided not to interfere in *secular* matters.

a—ale; ă—add; ä—arm; á—ask, ē—eve; ĕ—end; ê—err, her; ə—allow; even; ī—ice; ĭ—ill; ō—oll; ŏ—odd; ô—orb; ōo—food; ŏo—foot, put; o—out; th—thin; ū—use; ŭ—up; zh—pleasure

sedate ADJ. composed; grave. The parents were worried because they felt their son was too quiet and *sedate*.

sedentary (*sĕd*-) ADJ. requiring sitting. Because he had a *sedentary* occupation, he decided to visit a gymnasium weekly.

sedulous ADJ. diligent. Stevenson said that he played the "*sedulous* ape" and diligently imitated the great writers of the past.

seethe V. be disturbed; boil. The nation was *seething* with discontent as the noblemen continued their arrogant ways.

seine (*sān*) N. net for catching fish. When the shad run during the spring, you may see fishermen with *seines* along the banks of our coastal rivers.

semblance N. outward appearance; guise. Although this book has a *semblance* of wisdom and scholarship, a careful examination will reveal many errors and omissions.

senility N. old age; feeblemindedness of old age. Most of the decisions are being made by the junior members of the company because of the *senility* of the president.

sensual ADJ. devoted to the pleasures of the senses; carnal; voluptuous. I cannot understand what caused him to drop his *sensual* way of life and become so ascetic.

sententious ADJ. terse; concise; aphoristic. After reading so many redundant speeches, I find his *sententious* style particularly pleasing.

sepulcher N. tomb. Annabel Lee was buried in the *sepulcher* by the sea.

sequester V. retire from public life; segregate; seclude. Although he had hoped for a long time to *sequester* himself in a small community, he never was able to drop his busy round of activities in the city.

serendipity N. gift for finding valuable things not searched for. Many scientific discoveries are a matter of *serendipity*.

serenity N. calmness; placidity. The *serenity* of the sleepy town was shattered by a tremendous explosion.

serrated (*sə-rā-təd*) ADJ. having a sawtoothed edge. The beech tree is one of many plants that have *serrated* leaves.

servile (*sêr*-*vəl*) ADJ. slavish; cringing. Uriah Heep was a very *servile* individual.

severance N. division; partition; separation. The *severance* of church and state is a basic principle of our government.

shackle V. chain; fetter. The criminal's ankles were *shackled* to prevent his escape. also N.

ā—ale; ă—add; ä—arm; à—ask; ē—eve; ĕ—end; ê—err, her; ə—allow; even; ī—ice; ĭ—ill; ō—oll; ŏ—odd; ô—orb; ōō—food; ŏŏ—foot; put; o—oŭt; th—thin; ū—use; ŭ—up; zh—pleasure

shambles N. slaughterhouse; scene of carnage. By the time the police arrived, the room was a *shambles*.

sheaf N. bundle of stalks of grain; any bundle of things tied together. The lawyer picked up a *sheaf* of papers as he rose to question the witness.

sheathe V. place into a case. As soon as he recognized the approaching men, he *sheathed* his dagger and hailed them as friends.

sherbet N. flavored dessert ice. I prefer raspberry *sherbet* to ice cream since it is less fattening.

shibboleth (*shĭb-*) N. watchword; slogan. We are often misled by *shibboleths*.

shimmer V. glimmer intermittently. The moonlight *shimmered* on the water as the moon broke through the clouds for a moment. also N.

shoal N. shallow place. The ship was stranded on a *shoal* and had to be pulled off by tugs.

shoddy ADJ. sham; not genuine; inferior. You will never get the public to buy such *shoddy* material.

sibling N. brother or sister. We may not enjoy being *siblings,* but we cannot forget that we still belong to the same family.

sidereal (*sī-dĭr-*) ADJ. relating to the stars. The study of *sidereal* bodies has been greatly advanced by the new telescope.

silt N. sediment deposited by running water. The harbor channel must be dredged annually to remove the *silt.*

ETYMOLOGY 26

RUPT (to break)
>**interrupt** break into
>**bankrupt** insolvent
>**rupture** a break

SCI (to know)
>**science** knowledge
>**omniscient** knowing all
>**conscious** aware

SCRIB, SCRIPT (to write)
>**transcribe** copy
>**script** writing
>**circumscribe** enclose, limit (write around)

SED, SESS, SID (to sit)
>**sedentary** inactive (sitting)

ā—ale; ă—add; ä—arm; à—ask, ē—eve; ĕ—end; ê—err, her; ə—allow; even; ī—ice; ĭ—ill; ō—oll; ŏ—odd; ô—orb; o͞o—food; o͝o—foot, put; o—out; th—thin; ū—use; ŭ—up; zh—pleasure

session meeting
residence place where one dwells

SENT, SENS (to think, to feel)
resent show indignation
sensitive showing feeling
consent agree

SEQUE, SECUT (to follow)
consecutive following in order
sequence arrangement
sequel that which follows

TEST—Word List 26—*Antonyms*

Each of the questions below consists of a word printed in italics, followed by five words or phrases numbered 1 to 5. Choose the numbered word or phrase which is most nearly opposite in meaning to the word in italics and write the number of your choice on your answer paper.

501. *scurrilous* 1 savage 2 scabby 3 decent 4 volatile 5 major
502. *sagacious* 1 foolish 2 bitter 3 voracious 4 veracious 5 fallacious
503. *rudimentary* 1 pale 2 fundamental 3 asinine 4 developed 5 quiescent
504. *sanguine* 1 choleric 2 sickening 3 warranted 4 irritated 5 pessimistic
505. *sadistic* 1 happy 2 quaint 3 kindhearted 4 vacant 5 fortunate
506. *ruddy* 1 robust 2 witty 3 wan 4 exotic 5 creative
507. *salvage* 1 remove 2 outfit 3 burn 4 lose 5 confuse
508. *sacerdotal* 1 religious 2 frank 3 authoritative 4 violent 5 lay
509. *rubicund* 1 dangerous 2 pallid 3 remote 4 indicative 5 nonsensical
510. *salubrious* 1 salty 2 bloody 3 miasmic 4 maudlin 5 wanted
511. *ruthless* 1 merciful 2 majestic 3 mighty 4 militant 5 maximum
512. *rotundity* 1 promenade 2 nave 3 grotesqueness 4 slimness 5 impropriety
513. *sallow* 1 salacious 2 ruddy 3 colorless 4 permitted 5 minimum
514. *rueful* 1 sad 2 content 3 capable 4 capital 5 zealous
515. *secular* 1 vivid 2 clerical 3 punitive 4 positive 5 varying
516. *shoddy* 1 superior 2 incomplete 3 inadequate 4 querulous 5 garrulous

ā—ale; ă—add; ä—arm; à—ask; ē—eve; ĕ—end; ê—err, her; ə—allow; even; ī—ice; ĭ—ill; ō—oll; ŏ—odd; ô—orb; o͞o—food; o͝o—foot, put; o—out; th—thin; ū—use; ŭ—up; zh—pleasure

517. *sedentary*   1 vicarious 2 loyal 3 accidental 4 active 5 afraid
518. *servile*   1 menial 2 puerile 3 futile 4 lowly 5 haughty
519. *sententious*   1 paragraphed 2 positive 3 posthumous 4 pacific 5 wordy
520. *senility*   1 virility 2 loquaciousness 3 forgetfulness 4 youth 5 majority

---

Word List 27   simian - sultry

simian ADJ. monkeylike. Lemurs are nocturnal mammals and have many *simian* characteristics, although they are less intelligent than monkeys.

simile (sĭm'-ə-lē) N. comparison of one thing with another, using the word *like* or *as*. We are constantly using *similes* and metaphors to convey our thoughts to others.

simulate V. feign. He *simulated* insanity in order to avoid punishment for his crime.

sinecure (sī-nĭ-kyoŏr) N. well-paid position with little responsibility. My job is no *sinecure;* I work long hours and have much responsibility.

sinister ADJ. evil. We must defeat the *sinister* forces that seek our downfall.

sinuous ADJ. winding; bending in and out; not morally honest. The snake moved in a *sinuous* manner.

skimp V. provide scantily; live very economically. They were forced to *skimp* on necessities in order to make their limited supplies last the winter.

skittish ADJ. lively; frisky. He is as *skittish* as a kitten playing with a piece of string.

skulk V. move furtively and secretly. He *skulked* through the less fashionable sections of the city in order to avoid meeting any of his former friends.

slake V. quench; sate. When we reached the oasis, we were able to *slake* our thirst.

sleazy ADJ. flimsy; unsubstantial. This is a *sleazy* material; it will not wear well.

sleeper N. something originally of little value or importance which in time becomes very valuable. Unnoticed by the critics at its publication, the eventual Pulitzer Prize winner was a classic *sleeper.*

ā—ale; ă—add; ä—arm; à—ask, ē—eve; ĕ—end; ê—err, her; ə—allow; even; ī—ice; ĭ—ill; ō—oll; ŏ—odd; ô—orb; oō—food; oŏ—foot, put; o—oüt; th—thin; ū—use; ŭ—up; zh—pleasure

sloth (*slôth*) N. laziness. Such *sloth* in a young person is deplorable.

slough (*slŭf*) V. cast off. Each spring, the snake *sloughs* off its skin.

slovenly (*slŭv-*) ADJ. untidy; careless in work habits. Such *slovenly* work habits will never produce good products.

sluggard N. lazy person. "You are a *sluggard,* a drone, a parasite," the angry father shouted at his lazy son.

sobriety N. soberness. The solemnity of the occasion filled us with *sobriety.*

sojourn N. temporary stay. After his *sojourn* in Florida, he began to long for the colder climate of his native New England home.

solecism N. construction that is flagrantly incorrect grammatically. I must give this paper a failing mark because it contains many *solecisms.*

solicitous ADJ. worried; concerned. The employer was very *solicitous* about the health of his employees as replacements were difficult to get.

soliloquy N. talking to oneself. The *soliloquy* is a device used by the dramatist to reveal a character's innermost thoughts and emotions.

solstice N. point at which the sun is farthest from the equator. The winter *solstice* usually occurs on December 21.

solvent ADJ. able to pay all debts. By dint of very frugal living, he was finally able to become *solvent* and avoid bankruptcy proceedings.

somnambulist N. sleepwalker. The most famous *somnambulist* in literature is Lady Macbeth; her monologue in the sleepwalking scene is one of the highlights of Shakespeare's play.

somnolent ADJ. half asleep. The heavy meal and the overheated room made us all *somnolent* and indifferent to the speaker.

sonorous (*-nōr-*) ADJ. resonant. His *sonorous* voice resounded through the hall.

soupçon (*sōōp-sōn*) N. suggestion; hint; taste. A *soupçon* of garlic will improve this dish.

spangle N. small metallic piece sewn to clothing for ornamentation. The thousands of *spangles* on her dress sparkled in the glare of the stage lights.

spasmodic ADJ. fitful; periodic. The *spasmodic* coughing in the auditorium annoyed the performers.

spatial ADJ. relating to space. It is difficult to visualize the *spatial* extent of our universe.

spawn V. lay eggs. Fish ladders had to be built in the dams to assist the salmon returning to *spawn* in their native streams. also N.

ā—ale; ă—add; ä—arm; à—ask, ē—eve; ĕ—end; ê—err, her; ə—allow; even; ī—ice; ĭ —ill; ō—oll; ŏ—odd; ô—orb; ōō—food; ŏŏ—foot, put; o—oŭt; th—thin; ū—use; ŭ—up; zh—pleasure

specious (*spē*-) ADJ. seemingly reasonable but incorrect. Let us not be misled by such *specious* arguments.

spectral ADJ. ghostly. We were frightened by the *spectral* glow that filled the room.

splenetic (*splĭ-nĕt*-) ADJ. spiteful; irritable; peevish. People shunned him because of his *splenetic* temper. spleen, N.

sporadic (-*răd*-) ADJ. occurring irregularly. Although there are *sporadic* outbursts of shooting, we may report that the major rebellion has been defeated.

sportive ADJ. playful. Such a *sportive* attitude is surprising in a person as serious as you usually are.

spurious ADJ. false; counterfeit. He tried to pay the check with a *spurious* ten-dollar bill.

squalid (*skwŏl*-) ADJ. dirty; neglected; poor. It is easy to see how crime can breed in such a *squalid* neighborhood.

squander V. waste. The prodigal son *squandered* the family estate.

stagnant ADJ. motionless; stale; dull. The *stagnant* water was a breeding ground for disease. stagnate, V.

staid ADJ. sober; sedate. His conduct during the funeral ceremony was *staid* and solemn.

stamina N. strength; staying power. I doubt that he has the *stamina* to run the full distance of the marathon race.

stanch (*stônch*) V. check flow of blood. It is imperative that we *stanch* the gushing wound before we attend to the other injuries.

statute N. law. We have many *statutes* in our law books which should be repealed.

stein N. beer mug. He thought of college as a place where one drank beer from *steins* and sang songs of lost lambs.

stellar ADJ. pertaining to the stars. He was the *stellar* attraction of the entire performance.

stentorian ADJ. extremely loud. The town crier had a *stentorian* voice.

stigmatize V. brand; mark as wicked. I do not want to *stigmatize* this young offender for life by sending him to prison.

stint N. supply; allotted amount; assigned portion of work. He performed his daily *stint* cheerfully and willingly. also, V.

stipend (*stī*-) N. pay for services. There is a nominal *stipend* attached to this position.

stoic (*stō -ĭk*) N. person who is indifferent to pleasure or pain. The doctor called her patient a *stoic* because he had borne the pain of the examination without whimpering. also ADJ.

stoke V. to feed plentifully. They swiftly *stoked* themselves, knowing they would not have another meal until they reached camp.

ā—ale; ă—add; ä—arm; à—ask, ē—eve; ĕ—end; ê—err, her; ə—allow; even; ī—ice; ĭ—ill; ō—oll; ŏ—odd; ô—orb; ōo—food; ŏo—foot, put; o—out; th—thin; ū—use; ŭ—up; zh—pleasure

stolid ADJ. dull; impassive. I am afraid that this imaginative poetry will not appeal to such a *stolid* person.

stratagem (*strǎt-*) N. deceptive scheme. We saw through his clever *stratagem.*

striated (*strī-āt*) ADJ. marked with parallel bands. The glacier left many *striated* rocks.

stricture N. critical comments; severe and adverse criticism. His *strictures* on the author's style are prejudiced and unwarranted.

strident (*strīd-*) ADJ. loud and harsh. She scolded him in a *strident* voice.

stringent (*strĭn-jənt*) ADJ. binding; rigid. I think these regulations are too *stringent.*

stupor N. state of apathy; daze; lack of awareness. In his *stupor,* the addict was unaware of the events taking place around him.

stymie V. present an obstacle; stump. The detective was *stymied* by the contradictory evidence in the robbery investigation. also N.

suavity (*swǎv-*) N. urbanity; polish. He is particularly good in roles that require *suavity* and sophistication.

subaltern (*-bôl-*) N. subordinate. The captain treated his *subalterns* as though they were children rather than commissioned officers.

subjugate V. conquer; bring under control. It is not our aim to *subjugate* our foe; we are interested only in establishing peaceful relations.

sublimate V. refine; purify. We must strive to *sublimate* these desires and emotions into worthwhile activities.

sublime ADJ. exalted; noble; uplifting. We must learn to recognize *sublime* truths.

sub rosa ADV. in strict confidence; privately. I heard of this *sub rosa* and I cannot tell you about it.

subsequent ADJ. following; later. In *subsequent* lessons, we shall take up more difficult problems.

subservient ADJ. behaving like a slave; servile; obsequious. He was proud and dignified; he refused to be *subservient* to anyone.

subsidiary ADJ. subordinate; secondary. This information may be used as *subsidiary* evidence but is not sufficient by itself to prove your argument. also N.

subsistence N. existence; means of support; livelihood. In these days of inflated prices, my salary provides a mere *subsistence.*

substantiate V. verify; support. I intend to *substantiate* my statement by producing witnesses.

ā—ale; ǎ—add; ä—arm; à—ask, ē—eve; ĕ—end; ê—err, her; ə—allow; even; ī—ice; ĭ—ill; ō—oll; ŏ—odd; ô—orb; ōō—food; ŏŏ—foot, put; o—out; th—thin; ū—use; ŭ—up; zh—pleasure

subterfuge N. pretense; evasion. As soon as we realized that you had won our support by a *subterfuge,* we withdrew our endorsement of your candidacy.

subtlety (*sŭt-l-tē*) N. nicety; cunning; guile; delicacy. The *subtlety* of his remarks was unnoticed by most of his audience.

subversive ADJ. tending to overthrow or ruin. We must destroy such *subversive* publications.

succinct (*sŭk-sĭngkt*) ADJ. brief; terse; compact. His remarks are always *succinct* and pointed.

succor N. aid; assistance; relief. We shall be ever grateful for the *succor* your country gave us when we were in need. also V.

succulent ADJ. juicy; full of richness. The citrus foods from Florida are more *succulent* to some people than those from California. also N.

suffuse V. spread over. A blush *suffused* her cheeks when we teased her about her love affair.

sully V. tarnish; soil. He felt that it was beneath his dignity to *sully* his hands in such menial labor.

sultry ADJ. sweltering. He could not adjust himself to the *sultry* climate of the tropics.

summation N. act of finding the total; summary. In his *summation,* the lawyer emphasized the testimony given by the two witnesses.

sumptuous ADJ. lavish; rich. I cannot recall when I have had such a *sumptuous* feast.

sunder V. separate; part. Northern and southern Ireland are politically and religiously *sundered.*

sundry ADJ. various; several. My suspicions were aroused when I read *sundry* items in the newspapers about your behavior.

ETYMOLOGY 27

SOLV, SOLUT (to loosen)
        absolve free from blame
        dissolute morally lax
        absolute complete (not loosened)
SPEC, SPECT (to look at)
        spectator observer
        aspect appearance
        circumspect cautious (looking around)

ā—ale; ă—add; ä—arm; à—ask, ē—eve; ĕ—end; ê—err, her; ə—allow; even; ī—ice; ĭ—ill; ō—oll; ŏ—odd; ô—orb; ōō—food; ŏŏ—foot, put; o—out; th—thin; ū—use; ŭ—up; zh—pleasure

TEST—Word List 27—Synonyms and Antonyms

Each of the following questions consists of a word printed in italics, followed by five words or phrases numbered 1 to 5. Choose the numbered word or phrase which is most nearly the same as or the opposite of the word in italics and write the number of your choice on your answer paper.

521. *squander*   1 fortify 2 depart 3 roam 4 preserve 5 forfeit
522. *somnolent*   1 stentorian 2 settled 3 half awake 4 soothed 5 ambulatory
523. *skittish*   1 tractable 2 inquiring 3 dramatic 4 vain 5 frisky
524. *sportive*   1 competing 2 playful 3 indignant 4 foppish 5 fundamental
525. *solvent*   1 enigmatic 2 bankrupt 3 fiducial 4 puzzling 5 gilded
526. *sloth*   1 penitence 2 filth 3 futility 4 poverty 5 industry
527. *spasmodic*   1 intermittent 2 fit 3 inaccurate 4 violent 5 physical
528. *sobriety*   1 inebriety 2 aptitude 3 scholasticism 4 monotony 5 aversion
529. *sleazy*   1 fanciful 2 creeping 3 substantial 4 uneasy 5 warranted
530. *solstice*   1 equinox 2 sunrise 3 pigsty 4 interstices 5 iniquity
531. *slovenly*   1 half-baked 2 loved 3 inappropriate 4 tidy 5 rapidly
532. *sinister*   1 unwed 2 ministerial 3 good 4 returned 5 splintered
533. *sonorous*   1 resonant 2 reassuring 3 repetitive 4 resinous 5 sisterly
534. *slough*   1 toughen 2 trap 3 violate 4 cast off 5 depart
535. *spurious*   1 genuine 2 angry 3 mitigated 4 interrogated 5 glorious
536. *stringent*   1 binding 2 reserved 3 utilized 4 lambent 5 indigent
537. *sublime*   1 unconscious 2 respected 3 exalted 4 sneaky 5 replaced
538. *stamina*   1 patience 2 pistils 3 weakness 4 fascination 5 patina
539. *sporadic*   1 seedy 2 latent 3 vivid 4 inconsequential 5 often
540. *suavity*   1 ingeniousness 2 indifference 3 urbanity 4 constancy 5 paucity

---

Word List 28   superannuated - transcribe

superannuated ADJ. retired on pension because of age. The *superannuated* man was indignant because he felt that he could still perform a good day's work.

ā—ale; ă—add; ä—arm; à—ask, ē—eve; ĕ—end; ê—err, her; ə—allow; evⱸn; ī—ice; ĭ—ill; ō—oll; ŏ—odd; ô—orb; o͞o—food; o͝o—foot, put; o—out; th—thin; ū—use; ŭ—up; zh—pleasure

supercilious ADJ. contemptuous; haughty. I resent your *supercilious* and arrogant attitude.

superficial ADJ. trivial; shallow. Since your report gave only a *superficial* analysis of the problem, I cannot give you more than a passing grade.

superfluity (*-floo ´-*) N. excess; overabundance. We have a definite lack of sincere workers and a *superfluity* of leaders.

supersede V. cause to be set aside; replace. This regulation will *supersede* all previous rules.

supine (*-pīn*) ADJ. lying on back. The defeated pugilist lay *supine* on the canvas.

suppliant (*sŭp -lē-*) ADJ. entreating; beseeching. He could not resist the dog's *suppliant* whimpering, and he gave it some food. also N.

supplicate V. petition humbly; pray to grant a favor. We *supplicate* your majesty to grant him amnesty.

supposititious ADJ. assumed; counterfeit; hypothetical. I find no similarity between your *supposititious* illustration and the problem we are facing.

surcease (*-sēs*) N. cessation. He begged the doctors to grant him *surcease* from his suffering.

surfeit (*sêr -fət*) V. cloy; overfeed. I am *surfeited* with the sentimentality of the average motion picture film.

surly (*sêr -lē*) ADJ. rude; cross. Because of his *surly* attitude, many people avoided his company.

surmise (*-mīz*) V. guess. I *surmise* that he will be late for this meeting. also N.

surreptitious ADJ. secret. News of their *surreptitious* meeting gradually leaked out.

surveillance (*-vā -*) N. watching; guarding. The FBI kept the house under constant *surveillance* in the hope of capturing all the criminals at one time.

sustenance N. means of support, food, nourishment. In the tropics, the natives find *sustenance* easy to obtain.

swathe (*swäth*) V. wrap around; bandage. When I visited him in the hospital, I found him *swathed* in bandages.

swelter V. be oppressed by heat. I am going to buy an air conditioning unit for my apartment as I do not intend to *swelter* through another hot and humid summer.

sycophantic (*sĭk-ə-fănt -*) ADJ. servilely flattering. The king enjoyed the *sycophantic* attentions of his followers.

sylvan ADJ. pertaining to the woods; rustic. His paintings of nymphs

---

ā—ale; ă—add; ä—arm; à—ask, ē—eve; ĕ—end; ê—err, her; ə—allow; even; ī—ice; ĭ—ill; ō—oll; ŏ—odd; ô—orb; ōō—food; ŏŏ—foot, put; o—oüt; th—thin; ū—use; ŭ—up; zh—pleasure

in *sylvan* backgrounds were criticized as overly sentimental.

synchronous (*sĭng*-) ADJ. similarly timed; simultaneous with. We have many examples of scientists in different parts of the world who have made *synchronous* discoveries.

synthesis N. combining parts into a whole. Now that we have succeeded in isolating this drug, our next problem is to plan its *synthesis* in the laboratory.

synthetic ADJ. artificial; resulting from synthesis. During the twentieth century, many *synthetic* products have replaced the natural products. also N.

tacit ADJ. understood; not put into words. We have a *tacit* agreement.

taciturn ADJ. habitually silent; talking little. New Englanders are reputedly *taciturn* people.

tactile ADJ. pertaining to the organs or sense of touch. His calloused hands had lost their *tactile* sensitivity.

tainted ADJ. contaminated; corrupt. Health authorities are always trying to prevent the sale and use of *tainted* food.

talisman N. charm. She wore the *talisman* to ward off evil.

tantalize V. tease; torture with disappointment. Tom loved to *tantalize* his younger brother.

tantrum N. fit of petulance; caprice. The child learned that he could have almost anything if he went into *tantrums*.

tautological ADJ. needlessly repetitious. In the sentence "It was visible to the eye," the phrase "to the eye" is *tautological*.

tawdry ADJ. cheap and gaudy. He won a few *tawdry* trinkets in Coney Island.

tedium N. boredom; weariness. We hope this radio will help overcome the *tedium* of your stay in the hospital.

temerity (-*mĕr'*-) N. boldness; rashness. Do you have the *temerity* to argue with me?

temperate ADJ. restrained; self-controlled. Noted for his *temperate* appetite, he seldom gained weight.

tempo N. speed of music. I find the conductor's *tempo* too slow for such a brilliant piece of music.

temporal ADJ. not lasting forever; limited by time; secular. At one time in our history, *temporal* rulers assumed that they had been given their thrones by divine right.

temporize V. avoid committing oneself; gain time. I cannot permit you to *temporize* any longer; I must have a definite answer today.

ā—ale; ă—add; ä—arm; à—ask; ē—eve; ĕ—end; ê—err, her; ə—allow; even; ī—ice; ĭ—ill; ō—oll; ŏ—odd; ô—orb; ōō—food; oŏ—foot, put; o—oŭt; th—thin; ū—use; ŭ—up; zh—pleasure

tenacious ADJ. holding fast. I had to struggle to break his *tenacious* hold on my arm. tenacity, N.

tenet N. doctrine; dogma. I cannot accept the *tenets* of your faith.

tentative ADJ. provisional; experimental. Your *tentative* plans sound plausible.

tenuous ADJ. thin; rare; slim. The allegiance of our allies is held by rather *tenuous* ties.

tenure N. holding of an office; time during which such an office is held. He has permanent *tenure* in this position.

tepid (*tĕp*-) ADJ. lukewarm. During the summer, I like to take a *tepid* bath.

terminate V. to bring to an end. When his contract was *terminated* unexpectedly, he desperately needed a new job.

terminus N. last stop of railroad. After we reached the railroad *terminus*, we continued our journey into the wilderness on saddle horses.

terrestrial ADJ. on the earth. We have been able to explore the *terrestrial* regions much more thoroughly than the aquatic or celestial regions.

terse ADJ. concise; abrupt; pithy. I admire his *terse* style of writing.

tertiary ADJ. third. He is so thorough that he analyzes *tertiary* causes where other writers are content with primary and secondary reasons.

testy ADJ. irritable; short-tempered. My advice is to avoid discussing this problem with him today as he is rather *testy*.

tether V. tie with a rope. Before we went to sleep, we *tethered* the horses to prevent their wandering off during the night.

theocracy N. government of a community by religious leaders. Some Pilgrims favored the establishment of a *theocracy* in New England.

therapeutic ADJ. curative. These springs are famous for their *therapeutic* qualities.

thermal ADJ. pertaining to heat. The natives discovered that the hot springs gave excellent *thermal* baths and began to develop their community as a health resort. also N.

thrall N. slave; bondage. The captured soldier was held in *thrall* by the conquering army.

threnody N. song of lamentation; dirge. When he died, many poets wrote *threnodies* about his passing.

throes N. violent anguish. The *throes* of despair can be as devastating as the spasms accompanying physical pain.

throttle V. strangle. The criminal tried to *throttle* the old man.

ā—ale; ă—add; ä—arm; à—ask, ē—eve; ĕ—end; ê—err, hẻr; ə—allow; even; ī—ice; ĭ—ill; ō—oll; ŏ—odd; ô—orb; ōō—food; ŏŏ—foot, put; o—out; th—thin; ū—use; ŭ—up; zh—pleasure

thwart V. baffle; frustrate. He felt that everyone was trying to *thwart* his plans.

timidity N. lack of self-confidence or courage. If you are to succeed as a salesman, you must first lose your *timidity*.

tipple V. drink (alcoholic beverages) frequently. He found that his most enjoyable evenings occurred when he *tippled* with his friends at the local pub.

tirade N. extended scolding; denunciation. Long before he had finished his *tirade,* we were sufficiently aware of the seriousness of our misconduct.

titanic ADJ. gigantic. *Titanic* waves beat against the shore during the hurricane.

tithe (*tĭth*) N. tax of one-tenth. Because he was an agnostic, he refused to pay his *tithes* to the clergy. also V.

titular (*tĭch* -) ADJ. nominal holding of title without obligations. Although he was the *titular* head of the company, the real decisions were made by his general manager.

toady V. flatter for favors. I hope you see through those who are *toadying* you for special favors. also N.

toga N. Roman outer robe. Marc Antony pointed to the slashes in Caesar's *toga.*

tome N. large volume. He spent much time in the libraries poring over ancient *tomes.*

topography N. physical features of a region. Before the generals gave the order to attack, they ordered a complete study of the *topography* of the region.

torpid ADJ. dormant; dull; lethargic. The *torpid* bear had just come out of his cave after his long hibernation.

torso N. trunk of statue with head and limbs missing; human trunk. This *torso,* found in the ruins of Pompeii, is now on exhibition in the museum in Naples.

tortuous ADJ. winding; full of curves. Because this road is so *tortuous,* it is unwise to go faster than twenty miles an hour on it.

touchy ADJ. sensitive; irascible. Do not discuss this phase of the problem as he is very *touchy* about it.

toxic ADJ. poisonous. We must seek an antidote for whatever *toxic* substance he has eaten.

tract N. pamphlet; a region of indefinite size. The King granted William Penn a *tract* of land in the New World.

tractable ADJ. docile. You will find the children in this school very *tractable* and willing to learn.

ā—ale; ă—add; ä—arm; à—ask; ē—eve; ĕ—end; ê—err, her; ə—allow; even; ī—ice; ĭ—ill; ō—oll; ŏ—odd; ô—orb; o͞o—food; o͝o—foot, put; o—out; th—thin; ū—use; ŭ—up; zh—pleasure

traduce V. expose to slander. His opponents tried to *traduce* the candidate's reputation by spreading rumors about his past.

tranquillity N. calmness; peace. After the commotion and excitement of the city, I appreciate the *tranquillity* of these fields and forests.

transcend V. exceed; surpass. This accomplishment *transcends* all our previous efforts. transcendental, ADJ.

transcribe V. copy. When you *transcribe* your notes, please send a copy to Mr. Smith and keep the original for our files. transcription, N.

ETYMOLOGY 28

TANG, TACT (to touch)
- **tangent** touching
- **contact** touching with, meeting
- **contingent** depending upon

TEMPOR (time)
- **contemporary** at the same time
- **extemporaneous** impromptu
- **temporize** to delay

TEN, TENT (to hold)
- **tenable** able to be held
- **tenacity** retention
- **tenure** holding of office

TERR (land)
- **terrestrial** pertaining to earth
- **subterranean** underground

TEST—Word List 28—Synonyms

Each of the following questions consists of a word printed in italics, followed by five words or phrases numbered 1 to 5. Choose the numbered word or phrase which is most nearly similar in meaning to the word in italics and write the number of your choice on your answer paper.

541. *superannuated*   1 senile 2 experienced 3 retired 4 attenuated 5 accepted
542. *surfeit*   1 belittle 2 cloy 3 drop 4 estimate 5 claim
543. *tacit*   1 spoken 2 allowed 3 neural 4 understood 5 unwanted

ā—ale; ă—add; ä—arm; à—ask, ê—eve; ĕ—end; ê—err, her; ə—allow; even; ī—ice; ĭ—ill; ō—oll; ŏ—odd; ô—orb; ōō—food; ŏŏ—foot, put; o—out; th—thin; ū—use; ŭ—up; zh—pleasure

544. *supercilious*   1 haughty 2 highbrow 3 angry 4 subservient 5 philosophic
545. *surreptitious*   1 secret 2 snakelike 3 nightly 4 abstract 5 furnished
546. *talisman*   1 chief 2 juror 3 medicine man 4 amulet 5 gift
547. *superficial*   1 abnormal 2 portentous 3 shallow 4 angry 5 tiny
548. *swathed*   1 wrapped around 2 waved 3 gambled 4 rapt 5 mystified
549. *tawdry*   1 orderly 2 meretricious 3 reclaimed 4 filtered 5 proper
550. *suppliant*   1 intolerant 2 swallowing 3 beseeching 4 finishing 5 flexible
551. *sycophantic*   1 quiet 2 recording 3 servilely flattering 4 frolicsome 5 eagerly awaiting
552. *tenacious*   1 fast running 2 intentional 3 obnoxious 4 holding fast 5 collecting
553. *supposititious*   1 irreligious 2 experimental 3 subjunctive 4 hypothetical 5 grammatical
554. *synthetic*   1 simplified 2 doubled 3 tuneful 4 artificial 5 fiscal
555. *tepid*   1 boiling 2 lukewarm 3 freezing 4 gaseous 5 cold
556. *tantalize*   1 tease 2 wax 3 warrant 4 authorize 5 total
557. *tenuous*   1 vital 2 thin 3 careful 4 dangerous 5 necessary
558. *temerity*   1 timidity 2 resourcefulness 3 boldness 4 tremulousness 5 caution
559. *tentative*   1 prevalent 2 certain 3 mocking 4 wry 5 experimental
560. *temporal*   1 priestly 2 scholarly 3 secular 4 sleepy 5 sporadic

---

Word List 29   **transgression - veer**

transgression N. violation of a law; sin. Forgive us our *transgressions*.
transient ADJ. fleeting; quickly passing away; staying for a short time. This hotel caters to a *transient* trade.
transition N. going from one state of action to another. During the period of *transition* from oil heat to gas heat, the furnace will have to be shut off.
translucent ADJ. partly transparent. We could not recognize the people in the next room because of the *translucent* curtains which separated us.
transmute V. change; convert to something different. He was unable to *transmute* his dreams into actualities.

a—ale; ā—add; ä—arm; à—ask; ē—eve; ĕ—end; ê—err, her; ə—allow; even; ī—ice; ĭ—ill; ō—oll; ŏ—odd; ô—orb; ōō—food; ŏŏ—foot, put; o—out; th—thin; ū—use; ŭ—up; zh—pleasure

transparent ADJ. permitting light to pass through freely; easily detected. Your scheme is so *transparent* that it will fool no one.

transpire V. exhale; become known; happen. In spite of all our efforts to keep the meeting a secret, news of our conclusions *transpired*.

travail (tra-vāl') N. painful labor. How long do you think a man can endure such *travail* and degradation without rebelling?

traverse V. go through or across. When you *traverse* this field, be careful of the bull.

travesty N. comical parody; treatment aimed at making something appear ridiculous. The decision the jury has arrived at is a *travesty* of justice.

treatise N. article treating a subject systematically and thoroughly. He is preparing a *treatise* on the Elizabethan playwrights for his graduate degree.

trek V. travel; migrate. The tribe *trekked* further north that summer in search of available game. also N.

tremor N. trembling; slight quiver. She had a nervous *tremor* in her right hand.

tremulous ADJ. trembling; wavering. She was *tremulous* more from excitement than from fear.

trenchant ADJ. cutting; keen. I am afraid of his *trenchant* wit for it is so often sarcastic.

trepidation N. fear; trembling agitation. We must face the enemy without *trepidation* if we are to win this battle.

tribulation N. distress; suffering. After all the trials and *tribulations* we have gone through, we need this rest.

tribunal N. court of justice. The decision of the *tribunal* was final.

tribute N. tax levied by a ruler; mark of respect. The colonists refused to pay *tribute* to a foreign despot.

trident (trīd'-) N. three-pronged spear. Neptune is usually depicted as rising from the sea, carrying his *trident* on his shoulder.

trilogy (trĭl'-) N. group of three works. Romain Rolland's novel *Jean Christophe* was first published as a *trilogy*.

trite ADJ. hackneyed; commonplace. The *trite* and predictable situations in many television programs alienate many viewers.

troth N. pledge of good faith especially in betrothal. He gave her his *troth* and vowed he would cherish her always.

truculent (trŭk'-ya-) ADJ. aggressive; savage. They are a *truculent* race, ready to fight at any moment.

truism N. self-evident truth. Many a *truism* is well expressed in a proverb.

ā—ale; ă—add; ä—arm; à—ask; ē—eve; ĕ—end; ê—err, her; a—allow; even; ī—ice; ĭ—ill; ō—oll; ŏ—odd; ô—orb; o͞o—food; o͝o—foot, put; o—out; th—thin; ū—use; ŭ—up; zh—pleasure

trumpery N. objects that are showy, valueless, deceptive. All this finery is mere *trumpery.*

tryst (*trĭst*) N. meeting. The lovers kept their *tryst* even though they realized their danger.

tumbrel N. a farm tipcart. The *tumbrels* became the vehicles which transported the condemned people from the prisons to the guillotine.

tumid ADJ. swollen; pompous; bombastic. I especially dislike his *tumid* style; I prefer writing which is less swollen and bombastic.

turbid ADJ. muddy; having the sediment disturbed. The water was *turbid* after the children had waded through it.

turbulence N. state of violent agitation. We were frightened by the *turbulence* of the ocean during the storm.

turgid (*têr-jəd*) ADJ. swollen; distended. The *turgid* river threatened to overflow the levees and flood the countryside.

turnkey N. jailer. By bribing the *turnkey,* the prisoner arranged to have better food brought to him in his cell.

turpitude N. depravity. A visitor may be denied admittance to this country if he has been guilty of moral *turpitude.*

tutelage N. guardianship; training. Under the *tutelage* of such masters of the instrument, he made rapid progress as a virtuoso.

tyro (*tī-rō*) N. beginner; novice. For a mere *tyro,* you have produced some marvelous results.

ubiquitous ADJ. being everywhere; omnipresent. You must be *ubiquitous* for I meet you wherever I go.

ulterior ADJ. situated beyond; unstated. You must have an *ulterior* motive for your behavior.

ultimate ADJ. final; not susceptible to further analysis. Scientists are searching for the *ultimate* truths.

ultimatum (*-māt'-*) N. last demand; warning. Since they have ignored our *ultimatum,* our only recourse is to declare war.

umbrage (*ŭm'-brĭj*) N. resentment; anger; sense of injury or insult. She took *umbrage* at his remarks.

unanimity N. complete agreement. We were surprised by the *unanimity* with which our proposals were accepted by the different groups.

unassuaged ADJ. unsatisfied; not soothed. His anger is *unassuaged* by your apology.

unassuming ADJ. modest. He is so *unassuming* that some people fail to realize how great a man he really is.

unbridled ADJ. violent. He had a sudden fit of *unbridled* rage.

ā—ale; ă—add; ä—arm; à—ask, ē—eve; ĕ—end; ê—err, her; ə—allow; even; ī—ice; ĭ—ill; ō—oll; ŏ—odd; ô—orb; ōō—food; oŏ—foot, put; o—oŭt; th—thin; ū—use; ŭ—up; zh—pleasure

uncanny ADJ. strange; mysterious. You have the *uncanny* knack of reading my innermost thoughts.

unconscionable (-*kŏnch*-) ADJ. unscrupulous; excessive. He found the
loan shark's demands *unconscionable* and impossible to
meet.

uncouth ADJ. outlandish; clumsy; boorish. Most biographers portray Lincoln as an *uncouth* and ungainly young man.

unction N. the act of anointing with oil. The anointing with oil of a person
near death is called extreme *unction*.

unctuous ADJ. oily; bland; insincerely suave. Uriah Heep disguised his
nefarious actions by *unctuous* protestations of his "'umility."

undulate V. move with a wavelike motion. The waters *undulated* in the
breeze.

unearth V. dig up. When they *unearthed* the city, the archeologists found
many relics of an ancient civilization.

unearthly ADJ. not earthly; weird. There is an *unearthly* atmosphere in his
work which amazes the casual observer.

unequivocal ADJ. plain; obvious. My answer to your proposal is an *unequivocal* and absolute "No."

unerringly ADV. infallibly My teacher *unerringly* pounced on the one
typographical error in my essay.

unfaltering ADJ. steadfast. She approached the guillotine with *unfaltering* steps.

unfeigned ADJ. genuine; real. I am sure her surprise was *unfeigned*.

ungainly ADJ. awkward. He is an *ungainly* young man.

unguent (*ŭng*-*gwənt*) N. ointment. Apply this *unguent* to the sore muscles before retiring.

unimpeachable ADJ. blameless and exemplary. His conduct in office was
unimpeachable.

uninhibited ADJ. unrepressed. The congregation was shocked by her
uninhibited laughter during the sermon.

unique ADJ. without an equal; single in kind. You have the *unique* distinction of being the first student whom I have had to fail in this
course.

unison N. unity of pitch; complete accord. The choir sang in *unison*.

unkempt ADJ. disheveled; with uncared-for appearance. The beggar was
dirty and *unkempt*.

unmitigated ADJ. harsh; severe; not lightened. I sympathize with you in
your *unmitigated* sorrow.

unruly ADJ. disobedient; lawless. The only way to curb this *unruly* mob
is to use tear gas.

ā—ale; ă—add; ä—arm; a—ask; ē—eve; ĕ—end; ê—err, her; ə—allow;
even; ī—ice; ĭ —ill; ō—oll; ŏ—odd; ô—orb; o͞o—food; o͝o—foot, put;
o—out; th—thin; ū—use; ŭ—up; zh—pleasure

unseemly ADJ. unbecoming; indecent. Your levity is *unseemly* at this time.

unsullied ADJ. untarnished. I am happy that my reputation is *unsullied*.

untenable ADJ. unsupportable. I find your theory *untenable* and must reject it.

unwitting ADJ. unintentional; not knowing. He was the *unwitting* tool of the swindlers.

unwonted ADJ. unaccustomed. He hesitated to assume the *unwonted* role of master of ceremonies at the dinner.

upbraid V. scold; reproach. I must *upbraid* him for his misbehavior.

upshot N. outcome. The *upshot* of the rematch was that the former champion proved that he still possessed all the skills of his youth.

urbane (-*bān*) ADJ. suave; refined; elegant. The courtier was *urbane* and sophisticated. urbanity, N.

usury N. lending money at illegal rates of interest. The loan shark was found guilty of *usury*.

uxorious (*ŭk-sōr*-) ADJ. excessively devoted to one's wife. His friends laughed at him because he was so *uxorious* and submissive to his wife's desires.

vacillation N. fluctuation; wavering. His *vacillation* when confronted with a problem annoyed all of us who had to wait until he made his decision.

vacuous ADJ. empty; inane. The *vacuous* remarks of the politician annoyed the audience, who had hoped to hear more than empty platitudes.

vagary (*vā*-) N. caprice; whim. She followed every *vagary* of fashion.

vainglorious ADJ. boastful; excessively conceited. He was a *vainglorious* and arrogant individual.

validate V. confirm; ratify. I will not publish my findings until I *validate* my results.

vanguard N. forerunners; advance forces. We are the *vanguard* of a tremendous army that is following us.

vantage N. position giving an advantage. They fired upon the enemy from behind trees, walls and any other point of *vantage* they could find.

vapid (*văp*-) ADJ. insipid; inane. He delivered an uninspired and *vapid* address.

variegated ADJ. many-colored. He will not like this blue necktie as he is addicted to *variegated* clothing.

vaunted ADJ. boasted; bragged; highly publicized. This much *vaunted* project proved a disappointment when it collapsed.

ā—ale; ă—add; ä—arm; å—ask, ē—eve; ĕ—end; ê—err, her; ə—allow; even; ī—ice; ĭ—ill; ō—oll; ŏ—odd; ô—orb; ōō—food; ŏŏ—foot, pṵt; o—oŭt; th—thin; ū—use; ŭ—up; zh—pleasure

veer v. change in direction. After what seemed an eternity, the wind *veered* to the east and the storm abated.

ETYMOLOGY 29

URB (city)

        urban pertaining to the city
        urbane polished, sophisticated (pertaining to a city dweller)
        suburban outside of the city

TEST—Word List 29—Antonyms

Each of the following questions consists of a word printed in italics, followed by five words or phrases numbered 1 to 5. Choose the numbered word or phrase which is most nearly opposite in meaning to the word in italics and write the number of your choice on your answer paper.

561. *unimpeachable* 1 fruitful 2 rampaging 3 faulty 4 pensive 5 thorough
562. *ulterior* 1 tipped 2 stated 3 sparking 4 uncompromising 5 corrugated
563. *transient* 1 carried 2 close 3 permanent 4 removed 5 certain
564. *ungainly* 1 ignorant 2 graceful 3 detailed 4 dancing 5 pedantic
565. *tyro* 1 infant 2 rubber 3 personnel 4 idiot 5 expert
566. *unfeigned* 1 pretended 2 fashionable 3 wary 4 switched 5 colonial
567. *turbulence* 1 reaction 2 approach 3 impropriety 4 calm 5 hostility
568. *unearth* 1 conceal 2 gnaw 3 clean 4 fling 5 reach
569. *turbid* 1 clear 2 improbable 3 invariable 4 honest 5 turgid
570. *ultimate* 1 competing 2 throbbing 3 poisonous 4 incipient 5 powerful
571. *trite* 1 correct 2 original 3 distinguished 4 premature 5 certain
572. *vaunted* 1 unvanquished 2 fell 3 belittled 4 exacting 5 believed
573. *unkempt* 1 bombed 2 washed 3 neat 4 shabby 5 tawdry
574. *unsullied* 1 tarnished 2 countless 3 soggy 4 papered 5 homicidal
575. *vacillation* 1 remorse 2 relief 3 respect 4 steadfastness 5 inoculation
576. *unruly* 1 chatting 2 obedient 3 definite 4 lined 5 curious
577. *untenable* 1 supportable 2 tender 3 sheepish 4 tremulous 5 adequate
578. *vanguard* 1 regiment 2 rear 3 echelon 4 protection 5 loyalty

ā—ale; ă—add; ä—arm; à—ask; ē—eve; ĕ—end; ê—err, her; ə—allow;
even; ī—ice; ĭ—ill; ō—oll; ŏ—odd; ô—orb; ōō—food; ŏŏ—foot, put;
o—oŭt; th—thin; ū—use; ŭ—up; zh—pleasure

579. *unseemly* 1 effortless 2 proper 3 conducive 4 pointed 5 informative
580. *unwitting* 1 clever 2 intense 3 sensitive 4 freezing 5 intentional

---

Word List 30 vegetate - zephyr

vegetate V. live in a monotonous way. I do not understand how you can *vegetate* in this quiet village after the adventurous life you have led.

vehement ADJ. impetuous; with marked vigor. He spoke with *vehement* eloquence in defense of his client.

vellum N. parchment. Bound in *vellum* and embossed in gold, this book is a beautiful example of the binder's craft.

venal (*vēn*-) ADJ. capable of being bribed. The *venal* policeman accepted the bribe offered him by the speeding motorist whom he had stopped.

veneer N. thin layer; cover. Casual acquaintances were deceived by his *veneer* of sophistication and failed to recognize his fundamental shallowness.

venerable ADJ. deserving high respect. We do not mean to be disrespectful when we refuse to follow the advice of our *venerable* leader.

venerate V. revere. In China, the people *venerate* their ancestors.

venial (*vē'-nē*-) ADJ. forgivable; trivial. We may regard a hungry man's stealing as a *venial* crime.

vent N. a small opening; outlet. The wine did not flow because the air *vent* in the barrel was clogged.

vent V. express; utter. He *vented* his wrath on his class.

ventral V. abdominal. We shall now examine the *ventral* plates of this serpent.

venturous ADJ. daring. The five *venturous* young men decided to look for a new approach to the mountain top.

veracious ADJ. truthful. I can recommend him for this position because I have always found him *veracious* and reliable.

verbiage N. pompous array of words. After we had waded through all the *verbiage,* we discovered that the writer had said very little.

verbose (-*bōs*) ADJ. wordy. This article is too *verbose;* we must edit it.

verdant ADJ. green; fresh. The *verdant* meadows in the spring are always an inspiring sight.

ā—ale; ă—add; ä—arm; à—ask. ē—eve; ĕ—end; ê—err, her; ə—allow;
even; ī—ice; ĭ—ill; ō—oll; ŏ—odd; ô—orb; ōō—food; ŏŏ—foot, put;
o—out; th—thin; ū—use; ŭ—up; zh—pleasure

verdigris N. a green coating on copper which has been exposed to the weather. Despite all attempts to protect the statue from the elements, it became coated with *verdigris*.

verity N. truth; reality. The four *verities* were revealed to Buddha during his long meditation.

vernal ADJ. pertaining to spring. We may expect *vernal* showers all during the month of April.

versatile ADJ. having many talents; capable of working in many fields. He was a *versatile* athlete; at college he had earned varsity letters in baseball, football, and track.

vertex N. summit. Let us drop a perpendicular line from the *vertex* of the triangle to the base.

vertigo (*vêr*-) N. dizziness. We test potential plane pilots for susceptibility to spells of *vertigo*.

vestige N. trace; remains. We discovered *vestiges* of early Indian life in the cave.

viand (*vī*-) N. food. There was a variety of *viands* at the feast.

vicarious ADJ. acting as a substitute; done by a deputy. Many people get a *vicarious* thrill at the movies by imagining they are the characters on the screen.

vicissitude N. change of fortune. I am accustomed to life's *vicissitudes,* having experienced poverty and wealth, sickness and health, and failure and success.

victuals (*vĭt-lz*) N. food. I am very happy to be able to provide you with these *victuals*.

vie V. contend; compete. When we *vie* with each other for his approval, we are merely weakening ourselves and strengthening him.

vigilance N. watchfulness. Eternal *vigilance* is the price of liberty.

vilify V. slander. Why is he always trying to *vilify* my reputation?

vindicate V. clear of charges. I hope to *vindicate* my client and return him to society as a free man.

vindictive ADJ. revengeful. He was very *vindictive* and never forgave an injury.

viper N. poisonous snake. The habitat of the horned *viper,* a particularly venomous snake, is in sandy regions like the Sahara or the Sinai peninsula.

virago (-*răg-ō*) N. shrew. Rip Van Winkle's wife was a veritable *virago*.

virile ADJ. manly. I do not accept the premise that a man is *virile* only when he is belligerent.

virtuoso N. highly skilled artist. Heifetz is a violin *virtuoso*.

ā—ale; ă—add; ä—arm; à—ask, ê—eve; ĕ—end; ê—err, her; ə—allow; even; ī—ice; ĭ—ill; ō—oll; ŏ—odd; ô—orb; ōō—food; ŏŏ—foot, put; o—oūt; th—thin; ū—use; ŭ—up; zh—pleasure

virulent (*vĭr-*) ADJ. extremely poisonous. The virus is highly *virulent* and has made many of us ill for days.

virus (*vī-*) N. disease communicator. The doctors are looking for a specific medicine to control this *virus*.

visage (*vĭz-*) N. face; appearance. The stern *visage* of the judge indicated that he had decided to impose a severe penalty.

viscid (*vĭs-əd*) ADJ. sticky; adhesive. This is a *viscid* liquid.

viscous (*vĭs-kŭs*) ADJ. sticky; gluey. Melted tar is a *viscous* substance.

visionary ADJ. produced by imagination; fanciful; mystical. He was given to *visionary* schemes which never materialized. also N.

vitiate (*vĭsh-ē-āt*) V. spoil the effect of; make inoperative. Fraud will *vitiate* the contract.

vitriolic ADJ. corrosive; sarcastic. Such *vitriolic* criticism is uncalled for.

vituperative ADJ. abusive; scolding. He became more *vituperative* as he realized that we were not going to grant him his wish.

vivacious ADJ. animated; gay. She had always been *vivacious* and sparkling.

vociferous ADJ. clamorous; noisy. The crowd grew *vociferous* in its anger and threatened to take the law into its own hands.

vogue N. popular fashion. Slacks became the *vogue* on many college campuses.

volatile (*vŏl-*) ADJ. evaporating rapidly; lighthearted; mercurial. Ethyl chloride is a very *volatile* liquid.

volition N. act of making a conscious choice. She selected this dress of her own *volition*.

voluble ADJ. fluent; glib. He was a *voluble* speaker, always ready to talk.

voluptuous ADJ. gratifying the senses. The nobility during the Renaissance led *voluptuous* lives.

voracious (*-rā'-*) ADJ. ravenous. The wolf is a *voracious* animal.

votary N. follower of a cult. He was a *votary* of every new movement in literature and art.

vouchsafe V. grant condescendingly; guarantee. I can safely *vouchsafe* you a fair return on your investment.

vulnerable ADJ. susceptible to wounds. Achilles was *vulnerable* only in his heel.

vying V. contending. Why are we *vying* with each other for his favors? vie, V.

waggish ADJ. mischievous; humorous; tricky. He was a prankster who, unfortunately, often overlooked the damage he could cause with his *waggish* tricks.

waive V. give up temporarily; yield. I will *waive* my rights in this matter in order to expedite our reaching a proper decision.

ā—ale; ă—add; ä—arm; à—ask, ē—eve; ĕ—end; ê—err, her; ə—allow; even; ī—ice; ĭ—ill; ō—oll; ŏ—odd; ô—orb; ōō—food; ŏŏ—foot, put; o—out; th—thin; ū—use; ŭ—up; zh—pleasure

wan ADJ. having a pale or sickly color; pallid. Suckling asked, "Why so pale and *wan,* fond lover?"

wane V. grow gradually smaller. From now until December 21, the winter equinox, the hours of daylight will *wane.*

wanton ADJ. unruly; unchaste; excessive. His *wanton* pride cost him many friends.

wary ADJ. very cautious. The spies grew *wary* as they approached the sentry.

wheedle V. cajole; coax; deceive by flattery. She knows she can *wheedle* almost anything she wants from her father.

whet V. sharpen; stimulate. The odors from the kitchen are *whetting* my appetite; I will be ravenous by the time the meal is served.

whimsical ADJ. capricious; fanciful; quaint. *Peter Pan* is a *whimsical* play.

whit N. smallest speck. There is not a *whit* of intelligence or understanding in your observations.

wily ADJ. cunning; artful. He is as *wily* as a fox in avoiding trouble.

winsome ADJ. agreeable; gracious; engaging. By her *winsome* manner, she made herself liked by everyone who met her.

witless ADJ. foolish; idiotic. Such *witless* and fatuous statements will create the impression that you are an ignorant individual.

witticism N. witty saying; facetious remark. What you regard as *witticisms* are often offensive to sensitive people.

wizardry N. sorcery; magic. Merlin amazed the knights with his *wizardry.*

wizened (*wĭz-*) ADJ. withered; shriveled. The *wizened* old man in the home for the aged was still active and energetic.

wont (*wônt*) N. custom; habitual procedure. As was his *wont,* he jogged two miles every morning before going to work.

worldly ADJ. engrossed in matters of this earth; not spiritual. You must leave your *worldly* goods behind you when you go to meet your Maker.

wraith (*rāth*) N. ghost; phantom of a living person. It must be a horrible experience to see a ghost; it is even more horrible to see the *wraith* of a person we know to be alive.

wreak V. inflict. I am afraid he will *wreak* his wrath on the innocent as well as the guilty.

wrest V. pull away; take by violence. With only ten seconds left to play, our team *wrested* victory from their grasp.

zealot (*zĕl-*) N. fanatic; person who shows excessive zeal. It is good to have a few *zealots* in our group for their enthusiasm is contagious.

zenith N. point directly overhead in the sky; summit. When the sun was

ā—ale; ă—add; ä—arm; à—ask; ē—eve; ĕ—end; ê—err, her; ə—allow; even; ī—ice; ĭ—ill; ō—oll; ŏ—odd; ô—orb; ōō—food; ŏŏ—foot, put; o—out; th—thin; ū—use; ŭ—up; zh—pleasure

at its *zenith,* the glare was not as strong as at sunrise and sunset.

zephyr N. gentle breeze; west wind. When these *zephyrs* blow, it is good to be in an open boat under a full sail.

ETYMOLOGY 30

VENI, VENT (to come)
> **intervene** come between
> **prevent** stop
> **convention** meeting

VIA (way)
> **deviation** departure from way
> **viaduct** roadway (arched)
> **trivial** trifling (small talk at crossroads)

VID, VIS (to see)
> **vision** sight
> **evidence** things seen
> **vista** view

VINC, VICT, VANQU (to conquer)
> **invincible** unconquerable
> **victory** winning
> **vanquish** defeat

VOC, VOCAT (to call)
> **avocation** calling, minor occupation
> **provocation** calling or rousing the anger of
> **invocation** calling in prayer

VOLV, VOLUT (to roll)
> **revolve** roll around
> **evolve** roll out, develop
> **convolution** coiled state

TEST—Word List 30 — Synonyms and Antonyms

Each of the questions below consists of a word printed in italics, followed by five words or phrases numbered 1 to 5. Choose the numbered word or phrase which is most nearly the same as or the opposite of the word in italics and write the number of your choice on your answer paper.

581. *vestige* 1 trek 2 trail 3 trace 4 trial 5 tract
582. *venturous* 1 timorous 2 confiscatory 3 lethal 4 tubercular 5 dorsal

---

ā—ale; ă—add; ä—arm; à—ask; ē—eve; ĕ—end; ê—err, her; ə—allow; even; ī—ice; ĭ—ill; ō—oll; ŏ—odd; ô—orb; o͞o—food; o͝o—foot; p̣ut; o—out; th—thin; ū—use; ŭ—up; zh—pleasure

583. *vehement* 1 substantial 2 regular 3 calm 4 cautious 5 sad
584. *verdant* 1 poetic 2 green 3 red 4 autumnal 5 frequent
585. *venerate* 1 revere 2 age 3 reject 4 reverberate 5 degenerate
586. *verity* 1 sanctity 2 reverence 3 falsehood 4 rarity 5 household
587. *venial* 1 unforgivable 2 unforgettable 3 unmistaken 4 fearful 5 fragrant
588. *vicarious* 1 substitutional 2 aggressive 3 sporadic 4 reverent 5 internal
589. *venal* 1 springlike 2 honest 3 angry 4 indifferent 5 going
590. *veracious* 1 worried 2 slight 3 alert 4 truthful 5 instrumental
591. *vellum* 1 schedule 2 scenario 3 parchment 4 monastery 5 victim
592. *visage* 1 doubt 2 personality 3 hermitage 4 face 5 armor
593. *vertex* 1 whirlpool 2 drift 3 vehicle 4 base 5 context
594. *virulent* 1 sensuous 2 malignant 3 masculine 4 conforming 5 approaching
595. *viand* 1 wand 2 gown 3 food 4 orchestra 5 frock
596. *viscid* 1 talkative 2 affluent 3 sticky 4 sweet 5 embarrassed
597. *vigilance* 1 bivouac 2 guide 3 watchfulness 4 mob rule 5 posse
598. *vindictive* 1 revengeful 2 fearful 3 divided 4 literal 5 convincing
599. *vilify* 1 erect 2 eulogize 3 better 4 magnify 5 horrify
600. *vindicate* 1 point out 2 blame 3 declare 4 evict 5 menace

ā—ale; ă—add; ä—arm; à—ask; ē—eve; ĕ—end; ê—err, her; ə—allow; even; ī—ice; ĭ —ill; ō—oll; ŏ—odd; ô—orb; o͞o—food; o͝o—foot, put; o—out; th—thin; ū—use; ŭ—up; zh—pleasure

4 The Word Relationship, Sentence Completion, and Reading Comprehension Questions

In addition to testing knowledge of vocabulary, the SAT verbal part includes questions involving word relationships, sentence completion, and reading comprehension.

The Word Relationship Question

Current examinations present two variations of this type of question:

Type 1. In each row of words, the first two words form a pair. The third word can be combined with one of the remaining words on the line to form a similar pair of words. The candidate must select the word that best completes the second pair.

ILLUSTRATION

mother : daughter :: father : 1. uncle 2. son 3. cousin 4. brother-in-law 5. aunt.

First, determine the relationship (parent : child) existing between the first two words. Furthermore, notice that you are given the female parent and the female offspring. To match "father," the male parent, look for the male offspring, "son." Number 2 is the correct answer.

Type 2. The College Entrance Examination Board uses a different form of relationship question. Instead of asking the candidate to match the third word with another word as in the illustration above, the question presents a pair of words followed by five additional pairs of words. The candidate must select the pair of words that best matches the relationship existing between the first two words.

ILLUSTRATION

ointment : burn :: 1. tears : consolation 2. consolation : grief 3. butter : bread 4. bread : meat 5. happiness : grief

If you decide that the relationship between the first two words is that an ointment is placed on a burn, you may choose 3 as the correct answer because butter is placed on bread. However, if you realize that an ointment is used to soothe the pain of a burn, you will probably choose 2 as the answer because consolation helps to soothe the anguish (the tears) of grief. The best answer is 2.

Long-Range Strategy: Continue to build up your vocabulary and to study the connotations, as well as the literal meanings, of words. Also, learn the common types of relationships that may exist between words:

1. Worker and article created
        carpenter : house
        writer : book
        composer : symphony

2. Worker and tool used
        carpenter : saw
        writer : typewriter
        surgeon : scalpel

3. Tool and object worked on
        pencil : paper
        saw : wood

4. Act the tool does to the object it works on
                saw : wood   (cuts)
                knife : bread   (cuts)
                brake : car   (stops)

5. Time sequence
            early : late
            dawn : twilight
            sunrise : sunset

6. Cause and effect
            germ : disease
            carlessness : accident
            explosion : debris

7. **Degree of intensity**
    tepid : hot
    joy : ecstasy
    admiration : love

8. **Class — species**
    furniture : chair
    insect : grasshopper
    mammal : whale
    dog : poodle

9. **Type — characteristic**
    cow : herbivorous
    tiger : carnivorous

10. **Grammatical relationships**
    I : mine   (first person nominative case : first person
        possessive case)
    wolf : vulpine   (noun : adjective)
    have : had   (present tense : past tense)
    alumnus : alumni   (masculine singular noun : masculine
        plural noun)

11. **Synonyms**
    lie : prevaricate
    kind : benevolent

12. **Antonyms**
    never : always
    love : hate
    fancy : simple
    real : fictional

13. **Homonyms**
    hour : our
    their : there
    wear : where

14. **Rhyming**
    had : bad
    some : come
    fall : tall

15. Person and thing he or she seeks
    alchemist : gold
    prospector : gold

16. Person and thing he or she learns to avoid
    child : fire
    pilot : reef

17. Part and whole
    soldier : regiment
    star : constellation

18. Sex
    duck : drake
    bull : cow

Tips to Help You Cope

1. Look first for the types of relationships that are easiest for you to spot, perhaps synonyms and antonyms.

2. If the first pair of words does not fit into a category that is obvious to you, search for a more subtle relationship.

3. Do not be misled if the choices are from different fields or areas, or seem to deal with different items, from the given pair. Study the given words until you see the connection between them; then search for the same relationship among the choices. Botanist : microscope :: carpenter : hammer, even though the two workers may have little else in common.

4. Bear in mind that more than one relationship can exist between words, as shown in the illustration under "Type 2" above.

5. Be guided by the parts of speech. If the first two words are two nouns, two verbs, etc., the correct answer will also consist of two words that are the same part of speech. An example is cow : ewe :: bovine : ovine.

6. If the question deals with persons, places, or events in a specialized field, draw on your background knowledge in that area.

Examples to Get You Started

ILLUSTRATION 1

   surgeon : scalpel :: satirist :   1. saw   2. knife   3. words
4. pride   5. suture

   A surgeon uses a scalpel to make an incision, to cut. A satirist cuts pride and arrogance by means of the words he uses. Therefore 3 is the best answer.

ILLUSTRATION 2

possess : lose ::   1. hesitate : advance   2. cease : recur
3. undertake : perform   4. continue : desist   5. produce : supply

You eliminate choices 3 and 5 immediately, for they present synonyms and you are looking for opposites in meaning. Choice 1 does not provide a clear opposite; choice 2 is good; choice 4 is best. The objection to choice 2 lies in the word "recur," which carries the sense of repeated activity; this is not found in the word "lose."

ILLUSTRATION 3

grayhound : fast ::   1. dog : bark   2. mouse : small
3. cat : pet   4. young : old   5. tall : giraffe

The answer must have the same pattern, noun : adjective, as the given pair. You would eliminate 1 as noun : verb, 3 as noun : noun, 4 as adjective : adjective, and 5 as adjective : noun. Number 2 is correct.

ILLUSTRATION 4

Jupiter : Zeus ::   1. god : goddess   2. Greek : Latin
3. Hera : Juno   4. Minerva : Pallas Athene   5. Jove : Zoroaster

This question calls for a knowledge of mythology. Jupiter is the Latin god; Zeus, the Greek god. Numbers 2 and 3 are incorrect because the order is reversed (Greek first instead of Latin). Choice 4 is best because Minerva (the Latin goddess of wisdom) is the counterpart of the Greek goddess, Pallas Athene.

PRACTICE EXERCISE   Answers given on page 224.

Select the lettered pair of words that are related to each other in the same way as the original pair of words are related to each other.

1. **haggard : obese ::**   (A) lonesome : pathetic   (B) gaunt : corpulent
   (C) jocund : gay   (D) defiant : belligerent   (E) error : eraser
2. **day : week ::**   (A) week : year   (B) second : hour   (C) week :
   month   (D) ephemeral : permanent   (E) time : duration
3. **spitz : dog ::**   (A) philosopher : stone   (B) whale : fish   (C) growth
   : cancer   (D) whale : mammal   (E) reptile : crocodile

4. **large : immense ::**   (A) zero : infinity   (B) mauled : battered   (C) dislike : hatred   (D) turgid : bloated   (E) quest : voyage

5. **poison : death ::**   (A) purgative : disease   (B) experience : knowledge   (C) growth : maturation   (D) beauty : cosmetics   (E) truth : beauty

6. **chauvinism : country ::**   (A) frugality : money   (B) patriotism : country   (C) gluttony : food   (D) jingoism : loyalty   (E) criticism : book

7. **frugal : parsimonious ::**   (A) joy : ecstasy   (B) caution : wisdom   (C) honor : loyalty   (D) poor : miserly   (E) eager : anxious

8. **mice : rice ::**   (A) doe : rye   (B) mice : berries   (C) fauna : flora   (D) cats : mice   (E) hate : love

9. **secular : clerical ::**   (A) factory hand : secretary   (B) intrepid : cautious   (C) conference : missionary   (D) mundane : spiritual   (E) labor : management

10. **convention : mores ::**   (A) antics : caprice   (B) corruption : maggots   (C) popularity : ephemeral   (D) books : library   (E) honesty : falsity

---

TEST — WORD RELATIONSHIPS

Complete the relationship in each question.

1. **fish : bird :: submarine :**   1. tank   2. bird   3. airplane   4. hangar

2. **lion : carnivorous :: man :**   1. herbivorous   2. omnipotent   3. mortal   4. omnivorous

3. **doctor : disease :: psychiatrist :**   1. imbecility   2. senility   3. maladjustment   4. poverty

4. **clock : second :: calendar :**   1. year   2. month   3. day   4. hour

5. **scissors : sever :: millstone :**   1. weighs   2. rolls   3. cuts   4. grinds

6. **frugal : parsimonious :: generous :**   1. benevolent   2. philanthropic   3. prodigal   4. miserly

7. **teacher : ignorance :: light :**   1. darkness   2. bulb   3. electricity   4. current

8. **dusk : dawn :: senility :**   1. childhood   2. adolescence   3. garrulity   4. magic

9. **cat : feline :: dog :**   1. masculine   2. canine   3. bovine   4. doggerel

10. **ocean : bay :: continent :**   1. island   2. archipelago   3. promontory   4. peninsula

Select the numbered pair of words that are related to each other in the same way as the original pair of words are related to each other.

11. **corpulence : stout ::** 1. baldness : hirsute 2. erudition : learned 3. gauntness : beautiful 4. steadfastness : mercurial 5. intelligent : wit

12. **gold : ore ::** 1. dear : cheap 2. iron : steel 3. pearls : oysters 4. steel : iron 5. intelligence : astuteness

13. **lariat : cowboy ::** 1. medicine : patient 2. scalpel : surgeon 3. manuscript : author 4. lawyer : client 5. spice : gourmet

14. **carelessness : accident ::** 1. assiduity : success 2. indifference : fruition 3. care : avoidance 4. writer : blot 5. thoughtlessness : oversight

15. **brake : automobile ::** 1. choke : carburetor 2. conscience : man 3. detergent : society 4. stop : horse 5. thinker : doer

16. **mason : wall ::** 1. doctor : cure 2. magician : magic 3. stranger : friendship 4. painter : mural 5. bricklayer : trowel

17. **halcyon : martial ::** 1. moon : Mars 2. military song : warlike 3. peaceful : warlike 4. soothed : worried 5. belligerent : fighting

18. **enigma : riddle ::** 1. labyrinth : maze 2. dilemma : alternatives 3. Sphinx : Egyptian 4. bull : matador 5. labyrinth : string

19. **soldier : carbine ::** 1. author : book 2. chemist : test tube 3. sailor : pirate 4. sailor : marine 5. knight : spear

20. **archipelago : island ::** 1. peninsula : strait 2. Oceania : Alaska 3. multitude : individual 4. nucleus : cerebrum 5. cell : nucleus

Answers

Practice Exercise

1. B	3. D	5. B	7. A	9. D
2. C	4. C	6. C	8. C	10. A

Test

1. 3	5. 4	9. 2	13. 2	17. 3
2. 4	6. 3	10. 4	14. 1	18. 1
3. 3	7. 1	11. 2	15. 2	19. 5
4. 3	8. 1	12. 3	16. 4	20. 3

The Sentence Completion Question

In the sentence completion question, a sentence with one or two words omitted appears on the question paper. Five possible words or groups of words are provided, from which the student is asked to select the best answer.

Long-Range Strategy: When you encounter a new word, don't just memorize its meaning in rote fashion. Study the way it is used, and then use it correctly yourself in three or more sentences. Try to work the word into conversations and discussions, even if it startles the other participants. The way to make a word your own is to use it.

Tips to Help You Cope

1. Think what the sentence means.

2. If the subject matter is specialized, that is, deals with an area such as art, biology, or history, take advantage of your knowledge in this field.

3. Before looking at the choices, try to complete the sentence with a word (or words) of your own that would make sense.

4. Examine the choices given. If any is the same as, or is a synonym for, your own word, select it as the answer.

5. If this doesn't work, reread the sentence to see whether a new interpretation is possible. Search for implications — hidden meanings rather than the obvious one.

6. Watch for "clue" words. "And" signals more of the same; "but," something different. Examples of other helpful clue words are "moreover," "similarly," "also," "however," "although," and "on the other hand."

7. When two words are missing, it is sometimes helpful to consider the second one first.

8. After you have made your selection, read the completed sentence to yourself to see whether it sounds logical.

Examples to Get You Started

ILLUSTRATION 1

Because the enemy had a reputation for engaging in sneak attacks, we were _____ on the alert. 1. inevitably 2. frequently 3. constantly 4. evidently 5. occasionally

The best answer is 3 (constantly). Neither "frequent" nor "occasional" periods of alertness would provide the necessary protection against sneak attacks at all times. "Constant" vigilance would have to be maintained. Choice 1 (inevitably) may be supported, but it is not as good as choice 3.

ILLUSTRATION 2

The simplest animals are those whose bodies are simplest in structure and which do the things done by all living animals, such as eating, breathing, moving, and feeling, in the most _____ way. 1. haphazard 2. bizarre 3. primitive 4. advantageous 5. unique

You should know from your knowledge of biology and your reading that *primitive* life forms were simple in structure and that the more complex forms evolved later. To secure the most *advantageous* way of conducting the activities of life, an animal would have to become specialized and complex. Thus choice 3 (primitive) is best because it develops the concept of simplicity discussed in the sentence. There is no justification for the other choices.

ILLUSTRATION 3

_____ has introduced the tremendous problem of the _____ of the hundreds of workers replaced by machines. 1. Specialization — relocation 2. Automation — retraining 3. Unemployment — education 4. Disease — recovery 5. Machinery — training

At first glance, answers 2 and 5 are possibilities. However, the placement of workers deprived of their jobs by modern machinery calls for their retraining (not their training) into more skilled activities. Moreover, the word "automation" is preferable to "machinery" because it connotes the replacement of men by machines. Number 2 is best.

PRACTICE EXERCISE   Answers given on page 230.

In each of the sentences below there is a blank space, indicating that a word has been omitted. Beneath the sentence are five lettered words; from these five words you are to choose the one word that, when inserted in the blank space, *best* fits in with the meaning of the sentence as a whole. In some sentences, two words are omitted; for these sentences, you are given five pairs of words. Select the pair that best completes the sentence.

1. I intend to wait for a more _____ occasion before I announce my plans.   (A) propitious   (B) prodigious   (C) pronounced   (D) pathetic   (E) positive

2. Your _____ attitude will alienate any supporters you may have won to your cause.   (A) fascinating   (B) altruistic   (C) logical   (D) truculent   (E) tortuous

3. In such a _____ grouping, a wide range of talent must be expected.   (A) casual   (B) formal   (C) homogeneous   (D) heathenish   (E) heterogeneous

4. A person who is _____ cannot be accused of being _____.   (A) dexterous — gauche   (B) glib — ribald   (C) magnanimous — charitable   (D) impolitic — partial   (E) reticent — shy

5. The size of the _____ controls the amount of _____ admitted.   (A) debt — interest   (B) aperture — light   (C) car — speed   (D) platform — people   (E) debt — mortgage

6. Disturbed by the _____ nature of the plays being presented, the Puritans closed the theaters in 1642.   (A) mediocre   (B) fantastic   (C) moribund   (D) salacious   (E) witty

7. The columnist was very gentle when he mentioned his friends, but he was bitter and even _____ when he discussed people who irritated him.   (A) laconic   (B) splenetic   (C) remorseful   (D) militant   (E) stoical

8. _____ with the waters of the melting snow, the rivers threatened to overflow their banks.   (A) Ineffable   (B) Chilled   (C) Turgid   (D) Filled   (E) Berserk

9. The sergeant suspected that the private was _____ in order to avoid going on the strenuous campaign scheduled for that morning.   (A) malingering   (B) proselytizing   (C) arrant   (D) agnostic   (E) piqued

10. Since you have convinced me of my error in ordering his execution, I am going to _____ the order for his death. **(A)** reaffirm **(B)** reiterate **(C)** reject **(D)** rescind **(E)** expiate

---

TEST — SENTENCE COMPLETION

In each of the sentences below there is a blank space, indicating that a word has been omitted. Beneath the sentence are five numbered words; from these five words you are to choose the one word that, when inserted in the blank space, best fits in with the meaning of the sentence as a whole. In some sentences, two words are omitted; for these sentences you are given five pairs of words. Select the pair that best completes the sentence.

1. Now that we have succeeded in isolating this drug and discovering its nature, our next problem is to plan its _____ in the laboratory. 1. amalgamation   2. synthesis   3. introduction   4. qualities   5. nature

2. The teacher suspected cheating as soon as he noticed the pupil's _____ glances at his classmate's paper. 1. overt   2. sporadic   3. furtive   4. futile   5. inconsequential

3. The _____ was noted for his _____. 1. hypocrite — honesty 2. braggart — modesty   3. craven — integrity   4. philanthropist — altruism   5. mercenary — benevolence

4. If you listen carefully, you can hear this simple _____ throughout the entire score 1. cadence   2. paean   3. banality   4. motif 5. trilogy

5. I am amazed to see such fine work done by a mere _____. 1. amateur   2. entrepreneur   3. tyro   4. despot   5. libertine

6. The sociologist maintained that the _____ and filth contributed to the delinquency in the _____ area. 1. crime — entire 2. squalor — redolent   3. terror — beseiged   4. litter — renovated   5. penury — slum

7. Your _____ remarks spoil the effect of your speech; try not to stray from your subject. 1. digressive   2. demoniac   3. discerning   4. disingenuous   5. disputatious

8. We need both ornament and implement in our society; we need the artist and the _____. 1. beautician 2. writer 3. artistic 4. artisan 5. engineer

9. When such _____ remarks are circulated, we can only blame and despise those who produce them. 1. adulatory 2. avid 3. rhetorical 4. redundant 5. reprehensible

10. We need more men of culture and enlightenment in our society; we have too many _____ among us. 1. pedants 2. philistines 3. moralists 4. ascetics 5. paragons

11. To be _____ is to be _____. 1. petulant — eager 2. avid — thirsty 3. parsimonious — niggardly 4. vacillating — resolute 5. phlegmatic — ardent

12. _____ his many hours of hard work at his bench, he realized that his progress was tenuous. 1. Despite 2. Because of 3. Through 4. Besides 5. By

13. It is difficult to enforce these rules because they are too _____. 1. subservient 2. truculent 3. pellucid 4. stringent 5. decrepit

14. A sanguine personality is the sign of the _____. 1. pessimist 2. optimist 3. philanthropist 4. profiteer 5. rationalist

15. Many educators argued that a _____ grouping of students would improve instruction as the range of student abilities would be limited. 1. heterogeneous 2. intensive 3. homogeneous 4. systematic 5. varied

16. As news of his indictment spread through the town, the citizens began to _____ him and to avoid meeting him. 1. ostracize 2. capitulate 3. desecrate 4. minimize 5. harass

17. These sporadic raids seem to indicate that the enemy is waging a war of _____ rather than attacking us directly. 1. fragments 2. attrition 3. intensity 4. barbarism 5. words

18. There are too many _____ and not enough serious workers. 1. sycophants 2. kleptomaniacs 3. tyros 4. recreants 5. dilettantes

19. As the debate continued, the speakers became more vehement and their remarks more _____. 1. pertinent 2. prolix 3. prolonged 4. acrimonious 5. ravenous

20. Many elderly people are capable of working, but they are kept from gainful employment by a _____ on the part of employers which leads them to believe that young people alone can give them adequate service. 1. philosophy 2. conviction 3. device 4. tendency 5. short-sightedness

Answers

Practice Exercise

1. A	3. E	5. B	7. B	9. A
2. D	4. A	6. D	8. C	10. D

Test

1. 2	5. 3	9. 5	13. 4	17. 2
2. 3	6. 5	10. 2	14. 2	18. 5
3. 4	7. 1	11. 3	15. 3	19. 4
4. 4	8. 4	12. 1	16. 1	20. 5

The Reading Comprehension Question

The purpose of this question is to test the candidate's ability to understand what he or she reads. Selections of varying length and difficulty are followed by multiple-choice questions that test comprehension.

Long-Range Strategy: Read, read, read — and not just the easy stuff. Read newspapers, magazines, and books; read prose, poetry, and drama; read recipes, charts, tables, maps, and train and bus schedules.

Tips to Help You Cope

1. Skim the passage.

2. Look at the questions, noting the type of information called for.

3. Read the passage, underlining important points, names, and so on.

4. Determine the central thought. Is there a topic sentence that expresses the main idea succinctly? What title would you give the passage?

5. Notice the specific details or statements that the writer gives to support the main idea.

6. Note the special techniques used by the author. These may include reasoning from experimental data (inductive method) or from principles accepted in advance (deductive method) and the use of examples, anecdotes, analogies, and comparisons.

7. Ferret out the meanings of key or unfamiliar words. If a word has more than one meaning, try to determine from the context exactly how the author is using it. If the word is strange, search the text for clues to its meaning.

8. Determine the writer's mood (e.g., confident, critical, frustrated, pessimistic, angry) in order to recognize emotional coloration of facts.

9. Determine the author's purpose. Is he or she seeking to inform, to persuade, to satirize, to evoke pity, to amuse, to arouse to action?

10. Some passages require you to go beyond the obvious, to look for the implications of what the author is saying and to draw inferences from the text. In such cases search for clues to the proper conclusion. A clue may be a name, a place, a date, an object, or an unusual word.

Examples to Get You Started

ILLUSTRATION 1

Too often we retire people who are willing and able to continue working, according to Federal Security Agency Administrator Oscar R.

Ewing in addressing the first National Conference on Aging, to point up the fact that chronological age is no longer an effective criterion in determining whether or not an individual is capable of working. The second World War proved this point when it became necessary to hire older experienced people to handle positions in business and industry vacated by personnel called to serve their country. As shown by production records set during the war period, the employment of older people helped us continue, and even better, our high level of production.

It was also pointed out at the conference that our life expectancy is increasing and that the over-65 group will jump from 11,500,000 now to twenty million in 1975. A good many of these people are capable of producing and have a desire to work, but they are kept from gainful employment by a shortsightedness on the part of many employers which leads them to believe that young people alone can give them adequate service. It is true that the young person has greater agility and speed to offer, but on the other hand there is much to be gained from the experience, steadfastness, and maturity of judgment of the elderly worker.

The title that best expresses the ideas of this passage is
1. Increased Efficiency of Elderly Workers
2. Misjudging Elderly Workers
3. Lengthening the Span of Life
4. New Jobs for the Aged
5. Production during World War II

Analysis of Passage

The author does not discuss the *increased* efficiency of elderly workers. He describes the useful and effective job they did during World War II. He does not maintain that their efficiency increased. Similarly, the author does not discuss *new* jobs for the aged. He discusses the inadvisability of dropping experienced and qualified workers because of age. Thus choices 1 and 4 introduce ideas not presented by the author and are, therefore, unsuitable as appropriate titles.

Choices 3 and 5 do appear in the text but only as illustrations of the major point the author is presenting. He tells us that the life span is increasing and that (the important thing) we will have many more qualified elderly workers in the future. He also tells us that production in World War II was maintained at a high level, but he uses this information to demonstrate that elderly people can perform satisfactorily when given the opportunity.

Throughout the passage, the author tells us that we are making a mistake when we retire elderly people. He talks of the experience, steadfastness, and maturity of judgment which these elderly workers have and which we ignore when we replace them with younger workers who can offer greater agility and speed. Thus we are guilty of seriously misjudging elderly workers. Choice 2 is the best title for this passage.

ILLUSTRATION 2

We all know people who would welcome a new American car to their stables, but one cannot expect to find a sports-car man among them. He cannot be enticed into such a circus float without feeling soiled. He resents the wanton use of chromium as much as he shudders at the tail fins, the grotesquely convoluted bumpers, and other "dishonest" lines. He blanches at the enormous bustle that adds weight and useless space, drags on ramps and curbstones, and complicates the process of parking even in the car's own garage. The attitude of the owner of a Detroit product is reflected in the efforts of manufacturers to "take the drive out of driving." The sports-car addict regards this stand as outrageous. His interest in a car, he is forever telling himself and other captive listeners, lies in the fun of driving it, in "sensing its alertness on the road," and in "pampering it as a thoroughbred."

The passage implies that sport cars are very
1. colorful
2. showy
3. maneuverable
4. roomy
5. grotesque

Analysis of Passage

If the owner of the sports car takes delight in "sensing its alertness on the road" he is finding pleasure in its maneuverability (choice 3). The sports car addict would object to the color, the show, the excessive roominess and the grotesque appearance of the Detroit product.

PRACTICE EXERCISE   Answers given on page 238.

Read the following paragraphs and answer the questions based on them.

Just why some individuals choose one way of adjusting to their difficulties and others choose other ways is not known. Yet what an individual does when he is thwarted remains a reasonably good key to the understanding of his personality. If his responses to thwartings are emotional explosions and irrational excuses, he is tending to live in an unreal world. He may need help to regain the world of reality, the cause-and-effect world recognized by generations of thinkers and scientists. Perhaps he needs encouragement to redouble his efforts. Perhaps, on the other hand, he is striving for the impossible and needs to substitute a worthwhile activity within the range of his abilities. It is the part of wisdom to learn the nature of the world and of oneself in relation to it and to meet each situation as intelligently and as adequately as one can.

1. The title that best expresses the ideas of this paragraph is: (A) Adjusting to Life (B) Escape from Reality (C) The Importance of Personality (D) Emotional Control (E) The Real Nature of the World

2. The writer argues that all should (A) substitute new activities for old (B) redouble their efforts (C) analyze their relation to the world (D) seek encouragement from others (E) avoid thwartings

Of the 197 million square miles making up the surface of the globe, 71 percent is covered by interconnecting bodies of marine water; the Pacific Ocean alone covers half the Earth and averages nearly 14,000 feet in depth. The *continents* — Eurasia, Africa, North America, South America, Australia, and Antarctica — are the portions of the *continental masses* rising above sea level. The submerged borders of the continental masses are the *continental shelves*, beyond which lie the deep-sea basins.

The oceans attain their greatest depths not in their central parts, but in certain elongated furrows, or long narrow troughs, called *deeps*. These profound troughs have a peripheral arrangement, notably around the borders of the Pacific and Indian oceans. The position of the deeps near the continental masses suggests that the deeps, like the highest mountains, are of recent origin, since otherwise they would have been filled with waste from the lands. This suggestion is strengthened by the fact that the deeps are frequently the sites of world-shaking earthquakes. For example, the "tidal wave" that in April, 1946, caused widespread destruction along Pacific coasts resulted from a strong earthquake on the floor of the Aleutian Deep.

The topography of the ocean floors is none too well known, since in great areas the available soundings are hundreds or even thousands of miles apart. However, the floor of the Atlantic is becoming fairly well known as a result of special surveys since 1920. A broad, well-defined ridge — the mid-Atlantic ridge — runs north and south between Africa and the two Americas, and numerous other major irregularities diversify the Atlantic floor. Closely spaced soundings show that many parts of the oceanic floors are as rugged as mountainous regions of the continents. Use of the recently perfected method of echo sounding is rapidly enlarging our knowledge of submarine topography. During World War II great strides were made in mapping submarine surfaces, particularly in many parts of the vast Pacific basin.

The continents stand on the average 2870 feet — slightly more than half a mile — above sea level. North America averages 2300 feet; Europe averages only 1150 feet; and Asia, the highest of the larger continental subdivisions, averages 3200 feet. The highest point on the globe, Mount Everest in the Himalayas, is 29,000 feet above the sea; and as the greatest known depth in the sea is over 35,000 feet, the maximum *relief* (that is, the difference in altitude between the lowest and highest points) exceeds 64,000 feet, or exceeds 12 miles. The continental masses and the deep-sea basins are relief features of the first order; the deeps, ridges, and volcanic cones that diversify the sea floor, as well as the plains, plateaus, and mountains of the continents, are relief features of the second order. The lands are unendingly subject to a complex of activities summarized in the term *erosion*, which first sculptures them in great detail and then tends to reduce them ultimately to sea level. The modeling of the landscape by weather, running water, and other agents is apparent to the keenly observant eye and causes thinking people to speculate on what must be the final result of the ceaseless wearing down of the lands. Long before there was a science of geology, Shakespeare wrote that "the revolution of the times makes mountains level."

3. The highest point on North America is   (A) 2300 feet above sea level   (B) in Mexico   (C) not mentioned in the passage   (D) 2870 feet above sea level   (E) higher than the highest point in Europe

4. The largest ocean is the   (A) Atlantic   (B) Pacific   (C) Indian   (D) Aleutian Deep   (E) Arctic

5. The science of geology was started   (A) by the Greeks   (B) in 1920   (C) during World War II   (D) April 1946   (E) after 1600

6. The peripheral furrows or *deeps* are found   (A) only in the Pacific and Indian oceans   (B) near earthquakes   (C) near the shore   (D) in the center of the ocean   (E) to be 14,000 feet in depth in the Pacific

7. The highest mountains are   (A) oldest   (B) in excess of 12 miles   (C) near the *deeps*   (D) relief features of the first order   (E) of recent origin

8. The continental masses   (A) comprise 29 per cent of the earth's surface   (B) consist of six continents   (C) rise above sea level   (D) are partially submerged   (E) are relief features of the second order

9. The *deeps* are subject to change caused by   (A) earthquakes   (B) erosion   (C) soundings   (D) weathering   (E) waste
10. From this selection, we may conclude that earthquakes   (A) occur in the *deeps*   (B) occur more frequently in newly formed land or sea formations   (C) cause erosion   (D) will ultimately "make mountains level"   (E) are caused by the weight of the water

---

TEST — READING COMPREHENSION

Read the following paragraphs and answer the questions based on them.

PASSAGE A

During the first year that Mr. Wordsworth and I were neighbours, our conversations turned frequently on the two cardinal points of poetry, the power of exciting the sympathy of the reader by a faithful adherence to the truth of nature, and the power of giving the interest of novelty by the modifying colours of imagination. The sudden charm, which accidents of light and shade, which moon-light or sunset diffused over a known and familiar landscape, appeared to represent the practicability of combining both. These are the poetry of nature. The thought suggested itself — (to which of us I do not recollect) — that a series of poems might be composed of two sorts. In the one, the incidents and agents were to be, in part at least, supernatural; and the excellence aimed at was to consist in the interesting of the affections by the dramatic truth of such emotions, as would naturally accompany such situations, supposing them real. And real in this sense they have been to every human being who, from whatever source of delusion, has at any time believed himself under supernatural agency. For the second class, subjects were to be chosen from ordinary life; the characters and incidents were to be such as will be found in every village and its vicinity, where there is a meditative and feeling mind to seek after them, or to notice them, when they present themselves.

In this idea originated the plan of the LYRICAL BALLADS; in which it was agreed, that my endeavours should be directed to persons and characters supernatural, or at least romantic; yet so as to transfer from our inward nature a human interest and a semblance of truth sufficient to procure for these shadows of imagination that willing suspension of disbelief for the moment, which constitutes poetic faith. Mr. Wordsworth, on the other hand, was to propose to himself as his object, to give the charm of novelty to things of every day, and to excite a feeling analogous to the supernatural, by awakening the mind's attention to the lethargy of custom, and directing it to the loveliness and the wonders of the world before us; an inexhaustible treasure, but for which, in consequence of the film of familiarity and selfish solicitude, we have eyes, yet see not, ears that hear not, and hearts that neither feel nor understand.

1. Samuel Coleridge, the author of this passage, felt that one characteristic of his poetry was its emphasis on   1. ordinary life   2. nature   3. the supernatural   4. the lethargy of custom   5. the sudden charm of the familiar

2. Familiarity often   1. breeds contempt   2. is an inexhaustible treasure   3. has novel elements   4. hides the beauty of the surroundings   5. is a shadow of the imagination

3. Coleridge wrote   1. none of the poems in *Lyrical Ballads*   2. some of the poems in *Lyrical Ballads*   3. half of the poems in *Lyrical Ballads*   4. most of the poems in *Lyrical Ballads*   5. all of the poems in *Lyrical Ballads*

4. The best title for this passage is   1. Suspension of Belief   2. A Great Collaboration   3. Adherence to Nature   4. Two Great Minds   5. Wordsworth and Coleridge

PASSAGE B

To stop science would create more problems than solutions. Aside from military considerations, it would be disastrous to freeze culture at its present high point. The highly technical civilization of the 20th century is like an airplane in flight, supported by its forward motion. It cannot stop without falling. If all the world's inhabitants, for instance, learn to use natural resources as fast as Americans do now, many necessary substances will be exhausted. Scientists confidently count on improvements, including atomic energy, to provide ample substitutes. Present techniques won't do it.

Where will man's curve of scientific progress take him ultimately? The surprises since 1900 have made scientists humble. They know that as science grows, it only penetrates deeper into mystery. Human knowledge may be visualized as an expanding sphere whose volume grows larger as its diameter increases. But the area of the sphere's surface, its frontier with the unknown, increases as the square of the diameter. Beyond that frontier — nobody can know, until the frontier advances.

5. The title that best expresses the ideas of this passage is   1. The Future of Science   2. New Frontiers   3. Progress Unlimited   4. The 20th Century   5. Our Technical Civilization

6. Scientists feel that improvements which can provide substitutes are required to   1. prevent useless loss of life   2. keep culture advancing   3. advance scientific knowledge   4. prevent exhaustion of basic materials   5. improve techniques of aviation

7. Scientists regard expanding scientific knowledge with   1. enthusiasm   2. despair   3. humility   4. pride   5. disgust

Answers

Practice Exercise

1. A	3. C	5. E	7. E	9. A
2. C	4. B	6. C	8. D	10. B

Test

1. 3	3. 2	5. 1	6. 4	7. 3
2. 4	4. 2			

5 The Test of Standard Written English

The Test of Standard Written English determines the candidate's ability to recognize the common errors that crop up in sentences.

Long-Range Strategy: Review the rules of grammar. In particular, be aware of the 10 common types of errors listed below.

| 1. **Incomplete sentences** | *Not:* Our school is famous for its teams. Especially the football team. |
| | *But:* Our school is famous for its teams, especially the football team. |

| 2. **Run-on sentences** | *Not:* He hit the ball, it was a homerun. |
| | *But:* He hit the ball. It was a homerun. |

| 3. **Lack of agreement between subject and verb** | *Not:* Each of the blocks are numbered. |
| | *But:* Each of the blocks is numbered. |

| 4. **Lack of agreement between pronoun and antecedent** | *Not:* Not one of the girls returned their gifts. |
| | *But:* Not one of the girls returned her gifts. |

| 5. **Wrong tense** | *Not:* When I worked for a month, I asked for a day off. |
| | *But:* When I had worked for a month, I asked for a day off. |

| 6. **Misuse of subjunctive mood** | *Not:* If I was President, things would be different. |
| | *But:* If I were President, things would be different. |

7. **Incorrect comparison of adjectives**	*Not:* Joe is taller than any boy in his class.
	But: Joe is taller than any other boy in his class.
	Not: Ann is the oldest of the two girls.
	But: Ann is the older of the two girls.

8. **Misuse of adjectives and adverbs**	*Not:* Bill dances good.
	But: Bill dances well.
	Not: I admire these kind of paintings.
	But: I admire this kind of paintings.
	Not: I feel badly about the accident.
	But: I feel bad about the accident.

| 9. **Dangling participles** | *Not:* Driving along the highway, the mountain came into view. |
| | *But:* Driving along the highway, I saw the mountain. |

| 10. **Lack of parallel structure** | *Not:* I like fishing, hunting, and to play golf. |
| | *But:* I like to fish, to hunt, and to play golf. |

Tips to Help You Cope

1. Bear in mind that the error, if there is one, occurs in the underlined portion of the sentence.

2. Look first for common errors, such as lack of agreement between subject and verb.

3. Remember that what is tested here is correct *written* English. The standards for spoken English are less rigorous.

Ten Typical Questions, with Answers Explained, to Get You Started

In each of the sentences below, there are four underlined words or phrases. If you think there is an error in usage, grammar, or punctuation in the underlined part, write the appropriate letter on your answer paper. If there is no error in any of the underlined parts, write E.

1. For modern man, the acquisition of facts is like a habit-forming
                                              (A)
   drug; the more he takes, the more craving he has.   No error
        (B)   (C)   (D)   (E)

2. This play is different than the one we saw last night.   No error
       (A)   (B)   (C)   (D)   (E)

3. The house looked it's age, despite our efforts to beautify it.   No error
                   (A)(B)   (C)   (D)   (E)

4. It may be difficult to find an acceptable definition of style; every critic
      (A)   (B)
   has their own.   No error
       (C)   (D)   (E)

5. Dozens of phrases can be offered to describe style, but perhaps the
       (A)   (B)
   best one is: "Style — it is the man."   No error
             (C)   (D)   (E)

6. The laborer today has greater leisure, is less provincial, enjoying the
               (A)   (B)   (C)
   fruits of his labors to a far greater degree than was hitherto
                          (D)
   possible.   No error
               (E)

7. This is <u>one</u> of the paintings <u>which</u> <u>is going</u> to be sold <u>at auction</u> this
      (A)   (B) (C)   (D)

afternoon. <u>No error</u>
         (E)

> Each of the sentences below has an underlined portion that may be correct or have an error in grammar, diction, style, punctuation or capitalization. From the five choices listed, select the one which you believe is correct.

8. In the normal course of events, <u>John will graduate high school and enter</u> college in two years.

  (A) John will graduate high school and enter
  (B) John will graduate from High School and enter
  (C) John will be graduated from High School and enter
  (D) John will be graduated from high school and enter
  (E) John will have graduated from high school and enter

9. The teacher asked, <u>"Have you read 'What makes Sammy Run'?"</u>

  (A) "Have you read 'What makes Sammy Run'?"
  (B) "Have you read 'What makes Sammy Run?'"
  (C) "Have you read 'What Makes Sammy Run'?"
  (D) "Have you read 'What Makes Sammy Run?'"
  (E) "Have you read What Makes Sammy Run?"

10. With the exception of <u>Frank and I, everyone in the class finished</u> the assignment before the bell rang.

  (A) Frank and I, everyone in the class finished
  (B) Frank and me, everyone in the class finished
  (C) Frank and me, everyone in the class had finished
  (D) Frank and I, everyone in the class had finished
  (E) Frank and me everyone in the class finished

Answers and Explanations

1. **C.** Lack of parallel structure. The sentence is better as: *The more he takes, the more he craves.*
2. **B.** *Different from* is the preferred form.
3. **A.** *It's* is the contraction for *it is*. The possessive pronoun is *its*.
4. **C.** Error in agreement. *Their* should be *his* (singular) to agree with *critic* (singular).
5. **E.** Sentence is correct.

6. **C.** Lack of parallel structure. Substitute a verb for the participle to parallel the preceding verbs. Sentence is better as: *The laborer today has greater leisure, is less provincial, and enjoys . . . .*

7. **C.** Error in agreement between pronoun and verb. The antecedent of *which* is paintings (plural). *Which* (plural) should be followed by *are going* (plural).

8. **D.** This corrects the two errors in the sentence — the idiom error (*to be graduated*) and the error in capitalization.

9. **C.** This corrects the two errors in the sentence — the capitalization of *Makes* and the placement of the question mark.

10. **C.** This corrects the two errors in the sentence — the error in case (*me* for *I*) and the error in tense (*had finished* for *finished*).

PRACTICE EXERCISE   Answers given on page 246.

In each of the ten sentences below, there are four underlined words or phrases. If you think there is an error in usage, grammar, or punctuation in the underlined part, write the letter on your answer paper. If there is no error in any of the underlined parts, write E on your answer paper.

1. The conditions governing the truce which has been arranged by the (A) (B) United Nations has not been revealed. No error (C) (D) (E)

2. Each one of the dogs in the show require a special kind of diet. (A) (B) (C) (D) No error (E)

3. By order of the Student Council, the wearing of jeans by we girls in (A) (B) (C) school has been permitted. No error (D) (E)

4. The major difficulty confronting the authorities was the reluctance (A) (B) of the people to talk; they had been warned not to say nothing (C) (D) to the police. No error (E)

5. We were <u>already</u> to leave for the amusement park when <u>John's car</u>
           (A)   (B)

     <u>broke down;</u> we <u>were forced</u> to postpone our outing.   <u>No error</u>
        (C)   (D)   (E)

6. We have heard that the <u>principal</u> has decided <u>whom</u> the prize winners
                                (A)   (B)

     <u>will be</u> and <u>will announce</u> the names in the assembly today.
      (C)   (D)

     <u>No error</u>
      (E)

7. She sang <u>like</u> she wished the <u>people</u> in the next <u>county</u> <u>to hear</u> her.
          (A)   (B)   (C)   (D)

     <u>No error</u>
      (E)

8. Although the news <u>had come</u> as a surprise to <u>all</u> in the room, every-
                    (A)   (B)

     one tried to do <u>their</u> work <u>as though</u> nothing had happened.
                   (C)   (D)

     <u>No error</u>
      (E)

9. The committee <u>had intended</u> <u>both</u> you and <u>I</u> to speak at the
               (A)   (B)   (C)

     assembly; however, only one of us will be able to talk.
        (D)

     <u>No error</u>
      (E)

10. "At that moment," John reported, "the teacher said, 'Speak louder.'"
               (A)   (B)   (C)   (D)

     <u>No error</u>
      (E)

Each sentence below has an underlined portion that may be
correct or grammatically incorrect. From the five choices listed,
select the one which you believe is correct, and write the letter
on your answer paper.

11. The child is <u>neither encouraged to be critical or to examine</u> all the evidence for his opinion.
- (A) neither encouraged to be critical or to examine
- (B) neither encouraged to be critical nor to examine
- (C) either encouraged to be critical or to examine
- (D) encouraged either to be critical nor to examine
- (E) not encouraged either to be critical or to examine

12. The process by which the community <u>influence the actions of its members</u> is known as social control.
- (A) influence the actions of its members
- (B) influences the actions of its members
- (C) had influenced the actions of its members
- (D) influences the actions of their members
- (E) will influence the actions of its members

13. To be sure, there would be scarcely no time left over for other things if school children <u>would have been expected to have considered</u> all sides of every matter on which they hold opinions
- (A) would have been expected to have considered
- (B) should have been expected to have considered
- (C) were expected to consider
- (D) will be expected to have been considered
- (E) were expected to be considered

14. <u>Examining the principal movements sweeping through the world, it can be seen</u> that they are being accelerated by the war.
- (A) Examining the principal movements sweeping through the world, it can be seen
- (B) Having examined the principal movements sweeping through the world
- (C) Examining the principal movements sweeping through the world can be seen
- (D) Examining the principal movements sweeping through the world, we can see
- (E) It can be seen examining the principal movements sweeping through the world

15. However many mistakes have been made in our past, the tradition of America, <u>not only the champion of freedom but also fair play,</u> still lives among millions who can see light and hope scarcely anywhere else.

(A) not only the champion of freedom but also fair play,

(B) the champion of not only freedom but also of fair play,

(C) the champion not only of freedom but also of fair play,

(D) not only the champion but also freedom and fair play,

(E) not the champion of freedom only, but also fair play,

Answer Key

1.	D	4.	D	7.	A	10.	E	13.	C
2.	C	5.	A	8.	C	11.	E	14.	D
3.	C	6.	B	9.	C	12.	B	15.	C

6 The Mathematics Part

An aptitude test attempts to discover how much ability you have to learn and use mathematics. It is not designed to find out how much mathematics you know; this is the purpose of an achievement test.

The questions on a mathematics aptitude test, of course, are about mathematics. Thus, the better you are able to use elementary mathematics the better you will be able to do on the SAT or on any other mathematics aptitude test. The people who make up the mathematics section of the SAT want to determine how fast you work, how accurately you can read questions and follow instructions, and how well you can understand the basic mathematical concepts. You can increase your grasp of elementary mathematics through practice.

Important Mathematical Definitions

Sum is the result of addition.

Difference is the result of subtraction.

Product is the result of multiplication.

In division, $\dfrac{\text{Dividend}}{\text{Divisor}} = \text{Quotient} + \dfrac{\text{Remainder}}{\text{Divisor}}$

A **fraction** is an indicated division.

A **decimal** is an indicated fraction with a denominator of 10, 100, 1000, ...

A **percent** is a fraction with a denominator of 100.

A **ratio** compares two quantities by dividing one by the other.

A **proportion** is an equation, both sides of which are fractions.

A **positive number** is one that is greater than zero; a **negative number** is one that is less than zero. The meaning and the use of **signed numbers** are basic in the study of algebra. Positive numbers are preceded by a plus sign $(+)$; negative numbers, by a minus sign $(-)$.

The Language of Algebra

In algebra, we use letters as well as numbers. When no sign appears between a combination of numbers and letters, it indicates that the items are to be multiplied. Thus $4abc$ means $4 \times a \times b \times c$.

Factor.   When two or more numbers or letters are multiplied together to yield a product, these numbers or letters are called the factors of the product. Thus 5 and 3 are the factors of 15, and 6, a, and b are the factors of $6ab$. Also, $(a + b)$ and $(a - b)$ are the factors of $a^2 - b^2$.

Coefficient.   Any factor of a term is called the coefficient of the remaining factors. In usual practice, the numerical value that is multiplied by the remaining terms is regarded as the coefficient. In $6ab$, 6 is regarded as the coefficient of ab; in abc, 1 is the coefficient of abc.

Exponent.   An exponent is a small number or letter written above and to the right of another number or letter. It indicates how many times the number or letter is multiplied by itself. Thus:

$$2^5 = 2 \times 2 \times 2 \times 2 \times 2 = 32$$
$$y^4 = y \times y \times y \times y$$

Solving Equations

An equation is a mathematical sentence which states that two expressions name the same number. Thus $4x = 20$ is an equation that is true when x is 5 and false when x is anything else.

A root (or solution) of an equation is a number that makes the equation true when used in place of the variable. The root of the equation $4x = 20$ is 5. Some equations have more than one root. The roots of the equation $x^2 - 7x + 12 = 0$ are 4 and 3.

Addition, subtraction, multiplication, or division of each side of an equation by the same quantity results in a new equation that has the same roots. (Division by 0, of course, is excluded here as in every other place in mathematics.) These operations are used on equations whose roots are not immediately apparent in order to find new equations that are simpler.

Example: If 4 is subtracted from one-fourth of a number, the result is 20. Find the number.

Let x = the number. Then the first sentence readily translates into the equation

$$\frac{1}{4}x - 4 = 20$$

This equation is solved by first multiplying both sides by 4 and then adding 16 to each side:

$$x = 96$$

To check, note that $\frac{1}{4}$ of 96 is 24, and when 4 is subtracted from 24 the result is 20.

Axioms Involving Inequalities

The whole is greater than any of its parts.

If equal quantities are added to unequal quantities, the sums are unequal in the same order.

If equal quantities are subtracted from unequal quantities, the remainders are unequal in the same order.

If unequal quantities are added to unequal quantities in the same order, the sums are unequal in the same order.

If unequal quantities are subtracted from unequal quantities, the remainders are unequal in the opposite order.

Doubles of unequals are unequal in the same order.

Halves of unequals are unequal in the same order.

If the first of three quantities is greater than the second, and the second is greater than the third, then the first is greater than the third.

Important Formulas

$$\text{Average} = \frac{\text{Sum of numbers}}{\text{Quantity of numbers}}$$

$$(\text{Rate})\,(\text{Time}) = \text{Distance}$$

$$\text{Time} = \frac{\text{Distance}}{\text{Rate}}$$

$$\text{Rate} = \frac{\text{Distance}}{\text{Time}}$$

$$\text{Percent Composition} = \frac{\text{Quantity dissolved}}{\text{Total quantity of mixture}} \times 100$$

$$\text{Part of task done} = \frac{\text{Time actually worked}}{\text{Time required to complete entire task}}$$

Tips on Solving Important Types of Problems

1. Fractions

Case 1. To find a number that is a fractional part of a given number, multiply the number by the fraction.

Example: Find $\frac{7}{8}$ of 48.

$$\frac{7}{\cancel{8}} \times \frac{\cancel{48}^{\,6}}{1} = 42$$

Example: Mr. Brown, who owns $\frac{3}{7}$ of the interest in a company, sells $\frac{1}{2}$ of his share to Mr. Wein. What part of the business does Mr. Wein own after completing this transaction?

$$\frac{1}{2} \times \frac{3}{7} = \frac{3}{14}$$

Case 2. To find what fractional part one number is of another, divide the number representing the part by the number representing the whole:

$$\frac{\text{Part}}{\text{Whole}} = \text{Fractional part}$$

Hint: In most problems, the *part* follows the word "is" and the *whole* follows the word "of."

Example: In a class of 26, there are 16 girls. What part of the class is made up of girls?

$$\frac{16}{26} = \frac{8}{13}$$

Example: What part of a quarter is a nickel?

$$\frac{\text{Nickel}}{\text{Quarter}} = \frac{5 \text{ cents}}{25 \text{ cents}} = \frac{5}{25} = \frac{1}{5}$$

Case 3. To find a number when a fractional part of it is known, divide the given part by the fraction:

$$\frac{\text{Part}}{\text{Fractional part}} = \text{Whole}$$

Note: Most students prefer to solve problems of this type algebraically.

Example: 6 is $\frac{2}{3}$ of what number?

$$\frac{6}{\frac{2}{3}} = 6 \div \frac{2}{3} \text{ or } \cancel{6}^{3} \times \frac{3}{\cancel{2}} = 9$$

Or algebraically, let x = the number:

$$\frac{2}{3}x = 6$$
$$x = 9$$

2. Percent

1. Substitute a letter (x, y, z, etc.) for the *unknown* quantity, such as "what," "what number," "what fraction," or "how many."
2. Substitute an equal sign for words such as "is equal to," "equals," or "is the equivalent of."
3. Apply the definition of "percent" as "hundredths." Thus $\frac{x}{100}$ is substituted for $x\%$, $\frac{3}{100}$ is substituted for 3%, etc.
4. Substitute parentheses (indicating multiplication) for such words as "of" or "part of." At this point you have set up the required equation.
5. Solve the equation.

Example: A book sold for $4.80 after being discounted by 20%. What was the list price?

List price × Rate of discount = Discount	(1)
List price − Discount = Net price	(2)

Let x = List price

(Using formula 1)	$x(.20)$ = discount
(Using formula 2)	$x - .20x = 4.80$
	$.80x = 4.80$
	$x = \textbf{\$6.00}$

or, since a discount of 20% of the list price was allowed, $4.80 represents 80% of the list price. Thus $.60 represents 1% of the list price, and $6.00 represents 100% (the whole) of the list price.

3. Averages

Case 1. To find the average of a group of numbers, add the numbers and divide the sum by the quantity of numbers added.

Example: A boy in a chemistry class reports the following readings on a thermometer during an experiment: 5°, 0°, −2°, 9°. What is the average temperature?

$$
\begin{array}{r}
5° \\
0° \\
-2° \\
9° \\
\hline
12° \text{ (sum)}
\end{array}
\qquad
\frac{12°}{4} = 3° \quad \text{(average)}
$$

Case 2. The sum is equal to the product of the average and the quantity of numbers.

Example: A student has an average of 80% for six semesters in high school. What average must he earn in his next semester so that his average at the end of the seventh semester will be 82%?

His present average being 80%, the sum is 80% × 6 or 480%. His desired average is 82% so that the sum will need to be 82% × 7 or 574%.

In his seventh term his average will have to be 574% − 480% or 94%.

Case 3. Weighted Averages. If two or more averages are combined into a single average, appropriate weight must be given each average.

Example: A student attended a certain high school for two semesters and earned an average of 90%. The same student earned an average of 85% in another school during a period of five terms. What is the scholastic average of this student for his high school work?

The sum in the first school is 90% × 2 or 180%.
The sum in the second school is 85% × 5 or 425%.
The sum for both schools is 180 + 425 or 605%.

Divide by the number of terms (7):
$$605\% \div 7 = 86.4\%$$

4. Motion

Problems involving motion can be solved by applying one of the following formulas:

$$\text{Distance} = \text{Rate} \times \text{Time} \qquad (1)$$

$$\text{Rate} = \frac{\text{Distance}}{\text{Time}} \qquad (2)$$

$$\text{Time} = \frac{\text{Distance}}{\text{Rate}} \qquad (3)$$

Example: How many miles can be covered in 3 hours by a train traveling at 45 miles per hour?

Apply formula 1:

$$\text{Distance} = \frac{45 \text{ miles}}{\text{hour}} \times 3 \text{ hours}$$
$$\text{Distance} = 135 \text{ miles}$$

Example: A motorist covers 93 miles in 3 hours. What is the average rate during this trip?

Apply formula 2:

$$\text{Rate} = \frac{93 \text{ miles}}{3 \text{ hours}} = \frac{31 \text{ miles}}{\text{hour}}$$

Example: How long will it take a plane to cover a distance of 900 miles if it maintains an average rate of 90 miles per hour?

Apply formula 3:

$$\text{Time} = \frac{900 \text{ miles}}{\frac{90 \text{ miles}}{\text{hour}}}$$

or $\quad 900 \text{ miles} \div \frac{90 \text{ miles}}{\text{hour}}$

or $\quad 900 \text{ miles} \times \frac{\text{hour}}{90 \text{ miles}}$

$= 10 \text{ hours}$

5. Ratio and Proportion

A *ratio* is an expression that compares two quantities by dividing one by the other. In a class with 10 girls and 13 boys, it can be said that the ratio of girls to boys is $10:13$ or $\frac{10}{13}$, or that the ratio of boys to girls is $13:10$ or $\frac{13}{10}$.

A *maximum ratio* is the ratio that has the largest numerical value. Since a ratio may be written as a fraction, to find the maximum ratio among a given number of cases determine which fraction has the greatest numerical value.

In any ratio the unit must be the same. Thus, to express the ratio of the length of a room to the width, both units of measurement must be the same.

Example: The dimensions of a room are: length 120 inches, width 1.2 feet. What is the ratio of the width to the length?

$$\frac{\text{Width}}{\text{Length}} = \frac{1.2 \text{ feet}}{120 \text{ inches}} = \frac{1.2 \text{ feet}}{10 \text{ feet}} = \frac{12}{100} = \frac{3}{25}$$

The ratio is therefore $3:25$.

Example: Two numbers are in the ratio of $7:3$. Their difference is 20. Find the numbers.

Since $7:3$ represents the reduced ratio, we can represent the original numbers by multiplying each number by n.

Let the smaller number $= 3n$.
Let the larger number $\;= 7n$.

$$7n - 3n = 20$$
$$4n = 20$$
$$n = 5$$
$$3n = 15;\ 7n = 35$$

A *proportion* is a statement of equality that exists between two ratios. For example, $\frac{1}{2} = \frac{5}{10}$ is a proportion. It consists of four terms. The first and last are called *extremes*. The second and third are called *means*. In the above example, 1 and 10 are the extremes; 2 and 5 are the means. In any proportion, the product of the means equals the product of the extremes:

$$\frac{1}{2} \nearrow\!\!\!\searrow \frac{5}{10}$$

$$(1)\,(10) = (2)\,(5)$$

The principles of ratio and proportion can help solve many problems. First decide whether a proportion exists. Then determine whether it is a direct proportion or an inverse proportion.

Direct proportion. Two variables are directly proportional if their corresponding values have a constant ratio. If one quantity is multiplied or divided by the same number, the ratio of the variables is unchanged.

Inverse proportion. Two variables are inversely proportional if an increase by multiplication in one variable results in a corresponding decrease in the other, and a decrease by division in one variable results in a corresponding increase in the other.

Example: One cup of crushed graham crackers can be obtained from 12 crackers. How many cups can be obtained from 36 such crackers?

This is obviously a direct proportion since the greater the number of crackers used, the greater will be the number of cups of crushed graham crackers.

$$\frac{1 \text{ cup}}{12 \text{ crackers}} = \frac{x \text{ cups}}{36 \text{ crackers}}$$
$$12x = 36$$
$$x = 3 \text{ cups}$$

Thus:

$$\frac{1 \text{ cup}}{12 \text{ crackers}} = \frac{3 \text{ cups}}{36 \text{ crackers}}$$

In this case, the ratio is $\frac{1}{12}$. Multiplying the quantities by 3 yields the ratio $\frac{3}{36}$, which is equal to $\frac{1}{12}$.

Example: If 4 boys can clear the snow around a house in 3 hours, how long will 8 boys working at the same rate take to perform this task?

Obviously, by increasing the number of boys, we will cut down on the time. This is an inverse proportion. Since the man power has been doubled, the time will be cut in half.

In an inverse proportion, if one quantity (4 boys) is the numerator of the first fraction, its related quantity (3 hours) is the denominator of the second fraction:

$$\frac{\text{Original number of boys}}{\text{New number of boys}} = \frac{\text{Time required by new number of boys}}{\text{Time required by original number of boys}}$$

$$\frac{4 \text{ boys}}{8 \text{ boys}} = \frac{x \text{ hours}}{3 \text{ hours}}$$

$$\frac{4}{8} = \frac{x}{3}$$

$$8x = 12$$

$$x = \frac{12}{8} \text{ or } 1\frac{1}{2} \text{ hours}$$

6. Mixtures and Solutions

Problems involving mixtures or solutions apply the principles of fractions. An important formula is:

$$\frac{\text{Quantity of substance dissolved}}{\text{Total quantity of solution}} = \frac{\text{Part of solution containing}}{\text{the dissolved substance}}$$

Example: A 10 gallon solution of disinfectant contains 1 gallon of disinfectant. What is the percent concentration of the solution?

$$\frac{1 \text{ gallon}}{10 \text{ gallons}} = \frac{1}{10} = 10\%$$

Example: How many pounds of pure salt must be added to 30 pounds of a 2% solution of salt and water to increase it to a 10% solution?

The given solution contains (2%) of 30 pounds of salt, or (.02)(30 pounds) or 0.6 pound of salt.

We must add a certain quantity of pure salt to the 30 pounds of solution so that:

$$\frac{\text{Quantity of salt}}{\text{Quantity of solution}} = 10\%$$

Let x = number of pounds of salt to be added to the quantity of salt already in the solution. Therefore the solution will now contain 30 pounds of solution plus x pounds of salt.

$$\frac{x + .6}{x + 30} = 10\%$$

$$\frac{x + .6}{x + 30} = \frac{1}{10}$$

$$10(x + .6) = x + 30$$

$$10x + 6 = x + 30$$

$$9x = 24$$

$$x = 2\frac{2}{3} \text{ pounds}$$

7. Work

Problems involving work are actually applications of the principles involving fractions. A student who has 4 hours of homework does $\frac{1}{4}$ of his task when he works 1 hour. A simple formula to remember is:

$$\frac{\text{Time actually spent working}}{\text{Time required to do the task}} = \text{Part of task done}$$

Example: A man can paint a room in 6 hours. His son can paint the same room in 8 hours alone. How long will it take the man and his son if they work together?

Let x = number of hours it will take if they work together.

In 1 hour the man would perform $\frac{1}{6}$ of the task. In 1 hour the son would perform $\frac{1}{8}$ of the task. Likewise, in x hours the man would perform $\frac{x}{6}$ part of the task. Since they will complete the *entire* task by each performing his part, we may say that the sum of the fractions equals 1 (the whole job):

$$\frac{x}{6} + \frac{x}{8} = 1$$

$$8x + 6x = 48$$

$$14x = 48$$

$$x = 3\frac{3}{7} \text{ hours}$$

Example: Mr. Jones can do a job in 10 days. After working 3 days he hires a helper and the two complete the task in 5 days. How long would it have taken the helper to complete the task alone?

Let x = number of days required by helper working alone to complete the task.

Mr. Jones completed $\frac{3}{10}$ of the task before he was joined by the helper. During the 5 day period when he was assisted by a helper he completed $\frac{5}{10}$ or $\frac{1}{2}$ of the task. If we assume that the helper could do the task in x days, then in 5 days he completed $\frac{5}{x}$ part of the entire task.

$$\frac{3}{10} + \frac{1}{2} + \frac{5}{x} = 1$$
$$3x + 5x + 50 = 10x$$
$$-2x = -50$$
$$x = 25 \text{ days}$$

Important Relationships in Geometry

Right Triangles

In a right triangle, $(\text{leg})^2 + (\text{leg})^2 = (\text{hypotenuse})^2$, or $a^2 + b^2 = c^2$.

In a 30°–60°–90° triangle:

The leg opposite the 30° angle equals one-half the hypotenuse.

The leg opposite the 60° angle equals $\frac{1}{2}$ the hypotenuse times $\sqrt{3}$.

The ratio of the shorter leg to the hypotenuse is $1:2$.

In a 45°–45°–90° triangle:

The hypotenuse equals a leg times $\sqrt{2}$.

The leg equals $\frac{1}{2}$ the hypotenuse times $\sqrt{2}$.

Equilateral Triangles

In an equilateral triangle, the altitude equals $\frac{1}{2}$ the side times $\sqrt{3}$.

Areas of Polygons

Area of a rectangle = bh.

Area of a square = s^2.

Area of a parallelogram = bh.

Area of a triangle = $\frac{1}{2}bh$.

Area of a right triangle = $\frac{1}{2}$ leg × leg.

Circles

Circumference of a circle = πD or $2\pi r$.

Length of an arc = $\frac{n}{360} \times 2\pi r$.

Area of a circle = πr^2.

Coordinate Geometry

Distance between two points = $\sqrt{(x_1 - x_2)^2 + (y_1 - y_2)^2}$.

Coordinates of midpoint of line = $\frac{1}{2}(x_1 + x_2), \frac{1}{2}(y_1 + y_2)$.

Quantitative Comparisons

In this type of question you are given two quantities, with information regarding either or both, and are asked to decide which, if either, is the greater quantity. Actually, these questions apply various principles of mathematics already covered in this chapter and involve less reading and less computation than the other types of multiple-choice questions. The directions state that diagrams are not necessarily drawn to scale, and that facts pertaining to one or both quantities are centered above both columns. After comparing the two quantities, one in one column and the other in another column, you choose

A   if the quantity in Column A is greater,
B   if the quantity in Column B is greater,

C   if the two quantities are equal,

D   if the relationship cannot be determined from the information given.

Observe that in these questions there are four choices as compared with five for the other types of questions. Therefore, in calculating, the penalty for guessing the formula is:

$$\text{Number correct} - \frac{1}{3}(\text{Number wrong}) = \text{Raw score}$$

Some Tips for Solving Quantitative Comparison Questions

1. When a problem involves a straightforward computation, eliminate choice D, which cannot possibly be correct. Thus, in cases of simple computation, your chances of making a correct guess are much better since the answer will be one out of three possible choices.
2. Bear in mind that you should consider negatives and zero for your answers. For example, if $x^2 = 25$, then $x = +5$ or -5.
3. Eliminate terms that appear in both Column A and Column B. For example, if both columns have the factors (5) (6) (7), then you should consider, for comparison, all other factors.
4. Remember that diagrams are not necessarily drawn to scale. A figure is not equilateral because it may *seem* to be so. Consider the data given before making any assumptions.
5. Maintain a reasonable rate of speed. Since these problems are not as time consuming as the other types, you are expected to finish more of them in a given length of time.

Examples

	Column A	Column B
1.	$10 - \dfrac{10}{.1}$	-90

Analysis

$\dfrac{10}{1}$ equals $\dfrac{100}{1}$ or 100

$10 - 100 = -90$

The correct answer is **C**.

2.   50% $\frac{1}{.02}$

Analysis

The value of $\frac{1}{.02}$ = 50

50 is greater than 50%

The correct answer is **B**.

---

3. In the J.J. High School the average mark on a uniform city-wide chemistry test was 70% in one class and 75% in another class.

At the K.K. High School the average mark in the two chemistry classes on the same test was 72.5%.

Analysis

Since we do not have the number of students involved in these various classes we may not assign equal weight to the averages given.

The correct answer is **D**.

In rectange $ABCD$, $AB = \pi$ and BC = diameter of circle O.

4.   Area of $ABCD$ Circumference of circle O

Analysis

Area of rectangle = length × width

Let d = diameter of circle and side BC

Area of rectangle $ABCD = \pi d$

Circumference of a circle = π × diameter

Circumference of circle $O = \pi d$

The correct answer is **C**.

---

5.   Perimeter of $ABCD$ Area of circle O

Analysis

Perimeter of $ABCD = \pi + \pi + d + d$

Area of circle = πr^2

Area of circle $O = \pi \left(\frac{d}{2}\right)\left(\frac{d}{2}\right)$ or $\frac{\pi d^2}{4}$

The correct answer is **D**.

PRACTICE EXERCISE   Answers given on page 265-268.

Select the correct answer from the choices below each question.

1. If the circumference of a circle increases from π inches to 2π inches, what change occurs in the area?
   (a) remains the same   (b) doubles   (c) triples
   (d) quadruples   (e) is halved

2. Suppose $ab = a^2$ and $a \neq 0$. Then $a - b = $?
   (a) -1 (b) 0   (c) 1   (d) 2   (e) 5

3. Suppose six integers are multiplied and the product is odd. Exactly how many of the integers must be odd?
   (a) 1   (b) 2   (c) 3   (d) 5   (e) 6

4. Suppose $z = \frac{3x}{y}$. What happens to z if x is doubled and y is tripled?
   (a) doubled   (b) tripled   (c) halved
   (d) multiplied by 6   (e) multiplied by a factor of $\frac{2}{3}$

5. If x must be greater than 4, which of the following must have the least value?
   (a) $\frac{4}{x + 1}$ (b) $\frac{4}{x - 1}$ (c) $\frac{4}{x}$ (d) $\frac{x}{4}$ (e) $\frac{x + 1}{4}$

6. Suppose $x^2 + y^2 = 2$ and $x^2 - y^2 = 2$. Find $x^4 - y^4$.
   (a) 0   (b) 2   (c) 4   (d) 5   (e) 8

7. Six consecutive integers are given. The sum of the first three is 27. What is the sum of the last three?
   (a) 29   (b) 30   (c) 32   (d) 33   (e) 36

8. If the points given in (a) through (e) are the endpoints of segments that have the other end at the origin, which segment has a midpoint that is farthest from the origin?
   (a) (3,3)   (b) (2,5)   (c) (1,6)   (d) (0,7)
   (e) (4,3)

9. The symbol $\begin{vmatrix} a & b \\ c & d \end{vmatrix}$ means $ad - bc$. What is the value of $\begin{vmatrix} 1 & 2 \\ 3 & 4 \end{vmatrix}$?
   (a) -2 (b) 0   (c) 2   (d) 1   (e) -4

10. A certain type of bacteria triples in number every 20 minutes. At the end of 5 hours there are x bacteria in the colony. How many hours more will it take until there are $27x$?
    (a) 1   (b) $1\frac{1}{3}$ (c) $1\frac{2}{3}$ (d) 2   (e) $\frac{2}{3}$

11. What number must be multiplied by $\dfrac{1}{\sqrt{2}}$ to give $\sqrt{2}$?

(a) 2   (b) $\sqrt{2}$ (c) $\dfrac{1}{2}$ (d) $\dfrac{1}{\sqrt{2}}$ (e) $\dfrac{\sqrt{2}}{2}$

12. A mathematical law states that the sum of the first n odd counting numbers is n^2. Which of the following is an example of this law?

(a) $1 + 3 = 4$ (b) $1 + 9 + 16 = 26$
(c) $1 + 2 = 3$ (d) $1 + 3 + 5 = 1 + 2(4)^2$
(e) $1 + 4 = 5$

13. Find the area of triangle ABC if, for each point (x,y) of line AB, $y = 2x - 8$.

(a) 100   (b) 121   (c) 144   (d) 169   (e) 132

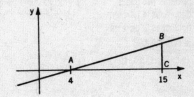

14. Suppose $a * b = c$ is true only if $b^c = a$. Find y when $64 * 4 = y$.

(a) $\dfrac{1}{2}$ (b) 2   (c) 3   (d) 4   (e) $\dfrac{1}{4}$

15. If $\neq$ means "is not equal to," what values of x make the following statement true?

$$3x - 1 \neq 2x$$

(a) $x = 1$ (b) $x = -1$ (c) $x \neq 1$
(d) $x > 1$ (e) $x < 1$

16. The number 4,554 is an example of a number of the form $xyyx$. Which of the following will always divide a number of this form?

(a) 2   (b) 3   (c) 6   (d) 9   (e) 11

17. A bag contains 28 pounds of sugar which is to be separated into packages containing 14 ounces each. How many such packages can be made?

(a) 2   (b) 4   (c) 8   (d) 16   (e) 32

18. Suppose $a = b + 3$. What is the value of $(a - b)^3$?

(a) 1   (b) 8   (c) 27   (d) 64   (e) 0

19. Suppose you know that $\sqrt{15}$ is approximately 3.89. Which of the following is the best approximation to $\sqrt{\dfrac{5}{3}}$?

(a) .2   (b) .41   (c) 1.29   (d) 6.10   (e) 3.66

20. Suppose you have 72 green marbles and 108 red marbles to sell. You decide to separate them into packages of the same size, each of which contains either all red or all green. What is the greatest number you can put in each package?

(a) 3　　　(b) 18　　　(c) 12　　　(d) 24　　　(e) 36

21. Which of the numbers in (a) through (e) is the greatest?

(a) $\dfrac{1 - \frac{1}{3}}{3}$　　(b) $\dfrac{-3}{-\frac{1}{3}}$　　(c) $\dfrac{-3}{\frac{1}{3}}$　　(d) 0　　(e) $\dfrac{3 - \frac{1}{3}}{3}$

22. If the length of a rectangle is increased by 20 percent and the width is decreased by 20 percent, what percent change occurs in the area?

(a) remains the same　　　(b) increases 5 percent
(c) decreases 4 percent　　　(d) increases 2 percent
(e) decreases 2 percent

23. Find the area of △ABC.

(a) $13\frac{1}{2}$　　(b) 12　　(c) 11　　(d) 9　　(e) $9\frac{1}{2}$

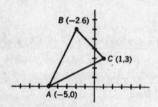

24. What percent of $\frac{1}{2}$ is $\frac{3}{4}$?

(a) 100%　　(b) 120%　　(c) 125%　　(d) 140%
(e) 150%

25. If $y = \dfrac{3x - 6}{x}$, for what values of x will y be positive?

(a) $x > 2$ or $x < 0$　　(b) only when x is positive
(c) only when x is negative　　(d) $-2 < x < 2$
(e) $-2 < x < 2$ but not zero

26. Which of the following is the square (second power) of $\sqrt{1 + \sqrt{1}}$?

(a) 1　　(b) 2　　(c) 4　　(d) 3　　(e) $1 + \sqrt{2}$

27. If AD and BC are parallel, what is the length of BC?

(a) x　　(b) x + y　　(c) x + 2y　　(d) 2x + y
(e) 2x + 2y

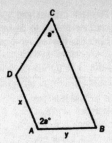

28. If $(.4)(y) = 5$, find $(4.44)(y)$.

    (a) 5.055   (b) .555   (c) 555   (d) 55.5   (e) 5.55

29. If $\dfrac{p \times p \times p}{p + p + p} = 6$, find p.

    (a) $\dfrac{1}{3}$ (b) $\dfrac{1}{9}$ (c) 27   (d) 3   (e) 9

30. Suppose $S(x)$ is defined as follows:

        $S(x) = 1$ when $x > 1$,

        $S(x) = x$ when $- \leq x \leq 1$, and

        $S(x) = -1$ when $x < 1$.

    What is the value of $S(5) + S(4) + S(0)$?

    (a) 1   (b) 0   (c) 3   (d) 2   (e) −1

Answers to Practice Exercise

1. **(d)** Since the circumference is doubled, the radius is doubled. The area is based on the square of the radius. Squaring the factor of 2 thus introduced makes the area change by a factor of 4.

2. **(b)** $ab = a^2$ means $0 = a^2 - ab = a(a - b)$. Divide both sides by a (which is given as not equal to 0), and you will find $a - b = 0$.

3. **(e)** If any of the integers is even, the product will have a factor of 2 and will be even.

4. **(e)** The pitfall that traps many students is the 3 in the numerator, which they cancel with the 3 that appears in the denominator when the denominator is tripled. If this is done, the result is $\dfrac{2x}{y}$, which is still $\dfrac{2}{3}\left(\dfrac{3x}{y}\right)$ or $\dfrac{2}{3}z$. The obvious solution is the true one.

5. **(a)** (d) and (e) can be excluded because greater values of x will increase the numerator and thereby the fraction. (a), (b), and (c) all have the same numerator so the least fraction will be the one with greatest denominator.

6. **(c)** $x^4 - y^4 = (x^2 + y^2)(x^2 - y^2) = (2)(2)$.

7. **(e)** The sum of the last three must be 9 more than the sum of the first three. You can see the pattern if we let x be the first of these integers.

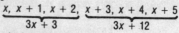

$$\underbrace{x,\ x + 1,\ x + 2,}_{3x\ +\ 3}\ \underbrace{x + 3,\ x + 4,\ x + 5}_{3x\ +\ 12}$$

8. **(d)** If the midpoint is farthest from the origin then the endpoint will be as well, so you need not find any midpoints. You could crank out the distances by formula, but a quick sketch gets the results in less time.

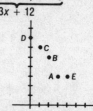

9. **(a)** This is easy. The pattern given is $1 \times 4 - 3 \times 2 = -2$.

10. **(a)** Since the question asks "how many more?" you can ignore the first 5 hours. In 20 minutes x will triple to $3x$ and in 20 more minutes this will triple to $3(3x)$. At the end of 1 hour, it will be $(3)(3)(3x)$ or $27x$.

11. **(a)** Divide $\sqrt{2}$ by $\dfrac{1}{\sqrt{2}}$ to get $\sqrt{2} \cdot \dfrac{\sqrt{2}}{1} = 2$ since $(\sqrt{2})(\sqrt{2}) = 2$.

12. **(a)** This is easy. Since each answer given uses only two or three terms ($n = 2$ or $n = 3$), you could write what the law states for the two cases and test: $1 + 3 = 2^2$ and $1 + 3 + 5 = 3^2$.

13. **(b)** This is easy. You have the length of the base, $15 - 4 = 11$, but need the height. The y-coordinate of b tells you the height. Since $y = 2x - 8$ for each point of the line and $x = 15$ at B, $y = 22$. Area $= \dfrac{1}{2}(11)(22) = 121$.

14. **(c)** By direct substitution into the formula given, you get $4^y = 64$. $64 = 4^3$ so $y = 3$.

15. **(c)** Any value that makes $3x - 1 \neq 2x$ true makes $3x - 1 = 2x$ false. The latter is true for $x = 1$ and false for $x \neq 1$.

16. **(e)** Other examples include 1221, 2332, etc. As you can see, 2 will not divide 1221 so neither will 6. 3 doesn't work with 2332 so neither will 9. Since one answer must be true, it must be (e). A proof would be complicated but is unnecessary.

17. **(e)** Changing pounds to ounces gives 28×16, but do not multiply it out since 14 will divide 28. $2 \times 16 = 32$.

18. **(c)** If $a = b + 3$, then $a - b = 3$ and. $(a - b)^3 = 3^3$.

19. **(c)** You must change $\sqrt{\dfrac{5}{3}}$ to a form that will use the given approximation of $\sqrt{15}$.

$$\sqrt{\frac{5}{3}} = \sqrt{\frac{5 \times 3}{3 \times 3}} = \frac{\sqrt{15}}{\sqrt{9}} = \frac{\sqrt{15}}{3} = \frac{3.87}{3} = 1.29$$

20. **(e)** $72 = 2 \times 2 \times 2 \times 3 \times 3$, $108 = 2 \times 2 \times 3 \times 3 \times 3$. By inspecting factors you can see that the greatest number which will divide both is $2 \times 2 \times 3 \times 3$.

21. **(b)** (a), (b), (e) are positive so (c) and (d) can be eliminated since they aren't. (e) is greater than (a) since $3 - \frac{1}{3}$ is greater than $1 - \frac{1}{3}$.

    (b) is 9. (e) is $\frac{2\frac{2}{3}}{3}$, which is $\frac{1}{3}$ of $2\frac{2}{3}$ and hence less than 1. A routine and lengthy approach is to simplify each of them.

22. **(c)** $(1.20L)(.80W) = .96LW$ is the new area or
    $$LW + .20LW - .20LW - .04LW$$

23. **(a)** You cannot find any base or height by simple methods so draw perpendiculars to the x-axis from B and C and then add and subtract the necessary pieces:

    (1) area of triangle $ABB' = \frac{1}{2}(3)(6) = 9$,

    (2) area of trapezoid $BB'C'C = \frac{1}{2}(6 + 3)3 = 13\frac{1}{2}$,

    (3) area of triangle $ACC' = \frac{1}{2}(6)(3) = 9$.

    Add (1) and (2), then subtract (3).

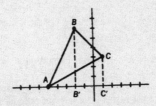

24. **(e)** $\frac{3}{4}$ is $\frac{1}{2}$ plus half of $\frac{1}{2}$ or 100% plus 50%.

25. **(a)** $\frac{3x - 6}{x} = 3 - \frac{6}{x}$, which will be positive as long as $3 > \frac{6}{x} \cdot \frac{6}{x}$ will be less than 3 when (1)x is negative, or (2)$x > 2$.

26. **(b)** $\sqrt{1} = 1$ so $\sqrt{1} + \sqrt{1} = \sqrt{1 + 1} = \sqrt{2}$, which when squared gives 2.

27. **(b)** Draw AP bisecting $\angle DAB$. $PC = x$ since $PADC$ is a parallelogram. $\angle APB$ has measure a° since $\angle APB$ and $\angle C$ are cor-

responding angles. $PB = y$ since $\angle PAB$ and $\angle BPA$ have the same measure.

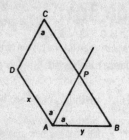

28. **(d)**

$$.4y = 5$$
$$.04y = .5 \text{ (multiply by .1)}$$
$$\underline{+\quad 4y = 50 \text{ (multiply by 10)}}$$
$$4.44y = 55.5$$

29. **(d)** $\dfrac{p^3}{3p} = \dfrac{p^2}{3}$, which is given to be 3. Thus $p^2 = 9$ and $p = 3$.

30. **(d)** From the three-part formula we can conclude $S(5) = 1$, $S(4) = 1$, $S(0) = 0$ so $1 + 1 + 0 = 2$.

7 Practice Scholastic Aptitude Test

This part is designed to give the student an idea of what to expect on the Scholastic Aptitude Test (SAT). The wise student will take this examination after thorough review of the earlier chapters and after doing the practice exercises that occur earlier in the book. The test should serve as a basis for analysis which, for some, may be a signal for the need for further drill before taking the tests that count and, for others, an indication that preparation for the SAT is adequate. Just as the weak student needs drill, the superior student often needs confidence. A good score on the test in this chapter should send the student into the examination room with such confidence.

The verbal section tests ability to reason with words and ideas and power to read rapidly and intelligently. The mathematics section tests ability to handle general number concepts rather than specific achievements in mathematics. The emphasis is on ability to apply fundamental mathematical knowledge to new situations. The standard written English portion tests the ability to communicate. This examination is different from other tests you have taken. The questions are all of the objective type with a penalty imposed for guessing. The score is determined by the number of correct answers made with deductions for incorrect answers. This situation is a new one, since in most regular school examinations the time factor is not important. In addition, the top-notch student has become accustomed to strive for perfection on school tests whereas most college entrance examinations are so constructed that only a few pupils can attain this goal. Economy of time is of utmost concern. It is best to work rapidly and carefully and not to waste time on questions that contain difficult or unfamiliar material. In the matter of guessing, it is advisable to leave a question unanswered rather than to spend too much time on it. This does not apply to what might be called "shrewd" guessing. You may sometimes eliminate certain possible answers to a question because of your general knowledge, and despite your inability to explain by good reasoning why you choose a specific answer, you feel that it is the correct one. Such a shrewd guess may be right and you should therefore give that answer.

To derive maximum benefit, the student should take this test in an examination room atmosphere. Find a quiet room and allow the *precise* time indicated for each section. Practice in taking tests has value in itself. The student who acquires the skill of taking an examination calmly is seldom guilty of misinterpreting questions, of losing valuable time because of tension caused by the test situation, or of not following examination directions.

Although the test in this chapter matches the SAT examination in that both are three-hour tests, many students preparing for the examination may be unwilling or unable to spend three hours at one sitting. They may decide to concentrate on one kind of test or may find that they have only an hour or a half-hour at a time to devote to their preparation for the SAT. However, the test is best taken during a complete, uninterrupted three-hour period so that the student will be prepared for the physical requirements of a long examination.

The various parts of each test are easily identified. Sections 1 and 4 are devoted to Verbal Aptitude; Sections 2 and 5 test Mathematical Aptitude; Section 3 tests ability in Standard Written English; Section 6 alternates between Math and Verbal Aptitude. On our model SAT, this section is a test of Mathematical Aptitude.

One thing to remember: the mathematical symbols used on the SAT may not conform to those used in your high school test, but the meaning should be very clear from the way the symbol is used in the question. This is especially true of questions about geometry. For example, in some texts *AB* is used to denote the line segment with endpoints at *A* and *B*. In others that same symbol,

AB, refers to the length of the segment. On the test, the line segment with endpoints at A and B is referred to as "line segment AB."

At times in your textbook you may have encountered questions about the symbols themselves. Such questions will not appear on the SAT. If you see a statement such as $\angle A = 60°$, which may have been considered an incorrect usage by the author of your textbook, do not reject the question as defective. You may assume that it has the simplest and most obvious meaning, that the degree measure of the angle with vertex A is 60.

After completing the test, score the answers. To evaluate your performance count the number of correct answers and the number of incorrect responses. To become accustomed to the procedure of penalizing for guessing, deduct ¼ for each incorrect answer, except in the quantitative comparison questions, where ⅓ is subtracted for each incorrect choice. For example, the student who finds that he or she has answered 24 of 30 questions and has 20 correct answers and 4 wrong answers should score the performance as follows:

$$20 - ¼(4) = 19 \text{ (Raw Score)}$$

The student who has answered 26 of the 30 questions in the allotted time and has made 8 errors should score that performance as follows:

$$18 - ¼(8) = 16 \text{ (Raw Score)}$$

While a Raw Score of 55 or 60 on the tests in these chapters is an indication of very superior performance, the Raw Score obtained in each case needs interpretation. The administrators of the College Entrance Examination Board indicate that this is a complicated task even for them, and that the significance of a particular score depends upon the caliber of the candidates who take the examination at that time. In addition, the meaning of a "good score" varies with individuals. For example, the student who takes the test for the award of a scholarship obviously must score very high. Likewise, the student who is seeking admission to a highly competitive "name" college must also attain a high score. More specifically, you can interpret the Raw Scores for the practice test in accordance with the following tables:

VERBAL SCORES

66 — 80	excellent
56 — 65	very good
41 — 55	average
28 — 40	passing
below 28	unsatisfactory

MATHEMATICAL SCORES

95 — 105	excellent
71 — 94	very good
50 — 70	average
45 — 49	passing
below 45	unsatisfactory

STANDARD WRITTEN ENGLISH SCORES

45 — 50	excellent
39 — 44	very good
34 — 38	average
25 — 33	passing
below 25	unsatisfactory

If you need more review, you should work with the most widely used college entrance review book — *Barron's How to Prepare for College Entrance Examinations*. This book of nearly 700 pages reviews, drills, and tests the verbal and mathematics phases of the SAT, the PSAT/NMSQT, and the CEEB Achievement Tests.

Answer Sheet

For each question, fill in the circle that corresponds to the answer you have chosen as correct.

Section 1

1. Ⓐ Ⓑ Ⓒ Ⓓ Ⓔ
2. Ⓐ Ⓑ Ⓒ Ⓓ Ⓔ
3. Ⓐ Ⓑ Ⓒ Ⓓ Ⓔ
4. Ⓐ Ⓑ Ⓒ Ⓓ Ⓔ
5. Ⓐ Ⓑ Ⓒ Ⓓ Ⓔ
6. Ⓐ Ⓑ Ⓒ Ⓓ Ⓔ
7. Ⓐ Ⓑ Ⓒ Ⓓ Ⓔ
8. Ⓐ Ⓑ Ⓒ Ⓓ Ⓔ
9. Ⓐ Ⓑ Ⓒ Ⓓ Ⓔ
10. Ⓐ Ⓑ Ⓒ Ⓓ Ⓔ
11. Ⓐ Ⓑ Ⓒ Ⓓ Ⓔ
12. Ⓐ Ⓑ Ⓒ Ⓓ Ⓔ
13. Ⓐ Ⓑ Ⓒ Ⓓ Ⓔ
14. Ⓐ Ⓑ Ⓒ Ⓓ Ⓔ
15. Ⓐ Ⓑ Ⓒ Ⓓ Ⓔ
16. Ⓐ Ⓑ Ⓒ Ⓓ Ⓔ
17. Ⓐ Ⓑ Ⓒ Ⓓ Ⓔ
18. Ⓐ Ⓑ Ⓒ Ⓓ Ⓔ
19. Ⓐ Ⓑ Ⓒ Ⓓ Ⓔ
20. Ⓐ Ⓑ Ⓒ Ⓓ Ⓔ
21. Ⓐ Ⓑ Ⓒ Ⓓ Ⓔ
22. Ⓐ Ⓑ Ⓒ Ⓓ Ⓔ
23. Ⓐ Ⓑ Ⓒ Ⓓ Ⓔ
24. Ⓐ Ⓑ Ⓒ Ⓓ Ⓔ
25. Ⓐ Ⓑ Ⓒ Ⓓ Ⓔ
26. Ⓐ Ⓑ Ⓒ Ⓓ Ⓔ
27. Ⓐ Ⓑ Ⓒ Ⓓ Ⓔ
28. Ⓐ Ⓑ Ⓒ Ⓓ Ⓔ
29. Ⓐ Ⓑ Ⓒ Ⓓ Ⓔ
30. Ⓐ Ⓑ Ⓒ Ⓓ Ⓔ
31. Ⓐ Ⓑ Ⓒ Ⓓ Ⓔ
32. Ⓐ Ⓑ Ⓒ Ⓓ Ⓔ
33. Ⓐ Ⓑ Ⓒ Ⓓ Ⓔ
34. Ⓐ Ⓑ Ⓒ Ⓓ Ⓔ
35. Ⓐ Ⓑ Ⓒ Ⓓ Ⓔ
36. Ⓐ Ⓑ Ⓒ Ⓓ Ⓔ
37. Ⓐ Ⓑ Ⓒ Ⓓ Ⓔ
38. Ⓐ Ⓑ Ⓒ Ⓓ Ⓔ
39. Ⓐ Ⓑ Ⓒ Ⓓ Ⓔ
40. Ⓐ Ⓑ Ⓒ Ⓓ Ⓔ
41. Ⓐ Ⓑ Ⓒ Ⓓ Ⓔ
42. Ⓐ Ⓑ Ⓒ Ⓓ Ⓔ
43. Ⓐ Ⓑ Ⓒ Ⓓ Ⓔ
44. Ⓐ Ⓑ Ⓒ Ⓓ Ⓔ
45. Ⓐ Ⓑ Ⓒ Ⓓ Ⓔ

Section 2

1. Ⓐ Ⓑ Ⓒ Ⓓ Ⓔ
2. Ⓐ Ⓑ Ⓒ Ⓓ Ⓔ
3. Ⓐ Ⓑ Ⓒ Ⓓ Ⓔ
4. Ⓐ Ⓑ Ⓒ Ⓓ Ⓔ
5. Ⓐ Ⓑ Ⓒ Ⓓ Ⓔ
6. Ⓐ Ⓑ Ⓒ Ⓓ Ⓔ
7. Ⓐ Ⓑ Ⓒ Ⓓ Ⓔ
8. Ⓐ Ⓑ Ⓒ Ⓓ Ⓔ
9. Ⓐ Ⓑ Ⓒ Ⓓ Ⓔ
10. Ⓐ Ⓑ Ⓒ Ⓓ Ⓔ
11. Ⓐ Ⓑ Ⓒ Ⓓ Ⓔ
12. Ⓐ Ⓑ Ⓒ Ⓓ Ⓔ
13. Ⓐ Ⓑ Ⓒ Ⓓ Ⓔ
14. Ⓐ Ⓑ Ⓒ Ⓓ Ⓔ
15. Ⓐ Ⓑ Ⓒ Ⓓ Ⓔ
16. Ⓐ Ⓑ Ⓒ Ⓓ Ⓔ
17. Ⓐ Ⓑ Ⓒ Ⓓ Ⓔ
18. Ⓐ Ⓑ Ⓒ Ⓓ Ⓔ
19. Ⓐ Ⓑ Ⓒ Ⓓ Ⓔ
20. Ⓐ Ⓑ Ⓒ Ⓓ Ⓔ
21. Ⓐ Ⓑ Ⓒ Ⓓ Ⓔ
22. Ⓐ Ⓑ Ⓒ Ⓓ Ⓔ
23. Ⓐ Ⓑ Ⓒ Ⓓ Ⓔ
24. Ⓐ Ⓑ Ⓒ Ⓓ Ⓔ
25. Ⓐ Ⓑ Ⓒ Ⓓ Ⓔ

Section 3

1. Ⓐ Ⓑ Ⓒ Ⓓ Ⓔ
2. Ⓐ Ⓑ Ⓒ Ⓓ Ⓔ
3. Ⓐ Ⓑ Ⓒ Ⓓ Ⓔ
4. Ⓐ Ⓑ Ⓒ Ⓓ Ⓔ
5. Ⓐ Ⓑ Ⓒ Ⓓ Ⓔ
6. Ⓐ Ⓑ Ⓒ Ⓓ Ⓔ
7. Ⓐ Ⓑ Ⓒ Ⓓ Ⓔ
8. Ⓐ Ⓑ Ⓒ Ⓓ Ⓔ
9. Ⓐ Ⓑ Ⓒ Ⓓ Ⓔ
10. Ⓐ Ⓑ Ⓒ Ⓓ Ⓔ
11. Ⓐ Ⓑ Ⓒ Ⓓ Ⓔ
12. Ⓐ Ⓑ Ⓒ Ⓓ Ⓔ
13. Ⓐ Ⓑ Ⓒ Ⓓ Ⓔ
14. Ⓐ Ⓑ Ⓒ Ⓓ Ⓔ
15. Ⓐ Ⓑ Ⓒ Ⓓ Ⓔ
16. Ⓐ Ⓑ Ⓒ Ⓓ Ⓔ
17. Ⓐ Ⓑ Ⓒ Ⓓ Ⓔ
18. Ⓐ Ⓑ Ⓒ Ⓓ Ⓔ
19. Ⓐ Ⓑ Ⓒ Ⓓ Ⓔ
20. Ⓐ Ⓑ Ⓒ Ⓓ Ⓔ
21. Ⓐ Ⓑ Ⓒ Ⓓ Ⓔ
22. Ⓐ Ⓑ Ⓒ Ⓓ Ⓔ

23. Ⓐ Ⓑ Ⓒ Ⓓ Ⓔ   37. Ⓐ Ⓑ Ⓒ Ⓓ Ⓔ

24. Ⓐ Ⓑ Ⓒ Ⓓ Ⓔ   38. Ⓐ Ⓑ Ⓒ Ⓓ Ⓔ

25. Ⓐ Ⓑ Ⓒ Ⓓ Ⓔ   39. Ⓐ Ⓑ Ⓒ Ⓓ Ⓔ

26. Ⓐ Ⓑ Ⓒ Ⓓ Ⓔ   40. Ⓐ Ⓑ Ⓒ Ⓓ Ⓔ

27. Ⓐ Ⓑ Ⓒ Ⓓ Ⓔ   41. Ⓐ Ⓑ Ⓒ Ⓓ Ⓔ

28. Ⓐ Ⓑ Ⓒ Ⓓ Ⓔ   42. Ⓐ Ⓑ Ⓒ Ⓓ Ⓔ

29. Ⓐ Ⓑ Ⓒ Ⓓ Ⓔ   43. Ⓐ Ⓑ Ⓒ Ⓓ Ⓔ

30. Ⓐ Ⓑ Ⓒ Ⓓ Ⓔ   44. Ⓐ Ⓑ Ⓒ Ⓓ Ⓔ

31. Ⓐ Ⓑ Ⓒ Ⓓ Ⓔ   45. Ⓐ Ⓑ Ⓒ Ⓓ Ⓔ

32. Ⓐ Ⓑ Ⓒ Ⓓ Ⓔ   46. Ⓐ Ⓑ Ⓒ Ⓓ Ⓔ

33. Ⓐ Ⓑ Ⓒ Ⓓ Ⓔ   47. Ⓐ Ⓑ Ⓒ Ⓓ Ⓔ

34. Ⓐ Ⓑ Ⓒ Ⓓ Ⓔ   48. Ⓐ Ⓑ Ⓒ Ⓓ Ⓔ

35. Ⓐ Ⓑ Ⓒ Ⓓ Ⓔ   49. Ⓐ Ⓑ Ⓒ Ⓓ Ⓔ

36. Ⓐ Ⓑ Ⓒ Ⓓ Ⓔ   50. Ⓐ Ⓑ Ⓒ Ⓓ Ⓔ

Section 4

1. Ⓐ Ⓑ Ⓒ Ⓓ Ⓔ   12. Ⓐ Ⓑ Ⓒ Ⓓ Ⓔ

2. Ⓐ Ⓑ Ⓒ Ⓓ Ⓔ   13. Ⓐ Ⓑ Ⓒ Ⓓ Ⓔ

3. Ⓐ Ⓑ Ⓒ Ⓓ Ⓔ   14. Ⓐ Ⓑ Ⓒ Ⓓ Ⓔ

4. Ⓐ Ⓑ Ⓒ Ⓓ Ⓔ   15. Ⓐ Ⓑ Ⓒ Ⓓ Ⓔ

5. Ⓐ Ⓑ Ⓒ Ⓓ Ⓔ   16. Ⓐ Ⓑ Ⓒ Ⓓ Ⓔ

6. Ⓐ Ⓑ Ⓒ Ⓓ Ⓔ   17. Ⓐ Ⓑ Ⓒ Ⓓ Ⓔ

7. Ⓐ Ⓑ Ⓒ Ⓓ Ⓔ   18. Ⓐ Ⓑ Ⓒ Ⓓ Ⓔ

8. Ⓐ Ⓑ Ⓒ Ⓓ Ⓔ   19. Ⓐ Ⓑ Ⓒ Ⓓ Ⓔ

9. Ⓐ Ⓑ Ⓒ Ⓓ Ⓔ   20. Ⓐ Ⓑ Ⓒ Ⓓ Ⓔ

10. Ⓐ Ⓑ Ⓒ Ⓓ Ⓔ   21. Ⓐ Ⓑ Ⓒ Ⓓ Ⓔ

11. Ⓐ Ⓑ Ⓒ Ⓓ Ⓔ   22. Ⓐ Ⓑ Ⓒ Ⓓ Ⓔ

23. Ⓐ Ⓑ Ⓒ Ⓓ Ⓔ   32. Ⓐ Ⓑ Ⓒ Ⓓ Ⓔ
24. Ⓐ Ⓑ Ⓒ Ⓓ Ⓔ   33. Ⓐ Ⓑ Ⓒ Ⓓ Ⓔ
25. Ⓐ Ⓑ Ⓒ Ⓓ Ⓔ   34. Ⓐ Ⓑ Ⓒ Ⓓ Ⓔ
26. Ⓐ Ⓑ Ⓒ Ⓓ Ⓔ   35. Ⓐ Ⓑ Ⓒ Ⓓ Ⓔ
27. Ⓐ Ⓑ Ⓒ Ⓓ Ⓔ   36. Ⓐ Ⓑ Ⓒ Ⓓ Ⓔ
28. Ⓐ Ⓑ Ⓒ Ⓓ Ⓔ   37. Ⓐ Ⓑ Ⓒ Ⓓ Ⓔ
29. Ⓐ Ⓑ Ⓒ Ⓓ Ⓔ   38. Ⓐ Ⓑ Ⓒ Ⓓ Ⓔ
30. Ⓐ Ⓑ Ⓒ Ⓓ Ⓔ   39. Ⓐ Ⓑ Ⓒ Ⓓ Ⓔ
31. Ⓐ Ⓑ Ⓒ Ⓓ Ⓔ   40. Ⓐ Ⓑ Ⓒ Ⓓ Ⓔ

Section 5

1. Ⓐ Ⓑ Ⓒ Ⓓ Ⓔ   16. Ⓐ Ⓑ Ⓒ Ⓓ Ⓔ
2. Ⓐ Ⓑ Ⓒ Ⓓ Ⓔ   17. Ⓐ Ⓑ Ⓒ Ⓓ Ⓔ
3. Ⓐ Ⓑ Ⓒ Ⓓ Ⓔ   18. Ⓐ Ⓑ Ⓒ Ⓓ Ⓔ
4. Ⓐ Ⓑ Ⓒ Ⓓ Ⓔ   19. Ⓐ Ⓑ Ⓒ Ⓓ
5. Ⓐ Ⓑ Ⓒ Ⓓ Ⓔ   20. Ⓐ Ⓑ Ⓒ Ⓓ
6. Ⓐ Ⓑ Ⓒ Ⓓ Ⓔ   21. Ⓐ Ⓑ Ⓒ Ⓓ
7. Ⓐ Ⓑ Ⓒ Ⓓ Ⓔ   22. Ⓐ Ⓑ Ⓒ Ⓓ
8. Ⓐ Ⓑ Ⓒ Ⓓ Ⓔ   23. Ⓐ Ⓑ Ⓒ Ⓓ
9. Ⓐ Ⓑ Ⓒ Ⓓ Ⓔ   24. Ⓐ Ⓑ Ⓒ Ⓓ
10. Ⓐ Ⓑ Ⓒ Ⓓ Ⓔ   25. Ⓐ Ⓑ Ⓒ Ⓓ
11. Ⓐ Ⓑ Ⓒ Ⓓ Ⓔ   26. Ⓐ Ⓑ Ⓒ Ⓓ
12. Ⓐ Ⓑ Ⓒ Ⓓ Ⓔ   27. Ⓐ Ⓑ Ⓒ Ⓓ
13. Ⓐ Ⓑ Ⓒ Ⓓ Ⓔ   28. Ⓐ Ⓑ Ⓒ Ⓓ
14. Ⓐ Ⓑ Ⓒ Ⓓ Ⓔ   29. Ⓐ Ⓑ Ⓒ Ⓓ
15. Ⓐ Ⓑ Ⓒ Ⓓ Ⓔ   30. Ⓐ Ⓑ Ⓒ Ⓓ

31. Ⓐ Ⓑ Ⓒ Ⓓ   34. Ⓐ Ⓑ Ⓒ Ⓓ
32. Ⓐ Ⓑ Ⓒ Ⓓ   35. Ⓐ Ⓑ Ⓒ Ⓓ
33. Ⓐ Ⓑ Ⓒ Ⓓ

Section 6

1. Ⓐ Ⓑ Ⓒ Ⓓ Ⓔ   21. Ⓐ Ⓑ Ⓒ Ⓓ
2. Ⓐ Ⓑ Ⓒ Ⓓ Ⓔ   22. Ⓐ Ⓑ Ⓒ Ⓓ
3. Ⓐ Ⓑ Ⓒ Ⓓ Ⓔ   23. Ⓐ Ⓑ Ⓒ Ⓓ
4. Ⓐ Ⓑ Ⓒ Ⓓ Ⓔ   24. Ⓐ Ⓑ Ⓒ Ⓓ
5. Ⓐ Ⓑ Ⓒ Ⓓ Ⓔ   25. Ⓐ Ⓑ Ⓒ Ⓓ
6. Ⓐ Ⓑ Ⓒ Ⓓ Ⓔ   26. Ⓐ Ⓑ Ⓒ Ⓓ
7. Ⓐ Ⓑ Ⓒ Ⓓ Ⓔ   27. Ⓐ Ⓑ Ⓒ Ⓓ
8. Ⓐ Ⓑ Ⓒ Ⓓ Ⓔ   28. Ⓐ Ⓑ Ⓒ Ⓓ
9. Ⓐ Ⓑ Ⓒ Ⓓ Ⓔ   29. Ⓐ Ⓑ Ⓒ Ⓓ
10. Ⓐ Ⓑ Ⓒ Ⓓ Ⓔ   30. Ⓐ Ⓑ Ⓒ Ⓓ
11. Ⓐ Ⓑ Ⓒ Ⓓ Ⓔ   31. Ⓐ Ⓑ Ⓒ Ⓓ
12. Ⓐ Ⓑ Ⓒ Ⓓ Ⓔ   32. Ⓐ Ⓑ Ⓒ Ⓓ
13. Ⓐ Ⓑ Ⓒ Ⓓ Ⓔ   33. Ⓐ Ⓑ Ⓒ Ⓓ
14. Ⓐ Ⓑ Ⓒ Ⓓ Ⓔ   34. Ⓐ Ⓑ Ⓒ Ⓓ
15. Ⓐ Ⓑ Ⓒ Ⓓ Ⓔ   35. Ⓐ Ⓑ Ⓒ Ⓓ
16. Ⓐ Ⓑ Ⓒ Ⓓ Ⓔ   36. Ⓐ Ⓑ Ⓒ Ⓓ
17. Ⓐ Ⓑ Ⓒ Ⓓ Ⓔ   37. Ⓐ Ⓑ Ⓒ Ⓓ
18. Ⓐ Ⓑ Ⓒ Ⓓ Ⓔ   38. Ⓐ Ⓑ Ⓒ Ⓓ
19. Ⓐ Ⓑ Ⓒ Ⓓ Ⓔ   39. Ⓐ Ⓑ Ⓒ Ⓓ
20. Ⓐ Ⓑ Ⓒ Ⓓ Ⓔ   40. Ⓐ Ⓑ Ⓒ Ⓓ

Typical Scholastic Aptitude Test

Section 1   45 QUESTIONS — 30 MINUTES

Each question below consists of a related pair of words or phrases, followed by five lettered pairs of words or phrases. Select the lettered pair that <u>best</u> expresses a relationship similar to that expressed in the original pair.

Example:

> YAWN : BOREDOM ::   (A) dream : sleep   (B) anger : madness
> (C) smile : amusement   (D) face : expression
> (E) impatience : rebellion   Ⓐ Ⓑ ● Ⓓ Ⓔ

1. **ostracism : censure** ::   (A) love : marriage   (B) success : promotion   (C) applause : approval   (D) editing : criticism   (E) loyalty : tribute

2. **cobbler : shoes** ::   (A) mechanic : automobile   (B) carpenter : saw   (C) apothecary : drugs   (D) spy : plans   (E) interrogator : questions

3. **propitiate : appease** ::   (A) disturb : agitate   (B) inaugurate : terminate   (C) illiterate : articulate   (D) mollify : incite   (E) irritate : soothe

4. **laconic : voluble** ::   (A) spartan : stern   (B) false : deceitful   (C) quiet : taciturn   (D) frozen : boiling   (E) noisy : shrill

5. **rooster : hen** ::   (A) duck : drake   (B) dog : cat   (C) gander : gosling   (D) swan : drake   (E) gander : goose

6. **rococo : simple** ::   (A) hackneyed : trite   (B) elaborate : ornate   (C) garish : showy   (D) baroque : plain   (E) ordinary : plain

7. **quart : pint** ::   (A) liter : meter   (B) pound : ton   (C) yard : inch   (D) minute : hour   (E) minute : second

8. **assurance : fear** ::   (A) opiate : pain   (B) opiate : dreams   (C) cigarette : nerves   (D) confidence : man   (E) narcotic : drug

9. **time : scythe** ::   (A) liberty : sickle   (B) justice : scales   (C) honesty : badge   (D) ignorance : chains   (E) freedom : mountain top

10. **felicity : sorrow** ::   (A) agility : skill   (B) agility : clumsiness   (C) concept : scheme   (D) congratulations : benediction   (E) ignorance : bliss

Each sentence below has one or two blanks, each blank indicating that something has been omitted. Beneath the sentence are five lettered words or sets of words. Choose the word or set of words that best fits the meaning of the sentence as a whole.

Example:

> Although its publicity has been . . . . . . , the film itself is intelligent, well-acted, handsomely produced, and altogether . . . .
> (A) tasteless..respectable   (B) extensive..moderate
> (C) sophisticated..amateur   (D) risqué..crude
> (E) perfect..spectacular   ● Ⓑ Ⓒ Ⓓ Ⓔ

11. His employers could not complain about his work because he was _____ in the performance of his duties.
    (A) derelict   (B) penetrating   (C) diversified   (D) assiduous
    (E) mandatory

12. He is much too _____ in his writings; he writes a page when a sentence should suffice.
    (A) diffuse   (B) pithy   (C) verbose   (D) benignant   (E) pleasant

13. Although I am not a (an) _____ , I am interested in the derivation of words.
    (A) entomologist   (B) graphologist   (C) historian   (D) numismatist   (E) lexicographer

14. Dr. Johnson with his _____ of _____ could be found at the tavern every evening.
    (A) coterie — friends   (B) bevy — accomplices   (C) group — critics   (D) dictionary — language   (E) paroxysms — joy

15. The noon _____ is a Spanish custom which we Americans cannot _____ .
    (A) luncheon — devour   (B) bull fight — tolerate   (C) siesta — avoid   (D) luncheon — enjoy   (E) siesta — imitate

16. To relieve his stomach distress, the doctor suggested that he take a _____ .
    (A) palliative   (B) paregoric   (C) ministration   (D) mendicant
    (E) migraine

17. You talk as though you were _____ .
    (A) ubiquitous   (B) omnipresent   (C) omniscient   (D) omnivorous   (E) nurtured

18. If you need additional _____, the person who reaches his quota will get a trip to Europe.
    (A) objective   (B) aims   (C) impetus   (D) incentive
    (E) prompting

19. A pessimist has a _____ outlook on life.
    (A) salubrious   (B) contemptuous   (C) intense   (D) placid
    (E) lugubrious

20. The evidence is not _____ to the issue at hand.

    (A) germane   (B) consistent   (C) inchoate   (D) luminous
    (E) manifest

Each question below consists of a word in capital letters, followed by five lettered words or phrases. Choose the word or phrase that is most nearly **opposite** in meaning to the word in capital letters. Since some of the questions require you to distinguish fine shades of meaning, consider all the choices before deciding which is best.

Example:

> GOOD: (A) sour (B) bad (C) red
> (D) hot (E) ugly   Ⓐ ● Ⓒ Ⓓ Ⓔ

21. PHLEGMATIC (A) tired (B) fancy (C) repetitious (D) active (E) indifferent

22. SALUTARY (A) harmful (B) respectful (C) disrespectful (D) beneficial (E) anxious

23. CULPABLE (A) touchable (B) blameless (C) irritated (D) noxious (E) careless

24. DEMURE (A) restrained (B) emotional (C) demonstrative (D) illiterate (E) intolerant

25. ORTHODOX (A) right (B) left (C) massive (D) plain (E) heretical

26. DISSUADE (A) exhort (B) extract (C) admonish (D) discourage (E) antagonize

27. SUCCOR (A) hindrance (B) tart (C) fakir (D) sweet (E) drink

28. OVERT (A) imposing (B) quiet (C) defamatory (D) clandestine (E) unhatched

29. LACKADAISICAL (A) sleepy (B) enthusiastic (C) monthly (D) languid (E) fortunate

30. SUAVE (A) tactless (B) smooth (C) scourish (D) urbane (E) authoritative

31. CRABBED (A) crowded (B) saccharine (C) sour (D) condemned (E) salty

32. CORROBORATION (A) proof (B) arrest (C) refutation (D) alibi (E) alias

33. DECORUM (A) ribaldry (B) balladry (C) high collar (D) solo (E) freedom

34. VIVACIOUS (A) surgical (B) lively (C) girlish (D) inactive (E) boyish

35. INGENUOUS (A) clever (B) stupid (C) naive (D) young (E) sophisticated

Each passage below is followed by questions based on its content. Answer all questions following a passage on the basis of what is stated or implied in that passage.

Our ignorance of the complex subject of social insurance was and remains colossal. For years American business leaders delighted in maligning the British social insurance schemes. Our industrialists condemned them without ever finding out what they were about. Even our universities displayed no interest. Contrary to the interest in this subject taken by organized labor abroad, our own labor movements bitterly opposed the entire program of social insurance up to a few years ago. Since the success of any reform depends largely upon a correct public understanding of the principles involved, the adoption of social insurance measures presented peculiar difficulties for the United States under our Federal type of government of limited powers, our constitutional and judicial handicaps, our long conditioning to individualism, the traditional hostility to social reform by both capital and labor, the general inertia, and our complete lack of trained administrative personnel without which even the best law can be ineffective. Has not bitter experience taught us that far more important than the passage of a law, which is at best only a declaration of intention, is a ready public opinion prepared to enforce it?

36. According to this writer, what attitude have we shown in this country toward social insurance?

(A) We have been extremely doubtful that it will work, but have been willing to give it a chance.   (B) We have opposed it on the grounds of a careful study of its defects.   (C) We have shown an unintelligent and rather blind antagonism toward it.   (D) We have been afraid that it would not work under our type of government.   (E) We have resented it because of the extensive propaganda in favor of it.

37. To what does the phrase, "our long conditioning to individualism," refer?

(A) Our habit of depending upon ourselves   (B) Our increasing dependence on the Federal Government   (C) Our long distrust of "big business"   (D) Our policies of high protective tariff   (E) Our unwillingness to accept reforms

38. Which of these ideas is expressed in this passage?

(A) the surest way to cure a social evil is to get people to pass a law against it.   (B) Legislation alone cannot effect social reforms.   (C) The American people are seriously uninformed about all social problems.   (D) Our type of government makes social reform practically impossible.   (E) Capital and labor retard social progress

The artist of the Renaissance was an all-round man. From his studio one could order a painting for the church altar, a carved wedding chest, a silver ewer, or a crucifix. The master of the workshop might be sculpturing a Venus for the Duke's garden while his apprentices were roughing-out a reredos for the new chapel. Many of the well-known painters of that golden period were goldsmiths, armorers, workers in glass, enamel or iron. The engineer was artist and the artist was engineer. The great Leonardo, famous today as the painter of *The Last Supper* and *Mona Lisa*, was perhaps equally well known in the 16th century for his engineering projects and his scientific experiments. Our own Thomas A. Edison pronounced him the greatest inventive genius of his time.

39. The title that best expresses the ideas of this paragraph is:
    (A) The great Leonardo   (B) Edison and 16th century scientists
    (C) The golden period   (D) Masters and apprentices   (E) Renaissance artists

40. Leonardo was famed as
    (A) a scientist   (B) an electrician   (C) a worker in glass   (D) a railroad engineer   (E) an apprentice

41. Artists of the Renaissance were
    (A) numerous   (B) many-sided   (C) honest   (D) wealthy   (E) lacking in thoroughness

The same high mental faculties which first led man to believe in unseen spiritual agencies, then in fetishism, polytheism, and ultimately in monotheism, would infallibly lead him, as long as his reasoning powers remained poorly developed, to various strange superstitions and customs. Many of these are terrible to think of — such as the sacrifice of human beings to a blood-loving god; the trial of innocent persons by the ordeal of poison or fire; witchcraft, etc. — yet it is well occasionally to reflect on these superstitions, for they show us what an infinite debt of gratitude we owe to the improvement of our reason to science, and to our accumulated knowledge.

42. According to this author we owe a debt of gratitude to science for our
    (A) accumulated knowledge   (B) higher mental faculties   (C) present judicial system of protecting the innocent   (D) departure from primitive superstitions   (E) powers of reflection

43. This passage most likely is part of a treatise on
    (A) witchcraft   (B) theology   (C) scientific method   (D) anthropology   (E) organic evolution

44. Select the statement which is true.
    (A) Monotheism motivated primitive people to the sacrifice of human beings   (B) Monotheism evolved with the development of the intellect   (C) Monotheism preceded the belief in unseen spiritual forces   (D) Monotheism was caused by the poor reasoning power of Man   (E) Monotheism preceded fetishism

45. From this passage we may infer that
(A) polytheism believed that there was a blood-loving god   (B) we can best appreciate the blessings of this century by examining the customs and superstitions of Primitive Man   (C) trial of innocent persons by the ordeal of poison was practiced until the development of modern religious concepts   (D) the author would condone witchcraft   (E) development of reasoning power had no effect on social customs

---

Section 2   25 QUESTIONS — 30 MINUTES

In this section solve each problem, using any available space on the page for scratchwork. Then decide which is the best of the choices given and blacken the corresponding space on the answer sheet.

The following information is for your reference in solving some of the problems.

Circle of radius r: Area $= \pi r^2$; Circumference $= 2\pi r$
  The number of degrees of arc in a circle is 360.
The measure in degrees of a straight angle is 180.

Definitions of symbols:

$=$ is equal to	$\leqq$ is less than or equal to
$\neq$ is unequal to	$\geqq$ is greater than or equal to
$<$ is less than	$\parallel$ is parallel to
$>$ is greater than	$\perp$ is perpendicular to

NOTE: Figures which accompany problems in this test are intended to provide information useful in solving the problems. They are drawn as accurately as possible EXCEPT when it is stated in a specific problem that its figure is not drawn to scale. All figures lie in the plane unless otherwise indicated. All numbers used are real numbers.

Triangle: The sum of the measures in degrees of the angles of a triangle is 180.

If $\angle CDA$ is a right angle, then

(1) area of $\triangle ABC = \dfrac{AB \times CD}{2}$

(2) $AC^2 = AD^2 + DC^2$

1. If 87955936 is divided by 284, the quotient is equal to exactly
   (A) 390701   (B) 309702   (C) 309703
   (D) 309704   (E) 309705

2. If $a = -6$, then $(a + 3)(a - 3)$ equals
   (A) -27 (B) 12   (C) 27   (D) 45   (E) 81

3. If $x = 3$, and $y = \frac{1}{6}$ then the value of x in terms of y is

   (A) $\frac{1}{2}y$ (B) $2y$ (C) $3\frac{1}{6}y$ (D) $6\frac{1}{3}y$ (E) $18y$

4. What is the value of $x - 2$, when $3x - 6 = 1$?
   (A) $\frac{1}{3}$ (B) $\frac{2}{3}$ (C) $\frac{5}{3}$ (D) 4   (E) 5

5. B and C are points on straight line AD, on which $AB = BC = CD$.
   What percent of AC is AD?
   (A) 1.5%   (B) 50%   (C) $66\frac{2}{3}\%$ (D) $133\frac{1}{3}\%$
   (E) 150%

6. A mixture of 17 parts of A, 3 parts of B and 4 parts of C weighs 72
   ounces. How many ounces of substance B are in this mixture?
   (A) 3.4   (B) 9   (C) 12   (D) 17   (E) 51

Questions 7 and 8:   A ship covered the following distances (in nautical
miles) on a recent Caribbean cruise:

New York — Curacao	1,770
Curacao — St. Maarten	630
St. Maarten — St. Thomas	100
St. Thomas — New York	1,500

7. What percent of the total distance covered on this cruise was covered
   from New York to Curacao?

   (A) 17.7%   (B) 22%   (C) $33\frac{1}{3}\%$ (D) $44\frac{1}{4}\%$
   (E) 50%

8. The distance from St. Maarten to St. Thomas may be expressed as
   160 statute miles. Approximately how many nautical miles
   equal 1 statute mile?
   (A) 0.625   (B) 0.89   (C) 0.9   (D) 1.14
   (E) 1.25

9. The area of each circle is 9π. What is the area of the shaded part?

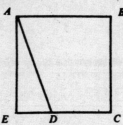

   (A) $36 - 9\pi$ (B) $36 - 36\pi$
   (C) $36\pi - 144$ (D) $144 - 9\pi$
   (E) $144 - 36\pi$

10. After purchasing a square sheet of plywood (area = 169 square feet), I found that I must cut off 2 feet from one of its edges in order to fit it onto the side of a wall. What is the area (in square feet) of this wall?

   (A) 117   (B) 121   (C) 143   (D) 165   (E) 167

11. The area of square $ABCE = x^2$ and $DC = y$. What is the area of triangle AED?

   (A) $\dfrac{x^2 - xy}{2}$ (B) $\dfrac{y(x - y)}{2}$ (C) $x^2 - xy$

   (D) $y^2 - xy$ (E) $xy - x^2$

12. If n and p are both odd numbers, which of the following numbers *must* be an even number?

   (A) $n + p$ (B) np (C) $np + 2$ (D) $n + p + 1$
   (E) $2n + p$

13. For the state football championship game, of the 30,000 tickets $\frac{1}{4}$ were sold at $3.00, $\frac{1}{3}$ were sold at $2.50, and the rest were sold at $1.25. How many were sold at $1.25?

   (A) 5,000   (B) 7,500   (C) 10,000   (D) 12,500
   (E) 25,000

14. The average weight of 3 boys is 53 pounds. No one of these boys weighs less than 51 pounds. What is the maximum weight (in pounds) of any one boy?

   (A) 53   (B) 55   (C) 57   (D) 59   (E) 61

15. If $a < b$ and $c < d$, then

   (A) $c + a < d + b$ (B) $c + a > d + b$ (C) $c = b$
   (D) $a = b$ (E) $ac = bd$

16. Mark can row downstream on the Saco River for 5 miles in 2 hours. It takes him 4 hours to return to his original departure point. What is Mark's average rate of speed (in miles per hour) for the round trip?

(A) $\frac{5}{6}$ (B) $1\frac{2}{3}$ (C) $1\frac{7}{8}$ (D) 3 (E) $3\frac{3}{4}$

17. Michael takes 20 minutes to cover a newspaper delivery route which Philip does on bicycle in $\frac{1}{4}$ hour. The average time (in hours) to do this task is

(A) $\frac{1}{7}$ (B) $\frac{2}{7}$ (C) $\frac{7}{24}$ (D) $\frac{1}{12}$ (E) $\frac{7}{12}$

18. Point $A(1,0)$ is drawn to $B(5,0)$ and is joined to $C(3,4)$. Which of the following is true?

(A) $CA = CB$ (B) $AB = BC$ (C) $AC = AB$
(D) $AC > BC$ (E) $AC < BC$

Questions 19-22: Use the following table:

Rank	Number of Employees	Wages Paid (in thousands)
Office Managers	5	$ 110
Factory Supervisors	25	$ 350
Assembly Workers	500	$ 600
TOTALS	530	$1060

19. The wages paid to managers make up what percent (to the nearest percent) of the total payroll?

(A) 5% (B) 9% (C) 10% (D) 11% (E) 42%

20. The average wage for all employees is

(A) $1,200 (B) $2,000 (C) $18,000
(D) $20,000 (E) $22,000

21. The ratio of the average salary of a manager to the average salary of an assembly worker is

(A) 3 to 55 (B) 11 to 60 (C) 11 to 6 (D) 60 to 11
(E) 55 to 3

22. If four of the managers are paid wages of x dollars each, then the remaining manager is paid

(A) $22,000 (B) $(110,000 - x)$
(C) $(110,000 - x)/4$ (D) $(110,000 - 4x)$
(E) $(22,000 - x)$

23. The base of an isosceles triangle is 16 units and each side is 10 units. What is the area of this triangle in square units?

(A) 24 (B) 36 (C) 48 (D) 50 (E) 100

24. If the area of rectangle R with altitude 4 feet is equal to the area of square S, which has a perimeter of 24 feet, then the perimeter of rectangle R equals

    (A) 9 feet   (B) 16 feet   (C) 24 feet   (D) 26 feet

    (E) 36 feet

25. There are 20 members on a football squad. In electing a captain and a co-captain, how many different outcomes of the election are possible?

    (A) 20   (B) 39   (C) 190   (D) 380   (E) 760

Section 3   50 QUESTIONS — 30 MINUTES

The questions in this section measure skills that are important to writing well. In particular, they test your ability to recognize and use language that is clear, effective, and correct according to the requirements of standard written English, the kind of English found in most college textbooks.

Directions: The following sentences contain problems in grammar, usage, diction (choice of words), and idiom.

    Some sentences are correct.
    No sentence contains more than one error.

You will find that the error, if there is one, is underlined and lettered. Assume that elements of the sentence that are not underlined are correct and cannot be changed. In choosing answers, follow the requirements of standard written English.

If there is an error, select the one underlined part that must be changed to make the sentence correct and blacken the corresponding space on your answer sheet.

If there is no error, blacken answer space (E) .

EXAMPLE:	SAMPLE ANSWER

The region has a climate <u>so severe that</u> plants
                A
growing there rarely <u>had been</u> more than twelve
   B   **C**
inches <u>high</u>. <u>No error</u>
    D   **E**
	Ⓐ Ⓑ ● Ⓓ Ⓔ

---

1. <u>Your</u> argument is no <u>different from</u> the <u>last speaker</u> who opposed the

   (A)   (B)   (C)   (D)

        legislation. <u>No error</u>

                 (E)

2. Please help me decide <u>which</u> of the two activities to choose — going to
                          (A)

    the theater with John <u>or</u> <u>to attend</u> <u>tonight's</u> dinner-dance at the
                          (B)   (C)   (D)

    hotel.   <u>No error</u>
             (E)

3. Shirley is very <u>fidgety</u>, <u>which</u> is an <u>annoying</u> <u>trait</u>.   <u>No error</u>
                   (A)   (B)   (C)   (D)   (E)

4. Every woman in the <u>ward</u> <u>hoped</u> that <u>their</u> child would be a normal and
                      (A)   (B)   (C)

    <u>healthy</u> baby.   <u>No error</u>
    (D)   (E)

5. When I have to decide <u>which</u> of two <u>applicants</u> for a job to hire, I find
                         (A)   (B)

    <u>myself giving</u> the position to the one who uses the <u>best</u> English.
    (C)   (D)

    <u>No error</u>
    (E)

6. <u>That</u> is the kind of <u>a house</u> <u>in which</u> I <u>should</u> like to live.   <u>No error</u>
   (A)   (B)   (C)   (D)   (E)

7. When you go shopping, will you please <u>bring</u> this note to the <u>manager of</u>
                         (A)   (B)   (C)

    the <u>grocery</u> department?   <u>No error</u>
        (D)   (E)

8. Charles <u>asked</u> <u>would I</u> go to the ball game with <u>him</u>.   <u>No error</u>
           (A)   (B)   (C) (D)   (E)

9. We were <u>particularly</u> frightened of <u>John</u> <u>driving</u> the <u>car</u> in the race.
           (A)   (B)   (C)   (D)

    <u>No error</u>
    (E)

10. <u>Because</u> I was seated on the <u>dais</u> just <u>in back of</u> the speaker, I could see
    (A)   (B)   (C)

    the <u>audience's</u> reaction to his vituperative remarks.   <u>No error</u>
        (D)   (E)

11. <u>During</u> the recent gasoline shortage, the <u>amount</u> of accidents on our
    (A)   (B)

    highways <u>decreased</u> <u>markedly</u>.   <u>No error</u>
             (C)   (D)   (E)

12. Having secured the ball on a fumble, we took advantage of our opponent's
    (A)   (B) (C)   (D)
         error and scored a field goal.   No error
                                              (E)

13. This is one of the things that annoy me.   No error
    (A)   (B)   (C)   (D)   (E)

14. Although I am willing to go along with your idea, I cannot enthuse much
        (A)   (B)   (C)
             over its chances of success.   No error
                         (D)   (E)

15. I was aggravated by the child's rudeness to the visiting dignitaries who
               (A)   (B)   (C)
             had come to visit our school.   No error
                  (D)   (E)

16. A complete system of checks and balances have been incorporated in
                   (A)   (B)   (C)
          our Constitution.   No error
          (D)   (E)

17. She is the only one of my friends who plan to attend the graduation ex-
                (A)   (B) (C) (D)
          ercises.   No error
                       (E)

18. Due to the excessively high interest rate on installment buying, it is
    (A)   (B)
             advisable to purchase things on a cash basis.   No error
                 (C)   (D)   (E)

19. The boys whom I predicted would win the contest have lived up to my
                  (A)   (B)   (C)   (D)
          expectations.   No error
                            (E)

20. When asked how long she had been a resident of the state, she replied,
                               (A)   (B)
          "I am living in this state for five years."   No error
              (C)   (D)   (E)

21. Owing to unfavorable weather, the party had to be postponed for a week.
    (A)   (B)   (C)   (D)
          No error
             (E)

22. Neither of the three applicants meets the requirements for this position.
    (A)   (B)   (C)   (D)
        No error
        (E)

23. When descending from 37,000 feet to make our landing, the pressure
         (A)   (B)   (C)
        affected our ears.   No error
        (D)   (E)

24. I am not certain if I should discuss my promotion with him or not.
              (A)   (B)   (C)   (D)
        No error
        (E)

25. He had a keen interest and wide knowledge of his esoteric subject.
             (A)   (B)   (C)   (D)
        No error
        (E)

Directions: In each of the following sentences, some part or all of the sentence is underlined. Below each sentence you will find five ways of phrasing the underlined part. Select the answer that produces the most effective sentence, one that is clear and exact, without awkwardness or ambiguity, and blacken the corresponding space on your answer sheet. In choosing answers, follow the requirements of standard written English. Choose the answer that best expresses the meaning of the original sentence.

Answer (A) is always the same as the underlined part. Choose answer (A) if you think the original sentence needs no revision.

EXAMPLE:	**SAMPLE ANSWER**
Laura Ingalls Wilder published her first book and she was sixty-five years old then.	Ⓐ ● Ⓒ Ⓓ Ⓔ
(A) and she was sixty-five years old then	
(B) when she was sixty-five years old	
(C) at age sixty-five years old	
(D) upon reaching sixty-five years	
(E) at the time when she was sixty-five	

26. Although I calculate that he will be here any minute, I cannot wait much
    longer for him to arrive.
        (A) Although I calculate that he will be here   (B) Although I reckon
        that he will be here   (C) Because I calculate that he will be here
        (D) Although I am confident that he will be here   (E) Because I am
        confident that he will be here

27. The scouts were told to take an overnight hike, pitch camp, prepare dinner, and that they should be in bed by 9 p.m.

   (A) to take an overnight hike, pitch camp, prepare dinner, and that they should be in bed by 9 p.m.   (B) to take an overnight hike, pitch camp, prepare dinner, and they should be in bed by 9 p.m.   (C) to take an overnight hike, pitch camp, prepare dinner, and be in bed by 9 p.m.   (D) to take an overnight hike, pitching camp, preparing dinner and going to bed by 9 p.m.   (E) to engage in an overnight hike, pitch camp, prepare dinner, and that they should be in bed by 9 p.m.

28. We want the teacher to be him who has the best rapport with the students.

   (A) We want the teacher to be him   (B) We want the teacher to be he   (C) We want him to be the teacher   (D) We desire that the teacher be him   (E) We anticipate that the teacher will be him

29. Did Alexander Pope write, "To err is human; to forgive, divine?"

   (A) write, "To err is human; to forgive, divine?"   (B) write that "To err is human; to forgive, divine?"   (C) write, "To err is human; to forgive, divine"?   (D) write: "To err is human; to forgive, divine?"   (E) write, "To err is human, to forgive divine"?

30. If he were to win the medal, I for one would be disturbed.

   (A) If he were to win the medal,   (B) If he was to win the medal,   (C) If he wins the medal,   (D) If he is the winner of the medal,   (E) In the event that he wins the medal,

31. She not only was competent but also friendly in nature.

   (A) She not only was competent but also friendly   (B) She not was only competent but friendly also   (C) She not only was competent but friendly also   (D) She was not only competent but also friendly   (E) She was not only competent but friendly also

32. The dean informed us that the applicant had not and never will be accepted by the college because of his high school record.

   (A) applicant had not and never will be accepted by the college because of his high school record.   (B) applicant had not and never would be accepted by the college because of his High School record.   (C) applicant had not been and never will be accepted by the college because of his high school record.   (D) applicant had not been and never would be accepted by the college because of his High School record.   (E) applicant had not been and never would be accepted by the college because of his high school record.

33. The government's failing to keep it's pledges will earn the distrust of all the other nations in the alliance.

   (A) government's failing to keep it's pledges   (B) government failing to keep it's pledges   (C) government's failing to keep its

pledges   (D) government failing to keep its pledges   (E) govern-
ments failing to keep their pledges

34. Her brother along with her parents insist that she remain in school.

     (A) insist   (B) insists   (C) are insisting   (D) were insisting
     (E) have insisted

35. Most students like to read these kind of books during their spare time.

     (A) these kind of books   (B) these kind of book   (C) this kind of
     books   (D) this kinds of books   (E) those kind of books

36. During the first year that he and I were neighbors, our conversations
     turned frequently on the two cardinal points of poetry: the power
     of exciting the sympathy of the reader by a faithful adherence to
     the truth of nature and the power to give the interest of novelty
     by the modifying colors of imagination.

     (A) power to give   (B) ability to give   (C) power to
     bestow   (D) ability to bestow   (E) power of giving

37. If I would have realized the danger involved in this assignment, I
     would not have asked you to undertake it.

     (A) If I would have realized   (B) If I should have realized
     (C) Had I realized   (D) When I realized   (E) Because I
     did not realize

38. Having the best record for attendance, the school awarded him a medal
     at graduation.

     (A) the school awarded him a medal   (B) the school award-
     ed a medal to him   (C) he was awarded a medal by the
     school   (D) a medal was awarded to him by the school
     (E) a school medal was awarded to him

39. Our company's keeping it's promises to the customers is of paramount
     importance to the stockholders.

     (A) Our company's keeping it's promises   (B) Our com-
     pany keeping it's promises   (C) Our company's keeping
     its promises   (D) Our company keeping its promises
     (E) Our companys keeping their promises

40. The principal along with the teachers and parents demand that the
     traffic department install a traffic light at the street crossing.

     (A) demand   (B) demands   (C) are demanding
     (D) were demanding   (E) have demanded

The questions in this section measure skills that are important to writing well.
In particular, they test your ability to recognize and use language that is clear,
effective, and correct according to the requirements of standard written English, the kind of English found in most college textbooks.

Directions: The following sentences contain problems in grammar, usage, diction (choice of words), and idiom.

> Some sentences are correct.
> No sentence contains more than one error.

You will find that the error, if there is one, is underlined and lettered. Assume that elements of the sentence that are not underlined are correct and cannot be changed. In choosing answers, follow the requirements of standard written English.

If there is an error, select the one underlined part that must be changed to make the sentence correct and blacken the corresponding space on your answer sheet.

If there is no error, blacken answer space Ⓔ .

EXAMPLE: **SAMPLE ANSWER**

The region has a climate <u>so severe that</u> plants   Ⓐ Ⓑ ⬤ Ⓓ Ⓔ
                          A

growing there rarely <u>had been</u> more than twelve
      B   **C**

inches <u>high.</u> <u>No error</u>
        D   **E**

---

41. <u>Everything</u> depended on <u>Joneses</u> <u>arriving</u> on time for the crucial dis-
    (A)   (B)   (C)   (D)
         sion. <u>No error</u>
                  (E)

42. Although he <u>is</u> in this country <u>only</u> two years, he talks <u>like</u> a native.
    (A)   (B)   (C)   (D)
         <u>No error</u>
           (E)

43. These cars are not ready for delivery as <u>they</u> come <u>off of</u> the assembly
                        (A)   (B)   (C)
         line; they must be tested before <u>they</u> can be sold.   <u>No error</u>
                                    (D)   (E)

44. The technique <u>discussed</u> in this article <u>enables</u> a student to learn
                     (A)   (B)
         <u>more quickly</u> and to remember for a longer <u>period</u> of time.
             (C)   (D)
         <u>No error</u>
           (E)

45. Everybody but you and he has joined the school organization.   No error
      (A)   (B)   (C)(D)   (E)

46. The population of California is larger than any state in the United States.
          (A)   (B)   (C)   (D)
      No error
      (E)

47. Reading quickly, the book was soon finished and returned to the library.
          (A)   (B) (C)   (D)
      No error
      (E)

48. He is wiser than us all.   No error
      (A) (B) (C)(D)   (E)

49. You can scarcely see the birds in the trees because of their protective
          (A)   (B)   (C)
      coloration.   No error
          (D)   (E)

50. The man who is laying in the aisle needs medical attention immediately.
          (A)   (B)   (C) (D)
      No error
      (E)

Section 4   40 QUESTIONS — 30 MINUTES

Each sentence below has one or two blanks, each blank indicating that something has been omitted. Beneath the sentence are five lettered words or sets
of words. Choose the word or set of words that best fits the meaning of the
sentence as a whole.

Example:

> Although its publicity has been . . . . . . , the film itself is intelligent, well-
> acted, handsomely produced, and altogether . . . .
> (A) tasteless..respectable   (B) extensive..moderate
> (C) sophisticated..amateur   (D) risqué..crude
>   (E) perfect..spectacular   ● Ⓑ Ⓒ Ⓓ Ⓔ

1. If one is tempted to reflect on the type of language which is used in polite
   society, and, more _____ , if one is inclined to interpret it
   literally, one must conclude that social intercourse involves a
   collection of _____ and a tissue of lies.
   (A) thoughtfully — saws   (B) especially — maxims   (C) essen-
   tially — aphorisms   (D) particularly — inanities · (E) violently
   — proverbs

2. It is said that the custom of shaking hands originated when primitive men held out empty hands to indicate that they had no _____ weapons and were thus _____ disposed.

  (A) lethal — clearly   (B) concealed — amicably   (C) hidden — harmoniously   (D) murderous — well   (E) secret — finally

3. In order to control and defeat the dreadful diseases which plague humanity, _____ activity is necessary.

  (A) concerted   (B) vital   (C) constant   (D) full   (E) indomitable

4. A leader, young or old, must have character traits which inspire others to accept his leadership. He must display courage, intelligence, and _____ .

  (A) wisdom   (B) bravery   (C) timorousness   (D) imbecility   (E) integrity

5. Such homely virtues as _____ , hard work, and simplicity appear old-fashioned in these days.

  (A) parsimony   (B) asceticism   (C) prodigality   (D) thrift   (E) wantonness

---

Each question below consists of a word in capital letters, followed by five lettered words or phrases. Choose the word or phrase that is most nearly opposite in meaning to the word in capital letters. Since some of the questions require you to distinguish fine shades of meaning, consider all the choices before deciding which is best.

Example:

> GOOD: (A) sour   (B) bad   (C) red
> (D) hot   (E) ugly   Ⓐ ● Ⓒ Ⓓ Ⓔ

6. **LICENTIOUS**   (A) moral   (B) permitted   (C) banal   (D) beginning   (E) nutlike

7. **RECALCITRANT**   (A) bellicose   (B) late   (C) stone-like   (D) mangy   (E) tractable

8. **IMPASSIVE**   (A) serene   (B) meager   (C) stationary   (D) agitated   (E) noble

9. **PROFILIGATE**   (A) dissolute   (B) extravagant   (C) staid   (D) masterly   (E) indicative

10. **PROLIX**   (A) full   (B) tapered   (C) terse   (D) insignificant   (E) angry

11. **PRODIGIOUS**   (A) intellectual   (B) formidable   (C) microscopic   (D) intense   (E) enormous

12. **SPECIOUS**   (A) typical   (B) false   (C) golden   (D) veracious   (E) contrary

13. **SEDULOUS** (A) imitative (B) seditious (C) diligent (D) indolent (E) contrary
14. **EFFETE** (A) festive (B) spent (C) energetic (D) elaborate (E) anxious
15. **NOCTURNAL** (A) musical (B) heavenly (C) earthly (D) deadly (E) daily

---

Each question below consists of a related pair of words or phrases, followed by five lettered pairs of words or phrases. Select the lettered pair that best expresses a relationship similar to that expressed in the original pair.

Example:

> YAWN : BOREDOM :: (A) dream : sleep (B) anger : madness
> (C) smile : amusement (D) face : expression
> (E) impatience : rebellion   Ⓐ Ⓑ ● Ⓓ Ⓔ

16. **policeman : criminal** :: (A) patient : doctor (B) officer : private (C) educator : ignorance (D) evangelist : sinner (E) doctor : patient
17. **archaic : modern** :: (A) stone : bomb (B) airplane : jet (C) pencil : pen (D) sword : scabbard (E) A-bomb : H-bomb
18. **benediction : anathema** :: (A) marriage : hatred (B) eulogy : vilification (C) elegy : lament (D) elegy : castigation (E) maudlin : sentimental
19. **crest : trough** :: (A) apex : summit (B) crown : throne (C) acme : zenith (D) peak : valley (E) honor : noble
20. **titanic : Lilliputian** :: (A) gigantic : monstrous (B) fancy : plain (C) oceanic : terrestrial (D) enormous : puny (E) powerful : wicked
21. **pain : sedative** :: (A) comfort : stimulant (B) grief : consolation (C) trance : narcotic (D) ache : extraction (E) arrest : warrant
22. **pork : pig** :: (A) beef : cow (B) rooster : chicken (C) mutton : sheep (D) steer : beef (E) lobster : crustacean
23. **maxim : epigram** :: (A) verbose : terse (B) adage : elegy (C) proverb : tombstone (D) proverb : essay (E) pithy : terse
24. **virus : cold** :: (A) serum : measles (B) infection : gangrene (C) microbe : incision (D) microbe : germ (E) virus : tuberculosis
25. **choleric : irascible** :: (A) wearisome : refreshing (B) angry : calm (C) bellicose : pacific (D) tiring : enervating (E) martial : marital

---

Each passage below is followed by questions based on its content. Answer all questions following a passage on the basis of what is stated or implied in that passage.

It is no secret that I am not one of those naturalists who suffer from cities, or affect to do so, nor do I find a city unnatural or uninteresting, or a rubbish heap of follies. It has always seemed to me there is something more than mechanically admirable about a train that arrives on time, a fire department that comes when you call it, a light that leaps into the room at a touch, and a clinic that will fight for the health of a penniless man and mass for him the agencies of mercy, the X-ray, the precious radium, the anesthetics and the surgical skill. For, beyond any pay these services receive, stands out the pride in perfect performance. And above all, I admire the noble impersonality of civilization that does not inquire where the recipient stands on religion or politics or race. I call this beauty, and I call it spirit — not some mystical soulfulness that nobody can define, but the spirit of man, that has been a million years a-growing.

26. The title that best expresses the ideas of this paragraph is:
    (A) The spirit of the city   (B) Advantages of a city home   (C) Disagreement among naturalists   (D) Admirable characteristics of cities   (E) Tolerance in the city

27. The services rendered by city agencies are given
    (A) only for pay   (B) on time   (C) only to people having a certain political background   (D) to everybody   (E) to the spirit of man

28. The author makes a defense of
    (A) cities   (B) prompt trains   (C) rural life   (D) nature   (E) free clinics

29. The aspect of city life most commendable to this author is its
    (A) punctuality   (B) free benefits   (C) impartial service   (D) mechanical improvement   (E) health clinics

30. The author implies that efficient operation of public utilities is
    (A) expensive   (B) of no special interest   (C) admired by most naturalists   (D) mechanically commendable   (E) spiritual in quality

The history of mammals dates back at least to Triassic time. Development was retarded, however, until the sudden acceleration of evolutional change that occurred in the oldest Paleocene. This led in Eocene time to increase in average size, larger mental capacity, and special adaptations for different modes of life. In the Oligocene Epoch, there was further improvement, with some appearance of some new lines and extinction of others. Miocene and Pliocene time was marked by culmination of several groups and continued approach toward modern characters. The peak of the career of mammals in variety and average large size was attained in the Miocene.

The adaptation of mammals to almost all possible modes of life parallels that of the reptiles in Mesozoic time, and except for greater intelligence, the mammals do not seem to have done much better than corresponding reptilian forms. The bat is doubtless a better flying animal than the pterosaur, but the dolphin and whale are hardly more fishlike than the ichthyosaur. Many swift-running mammals of the plains, like the horse and the antelope, must excel any of the dinosaurs. The tyrannosaur was a more ponderous and powerful carnivore than any flesh-eating mammal, but the lion or tiger is probably a more efficient and dangerous beast of prey because of a superior brain. The significant point to observe is that different branches of the mammals gradually fitted themselves for all sorts of life, grazing on the plains and able to run swiftly (horse, deer, bison), living in rivers and swamps (hippopotamus, beaver), dwelling in trees (sloth, monkey), digging underground (mole, rodent), feeding on flesh in the forest (tiger) and plain (wolf), swimming in the sea (dolphin, whale, seal) and flying in the air (bat). Man is able by mechanical means to conquer the physical world and adapt himself to almost any set of conditions.

This adaptation produces gradual changes of form and structure. It is biologically characteristic of the youthful, plastic stage of a group. Early in its career, an animal assemblage seems to possess capacity for change, which, as the unit becomes old and fixed, disappears. The generalized types of organisms retain longest the ability to make adjustments when required, and it is from them that new, fecund stocks take origin — certainly not from any specialized end products. So, in the mammals, we witness the birth, plastic spread in many directions, increasing specialization, and in some branches, the extinction, which we have learned from observation of the geologic record of life is a characteristic of the evolution of life.

31. The aboreal mammal mentioned in the passage is the
    (A) bison   (B) deer   (C) beaver   (D) mole   (E) sloth

32. From this passage, we may conclude that the pterosaur
    (A) resembled the bat   (B) was a mammal that lived in the Mesozoic period   (C) was a flying reptile   (D) lived in the sea   (E) evolved during the Miocene period

33. The greatest number of forms of mammalian life is found in the
    (A) Triassic period   (B) Eocene period   (C) Oligocene Epoch   (D) Pliocene period   (E) Miocene period

34. That the mammals which succeeded the reptiles in geologic time were superior is illustrated by the statement that
    (A) the tiger has a brain that surpasses that of the tyrannosaur   (B) the deer runs more swiftly than the lion   (C) the whale is more fishlike than the ichthyosaur   (D) the tiger is more powerful than the carnivorous reptiles   (E) the dinosaurs were slow moving animals

35. *Saur* in such words as pterosaur, dinosaur, and tyrannosaur probably means

(A) large   (B) reptilian   (C) living in Mesozoic time   (D) inefficient   (E) defunct

36. The statements made by the writer are based on evidence

(A) developed by Charles Darwin   (B) found by comparing animals and reptiles   (C) found by going to different time periods (D) that cannot be definitely established   (E) gained by studying fossil remains

37. Man has been able to adjust himself to his environment better than other animals

(A) because he is stronger   (B) because he can swim and walk (C) because he was developed in Pliocene time   (D) because he can adjust to his environment   (E) because he can utilize mechanical devices

We now know that what constitutes practically all of matter is empty space; relatively enormous voids in which revolve with lightning velocity infinitesimal particles so utterly small that they have never been seen or photographed. The existence of these particles has been demonstrated by mathematical physicists and their operations determined by ingenious laboratory experiments. It was not until 1911 that experiments by Sir Ernest Rutherford revealed the architecture of the mysterious atom. Moseley, Bohr, Fermi, Millikan, Compton, Urey, and others have also worked on the problem. Matter is composed of molecules whose average diameter is about 1/125 millionth of an inch. Molecules are composed of atoms so small that about five million could be placed in a row on the period at the end of this sentence. Long thought to be the ultimate, indivisible constituent of matter, the atom has been found to consist roughly of a proton, the positive electrical element in the atomic nucleus, surrounded by electrons, the negative electric elements swirling about the proton.

38. The center of the atom, according to this passage,

(A) contains one electron   (B) was seen as early as 1911   (C) has not yet been seen by the naked eye   (D) is about the size of a period   (E) might be photographed under microscopes.

39. The paragraph indicates that the atom

(A) is the smallest particle   (B) is very little larger than a molecule (C) is composed of several particles   (D) has been seen   (E) is empty space

40. Scientists agree that molecules are

(A) voids   (B) the most mysterious particles   (C) not divisible (D) not basically composed of electric elements   (E) huge compared with electrons

Section 5   35 QUESTIONS — 30 MINUTES

In this section solve each problem, using any available space on the page for scratchwork. Then decide which is the best of the choices given and blacken the corresponding space on the answer sheet.

The following information is for your reference in solving some of the problems.

Circle of radius r: Area = πr^2; Circumference = $2\pi r$
The number of degrees of arc in a circle is 360.
The measure in degrees of a straight angle is 180.

Definitions of symbols:

= is equal to	≤ is less than or equal to
≠ is unequal to	≥ is greater than or equal to
< is less than	‖ is parallel to
> is greater than	⊥ is perpendicular to

NOTE: Figures which accompany problems in this test are intended to provide information useful in solving the problems. They are drawn as accurately as possible EXCEPT when it is stated in a specific problem that its figure is not drawn to scale. All figures lie in the plane unless otherwise indicated. All numbers used are real numbers.

Triangle: The sum of the measures in degrees of the angles of a triangle is 180.

If $\angle CDA$ is a right angle, then

(1) area of $\triangle ABC = \dfrac{AB \times CD}{2}$

(2) $AC^2 = AD^2 + DC^2$

1. Out of a group of 80 applicants for a civil service examination, 20 persons failed to appear for the first part of this test. What percent of the total applicants did appear for this part of the test?
    (A) 4   (B) 16   (C) 25   (D) 60   (E) 75

2. A class has b number of boys and g number of girls. The ratio of girls to boys is

    (A) bg (B) $\dfrac{b}{g}$ (C) $\dfrac{b}{b+g}$ (D) $\dfrac{g}{b}$ (E) $\dfrac{g}{b+g}$

3. What is the value of $\sqrt{\frac{1}{16} + \frac{1}{9}}$?

(A) $\frac{1}{7}$ (B) $\frac{2}{7}$ (C) $\frac{25}{144}$ (D) $\frac{5}{12}$ (E) $\frac{7}{12}$

4. The fraction $\frac{a+b}{b}$ equals

(A) a (B) $\frac{a}{b} + b$ (C) $\frac{a}{b} + 1$ (D) $a^2 + 1$

(E) $\frac{a+b}{a}$

5. How many kilometers are there in 12 miles? (1 kilometer = $\frac{5}{8}$ mile.)

(A) 7.2   (B) 7.5   (C) 19.2   (D) 19.5   (E) 22.3

6. Having installed a new gas tank in my car, the attendant took $1\frac{3}{4}$ minutes to completely fill my gas tank. What part of the tank would have been filled if he had stopped after a full minute?

(A) $\frac{2}{7}$ (B) $\frac{3}{7}$ (C) $\frac{4}{7}$ (D) $\frac{3}{4}$ (E) $\frac{5}{7}$

7. If I can purchase 2 items for $c¢$, at the same rate, how many items will I receive for $x¢$?

(A) $\frac{c}{2x}$ (B) $\frac{2c}{x}$ (C) $\frac{cx}{2}$ (D) $2cx$ (E) $\frac{2x}{c}$

8. Which of the following statements is always true?
   I. A root of a negative number may be a real number.
   II. The positive square root of a number is smaller than the number.
   III. A binomial multiplied by a binomial yields a trinomial.
   (A) only I   (B) only II   (C) only III   (D) II and III
   (E) all are true

9. The radius of the pool in Shelter Rock Park is twice the radius of the pool in Martin's backyard. The area of the pool in the park is how many times the area of Martin's pool?

(A) $\frac{1}{4}$ (B) $\frac{1}{2}$ (C) 2   (D) 4   (E) 8

10. $BD \perp BE$ and $\angle DBA \triangleq 70$. What is the value of x?

(A) 20   (B) 110   (C) 120
(D) 160   (E) 290

11. What is the value of x?
(A) 5   (B) 6   (C) 7
(D) 8   (E) 9

12. In isosceles triangle *ABC*, *BD* and *CD* are the bisectors of the base angles. The vertex angle has a measure of 70°. Find the value of *x*.

(A) 35   (B) 70   (C) 100

(D) 125   (E) 155

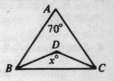

Questions 13-17 are based on the following:

Five executives of a European corporation hold a conference in Rome.

Mr. A can speak Spanish and Italian.

Mr. B understands Spanish and English.

Mr. C converses in English and Italian.

Mr. D speaks French and understands Spanish quite well.

Mr. E, a native Italian, can also speak French.

13. Which of the following can act as interpreter when Mr. C and Mr. D wish to confer?

(A) only Mr. A   (B) only Mr. B   (C) only Mr. E

(D) Mr. A or Mr. B   (E) any of the other three executives

14. Which of the following cannot converse between them without an interpreter?

(A) Mr. B and Mr. E   (B) Mr. A and Mr. B   (C) Mr. A and Mr. C   (D) Mr. B and Mr. D   (E) Mr. A and Mr. E

15. Besides Mr. E, which of the following can converse with Mr. D without an interpreter?

(A) only Mr. A   (B) only Mr. B   (C) only Mr. C

(D) Mr. A and Mr. B   (E) Mr. A, Mr. B, and Mr. C

16. If a sixth executive is brought in, to be understood by the maximum number of the original five, he should be fluent in

(A) English and French   (B) Italian and English

(C) French and Italian   (D) Italian and Spanish

(E) English and Spanish

17. Of the languages spoken at this conference, which are the two least common?

(A) English and Spanish   (B) English and French

(C) Italian and Spanish   (D) English and Italian

(E) French and Spanish

18. How much paper (in terms of π) is wasted if the largest possible circle with a diameter of *d* is cut out of the square?

(A) $d - \pi d^2$ (B) $\dfrac{d^2 \pi}{4}$

(C) $\dfrac{\pi d^2}{4} - d^2$ (D) $\dfrac{4d^2 - \pi d^2}{4}$

(E) $\dfrac{16d^2 - \pi d^2}{4}$

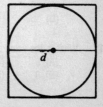

Questions 19–35 each consist of two quantities, one in Column A and one in Column B. You are to compare the two quantities and on the answer sheet blacken space

    A if the quantity in Column A is greater;
    B if the quantity in Column B is greater;
    C if the two quantities are equal;
    D if the relationship cannot be determined from the information given.

Notes: 1. In certain questions, information concerning one or both of the quantities to be compared is centered above the two columns.
        2. A symbol that appears in both columns represents the same thing in Column A as it does in Column B.
        3. Letters such as x, n, and k stand for real numbers.

Column A	Column B
19.	$(a)(b) = 0$
a	b

Column A	Column B
20.	$xy = 5$
	$x^2 + y^2 = 7$
$(x + y)^2$	17

Column A	Column B
21. $\sqrt{0.3}$	0.49

Column A	Column B
22. one-half of one percent	0.05

Column A	Column B
23.	$x = 2,\ y = 3,\ z = 7$
$x(y + z)$	$xz + y$

24.

AGFC and BEDC are rectangles

Perimeter of AGFC	Perimeter of shaded region

	Column A	Column B

25.

$$x > 0$$

$2x^2$	$(2x)^2$

26.

Basketball Player	Points Scored in Game
A	20
B	8
C	22
D	14
E	2

Average score of all players	Points scored by player D

27.

AB and CD are parallel lines

Area of triangle PCD	Area of triangle RCD

28.

x	y

29.

$$5x = 729$$
$$3y = 729$$

x	y

Column A	Column B

30.   In 19 years from now Mark will be three times as old as Philip is now. Michael is 3 years younger than Mark.

Michael's age now	Philip's age now

31.
$$1 < a < 5$$
$$1 < b < 5$$

$b - a$	$a - b$

---

32. $3\frac{1}{2}\%$ | $\dfrac{35}{1000}$ |

33.
$$\frac{1}{A} = \frac{1}{x} + \frac{1}{y}$$

A	$\dfrac{xy}{x+y}$

---

34. $x < -1$

x	$\dfrac{1}{x}$

---

35. $a > 1$ and $b > 1$

$\dfrac{a^2 - b^2}{(a-b)^2}$	$\dfrac{a+b}{a-b}$

Section 6   40 QUESTIONS — 30 MINUTES

In this section solve each problem, using any available space on the page for scratchwork. Then decide which is the best of the choices given and blacken the corresponding space on the answer sheet.

The following information is for your reference in solving some of the problems.

Circle of radius r: Area $= \pi r^2$; Circumference $= 2\pi r$
    The number of degrees of arc in a circle is 360.
The measure in degrees of a straight angle is 180.

Definitions of symbols:

= is equal to	$\leqq$ is less than or equal to
$\neq$ is unequal to	$\geqq$ is greater than or equal to
< is less than	‖ is parallel to
> is greater than	⊥ is perpendicular to

NOTE: Figures which accompany problems in this test are intended to provide information useful in solving the problems. They are drawn as accurately as possible EXCEPT when it is stated in a specific problem that its figure is not drawn to scale. All figures lie in the plane unless otherwise indicated. All numbers used are real numbers.

Triangle: The sum of the measures in degrees of the angles of a triangle is 180.

If $\angle CDA$ is a right angle, then

(1) area of $\triangle ABC = \dfrac{AB \times CD}{2}$

(2) $AC^2 = AD^2 + DC^2$

1. $12 = 1\frac{1}{3}(?)$

    (A) 3 (B) 4 (C) 8 (D) 9 (E) 16

2. If one pie serves seven people, how many pies are needed to serve a banquet of 91 people?

    (A) 7 (B) 9 (C) 13 (D) 15 (E) 637

3. Which of the following is the next smaller than $\frac{1}{2}$?

    (A) $\frac{1}{5}$ (B) $\frac{2}{5}$ (C) $\frac{3}{5}$ (D) $\frac{16}{25}$ (E) $\frac{13}{25}$

4. $\dfrac{a+b}{a-b} \div \dfrac{b+a}{b-a} = ?$

    (A) −1 (B) 0 (C) 1 (D) $a + b$ (E) $a - b$

5. How many feet are there in 7.2 inches?

    (A) $\frac{1}{6}$ (B) $\frac{7}{12}$ (C) $\frac{3}{5}$ (D) $\frac{5}{3}$ (E) 6

6. Which is the smallest of the following?

    (A) $\frac{1}{.4}$ (B) $\frac{5}{8}$ (C) $(.2)^2$ (D) $\frac{9}{100}$ (E) $\sqrt{1.44}$

7. A car uses a gallon of gasoline in traveling 15 miles. Another automobile can travel m miles on a gallon of gasoline. How many miles can the second travel on the amount of gasoline required by the first car in going 60 miles?

(A) $\frac{m}{4}$ (B) m (C) $4m$ (D) $\frac{m}{9}$ (E) $9m$

8. A box of 12 tablets costs 21 cents. The same brand is packaged in bottles containing 100 tablets and sells for $1.50 per bottle. How much is saved per dozen, by purchasing the larger amount?

(A) 3¢   (B) 4¢   (C) 30¢   (D) 36¢   (E) 40¢

9. A man can do $\frac{1}{8}$ of a piece of work in one day. How much of it can he do in x days?

(A) $\frac{x}{8}$ (B) $\frac{8}{x}$ (C) $x + 8$ (D) $8 - x$ (E) $8x$

10. If the length of a rectangle is $3u + 2v$, and its perimeter is $10u + 6v$, what is its width?

(A) $v + 2u$ (B) $2v + 4u$ (C) $2v + \frac{7}{2}u$ (D) $4v + 7u$

(E) $6v + 10u$

11. $W = i^2r$ $r = \frac{E}{i}$ Find E in terms of W and r.

(A) $\frac{1}{Wr}$ (B) Wr (C) $\sqrt{Wr}$ (D) $\frac{W}{r}$ (E) w^2r^2

12. At 10 A.M. water begins to pour into a cylindrical can 14 inches high and 4 inches in diameter at the rate of 8 cubic inches every 10 minutes. At what time will it begin to overflow?   (Use $\pi = \frac{22}{7}$.)

(A) 1:20 P.M.   (B) 1:40 P.M.   (C) 3:40 P.M.   (D) 6:20 P.M.
(E) 6:40 P.M.

13. The length of a rectangle is increased by 50%. By what per cent would the width have to be decreased to maintain the same area?

(A) $33\frac{1}{3}$ (B) 50   (C) $66\frac{2}{3}$ (D) 150

(E) 200

14. Radius $OA = 6.5$ Chord $AC = 5$ Area of triangle ABC equals

(A) 16   (B) 18   (C) 24   (D) 30
(E) 36

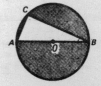

15. A man travels in his yacht downstream at d knots and returns the same distance upstream at u knots. What is his average rate (in knots) for the round trip?

(A) $\dfrac{du}{2}$ (B) $\dfrac{d+u}{2}$ (C) $\dfrac{du}{d+2}$ (D) $\dfrac{2du}{d+u}$ (E) $\dfrac{d+u}{2du}$

16. $ab - 2cd = p$ $ab - 2cd = q$ $6cd - 3ab = r$ $\dfrac{p}{r} = ?$

(A) -3 (B) $-\dfrac{1}{3}$ (C) $\dfrac{1}{3}$ (D) 1 (E) 3

17. In a certain office, ⅓ of the workers are women, ½ of the women are married, and ⅓ of the married women have children. If ¾ of the men are married and ⅔ of the married men have children, what part of the workers are without children?

(A) $\dfrac{5}{18}$ (B) $\dfrac{4}{9}$ (C) $\dfrac{17}{36}$ (D) $\dfrac{11}{18}$ (E) $\dfrac{2}{3}$

18. The distance between point P (3,0) and point Q is 5. The coordinates of point Q could be any of the following except

(A) (3,−5) (B) (3,5) (C) (0,8) (D) (0,−8) (E) (−2,0)

19. The coordinates of A and B are $(2a, 2b)$ and $(4a, 6b)$, respectively. The coordinates of the midpoint of AB in terms of a and b are

(A) $(3a, 4b)$ (B) $(3b, 4a)$ (C) $(6a, 8b)$ (D) $(6b, 8a)$

(E) $(3a, 6b)$

20. The vertices of rectangle $ABCD$ are the points A (0,0), B (8,0), C (8,k), D (0,5). k equals

(A) 4 (B) 5 (C) 6 (D) 3 (E) 2

Questions 21–40 each consist of two quantities, one in Column A and one in Column B. You are to compare the two quantities and on the answer sheet blacken space

    A if the quantity in Column A is greater;
    B if the quantity in Column B is greater;
    C if the two quantities are equal;
    D if the relationship cannot be determined from the information given.

Notes: 1. In certain questions, information concerning one or both of the quantities to be compared is centered above the two columns.
        2. A symbol that appears in both columns represents the same thing in Column A as it does in Column B.
        3. Letters such as x, n, and k stand for real numbers.

	COLUMN A	COLUMN B
21.	$\dfrac{1}{7}$	.0142
22.	$\sqrt{\dfrac{1}{.25}}$	2
23.	5% of 500	2.5
24.	Time elapsed from 2:55 P.M. to 3:15 P.M. on the same afternoon	$\dfrac{1}{3}$ hour

25. $\dfrac{(15)(16)}{x} = (5)(4)(3)$

	COLUMN A	COLUMN B
	x	4

26. $\dfrac{1}{x} = \sqrt{.09}$

	COLUMN A	COLUMN B
	x	$3\dfrac{1}{3}$

27. $a + 2b = 1\dfrac{1}{3}$

$a - b = \dfrac{1}{3}$

	COLUMN A	COLUMN B
	$3b$	1
28.	$\dfrac{x - y}{-z}$	$\dfrac{y - x}{z}$

29. $x = 0$ and $y > 0$

	COLUMN A	COLUMN B
	$\dfrac{9x^2y^2}{27}$	$\dfrac{1}{3}$
30.	$\dfrac{4}{5}$ quart	$\dfrac{1}{5}$ gallon

$a : b = c : d$
This concerns #31– #34

	COLUMN A	COLUMN B
31.	$\dfrac{b}{a}$	$\dfrac{d}{c}$
32.	$a + b$	$c + d$
33.	bc	ad

COLUMN A	COLUMN B
34. $\dfrac{a}{c}$	$\dfrac{b}{d}$

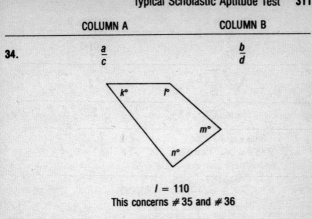

$l = 110$
This concerns #35 and #36

	COLUMN A	COLUMN B
35.	l	n
36.	$k + m$	$l + n$

The area of triangle *ABC* = 72
The measure of angle *A* is equal
to the measure of angle *C*, which
is 45 degrees. This information
concerns #37– #40.

	COLUMN A	COLUMN B
37.	Length of *AB*	Length of *BC*
38.	Length of *AB*	Length of *AC*
39.	Length of *AB*	12
40.	Length of *AC* + length of *BC*	Length of *AB*

8 SAT Answer Key and Answer Explanations

Section 1

1. C	10. B	19. E	28. D	37. A
2. A	11. D	20. A	29. B	38. B
3. A	12. C	21. D	30. A	39. E
4. D	13. E	22. A	31. B	40. A
5. E	14. A	23. B	32. C	41. B
6. D	15. E	24. C	33. A	42. D
7. E	16. B	25. E	34. D	43. C
8. A	17. C	26. A	35. E	44. B
9. B	18. D	27. A	36. C	45. B

Section 2

1. D	6. D	11. A	16. B	21. E
2. C	7. D	12. A	17. C	22. D
3. E	8. A	13. D	18. A	23. C
4. A	9. E	14. C	19. C	24. D
5. E	10. C	15. A	20. B	25. D

Section 3

1.	D	11.	B	21.	E	31.	D	41.	B
2.	C	12.	E	22.	A	32.	E	42.	B
3.	C	13.	E	23.	A	33.	C	43.	C
4.	C	14.	C	24.	B	34.	B	44.	E
5.	D	15.	A	25.	B	35.	C	45.	C
6.	B	16.	B	26.	D	36.	E	46.	D
7.	B	17.	D	27.	C	37.	C	47.	A
8.	B	18.	A	28.	A	38.	C	48.	C
9.	B	19.	A	29.	C	39.	C	49.	E
10.	C	20.	C	30.	A	40.	B	50.	B

Section 4

1.	D	9.	C	17.	A	25.	D	33.	E
2.	B	10.	C	18.	B	26.	D	34.	A
3.	A	11.	C	19.	D	27.	D	35.	B
4.	E	12.	D	20.	D	28.	A	36.	E
5.	D	13.	D	21.	B	29.	C	37.	E
6.	A	14.	C	22.	C	30.	E	38.	C
7.	E	15.	E	23.	E	31.	E	39.	C
8.	D	16.	D	24.	B	32.	C	40.	E

Section 5

1.	E	8.	A	15.	D	22.	B	29.	B
2.	D	9.	D	16.	D	23.	A	30.	D
3.	D	10.	D	17.	B	24.	C	31.	D
4.	C	11.	C	18.	A	25.	B	32.	C
5.	C	12.	D	19.	D	26.	B	33.	C
6.	C	13.	E	20.	C	27.	C	34.	B
7.	E	14.	A	21.	A	28.	A	35.	C

Section 6

1. D	9. A	17. D	25. C	33. C
2. C	10. A	18. D	26. C	34. C
3. B	11. C	19. A	27. C	35. D
4. A	12. B	20. B	28. C	36. D
5. C	13. A	21. A	29. B	37. C
6. C	14. D	22. C	30. C	38. B
7. C	15. D	23. A	31. C	39. C
8. A	16. B	24. C	32. D	40. A

Answers Explained

Section 1

1. **C** *Ostracism* (banishment from society) is a form of *censure* (expression of disapproval). *Applause* is a demonstration of *approval*.

2. **A** A *cobbler* repairs *shoes* and a *mechanic* repairs *automobiles*.

3. **A** *Propitiate* and *appease* are synonyms; likewise, *disturb* and *agitate* are synonyms.

4. **D** *Laconic* and *voluble* are antonyms; likewise, *frozen* and *boiling* are antonyms.

5. **E** *Rooster* and *gander* are male; *hen* and *goose*, female.

6. **D** *Rococo* and *baroque* are synonyms and are the opposite of *simple* and *plain*.

7. **E** In measuring liquids, (liquid measure) *pint* immediately precedes *quart*; in measuring time, *second* immediately precedes *minute*.

8. **A** *Assurance* will allay *fear* and an *opiate* will allay *pain*.

9. **B** The symbol of *time* is a bearded gentleman carrying a *scythe*; the symbol of *justice* is a blindfolded lady carrying a *scale*.

10. **B** *Felicity* (bliss) and *sorrow* are antonyms; *agility* and *clumsiness* are antonyms.

11. **D** *Assiduous* means diligent.

12. **C** *Verbose* means overly wordy.

13. **E** A *lexicographer* (writer of dictionaries) would be interested in the derivation of words.

14. **A** Dr. Johnson would be surrounded most probably by a *coterie* (select circle) of friends.

15. **E** One custom observed in Spain but not in America is the mid-day rest or *siesta*.

16. **B** A *paregoric* would be the most suitable remedy.

17. **C** *Omniscient* means all-knowing.

18. **D** The bonus of a trip to Europe would provide an *incentive*.

19. **E** A pessimist has a doleful or *lugubrious* outlook.

20. **A** *Germane*, meaning pertinent, is the only appropriate choice.

21. **D** The opposite of *phlegmatic* (sluggish) is *active*.

22. **A** The opposite of *salutary* (wholesome, beneficial) is *harmful*.

23. **B** The opposite of *culpable* (blameworthy) is *blameless*.

24. **C** A *demure* (markedly quiet and unexcited) person is not *demonstrative*.

25. **E** The opposite of *orthodox* (holding correct views) is *heretical* (unorthodox).

26. **A** The opposite of *dissuade* (discourage) is *exhort* (urge on).

27. **A** The opposite of *succor* (aid, assistance) is *hindrance*.

28. **D** An *overt* (unconcealed) act is not *clandestine* (done secretly).

29. **B** A *lackadaisical* person lacks enthusiasm. He is not *enthusiastic*.

30. **A** A *suave* individual is polite and polished. He would not be *tactless*.

31. **B** Crabbed (grouchy, irritable) is the opposite of saccharine (cloyingly sweet in expression).

32. **C** Corroboration (support with additional proof) and refutation (proof of error or falsity) are opposites.

33. **A** Decorum (propriety of speech, behavior, etc.) and ribaldry (vulgarity in speech, etc.) are opposites.

34. **D** Vivacious (lively) and inactive are opposites.

35. **E** The opposite of *ingenuous* (young, naive) is sophisticated.

36. **C** The passage describes the extreme lack of interest in and knowledge of social insurance. Choice C sums this up.

37. **A** Americans have always been proud of our "rugged individualism." Choice A is best.

38. **B** The last sentence supports Choice B.

39. **E** The passage discusses the versatility of all Renaissance artists. Choice E is best.

40. **A** The next-to-the-last sentence discusses Leonardo's fame as an engineer and scientist.

41. **B** Another way of describing an "all-around Man" (sentence 1) is that he is "many-sided."

42. **D** The last portion of the paragraph reminds us of the "terrible" things we did because of superstition.

43. **C** Since the passage ends with a note of gratitude to science, we may assume that the author will continue to discuss science and scientific methods.

44. **B** The opening sentence supports Choice B.

45. **B** The use of the words "it is well to reflect occasionally" in the last sentence supports Choice B. An examination of the other choices reveals that they are all false according to the passage.

Section 2

1. **D** Time does not permit actually doing the long division. Also, bear in mind that this is not an arithmetic test. Observe that the dividend ends with a 6 and the divisor ends with a 4. Only one choice ends in a 4.

2. **C**
$$(a + 3)(a - 3) = a^2 - 9$$
Substitute value of a:
$$(-6)(-6) - 9$$
$$+36 - 9 = 27.$$

The time-consuming method is to substitute the values given and multiply. $(-6 + 3)(-6 - 3)$, which equals $(-3)(-9)$ or $+27$. In incorrect choice (B) algebraic addition is done incorrectly and multiplication is not done. In (C) one fails to observe the signed number properties $(+)(+) = +$ and $(-)(-) = +$ and $(-)(+) = -$. (D) and (E) fail to add algebraically.

3. **E**
$$y = \frac{1}{6}$$
$$6y = 1$$
$$18y = 3$$
Since $x = 3$ (given)
then $x = 18y$ (things equal to the same thing are equal).

4. **A**
$$3x - 6 = 1$$
Then $x - 2 = \frac{1}{3}$ (dividing by 3).

5. **E** $\dfrac{AD}{AC} = \dfrac{3 \text{ of the equal units}}{2 \text{ of the equal units}} = 1\frac{1}{2}$ or 150%.

6. **D** Substance B makes up $\frac{3}{24}$ or $\frac{1}{8}$ of the total mix. $\frac{1}{8}$ of 72 ounces equals 9 ounces.

7. **D**   The total distance covered during the cruise was 4,000 nautical miles. The part covered from New York to Curaçao was

$$\frac{1770}{4000} = \frac{44.25}{100} = 44.25\%$$

8. **A**   Let x = number of nautical miles in 1 statute mile. Set up a proportion:

$$\frac{\text{nautical mile}}{\text{statute mile}} = \frac{100}{160} = \frac{x}{1} = \frac{5}{8} = 0.625.$$

9. **E**   Since the area of each circle = 9π, then the radii of each circle = 3 and the diameter of each circle = 6. Each side of the square = two diameters or 12. The area of the square = 144. The shaded area constitutes the area of the square minus the area of the 4 circles (4 times 9π).

10. **C**

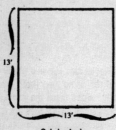
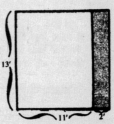

Original size
of plywood

Shaded part shows
part cut to fit wall.

Area of wall = $(13')(11')$ or 143 square feet.

11. **A**   Since the area of the square = x^2, each side = x. ED, the base of triangle $AED = x - y$ since $EC = x$ and $DC = y$. Area of triangle $AED = \frac{1}{2}(AE)(ED)$ or

$\frac{1}{2}(x)(x - y)$ or

$\frac{x^2 - xy}{2}$.

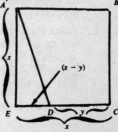

12. **A**   Odd numbers are of the form $2x + 1$, where x is an integer. Thus, if $n = 2x + 1$ and $p = 2k + 1$, then $n + p = 2x + 1 + 2k + 1 \doteq 2x + 2k + 2$, which is even. Using $n = 3$ and $p = 5$, all the other choices give an odd number. In general, if a problem involves odd or even numbers, try using the fact that odd numbers are of the form $2x + 1$ and even numbers of the form $2y$, where x and y are integers.

13. **D** The time-consuming method would calculate the number sold at
$3 ($\frac{1}{4}$ of 30,000) and add the number sold at $2.50 ($\frac{1}{3}$ of 30,000)
and subtract that from 30,000. The suggested method first alerts
you to the fact that you may disregard the prices in your computation, for the problem could have referred to color of tickets.
$\frac{1}{4} + \frac{1}{3}$ or $\frac{7}{12}$ of the tickets in the upper price ranges were sold,
so that the rest or $\frac{5}{12}$ of 30,000 or 12,500 were sold at $1.25.

14. **C** Since the average of the 3 persons is 53, the total weight of the
3 is 159. Since we are looking for the maximum weight for one
boy, we should assume the minimum weight for the other 2. (A)
and (B) fail to do so. Assume two of them each weigh 51 pounds
for a total of 102, leaving 57 pounds for the third boy. Choice (D)
leaves 100 pounds to be divided between the other 2, which
is impossible since each must have a minimum weight of 51
pounds. (E) is incorrect for the same line of reasoning.

15. **A** Recall the basic principles of inequalities. Choice (A) is correct
since, if two inequalities are of the same type (both greater or
both less), adding the respective sides gives the same type of
inequality. Choice (B) is incorrect since inequalities are reversed
if you multiply or divide by a negative number. Choices (C), (D)
and (E) are not consistent with the given information.

16. **B** Mark traveled 10 miles in 6 hours. Substitute in the formula:

$$\text{Rate} = \frac{\text{Distance (in miles)}}{\text{Time (in hours)}}$$

Choice (C) is incorrect. The rate going may not be averaged
with the rate returning since the time spent returning was twice
as much as the time spent at the faster rate going downstream.
Choice (D) gives the sum of the rates.

17. **C** Note that Michael's time is expressed in minutes while the
answer is to be expressed in hours. Change 20 minutes to $\frac{1}{3}$ of
an hour. The incorrect choice (E) is the sum of $\frac{1}{3}$ and $\frac{1}{4}$ ($\frac{7}{12}$).

$$\text{Average} = \frac{\text{Sum}}{\text{Number of cases}} \text{ or } \frac{7}{12} \div 2 \text{ or } \frac{7}{24}.$$

Choice (A) adds the denominators and choice (B) adds numer-
ators and denominators. Recall that, in adding fractions, nu-
merators are added with common denominators.

18. **A**   Observe that an isosceles triangle is formed.

19. **C**   The total payroll is $1,060,000, and the wages paid to managers = $110,000. 110,000/1,060,000 = 11/106 = .10 (rounding to the nearest hundredth) or 10%.

20. **B**   The average wage is $1,060,000 divided by 530 or $2,000.

21. **E**   The average salary of a manager is $110,000/5 or $22,000. The average salary of an assembly worker is $600,000 divided by 500 or $1,200. So the ratio is 220 to 12 or 55 to 3.

22. **D**   All 5 managers together earn $110,000. Since each one of the four makes x dollars, the remaining manager is paid $(110,000 - 4x)$.

23. **C**   Draw altitude AH, which bisects BC. Therefore BH equals 8. In right triangle ABH, since AB equals 10 and BH equals 8, then AH equals 6. The area of ABC equals $\frac{1}{2}$ (base) (altitude) or $\frac{1}{2}$(16)(6) or 48 units. In choice

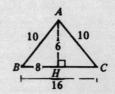

(A) area of triangle ABH is given. In (D) and (E) the formula for area of right triangles was applied. Recall that in right triangles one leg may be regarded as the base and the other leg may be regarded as the altitude. In (E) an additional error was committed by failing to multiply by $\frac{1}{2}$.

24. **D**   Since the perimeter of the square is 24, each side is 6 and its area is 36. Since the area of R is also 36 and its altitude is 4, its base is 9 (note this is incorrect choice A). The perimeter of R is (2)(4) + (2)(9) or 26 feet. Choice (E) gives the area of R. Choice (B) fails to consider R a rectangle. Choice (C) assumes that the base of R equals the side of the square.

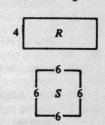

25. **D** Since there are 20 members on the squad, any one of these may be elected captain. Since the elected captain may not also be co-captain, any one of the remaining 19 squad members is left as a possible co-captain. Therefore there are (20)(19) or 380 different outcomes of this election. Choice (A) fails to account for the fact that one election can occur in 20 different ways and is followed by a second election that can occur in (20 − 1) or 19 different ways.

Section 3

1. **D** Faulty comparison. Do not compare a person with a thing. Correct form: *Your argument is no different from that of the last speaker* . . .

2. **C** Violation of parallel structure. Change *to attend* to *attending*.

3. **C** Faulty reference. *Which* should not refer to a clause.

4. **C** Lack of agreement. Woman (singular) requires a singular pronoun.

5. **D** Faulty comparison. When comparing two persons or things, use the comparative form (*better*) instead of the superlative (*best*).

6. **B** Faulty diction. Omit the article (a) in *this kind of a* . . .

7. **B** Faulty diction. Use *take* instead of *bring*.

8. **B** Faulty diction. Change *would I go* to *whether I would go*.

9. **B** Wrong case. Change *John* to *John's*.

10. **C** Faulty diction. Use *behind* instead of *in back of*.

11. **B** Faulty diction. Change *amount* to *number*.

12. **E** Sentence is correct.

13. **E** Sentence is correct.

14. **C** Faulty diction. Change *enthuse* to *be enthusiastic*.

15. **A** Faulty diction. Use *annoyed* or *irritated* instead of *aggravated*.

16. **B** Error in agreement. A *system has been incorporated* is correct.

17. **D** Error in agreement. The antecedent of *who* is *one*. Change *plan* to *plans*.

18. **A** Error in diction. Do not use *due to* when you mean *because of*.

19. **A** Error in case. Use *who* because it is the subject of *would win*.

20. **C** Error in tense. Substitute *have lived* for *am living*.

21. **E** Sentence is correct.

22. **A** Faulty diction. Do not use *neither* when discussing more than two items. Substitute *none*.

23. **A** Dangling participle. Change to a subordinate clause — *When we descended* . . .

24. **B** Faulty diction. Use *if* to indicate a condition. Substitute *whether*.

25.   **B**   Omission of important word. Sentence is better as: *He had a keen interest in and a wide knowledge of his esoteric subject*.

26.   **D**   Do not use *calculate* when you mean *think*.

27.   **C**   This sentence does not violate parallel structure.

28.   **A**   Sentence is correct.

29.   **C**   Improper punctuation of direct quotation. Choice C is correct.

30.   **A**   Sentence is correct.

31.   **D**   This choice eliminates the error in parallel structure.

32.   **E**   Omission of important word is corrected in Choice E.

33.   **C**   Error in the possessive form of *government* and *it*.

34.   **B**   Error in agreement. *Her brother . . . insists* is correct.

35.   **C**   Error in agreement. *Kind* is singular and requires a singular modifier (*this*).

36.   **E**   This preserves the parallel structure in the sentence.

37.   **C**   The past perfect tense is required in an "if" clause.

38.   **C**   The dangling participle construction is corrected in (C).

39.   **C**   *Company's* and *its* are the correct possessive case forms.

40.   **B**   The verb should agree with its subject (*principal*) in number.

41,   **B**   Wrong case. The possessive case of *Jones* is *Jones's*.

42.   **B**   Wrong tense. Change *is* to *has been*.

43.   **C**   Faulty diction. Delete *of*.

44.   **E**   Sentence is correct.

45.   **C**   Error in case. Substitute *him* for *he*.

46.   **D**   Faulty comparison. Change *any state* to *that of any other state*.

47.   **A**   Dangling participle. Change *Reading quickly* to *Because he was a quick reader*.

48.   **C**   Incorrect case. Change *us* to *we*.

49.   **E**   Sentence is correct.

50.   **B**   Wrong word. Use *lying* instead of *laying*.

Section 4

1.   **D**   *Inaninities* (words which are empty and senseless) is the only word which can go with the expression "a pack of lies." *Saws*, *maxims*, *aphorisms* and *proverbs* cannot be called *lies*.

2.   **B**   The showing of a lack of *concealed* weapons revealed that people were friendly or *amicably* disposed.

3.   **A**   This question calls for judgment since all the choices seem good. However, a *concerted* or joint effort where everyone does his best is most likely to produce the desired results.

4.   **E**   We can eliminate Choices C and D because they are undesirable traits. Choices A and B are synonyms of things mentioned in the

5. **D** *Thrift* is a virtue not mentioned in the sentence.
   sentence and are repetitious. Choice E represents a new and desirable trait.

6. **A** The opposite of *licentious* (immoral) is *moral*.

7. **E** The opposite of *recalcitrant* (refusing compliance) is *tractable* (willing to conform or comply).

8. **D** The opposite of *impassive* (devoid of emotion) is *agitated*.

9. **C** The opposite of *profligate* (dissolute) is *staid* (sober).

10. **C** The opposite of *prolix* (long-winded) is *terse* (concise).

11. **C** The opposite of *prodigious* (enormous) is *microscopic* (tiny).

12. **D** The opposite of *specious* (seemingly plausible) is *veracious* (true).

13. **D** The opposite of *sedulous* (persevering) is *indolent* (lazy).

14. **C** The opposite of *effete* (worn out) is *energetic*.

15. **E** The opposite of *nocturnal* (nightly) is *daily*.

16. **D** The *policeman* fights the *criminal* and the *evangelist* fights the *sinner*.

17. **A** The *stone* was a weapon used in ancient or *archaic* times; the *bomb*, a weapon used in *modern* times.

18. **B** *Benediction* (blessing) and *anathema* (curse) are opposites; *eulogy* (praise) and *vilification* (abuse) are opposites.

19. **D** The *crest* of a wave may be compared to a *peak* and the *trough* to a *valley*.

20. **D** *Titanic* means *enormous* and *Lilliputian* means *puny*.

21. **B** Just as a *sedative* will quiet or reduce *pain*, *consolation* will quiet or reduce *grief*.

22. **C** The meat of a *pig* is called *pork*; the meat of a *sheep* is called *mutton*.

23. **E** *Maxims* and *epigrams* are *pithy* and *terse* statements.

24. **B** The common *cold* is caused by a *virus*; *gangrene* is caused by *infection*.

25. **D** *Choleric* and *irascible* (easily angered) are synonyms; *tiring* and *enervating* are synonyms.

26. **D** Throughout the passage, the author mentions characteristics of a city which he finds admirable.

27. **D** The reference to the "penniless man" and "noble impersonality" indicate that the services are given to everybody.

28. **A** This passage is a defense of cities.

29. **C** The use of the expression "and above all" in the next-to-last sentence emphasizes the author's pleasure with the impartial service.

30. **E** The last sentence justifies Choice E.

31. **E** In the second paragraph, the author mentions two arboreal (living in trees) mammals — the sloth and the monkey.

32. **C** In the second paragraph the author shows how the adaptation of mammals parallels that of ancient reptiles. As an illustration, he compares the flying abilities of the bat (a mammal) with those of the ptersosaur (a reptile).

33. **E** See the last sentence of the first paragraph.

34. **A** In the second paragraph, the author points out the superiority of the mammals to the reptiles and in the discussion of the tyrannosaur and the tiger, the author attributes the tiger's superiority to a "superior brain."

35. **B** Since these three animals were reptiles, we may assume that saur means reptile.

36. **E** The last sentence of the passage supports Choice E.

37. **E** The last sentence of the second paragraph supports Choice E.

38. **C** Choice C is supported by the opening sentence.

39. **C** The particles that make up the atom are mentioned in the opening and closing sentences.

40. **E** Molecules are much larger than atoms and even larger than electrons.

Section 5

1. **E** 60 out of 80 applicants did appear.

$$\frac{60}{80} = \frac{3}{4} = 75\%$$

Choice (C) does not answer the question. It gives the percent of the total applicants that failed to appear. Choices (A) and (D) result from guessing by dividing or subtracting the numerals given. Choice (B) evidently tries multiplication and then rounds off zeros to change to percent. This simple problem illustrates the danger of wild guessing.

2. **D** Ratio is a comparison of two quantities by division in correct order. Unlike the correct choice (D), in (B) the ratio of boys to girls is given. Choice (C) gives the part of the number of boys in the entire class and (E) gives the part of the number of girls in the entire class. This question does not ask for that information.

3. **D** $$\sqrt{\frac{1}{16} + \frac{1}{9}} = \sqrt{\frac{25}{144}} \text{ or } \frac{5}{12}$$

Choice (E) incorrectly answers the question

$$\sqrt{\frac{1}{16}} + \sqrt{\frac{1}{9}}$$

which is $\frac{1}{4} + \frac{1}{3}$ or $\frac{7}{12}$. Choices (A) and (B) incorrectly add $\frac{1}{4} + \frac{1}{3}$. Choice (C) fails to extract the square root.

4. **C** The fraction $\frac{a + b}{b}$ may be written as $\frac{a}{b} + \frac{b}{b}$. Since $\frac{b}{b} = 1$, the correct choice is (C). Choice (A) subtracts b from numerator and denominator. Recall that in multiplying (or dividing) an equal quantity by the numerator and denominator of a fraction we are actually multiplying (or dividing) by 1.

5. **C** Conversion problems involve ratio and proportion. Kilometers bear a direct ratio to miles, since 1 kilometer = $\frac{5}{8}$ of a mile.

Let x = the number of kilometers in 12 miles.

$$\frac{\text{Kilometers}}{\text{Miles}} = \frac{1}{\frac{5}{8}} = \frac{x}{12}$$

$$\frac{5}{8}x = 12$$

$$\left(\frac{8}{5}\right)\frac{5}{8}x = 12\left(\frac{8}{5}\right)$$

$$x = \frac{96}{5} = 19\frac{1}{5} \text{ or}$$

$$19.2 \text{ kilometers}$$

Note that the incorrect choices (A) and (B) fail to keep the correct order of kilometers:miles. Those who choose (D) evidently perform the operations, and when the numeral 5 appears as a remainder of the division of 96 by 5 they carelessly choose 19.5 as their answer.

6. **C** Since the tank was completely filled in $1\frac{3}{4}$ minutes, it would be be proportionately less full in 1 minute.

$$\frac{\text{Time (in minutes)}}{\text{Part filled}} = \frac{1\frac{3}{4}}{1} = \frac{1}{x}$$

$$\frac{7}{4}x = 1$$

$$x = \frac{4}{7}$$

Choice (B) gives the part not filled in the 1 minute. Choice (D) gives the time not used to completely fill the tank.

7. **E**   The time-consuming method is to find the cost of one item $\left(\frac{c}{2}\right)$ ¢ and divide the amount of money available (x¢) by the cost of one item. Choice (C) multiplies. The quick method sets up a proportion:

$$\frac{\text{Number of items purchased}}{\text{Cost (in cents)}} = \frac{2}{c} = \frac{?}{x}$$

$$(c)(?) = 2x \text{ and } ? = \frac{2x}{c}$$

8. **A**   I is true, e.g., $\sqrt[3]{-8} = -2$

II is false; $\sqrt{\frac{1}{4}}$ is not smaller than $\frac{1}{4}$

$\sqrt{\frac{1}{4}} = \frac{1}{2}$; $\frac{1}{2}$ is larger than $\frac{1}{4}$

III is false; $(A - B)(A + B) = A^2 - B^2$

9. **D**   This problem tests your ability to apply the formula used to find areas of circles. Since the area of a circle is πR^2, any change in R will affect the area by that quantity squared. Since we are concerned with area, we are evidently concerned with the area of the empty pool or its floor. Since the radius is doubled, the area will be 4 times as much. Some of the incorrect choices are caused by confusion between the effect on the circumference by changes in radius. Since the formula for circumference is $C = \pi D$ or $2\pi r$, any change in radius or diameter will affect the circumference in the same numerical way.

10. **D**   Since angle DBE is a right angle, angle ABE is the complement of angle DBA and has a measure of $90° - 70°$ or $20°$. Choice (A) does not complete the question. Since ABC is a straight line, $x = 180° - 20°$ or $160°$.

11. **C**   Draw $BF \perp EC$
$BF = AD = 4$
$ED = 3$ and $FC = 3$
$DF = 13 - 6$ or 7
$AB = DF = 7$

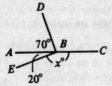

12.   **D**   Since $\angle A \triangleq 70$, then $\angle ABC + \angle ACB \triangleq 110$ or each $\triangleq 55$, and each bisected angle (*DBC* and *DCB*) has a measure of $\frac{55}{2}$ degrees. In triangle *DBC*, the measure of $\angle BDC + \angle DCB + \angle DBC$ is 180 degrees. Since $\angle DBC + \angle DCB \triangleq 55$, $x = 180 - 55$ or 125.

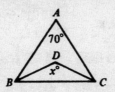

For 13-17:   Summarize the facts.
  Spanish is spoken by 3 — A, B, D.
  Italian is spoken by 3 — A, C, E.
  English is spoken by 2 — B, C.
  French is spoken by 2 — D, E.

13.   **E**   When C and D converse they can use English, Italian, French, and Spanish between them. Mr. A speaks Spanish and Italian. Mr. B speaks English and Spanish. Mr. E speaks French and Italian.

14.   **A**   Mr. B understands English and Spanish, while Mr. E speaks two other languages, French and Italian.

15.   **D**   Mr. A and Mr. B can converse in Spanish.

16.   **D**   Three executives speak Spanish (Messrs. A, B, and D). The other executives (Messrs. C and E) speak Italian.

17.   **B**   English is spoken by two executives (Messrs. B and C), and French is spoken by two executives (Messrs. D and E). English and Spanish are spoken by 5. Italian and Spanish are spoken by 5. English and Italian are spoken by 5. French and Spanish are spoken by 5.

18.   **A**   The paper wasted is the difference between the area of the square and the area of the circle. Note choice (C) gives the difference of the circle from the square. Since we are cutting the largest possible circle, the diameter must equal the side of the square. The area of the square is d^2 and the radius of the circle is $\frac{d}{2}$ and the area

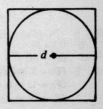

of the circle is $\pi \left(\dfrac{d}{2}\right)^2$ or $\dfrac{\pi d^2}{4}$. Note that choice (B) gives the area of the circle only. The correct solution is

$$d^2 - \left(\dfrac{d}{2}\right)^2 \pi$$

$$\dfrac{d^2}{1} - \dfrac{\pi d^2}{4}$$

$$\dfrac{4d^2}{4} - \dfrac{\pi d^2}{4}$$

$$\dfrac{4d^2 - \pi d^2}{4}$$

19. **D** Both, either, or neither a or b may be equal to zero.

20. **C** $(x + y)^2 = x^2 + 2xy + y^2$
Substitute $xy = 5$ and $x^2 + y^2 = 7$
$2xy = 10$ and $x^2 + y^2 = 7$
$x^2 + 2xy + y^2 = 17$.

21. **A** $\sqrt{0.3} = .5+$; $.5+ > .49$.

22. **B** $1\% = .01$ and $\dfrac{1}{2}\% = .005$; $.05 > .005$.

23. **A** Substitute values given: $x(y + z) = 2(3 + 7)$ or 20
$xz + y = (2)(7) + 3$ or 17.

24. **C** Perimeter of $AGFC = AG + GF + FC + AC$
Perimeter of shaded part $= AG + GF + FD + ED + BE + AB$
Since both figures are rectangles, $ED = BC$ and $BE = CD$.
$AC = AB + BC$ and $FC = CD + DF$.

25. **B** Since x is positive, $2x^2 = (2)(x)(x)$ and $(2x)^2 = 4x^2$ or $(4)(x)(x)$.

26. **B** The team scored a total of 66 points in this game. The average for all players is therefore $66 \div 6$ or 11 points. Player D scored 14 points, which is better than the average for the entire team.

27. **C** Both triangles have a common base (CD). Both triangles have equal altitudes since perpendiculars between parallel lines are equal.

28. **A** $2x = 3y$
$x = \dfrac{3}{2}y$ or $x = 1\dfrac{1}{2}$ times y

29. **B** Things equal to the same thing are equal to each other. Therefore $5x = 3y$ and $x = \dfrac{3}{5}y$

30. **D** Let $x =$ Mark's age now
Let $y =$ Philip's age now
Let $z =$ Michael's age now

From the first sentence we may write the equation: $x + 9 = 3y$, and from the second sentence the equation: $x = z + 3$. With three unknowns we must have 3 different equations in order to solve the unknowns.

31. **D** You may assume that a and b have values in the range of 2 to 4. The substitution of any of these values in $b - a$ and $a - b$ may produce many possibilities.

32. **C** $3\frac{1}{2}\% = 3.5\% = \frac{3.5}{100}$ or $\frac{35}{1000}$

33. **C** $\frac{1}{A} = \frac{1}{x} + \frac{1}{y}$

$\frac{1}{A} = \frac{x + y}{xy}$

$A = \frac{xy}{x + y}$ (reciprocals of equals are equal)

34. **B** Since x has a negative value, let $x = -5$.

$$\frac{1}{-5} = 1 \div -5 \text{ or } -0.2$$

$$-.02 > -5.0$$

35. **C** $\frac{a^2 - b^2}{(a - b)^2} = \frac{(a + b)\cancel{(a - b)}}{(a - b)\cancel{(a - b)}} = \frac{a + b}{a - b}$

Section 6

1. **D** $12 = 1\frac{1}{3}(x)$

$12 = \frac{4}{3}x$

$\frac{4}{3}x = 12$

$4x = 36$

$x = 9$

2. **C** $\frac{\text{quantity of pie}}{\text{number of people served}} = \frac{1}{7} = \frac{x}{91}$

$7x = 91$

$x = 13$

3. **B** $\frac{1}{5} = 20\%$; $\frac{2}{5} = 40\%$; $\frac{3}{5} = 60\%$; $\frac{16}{25} = 64\%$; $\frac{13}{25} = 52\%$

$\frac{2}{5}$ is next smaller than $\frac{1}{2}$ or 50%

4. **A** $\dfrac{a+b}{a-b} \div \dfrac{b+a}{b-a}$

   $\dfrac{a+b}{a-b} \cdot \dfrac{b-a}{b+a}$

   $\dfrac{a+b}{a-b} \cdot \dfrac{-a+b}{a+b}$

   $\dfrac{a+b}{a-b} \cdot \dfrac{-\,a-b}{a+b}$

   $\dfrac{a+b}{\cancel{a-b}} \cdot \dfrac{-\cancel{a-b}}{a+b}$ or -1

5. **C** $\dfrac{\text{feet}}{\text{inches}} = \dfrac{1}{12} = \dfrac{x}{7.2}$

   $12x = 7.2$

   $120x = 72$

   $x = \dfrac{72}{120}$ or $\dfrac{3}{5}$

6. **C** $\dfrac{1}{.4} = \dfrac{10}{4} = 2\dfrac{1}{2}$ or 250%

   $\dfrac{5}{8} = 62\dfrac{1}{2}\%$

   $(.2)^2 = .04 = 4\%$

   $\dfrac{9}{100} = 9\%$

   $\sqrt{1.44} = 1.2 = 120\%$

   4% or $(.2)^2$ is smallest

7. **C**   First car uses 1 gallon for 15 miles. Therefore, it uses 4 gallons for 60 miles. Since the second car can travel m miles on one gallon, it can travel $4m$ miles on 4 gallons.

8. **A**   When purchased in box of 12, cost per tablet is $\dfrac{21¢}{12}$ or $1\dfrac{3}{4}¢$.

   When purchased in bottle of 100, cost per tablet is $\dfrac{\$1.50}{100}$ or

   $1\dfrac{1}{2}¢$. Saving per tablet by purchasing in bottle is $1\dfrac{3}{4}¢ - 1\dfrac{1}{2}¢$

   $1\dfrac{1}{4}¢$. Therefore saving per dozen = $12\left(\dfrac{1}{4}¢\right)$ or 3¢.

9. **A**   If a man does $\dfrac{1}{8}$ of his work in one day, in x days he will do x times

   as much or $\dfrac{x}{8}$.

10. **A**   Perimeter of rectangle = 2 (Length) + 2 (Width)

Let x = the width

Perimeter of rectangle = $2(3u + 2v) + 2x$

Perimeter of rectangle = $6u + 4v + 2x$

$10u + 6v = 6u + 4v + 2x$

$4u + 2v = 2x$

$x = 2u + v$

11. **C** $r = \dfrac{E}{i}$

$ir = E$

$i = \dfrac{E}{r}$

$W = i^2 r$

$W = \dfrac{E}{r} \cdot \dfrac{E}{r} \cdot r$ (Substitution)

$W = \dfrac{E^2}{r}$

$Wr = E^2$

$E = \sqrt{Wr}$

12. **B**   Volume of water in can = (area of base) (height)

Volume of water in can = (π) (radius)^2 (height)

Volume of water in can = $(\frac{22}{7})$ (4) (14) or 176 cubic inches

To find time for 176 cubic inches we have a direct proportion.

Let x = number of minutes required for 176 cubic inches

$\dfrac{\text{cubic inches}}{\text{minutes}} = \dfrac{8}{10} = \dfrac{176}{x}$

$8x = 1760$

$x = 220$ minutes

Since 220 minutes equals 3 hours and 40 minutes, the water which began to flow at 10 A.M. will begin to overflow at 1:40 P.M.

13. **A**   Area of original rectangle = lw

Length of new rectangle = $l + \frac{1}{2}l$

Let x = decrease in width

Width of new rectangle = $w - x$

Area of new rectangle = $(l + \frac{1}{2}l)\,(w - x) = lw$

$\left(\dfrac{3}{2}l\right)\left(w - x\right) = lw$

$$\frac{3lw}{2} - \frac{3lx}{2} = lw$$

$$3lw - 3lx = 2lw$$

$$-3lx = 2lw - 3lw$$

$$-3lx = -lw$$

$$-3x = -\frac{lw}{l}$$

$$3x = w$$

$$x = \frac{1}{3}w \text{ or } 33\frac{1}{3}\%w$$

14. **D** Radius $AO = 6.5$

Diameter $AB = 13$

Angle C is a right angle (an angle inscribed in a semi-circle is a right angle). Triangle ABC is a right triangle.

$$(13)^2 = (5)^2 + (CB)^2$$

$$169 = 25 + (CB)^2$$

$$(CB)^2 = 144$$

$$CB = 12$$

Area of triangle $ABC = \frac{1}{2}(AC)(CB)$

Area of triangle $ABC = \frac{1}{2}(5)(12)$ or 30

15. **D** Let x = distance (one way) traveled by yacht.

$$\frac{\text{Distance}}{\text{Rate}} = \text{Time}$$

$$\frac{x}{d} = \text{Time (downstream)}$$

$$\frac{x}{u} = \text{Time (upstream)}$$

$$\frac{x}{d} + \frac{x}{u} \text{ or } \frac{ux + dx}{du} \quad \text{(Total time)}$$

$$2x = \text{total distance}$$

$$\frac{\text{Total distance}}{\text{Total time}} = \text{average rate for the round trip}$$

$$\frac{2x}{\frac{ux + dx}{du}} = \text{average rate for the round trip}$$

$$= 2x + \frac{ux + dx}{du}$$

$$= 2x \cdot \frac{du}{ux + dx}$$

$$= 2x \cdot \frac{du}{x(u + d)}$$

$$= \frac{2du}{u + d}$$

16. **B** $p = ab - 2cd$
$3p = 3ab - 6cd$
$-3p = -3ab + 6cd$
$r = -3ab + 6cd$
$-3p = r$ (things equal to the same thing are equal to each other)

$\dfrac{-3p}{r} = 1$ (division by r)

$\dfrac{p}{r} = -\dfrac{1}{3}$ (division by -3)

$ab - 2cd = q$ is irrelevant

17. **D** $\dfrac{1}{2}$ of $\dfrac{1}{3}$ or $\dfrac{1}{6}$ of the workers are married women

$\dfrac{1}{3}$ of $\dfrac{1}{6}$ or $\dfrac{1}{18}$ of the women workers have children

Since $\dfrac{1}{3}$ of the workers are women, $\dfrac{2}{3}$ of the workers are men

$\dfrac{3}{4}$ of $\dfrac{2}{3}$ or $\dfrac{1}{2}$ of the workers are married men

$\dfrac{2}{3}$ of $\dfrac{1}{2}$ or $\dfrac{1}{3}$ of the male workers have children

$\dfrac{1}{18} + \dfrac{1}{3}$ or $\dfrac{7}{18}$ of the workers have children

Therefore $\dfrac{11}{18}$ of the workers do not have children

18. **D**   If two points have one coordinate the same, the distance between them is the difference between the two other coordinates.

(A) $0 - (-5) = 5$ (B) $5 - 0 = 5$ (C) $8 - 3 = 5$
(D) $3 - (-8) \neq 5$ (E) $3 - (-2) = 5$

19. **A** Use the formulas:

$$x \text{ mid.} = \frac{x_1 + x_2}{2} \text{ and } y \text{ mid.} = \frac{y_1 + y_2}{2}.$$

In this case, $x_1 = 2a$, $x_2 = 4a$, $y_1 = 2b$, $y_2 = 6b$.

$$x \text{ mid.} = \frac{2a + 4a}{2} = \frac{6a}{2} = 3a$$

$$y \text{ mid.} = \frac{2b + 6b}{2} = \frac{8b}{2} = 4b$$

20. **B** k is the y-coordinate of point C. Point C is the same distance above the x-axis as is point D. The y-coordinate of point D is 5. Therefore, the y-coordinate of point C is 5. Thus, $k = 5$.

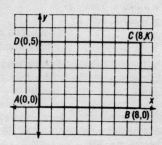

21. **A** $\frac{1}{7} = .142+$ $.142 > .0142$

22. **C** $\sqrt{\dfrac{1}{.25}} = \sqrt{\dfrac{100}{25}} = \sqrt{4} = 2$

23. **A** 5% of 500 = 25

24. **C** Between 2:55 and 3:15, 20 minutes (or $\frac{1}{3}$ of an hour) elapse.

25. **C** Since 15 is common to both columns, consider only $\dfrac{16}{x} = 4$.

Since $4x = 16$, $x = 4$.

26. **C** $\dfrac{1}{x} = \sqrt{.09}$ and $\dfrac{1}{x} = .3$

$.3x = 1$

$3x = 10$ and $x = 3\frac{1}{3}$

27. **C** $a + 2b = 1\frac{1}{3}$

$\dfrac{-a + b = -\frac{1}{3} < -1}{3b = 1}$

28. **C** Multiply by $\frac{-1}{-1}$. $\frac{x-y}{-z} = \frac{-x+y}{z}$ or $\frac{y-x}{z}$

29. **B** If x = zero, the numerator equals 0 and the value of the fraction equals zero regardless of the value of y.

30. **C** 4 quarts = 1 gallon

   1 quart $= \frac{1}{4}$ gallon

   $\frac{4}{5}$ quart $= \left(\frac{4}{5}\right)\left(\frac{1}{4}\right)$ or $\frac{1}{5}$ gallon

31. **C** $a:b = c:d$ or, $\frac{a}{b} = \frac{c}{d}$ Because reciprocals of equals are equal $\frac{b}{a} = \frac{d}{c}$.

32. **D** No information is given about the individual values of a, b, c, d.

33. **C** See #31. $\frac{a}{b} = \frac{c}{d}$

34. **C** With this given proportion, if we multiply the means and the extremes we get $bc = ad$. This satisfies the proportion as explained in #33.

35. **D** We may not assume that this quadrilateral is a parallelogram and we have no basis for determining the value of n, the angle opposite the one with the measure given as 110. We do know that $k + l + m + n = 360$.

36. **D** See #35.

37. **C** Since the measure of angle A equals the measure of angle C (45°) angle B must be a right angle. Sides AB and BC lie opposite equal angles.

38. **B** AB lies opposite the angle that has a measure of 45° while AC lies opposite the right angle. $AC > AB$.

39. **C** The area of triangle $ABC = \frac{1}{2}(AB)(BC)$

   Let $x = AB = BC$

   Area $= \frac{1}{2}x^2 = 72$

   $x^2 = 144$

   $x = 12$

40. **A** A straight line is the shortest distance between two points.

Answers to Word Tests

Word Test 1 (page 44)

1. 5	8. 1	15. 1
2. 4	9. 3	16. 2
3. 2	10. 2	17. 3
4. 5	11. 1	18. 4
5. 1	12. 3	19. 1
6. 5	13. 5	20. 1
7. 3	14. 4	

Word Test 2 (page 50)

21. 2	28. 2	35. 4
22. 2	29. 2	36. 5
23. 4	30. 3	37. 5
24. 5	31. 4	38. 4
25. 5	32. 4	39. 3
26. 1	33. 3	40. 2
27. 1	34. 4	

Word Test 3 (page 57)

41. 2	48. 4	55. 3
42. 3	49. 4	56. 4
43. 1	50. 5	57. 2
44. 4	51. 4	58. 3
45. 5	52. 3	59. 3
46. 3	53. 1	60. 4
47. 3	54. 2	

Word Test 4 (page 63)

61. 4	68. 3	75. 2
62. 5	69. 4	76. 2
63. 2	70. 5	77. 1
64. 1	71. 4	78. 3
65. 3	72. 4	79. 2
66. 2	73. 2	80. 1
67. 2	74. 1	

Word Test 5 (page 69)

81. 2	88. 3	95. 4
82. 5	89. 5	96. 2
83. 2	90. 3	97. 3
84. 5	91. 3	98. 1
85. 4	92. 3	99. 5
86. 2	93. 1	100. 1
87. 4	94. 4	

Word Test 6 (page 75)

101. 2	108. 2	115. 3
102. 1	109. 1	116. 2
103. 1	110. 4	117. 4
104. 4	111. 1	118. 4
105. 5	112. 5	119. 5
106. 1	113. 5	120. 4
107. 1	114. 4	

Word Test 7 (page 81)

121. 5	128. 4	135. 2
122. 1	129. 3	136. 2
123. 5	130. 2	137. 3
124. 3	131. 3	138. 4
125. 1	132. 5	139. 4
126. 1	133. 1	140. 4
127. 1	134. 2	

Word Test 8 (page 87)

141. 4	148. 3	155. 1
142. 1	149. 1	156. 5
143. 3	150. 5	157. 5
144. 2	151. 4	158. 3
145. 2	152. 4	159. 2
146. 2	153. 1	160. 3
147. 1	154. 2	

Word Test 9 (page 92)

161. 3	168. 3	175. 4
162. 3	169. 2	176. 1
163. 2	170. 2	177. 3
164. 3	171. 3	178. 2
165. 4	172. 3	179. 4
166. 3	173. 1	180. 2
167. 4	174. 1	

Word Test 10 (page 99)

181. 3	188. 2	195. 5
182. 3	189. 2	196. 1
183. 3	190. 5	197. 4
184. 3	191. 1	198. 1
185. 4	192. 4	199. 3
186. 5	193. 5	200. 2
187. 4	194. 1	

Word Test 11 (page 105)

201. 3	208. 1	215. 2
202. 3	209. 3	216. 5
203. 4	210. 4	217. 1
204. 5	211: 2	218. 2
205. 1	212. 2	219. 3
206. 1	213. 1	220. 1
207. 5	214. 5	

Word Test 12 (page 110)

221. 1	228. 5	235. 1
222. 4	229. 3	236. 3
223. 3	230. 1	237. 2
224. 2	231. 3	238. 5
225. 1	232. 4	239. 5
226. 3	233. 1	240. 2
227. 1	234. 4	

Word Test 13 (page 116)

241. 3	248. 1	255. 3
242. 5	249. 3	256. 2
243. 1	250. 2	257. 1
244. 2	251. 4	258. 3
245. 2	252. 4	259. 2
246. 4	253. 1	260. 2
247. 3	254. 5	

Word Test 14 (page 122)

261. 4	268. 1	275. 2
262. 2	269. 3	276. 1
263. 1	270. 2	277. 2
264. 1	271. 1	278. 2
265. 3	272. 1	279. 4
266. 4	273. 3	280. 3
267. 5	274. 5	

Word Test 15 (page 127)

281. 2	288. 1	295. 1
282. 4	289. 4	296. 1
283. 2	290. 1	297. 4
284. 1	291. 2	298. 3
285. 1	292. 3	299. 2
286. 3	293. 3	300. 2
287. 3	294. 2	

Word Test 16 (page 133)

301. 2	308. 2	315. 1
302. 5	309. 2	316. 2
303. 2	310. 5	317. 1
304. 2	311. 2	318. 2
305. 5	312. 1	319. 4
306. 3	313. 3	320. 2
307. 1	314. 3	

Word Test 17 (page 139)

321. 3	328. 2	335. 3
322. 4	329. 5	336. 4
323. 5	330. 1	337. 5
324. 2	331. 2	338. 5
325. 1	332. 4	339. 2
326. 5	333. 5	340. 3
327. 2	334. 1	

Word Test 18 (page 145)

341. 3	348. 2	355. 5
342. 3	349. 5	356. 2
343. 1	350. 1	357. 2
344. 2	351. 1	358. 1
345. 4	352. 1	359. 1
346. 2	353. 2	360. 4
347. 1	354. 4	

Word Test 19 (page 150)

361. 2	368. 5	375. 3
362. 2	369. 2	376. 1
363. 5	370. 3	377. 4
364. 3	371. 3	378. 3
365. 1	372. 1	379. 1
366. 2	373. 3	380. 2
367. 5	374. 3	

Word Test 20 (page 156)

381. 1	388. 4	395. 3
382. 3	389. 2	396. 3
383. 1	390. 3	397. 1
384. 5	391. 2	398. 3
385. 4	392. 4	399. 3
386. 1	393. 2	400. 3
387. 1	394. 2	

Word Test 21 (page 162)

401. 2	408. 3	415. 5
402. 4	409. 4	416. 4
403. 1	410. 5	417. 3
404. 3	411. 4	418. 2
405. 3	412. 5	419. 5
406. 3	413. 1	420. 2
407. 2	414. 2	

Word Test 22 (page 168)

421. 2	428. 1	435. 1
422. 3	429. 4	436. 5
423. 3	430. 1	437. 3
424. 4	431. 1	438. 5
425. 5	432. 2	439. 3
426. 5	433. 5	440. 2
427. 1	434. 1	

Word Test 23 (page 175)

441. 3	448. 4	455. 5
442. 1	449. 5	456. 1
443. 2	450. 2	457. 5
444. 4	451. 1	458. 1
445. 3	452. 3	459. 1
446. 3	453. 4	460. 3
447. 2	454. 5	

Word Test 24 (page 180)

461. 2	468. 3	475. 2
462. 3	469. 2	476. 5
463. 2	470. 1	477. 1
464. 5	471. 1	478. 2
465. 4	472. 4	479. 4
466. 3	473. 2	480. 3
467. 4	474. 5	

Word Test 25 (page 186)

481. 2	488. 2	495. 1
482. 4	489. 2	496. 2
483. 3	490. 4	497. 3
484. 5	491. 1	498. 1
485. 1	492. 3	499. 1
486. 1	493. 4	500. 1
487. 4	494. 2	

Word Test 26 (page 192)

501. 3	508. 5	515. 2
502. 1	509. 2	516. 1
503. 4	510. 3	517. 4
504. 5	511. 1	518. 5
505. 3	512. 4	519. 5
506. 3	513. 2	520. 4
507. 4	514. 2	

Word Test 27 (page 198)

521. 4	528. 1	535. 1
522. 3	529. 3	536. 1
523. 5	530. 1	537. 3
524. 2	531. 4	538. 3
525. 2	532. 3	539. 5
526. 5	533. 1	540. 3
527. 1	534. 4	

Word Test 28 (page 203)

541. 3	548. 1	555. 2
542. 2	549. 2	556. 1
543. 4	550. 3	557. 2
544. 1	551. 3	558. 3
545. 1	552. 4	559. 5
546. 4	553. 4	560. 3
547. 3	554. 4	

Word Test 29 (page 209)

561. 3	568. 1	575. 4
562. 2	569. 1	576. 2
563. 3	570. 4	577. 1
564. 2	571. 2	578. 2
565. 5	572. 3	579. 2
566. 1	573. 3	580. 5
567. 4	574. 1	

Word Test 30 (page 214)

581. 3	588. 1	595. 3
582. 1	589. 2	596. 3
583. 3	590. 4	597. 3
584. 2	591. 3	598. 1
585. 1	592. 4	599. 2
586. 3	593. 4	600. 2
587. 1	594. 2	